# MARKET MANAGE
# PROJECT BUSINESS DEVEL

*Market Management and Project Business Development* is a guide to managing markets through the theory and practice of marketing and selling projects in business.

Successfully marketing and selling a project to investors is so crucial an element of managing the project business and project management that it dictates whether projects are secured, how they are delivered and how clients are managed. Marketing and business development are not separate functions; they permeate other functions to secure and deliver value, and improve performance in profitable ways. Market management strategy cascades down the project business hierarchy to meet the project at the front of the strategic front-end. It carries on throughout project lifecycles and beyond as part of client management and programme management for the project business. The effective management of project businesses thinks of the client and service experience as well as the project as the prime foci, extending the competent project manager's skills set, the capabilities of the organization and project execution.

This book provides a unique set of key principles and guidelines to business-to-business (B2B) marketing, setting out a range of theoretical developments and applying them throughout to practical application and through cases to link theory to practice. Smyth structures his guide through the stages in the process of marketing a project from developing organizational and project capabilities to add value, from inception to the delivery of benefits and impact in use, covering a range of approaches: the marketing mix, relationship marketing and its project marketing variant, entrepreneurial marketing and the service-dominant logic.

This book is valuable reading for all students and specialists in project management, as well as project managers in business management. It indeed carries many lessons for any industry delivering highly specific assets and services to contract.

**Hedley Smyth** is Director of Research for the Bartlett School of Construction and Project Management, University College London. He has worked extensively in industry and academia and has been published in many leading journals and authored a wide range of books.

This book pulls together developments in marketing, business development and project management to provide an in-depth, rigorous analysis of how both horizontal and vertical integration is crucial to garner competitive advantage and value creation in the market place. Ten substantive issues are presented to advance this cause, refocusing on how project businesses manage markets. This book is strongly recommended for anyone who wishes to learn about conceptual development of these issues, rebalancing emphasis in application and implementation rigour in practice.

*Professor Low Sui Pheng, Director, Centre for Project Management and Construction Law, Department of Building, National University of Singapore, Singapore*

This book provides an essential reference for students, researchers and professionals interested in understanding the pivotal role of projects in marketing and business development. Not only is this essential reading for anyone interested in the project business, it also provides deep practical insights for managers of project-based enterprises.

*Professor Andrew Davies, Chair in the Management of Projects, School of Construction and Project Management, The Bartlett, UCL, UK*

This book is an essential text for anyone studying, researching or practising marketing of projects and business development of project organizations. The author brings a wealth of expertise of research and practice to produce a comprehensive and insightful volume which is both provocative and forward-looking. Together with its companion book, *Relationship Management and the Management of Projects*, this text provides thorough analysis of project clients, supply participants and their performance-related relationships.

*Professor Richard Fellows, School of Civil and Building Engineering, Loughborough University, UK*

# MARKET MANAGEMENT AND PROJECT BUSINESS DEVELOPMENT

*Hedley Smyth*

Routledge
Taylor & Francis Group
LONDON AND NEW YORK

First published 2015
by Routledge
2 Park Square, Milton Park, Abingdon, Oxon OX14 4RN

and by Routledge
711 Third Avenue, New York, NY 10017

*Routledge is an imprint of the Taylor & Francis Group, an informa business*



*British Library Cataloguing-in-Publication Data*
A catalogue record for this book is available from the British Library

*Library of Congress Cataloging-in-Publication Data*
Smyth, Hedley.
Market management and project business development / Hedley Smyth.
pages cm
Includes bibliographical references and index.
1. Project management. 2. Marketing. I. Title.
HD69.P75S6144 2014
658.8–dc23
2014010600

ISBN: 978-0-415-70508-0 (hbk)
ISBN: 978-0-415-70509-7 (pbk)
ISBN: 978-1-315-88999-3 (ebk)

Typeset in Bembo
by Apex CoVantage, LLC

Printed and bound by CPI Group (UK) Ltd, Croydon, CR0 4YY

This book is dedicated to Sue

# CONTENTS

# FIGURES

# TABLES

# FACT BOXES

# PREFACE

Markets are changing in time and space in response to globalization, economic cycles, as well as local conditions by place, environment and sector. Firms are undergoing fundamental changes in response to these new and sophisticated demands. One of the understated aspects of change in management theorization and investigation is the extent to which the project has become a primary delivery channel, estimates placing the contribution as high as 25–35 per cent GDP. Project businesses have been increasingly addressing market management at the operational level and at the front-end through marketing and 'business development'. Adopting market management and marketing theory in project markets requires care and 'translation' to fit into project businesses and project contexts.

The book addresses market management by linking *marketing*, the *management of projects* and *capability development* for effectiveness in the market. The book poses a number of important questions that challenge the project domain as a discipline and in practice. The answers provided through current practice have significant implications for clients, owners and society at large.

*To what extent are markets managed by project businesses?* Are project businesses market makers or takers, initiators or followers, active or passive recipients? It may not matter as long as firms survive or at least survive for the tenure of current management. But it does matter for shareholders and it does matter for clients. Long-term performance depends upon how well clients are served and how financially successful any project business is.

*In what ways is the market managed at an operational level through marketing and sales or business development?* How are marketing and business development implemented so as to improve market management? The paradigms and conceptual approaches, the structures, systems and procedures applied pose important choices. The choices affect the ability to manage the market, improve performance and meet client needs. The choices affect the survival and competitive strength of project businesses through differentiation and through head-on competition.

*What is the extent of the issues between the theoretical principles applied in practice and the theory?* The extent of any issues suggests there is either room for improvement or scope to show theory wrong. This is a challenge to read on for there is, I shall ague, uncharted terrain to be explored and mapped. The book can achieve some of the theoretical side, translating general management theory into the project context, but only industry can generate outcomes in practice. Businesses, policy arenas, other communities and the environment are all affected as to how well clients are served.

The book builds upon what has gone before and updates market management, marketing and business development in theoretically and practically challenging ways, using both knowledge of the project domain and new empirical material collected over recent years. Moreover, it meets the challenge of placing this in the broader corporate context – the project business. The *aim* is therefore to set out how theoretical developments and developments in practice apply in the asset-specific markets of projects. The main *objectives* are to improve understanding of market management, marketing and business development in project businesses from the viewpoint of academe and practice, and improve understanding of the implications for the overall management of the project business.

The gestation of this book goes back a long way. Some grows out of the years spent in project businesses associated with the built environment – construction, development, as well as working in the professions. Some of it grows out of the years spent undertaking my doctorate and research publications across a range of outlets. My work at UCL's Bartlett Faculty of the Built Environment over a couple of decades has proved influential through staff and students. I have particularly been influenced by the work of Graham Ive, Peter Morris and the work undertaken with Stephen Pryke. This book is one of a pair that are interrelated and mutually reinforcing. The other book, *Relationship Management and the Management of Projects*, arguably has broader significance in the study of management and project management, but in many ways, it grows out of the same issues addressed here.

The book is written to provide a challenge in ways that will help inform future research, have an influence through teaching and upon reflective practitioners.

H. S.
London, UK

# ACKNOWLEDGEMENTS

I would like to thank The Bartlett School of Construction and Project Management at UCL for supporting this endeavour, especially for the sabbatical. Peter Morris encouraged me to develop the work and take a sabbatical. Subsequent support came from Andrew Edkins as Director. My colleagues have carried the burden of my absence, especially for administrative duties, exam marking and supervision. I particularly single out Satu Teerikangas, Stephen Pryke, John Kelsey and Illona Kusuma for their support. I wish to thank colleagues at PBI in Finland, who hosted me during some of the writing period, especially Kim Wikström and Magnus Gustafsson, and similarly the BI Norwegian Business School, who also accommodated me while writing, especially Jonas Söderlund and Anne Live Vaagaasar. I have been fortunate to work with other scholars on publications that have underpinned parts of this work. They are cited in the book, and I thank them for their help and insight. I would also like to thank Tim Fitch of Invennt for facilitating a number of opportunities for research, those from many companies who provide access and their time, and three government-funded Knowledge Transfer Partnerships between UCL and other organizations. I thank Andy Davies, Grant Mills, Tim Fitch and Laurence Lecoeuvre for their valuable comments and feedback on an earlier draft of the book.

# ABBREVIATIONS

| | |
|---|---|
| € | euros or eurodollars |
| £ | British pounds sterling |
| 4Ps | product, price, place, promotion |
| 30Rs | thirty types of relationships |
| APM | Association of Project Management |
| B2B | business-to-business |
| B2C | business-to-customer |
| BDM | business development management |
| BDMs | business development managers |
| BIM | building information modelling |
| BoK | body of knowledge |
| BOOT | build, own, operate and transfer |
| BU | business unit |
| CapEx | capital expenditure |
| CEO | chief executive officer |
| CLV | customer or client lifetime value |
| CPV | client perceived value |
| CRM | customer or client relationship management |
| DART | dialogue, access, risk assessment, transparency |
| DMU | decision-making unit |
| D-U-C | discontinuity, uniqueness, complexity |
| ECI | early contractor involvement |
| ENR | Engineering News-Record |
| EPC | Engineering, Procurement and Construction |
| F2F | face-to-face |
| FM | facilities management |
| GDP | gross domestic product |

| | |
|---|---|
| GNP | gross national product |
| H&S | health and safety |
| HRM | human resource management |
| IT | information technology |
| KAM | key account management |
| KM | knowledge management |
| KPIs | key performance indicators |
| M&O | manufacturer and operator |
| MoP | management of projects |
| NPV | net present value |
| O&M | Operations and Maintenance |
| OpEx | operational expenditure |
| OTC | over-the-counter |
| $P^3M$ | project, programme and portfolio management |
| PFI | public finance initiative |
| PM | project management |
| PMBoK® | Project Management Body of Knowledge |
| PMI | Project Management Institute |
| PPP | public private partnerships |
| R&D | research and development |
| RBV | resourced-based view of the firm |
| RFP | request for proposal |
| RM | relationship management |
| ROCE | return on capital employed |
| ROI | return on investment |
| ROMI | return on marketing investment |
| SCM | supply chain management |
| S-DL | service-dominant logic |
| SI | substantive issue |
| SPV | Special Purpose Vehicle |
| SWOT | strengths, weaknesses, opportunities, threats |
| TMOs | temporary multi-organizational project teams |
| UK | United Kingdom |
| VRIN | valuable, rare, inimitable and non-substitutable |

# 1

# THE SHADOW OF THE PAST

## Introduction

*Don't You Just Know It* is the title of the New Orleans rhythm and blues number written by Huey 'Piano' Smith that was performed with the Clowns. It lends a lighthearted way of starting a serious endeavour. The song title points towards something we are already supposed to know, yet need reminding about, so it can be effectively developed. So it is with market management and business development. We *think* we know about market management and business development, especially marketing and selling, that is, how project businesses manage this. Yet the level of awareness and current practice continues to lag a long way behind trends in theory and general practice. For example, marketing and sales or *business development management* (BDM) are frequently organized as separate activities. They are often found to be isolated functionally and in the organizational culture (Smyth and Kusuma, 2013). On the ground, there remains a lack of awareness at senior management of the ways of thinking and systematic implementation of marketing principles in many project businesses.

The truth is that awareness and understanding amongst researchers about these functions still remains low. Research frequently excludes this area yet poses challenges. First, project management research tends to conceive market management to be something separate and high level in the hierarchy. Yet, marketing and BDM is conceptually perceived as a peripheral activity that needs drawing into project management. The actual position is the exact opposite where the project is the *delivery channel* in terms of marketing within which project management provides the logistics. Second, *management of projects* (MoP) research to date has largely overlooked marketing and BDM as being introduced into project lifecycles at the front of the front-end on the supply side. Third, project management renders a *service* to the client, especially if the project business is a systems integrator. There remains a strong tendency to mainly focus upon the tangible 'product' and artifacts. The emphasis of this book is to addresses market management through the *marketing* lens, linking it to MoP and *capability development* for effective market management and business development.

Market management sets the scene for business growth; then, the operational level is charged with delivering value profitably. Many traditional project management textbooks have us believe project management is where value is added. Market management strategically informs how the project front-end strategically mobilizes the business aims at the micro level and coordinates activities to deliver value profitably. The front of the front-end is where value first begins to be levered in practice. This is where marketing engages through BDM and where value begins to be identified and added from the supply side. A chief executive of an international main contractor recently stated *value is largely identified pre-prequalification*, constraining subsequent opportunities for *it is hard to shoehorn those things in post-prequalification*. We may disagree with this stark representation, but a point is made. Like the blues number, *Don't You Just Know It*, that is located on the cusp of rock, it is good to go back to the roots yet view the current changes and much excellent research through another lens. And so starts the examination of market management and project business development.

This book is therefore *about* businesses that undertake projects. These firms have been given various labels, for example, project-based suppliers, P-form organizations, project business and main contractors. The term *project-based organization* (e.g. Hobday, 2000) includes firms that source in-house. P-form and project business tend to stress the internal management logic (e.g. Söderlund and Tell, 2009; Wikström et al., 2009). *Project business* is the term mainly used here, although *supplier* and *main contractor* are used to emphasize particular contextual features. Project businesses are specialist producers and service providers undertaking projects, which is the primary mode of organizing. They can be divided into three:

1. *The systems integrator* – the project business that does not produce a direct artifact, but acts as the coordinating mechanism between the client, advisors, subcontractors and other suppliers in order to identify, lever and deliver value that comprises holistic solutions. This is largely a service function (Page and Siemplenski, 1983; Galbraith, 2002; Davies et al., 2007).
2. *The solutions seller* – the project business offering advisory role and professional services (Mattson, 1973; Davies et al., 2007).
3. *The systems seller* – the project business that does produce direct artifacts, frequently comprise bundled complex components and service content of a specialist nature provided by specialist advisors and producers (Davies et al., 2007).

These firms solicit for contracts in a competitive marketplace. Securing sufficient workflow is far from straightforward and operate in diverse sectors each with their own demands, ranging from construction (e.g. Eccles, 1981), shipbuilding (e.g. Martinsuo and Ahola, 2010), oil and gas (e.g. Merrow, 2011), and IT (e.g. Sauer and Reich, 2009) to sectors such as fashion (Uzzi, 1997), film (e.g. DeFillippi and Arthur, 1998; Bechky, 2006), media (e.g. Miles and Snow, 1986; Windeler and Sydow, 2001) and events management (Pitsis et al., 2003). They apply marketing and other business procedures to secure contracts from courting, prequalification, bidding and for delivering the value offered. A systematic approach supports these processes, comprising nested coordination mechanisms and routines to operationalize the system. Systems draw together market management and marketing activities with other functions and their subsystems to achieve integration to effectively deliver value in profitable ways. *Coordinating mechanisms* are dynamic procedures comprising, for example consistent organizational behaviour and behavioural programmes, to guide action in relatively stable ways (Jarzabkowski et al., 2012: 907). Some procedures are *routines*, which are about how activities are conducted at a more detailed level (Parmigiani and Howard-Grenville, 2011), for example specific actions and implementing codes of conduct. Systems and procedures (coordinating mechanisms and routines) yield capabilities and support competencies that affect marketing inputs and outputs that can be decisive in the marketplace for delivering performance at a high level.

A practical issue is that there are weak coordination mechanisms between marketing and other functions within the 'corporate centre' of many project businesses, and between the 'corporate centre' and projects. Project businesses are structured around the project as the prime unit of management rather than complementary foci upon managing the business to manage markets, clients and service provision. The marketing and sales are often seen as separate from any project and are further subdivided, consigning marketing to corporate communications (e.g. Preece et al., 1998) as it is further removed from projects than sales or BDM. Yet *marketing and BDM* provide a conceptual interface between market management and portfolio, programme and project management ($P^3M$) and is the term used in the book to show:

1. marketing and BDM are conceptually inseparable activities, theoretically related for integration in practice;
2. marketing and BDM involve vertical integration, a strategy-to-tactics dimension that is implemented top-down and refined bottom-up;
3. marketing and BDM involve horizontal integration, operating sequentially in tandem with and as part of programme management along project lifecycles.

It should be clear by this point that marketing is about business performance. It feeds performance as well as being a function that is performed well or not. While this book is about current theoretical knowledge and practice as applied, discussing how the theory–practice connection is articulated inevitably leads to exploring normative content for practice and hence the prescriptive contribution. All management research has an implicit, sometimes explicit, normative component. This book takes the long view of recent shifts in practice and uses a wide angled lens to take the field out of the *shadows of the past* (Artto et al., 2011; cf. Poppo et al., 2008).

## Aims and objectives

### *Aims*

An overarching *aim* of the book is to set out how theoretical developments apply in practice within this asset specific market. The *main aim* is focus upon *market management* and *business development*, in particular through marketing and sales. Market management and business development cover strategic options from strategic positioning, the business logic and models applied to growth through diversification, vertical integration, acquisitions and marketing. These activities involve the injection of new capital (share issues or loans) or come from excellent performance through profitability (especially return on capital employed and margins). Marketing and sales or marketing and BDM provide an important resource for securing work, generating excellent performance, profit and growth. Marketing and BDM are a prime means for project businesses to manage and develop their markets, and the extent to which they do and in what ways they do is examined in the book.

A *specific aim* is to focus upon marketing and BDM as a key part of strategic positioning that reaches down the hierarchy to operational performance and into the front of the project front-end, along project lifecycles, and finally into the post-project or programme period. Projects are also part of marketing, that is, projects as the *delivery channel* from the client viewpoint that gives rise to specialist project businesses, which links to marketing and BDM as follows:

> Client delivery channel → Client management of projects → Project business → Marketing and BDM → Project business management of projects

Marketing and BDM along project lifecycles is as much about client management as it is about programme and project management, adding a complementary client-centric approach to the primary task focus of project organizations (Handy, 1997; Pryke and Smyth, 2006). What is meant by a task focus is that project management and associated tasks are seen as an end in themselves, whereas a client-centric lens sees it as a means to serve. Client management extends beyond the life of any particular project and beyond both programme management and the allocation of resources as part of portfolio management ($P^3M$) to a broader corporate level, referred to in the book as the 'corporate centre'. The book therefore considers three aspects: corporate management of the project business, marketing and business development which reaches down from strategy into project lifecycles and the management of projects from the front of the front-end to post-execution.

Research into market management generally and marketing and BDM specifically has been growing yet remains sporadic. It barely touches mainstream project management (Pinto and Covin, 1992; Turner, 1995). There is a lack of conceptual awareness of the role and relevance to project management. There has been a growing interest amongst research academics in drawing upon marketing references, particularly since the mid-1990s (Turner et al., 2011). Yet researchers focusing at the front-end tend to adopt a narrow functional approach (Pryke and Smyth, 2006), looking forwards to how definition and scoping as project strategy affect execution in terms of matters such as value and risk (e.g. Morris, 1994; 2013), and it is often undertaken with a client-side bias that fails to locate supply side marketing and BDM prior to any project at the front of the front-end of projects. Researchers who have contributed to research in the field of marketing and BDM include Pinto (Pinto and Covin, 1992; Pinto and Rouhiainen, 2001), Cova (e.g. Cova and Holstius, 1993; Cova and Salle, 2005; 2006; 2011), Skaates and Tikkanen (e.g. Skaates et al., 2002a; 2002b; 2003; Skaates and Tikkanen, 2003a; Skaates and Seppänen, 2005), Smyth (e.g. Smyth, 2000; Skitmore and Smyth, 2007; Smyth and Edkins, 2007; Smyth and Fitch, 2009; Smyth and Kioussi, 2011a) and Preece (e.g. Preece et al., 1998; 2003). This body of work proves a valuable resource for the development of marketing in ways, it is hoped, that will begin to address some of the substantive issues in research and practice.

This book poses a number of important questions that provide challenges in the project domain as a discipline and to its application in practice:

1. *To what extent are markets managed by project businesses?* Market forces are strong, and individual firms are not market makers; they influence the market context from the bottom-up. As market followers, the first task is survival (Skitmore and Smyth, 2007), whether that is interpreted as short-term shareholder value or return on investment with an eye to medium-term tenure of current management and the long-term health of the business (Smyth and Lecoeuvre, 2014). Performance, especially long-term, depends upon how well clients are served and how successful the project business is financially. Client businesses, other client organizations, policy arenas, communities and the environment are all affected by the value delivered in terms of technical content and service.
2. *In what ways is the market managed through marketing and BDM?* The 'palette of paradigms' and conceptual approaches within the chosen paradigm influence organizational structures, shape systems and procedures. The choices and degree of alignment across the range of project business functions – the business model or logic (e.g. Vargo and Lusch, 2004; cf. Wikström et al., 2009) – affect the ability to manage the market, improve performance and meet client needs. How marketing and BDM are implemented increases the scope for and improves market management.
3. *What is the extent of the issues between the theoretical principles applied in practice and the theory?* The extent to which fleshing out the substance and amplifying partial practice suggests there is either room for improvement or scope to show theory to be wrong. As research in project management has failed to sufficiently integrate market management, marketing and BDM with MoP, it is remains hard to assess the extent to which it is wrong. The research carried

out by the cited authors clearly demonstrates the need to 'translate' mainstream marketing theory for conceptual and practical applicability in project markets, that is, actionable knowledge (cf. Romme, 2003). As project businesses have largely remained upon transactional territory, the application of marketing paradigms has been narrow. The book attempts to contribute to the discussion on the theoretical side, examine practice, assess transitions and assess the scope for future developments.

The chapter addresses:

A. A theoretical and applied focus upon measures (and changes) that can be made – the internal functions that are under management guidance and control.
B. Theory and concepts are highly practical, yet application can be challenging – if it was all easy, it would have been done long ago, yet application can have a profound effect upon business performance.
C. Profound and positive effects on business performance involve other functions and processes to be aligned, and where necessary, mutually adjusted and configured for effective performance including satisfying work for staff as well as clients.

Performance arises out of a client and service focus complementing the traditional and dominant project execution focus. In this way, the book makes an important contribution to MoP (cf. Morris and Hough, 1987; Morris, 1994; 2013). It adds to the call for the front-end emphasis, and for this to be complemented by a back-end emphasis for benefits delivery and evaluation (cf. Morris et al., 2000; Edkins et al., 2008) and as part of client management within marketing and BDM.

The book also contributes to the areas of systematic integration and capability development in project businesses (e.g. Hobday, 2000; Davies, 2004; Brady et al., 2005; Davies et al., 2007). The value offered and delivered is an important part of marketing. Value, meaning meeting requirements against time–cost–quality/scope or *value added* and *added value* above this level are key marketing issues for securing work, and especially for repeat business. Value and repeat business feed into market management. This book brings together the demand side research emphasis from the MoP domain with the supply side emphasis upon capabilities as a key to understanding how to manage the market and develop project businesses through the marketing lens. There are resource commitments to market management and business development. This depends upon the selection from the 'palette of paradigms' to approach marketing and BDM. For example, the traditional transactional marketing mix paradigm appears cheap short-term, yet tends to be more costly with lost opportunities long-term. The reverse is the case for relationship marketing, although it poses more management challenges.

On the supply side, projects provide an administrative approach to production that gives scope for individuals to flourish outside conventional bureaucratic constraints (e.g. Christensen and Kreiner, 1997, cited in Lindgren and Packendorff, 2003a). From a market management and marketing perspective, the project is a delivery channel for the demand side. Yet structuring and guidance through power and routines are needed to govern project practices (e.g. Kadefors, 1995). Outsourced projects to project businesses typically comprise at least three types of organizational actors: the client, the project business, and the project team. The project focus of most project management textbooks tends to emphasize the temporary nature of the project. This overlooks the more enduring and stable client and supplier organizations that frame the project (Winch, 2013). Only the project team comprising the TMO (Cherns and Bryant, 1984) or broader coalition (Winch, 2002) is temporary. Marketing and BDM is an interface and involves achieving a balance between the stable and temporary organizations. This is organized through systems and procedures for effective performance, including securing projects, yet it extends beyond the temporary nature of any one programme or project.

A great deal of attention has been given to the marketing of services in recent decades in the management literature. It seems surprising therefore to see leading authors state: *There is more emphasis on rhetoric than actions. In fact, we estimate that less than one service organization in five has a deep understanding of its customer base and an effective strategic marketing plan based upon this understanding* (McDonald et al., 2011: 3). It has been claimed many businesses fail to recognize the extent to which they are *service providers* – deeds, processes and performance that render (product) benefits (e.g. Zeithaml and Bitner, 1996; Vargo and Lusch, 2004), service being defined in terms of: *Services are economic activities offered by one party to another, most commonly employing time-based performances to bring about desired results in recipients themselves or in objects or other assets* (Fitzsimmons and Fitzsimmons, 2011: 4).

Project businesses largely see themselves as producers of tangible outputs rather than service providers (Smyth, 2000; 2013b). Most project businesses subcontract large proportions of the work. To the extent they do, they are service providers. Indeed, many project businesses are only service providers in project execution, the *systems integrator* role (Davies et al., 2007), which sometimes extends to managing the facilities provided. McDonald et al. (2011) also say that 90 per cent of chief executives of service organizations claim they manage customer- or market-orientated organizations, yet when asked about their own suppliers, they only recognized 5–10 per cent as being market orientated. The mismatch suggests an optimism bias among managers as to the service capability of their firm.

There is a need to link marketing to operations to ensure intent is delivered. In project businesses, this is where marketing comes down the hierarchy to meet the horizontal operations of managing projects over their lifecycles. Marketing conceptually meets the project lifecycle at the front of the front-end from a management of projects (MoP) perspective. It thus links the institutional level with MoP.

Morris et al. (2011) in *The Oxford Handbook of Project Management* argue there are three waves of project management, and we are currently addressing the emergence and development of the third wave concerning the institutional context (see also Morris and Geraldi, 2011). Morris (2013) states there are three issues that project management particularly needs to address in academia and practice: *value*, *context* and *impact*. *Value* is meant in terms of the benefits configured at the front-end and delivered during execution. In terms of marketing, value provides one of two key driving motives. The configuration of the value offered and delivered is how project businesses get profitable work. *Context* is meant as all the specific features for the project and in its environment that influence how the project strategy is formed at the front-end and implemented during execution. In terms of marketing and BDM, context is key as to why every project is unique and how value is configured and how projects are shaped. Understanding client needs, especially beyond the requirements documentation (Turkulainien et al., 2013) that is the 'deep understanding' referred to above (MacDonald et al., 2011), is key in marketing. *Impact* is meant in terms of project usefulness for the client business, stakeholders and society. Impact flows from the benefits delivered and shifts the focus from project management as the means to the usefulness of the project. This is part of customer delight. From the marketing perspective, this represents a shift from the pre-occupation with the tasks at hand in execution to a complementary client-centric view. A client-centric view links with front-end strategy and is formulated to achieve project goals and generate value that has impact. It is outward focused and engages with industrial networks to deliver value (e.g. Håkansson and Snehota, 1995; 2006; Christopher et al., 2002) and is therefore both forming as well as being part of the institutional context.

Identifying value at the front of the front-end is a strategic market issue that is initiated and in part operationalized through the marketing function. It is a tactical challenge to those undertaking the selling, the business development managers (BDMs). Many project management academics approach this issue primarily from the client perspective (e.g. Morris, 2013; Edkins et al., 2013), yet from the supplier perspective, the challenges are also considerable. They are underplayed and misunderstood in research and practice. Compared to the more '*mechanistic*' world of mainstream production (cf. Burns and Stalker, 1961), projects pose problems because *what is happening is typically complex, intangible and uncertain: management here is a lot less easy to explicate* (Edkins et al., 2013: 74). Edkins and his colleagues (2013) found application of a more instinctive approach (cf. Dreyfus and Dreyfus, 2005). This instinctive and intuitive sense making is important, yet improving awareness and articulating understanding improves performance and goes beyond rationalistic and mechanistic pursuit of narrow prescriptions (cf. PMI, 2013). Success in projects is based on human factors rather than merely upon on tools and techniques (e.g. Slevin and Pinto, 1986; Morris, 2013).

Success in projects is based upon an equal focus upon the client and projects rather than projects as the primary unit of management. Project businesses exist to *serve* clients. Client consideration changes decisions taken on projects, especially when the client is considered in terms of their client lifetime value or CLV, which is the amount of turnover and profit generated over the (estimated) period over which a client is providing work. This depends upon retention rates and may span several programmes on the client side. The flow may not be continuous. CLV provides a different unit of business analysis than the project focus and acts back to affect project management decisions from a long-term perspective.

## Objectives

Marketing and BDM offers a particular focus to facilitate integrated functioning in asset specific markets, including project businesses (Bessom, 1975). How this is achieved through research-informed practice involves drilling down to scope the objectives for the book. The main *objectives* are to:

1. Improve understanding of marketing and BDM in project businesses from the viewpoint of academe in research and learning in practice;
2. Improve selection of the most appropriate marketing paradigm, approach and detailed implementation from theory to project business practice;
3. Improve understanding of the implications of BDM practices for the overall management of project businesses.

Achieving these objectives for research and practice involves engagement with *enabling effort* in project businesses, the *securing of results* and *evaluation of outcomes. Enabling effort* involves awareness creation, alignment of value demanded and supplied, inducing a strong corporate brand, and building the social capital of the project business. *Securing results* involves proactive creation of new needs and demands, consistent service performance, improving CLV to increase market share, profitability, hence shareholder value. *Outcome evaluation* involves benefits delivery to clients, stakeholders and for some projects society at large. Outcomes are about the use value of projects and what is needed to achieve impact. These are seldom evaluated by project businesses, yet are important considerations for differentiation in the market. If projects are about imagining and realizing the 'future perfect', then it is reasonable to evaluate how 'perfect' the materialized future is (cf. Pitsis et al., 2003).

Management conceptually and practically addresses these issues through determining the organizational mission, setting goals and objectives, examining growth options and capturing these in a documented market plan (e.g. McDonald et al., 2011). The choice of paradigm may constitute the next step. A paradigm is a thought pattern or worldview that informs concepts, theories and practice. A paradigm can therefore be seen as a lens through which people make sense of their world. There are three main marketing approaches, the 'palette of paradigms':

1. Marketing mix: the transactional paradigm,
2. Relationship marketing: the systematic and behavioural paradigm,
3. Entrepreneurial marketing: an emergent conceptualization.

The marketing mix paradigm is somewhat outdated, yet still dominates many project businesses and even those in transition retain strong transactional practices. Therefore the marketing mix is retained for these reasons. Relationship marketing has developed a project business variant called *project marketing*, and relationship marketing is also developing into and is being absorbed by a broader 'paradigm' that brings a series of theoretical issues together under the *service-dominant logic*, sometimes also referred to as the *service logic*. Each of these is reviewed and 'translated' into the project business context in its own chapter: the *marketing mix* in **Chapter 3**, *relationship marketing* in **Chapter 4**, *project marketing* in **Chapter 5**, *entrepreneurial marketing* in **Chapter 6** and the *service-dominant logic* in **Chapter 10.**

## Defining the scope

The first task is to establish the meaning of terms, yet there are competing definitions, some being contested.

### *Definition and scope of terms*

The term *market* embodies many levels and multiple meanings, which are not always made clear (Hodgson, 1988; White 1993). Markets are made and not pre-given, being socially constructed and constantly renegotiated (cf. Polanyi 1944; Abolafia, 1996). In the marketing context, 'market' is defined as *the aggregation of all products or services which customers regard as capable of satisfying the same need* (McDonald et al., 2011: 113), a meaning pitched between a sector and an exchange, sometimes defined in terms as a segment or niche. Within some project markets, it may also be defined by procurement route and contract type, for example projects in property development markets. Market in the context of this book will refer to project businesses in general and by sector, for example oil and gas or IT, and at the level of the exchange between supplier and client or customer.

Project markets exhibit a considerable level of dysfunction, manifested at sector and project levels as high failure rates. For example amongst 300 industrial global megaprojects, 65 per cent were deemed to fail when measured against business objectives. In some industrial sectors, the level is as high as 75 per cent (Porter, 2011). Current projects are more complex in content and will become more so. Context adds complexity, for example the urban environment for infrastructure renewal. The context is also more complex organizationally in terms of the range of sophisticated and engaged stakeholders and the regulatory regimes to which organizations are required to comply. Crowded markets of intense competition provide insufficient room for project businesses to adjust in order to develop capacity and capabilities to meet increasing complexity. Market forces are strong, yet self-induced passivity towards developing differentiating capabilities is largely the result of serving shareholders ahead of clients. The two specific financial outcomes are sought. *Profit margins* increase shareholder value, through some combination of distribution to shareholders and investment into the business to fuel future growth. However, many project businesses make more money from the managing the return on capital employed than they do from the ability to raise margins. Increase in *market share* is linked to increasing turnover, hence the mass of profits for distribution to owners and for investment. Increased market share comes from market penetration in existing markets plus diversification into new markets. Increased market share comes from being more effective at satisfying clients by meeting requirements against time, cost and quality or scope and especially by adding value.

Differentiating the offer in the marketplace helps to grow market share where the configured value aligns with what is valued by the client base. Differentiation helps 'create uncontested space' and 'make competition irrelevant' in what is sometimes termed 'blue ocean strategy' (Kim and Mauborgne, 2004). The first aim of market management, especially for project businesses, is survival in the boom–bust cycle and 'lumpiness' of demand in the market at any time (Skitmore and Smyth, 2007). The second market management aim is investment to create a competitive advantage, for example developing specialist technical skills and expertise that constitute excellent *threshold competencies* (Hamel and Prahalad, 1994) and specialist skills and expertise that extend beyond the operational *raison d'être* to help articulate the efficiency and effectiveness of the business that are called *core competencies* (Hamel and Prahalad, 1994) or enhanced processes that underpin and articulate efficiency and effectiveness, called *dynamic capabilities* (e.g. Teece et al., 1997). In recession, restructuring and delayering need to be balanced with selective and nuanced investment, particularly around organic and geographic expansion through mergers and acquisitions. Fact Box 1.1 illustrates this trend by mapping the process at the upper end of the British construction industry amongst the major contractors. This leads to the need to define market management.

## *Market management*

How can firms create competitive advantage? A great deal of attention has been given to competitive advantage in management studies. Theories have been developed to address the question as to how advantage is created. Two commonly mobilized theories illustrate the point. First, Porter's (1979) five forces model analyzes the extent of advantage and disadvantage through buyer bargaining power, supplier bargaining power, threats of market entry, threats of product substitution and the degree of rivalry amongst competitors. The prime focus is market forces. Porter (1980) complemented this analysis with the focus a firm adopts – cost and hence price focus, and differentiation focus – and how value is levered and managed internally through the value chain. Second, the resource-based view (RBV) evaluates how bundles of resources are allocated within a firm, which will shape its ability to effectively differentiate itself or compete against other firms (e.g. Penrose, 1959; Wernerfelt, 1984; Barney, 1991; 2003; Teece et al., 1997). RBV focuses upon internal factors that are in the control of management. Core competencies and dynamic capabilities reside within the RBV; indeed, certain marketing

## FACT BOX 1.1 COMPETITIVE STAKES AND PROJECT BUSINESS DEVELOPMENT

The British construction industry grew in the rearmament period, was transformed during defense-related construction during the Second World War and grew during reconstruction postwar, subsequently expanding overseas, especially into Middle Eastern markets. The leading contractors were prominent in the international league tables presented in *Engineering News-Record* (*ENR*) over the next three decades. The present position provides a contrasting picture. The top 10 global contractors comprise 5 Chinese contractors, 2 French owned, 1 Spanish, 1 German and 1 US contractor in descending order of national appearance. The first British contractor appears 23rd on the list.

There has been a long-term trend of low investment and even divestment compared to contractors from other markets. British market share had shrunk back by the onset of the recession of the early 1990s. Over the 1993–1996 recession period, overseas divestment by British contractors, coupled with organic geographical expansion by mainland European contractors and takeover activity saw the British contractors lose nearly 19 per cent market share amongst the top 10 and nearly 20 per cent market share amongst the top 50 European-owned contractors. Having had over 23 per cent of the market amongst the top 10 European contractors in 1993, it was 0 per cent by 2008, yet crept up to 7.9 per cent by 2012.

Amongst leading UK contractors, divestment eroded market share by over 18 per cent compared to European counterparts in the recession between 1993 and 1996. Many leading mainland European contractors invested in geographical coverage over the same period. They now dominate the UK market and have restructured in ways to protect market share between 2008 and 2013, although have not always restructured to maintain marketing capabilities in terms of services. The largest British contractor was included in the top 10, but it reported in March 2013 it was planning to sell most of its European businesses. The business case was said to be the ongoing uncertainty in the Eurozone. Stepping back from the decision of this project business, it follows the pattern of divestment and shrinkage in market share during recession, whilst contractors on the European mainland have selectively invested. Overall, British owned contractors have lost nearly 4 per cent market share against the top 50 European-owned contractors since the 'credit crunch' recession commenced.

At one level, ownership does not matter – look at the car industry, which thrives in the United Kingdom. In construction, there are excellent European contractors in the United Kingdom. But it might say something about the ability of British management to make strategic decisions on market management and business development. It might also say something about the ability or desire of shareholders to guide management in the long term.

*Sources*: *Building* (1994; 1997) cited in Smyth (1998); *Building Magazine* (2009); Smyth (2010a; 2013a).

paradigms can be seen as functioning within this view (e.g. **Chapter 4**). Senior managers apply theories and models. They tend to be quite pragmatic in so doing, being prepared to learn from and adapt to emergent factors (Brews and Hunt, 1999), placing more emphasis upon the tactical issues. Issues of fit, alignment and integration become important in implementation and are important under RBV, particularly with core competency and dynamic capability theories (e.g. Prahalad and Hamel, 1990; Teece et al., 1997). *Core competency* theory sees how advantageous competencies arise from practice and that can be developed that go beyond those needed to be in a particular business (e.g. Prahalad and Hamel, 1990; Hamel and Prahalad, 1994), for example in marketing or creative environmental sustainability for added project value. *Dynamic capabilities*, similarly, involve developing efficient and effective processes that mobilize otherwise untapped potential to advantage (Helfat, 1997; Teece et al., 1997; Eisenhardt and Martin, 2000), for example routines between marketing and procurement for the creative management of value leverage in supply chains that aligns with client expectations. In project environments there are organizational capabilities (Davies and Brady, 2000), including marketing capabilities (Möller, 2006), as well as project capabilities (Brady and Davies, 2004) that can become organizational ones through $P^3M$.

The benefits may be cost reduction or added value for clients. Lean production is an example of more efficient and effective working. However, practitioners have tended to corrupt the application to squeeze costs and reduce investment (cf. value management and engineering). This may work short-run but the long-run economic principle holds that a return can only be yielded on an investment. Reducing capacity without investment can lead to the 'anorexic organization' (Radnor and Boaden, 2004). This is pertinent to project businesses where some firms have become *hollowed out* (Green et al., 2008). Project businesses frequently show reluctance to invest, at worst becoming hollowed-out firms to the extent they lack flexibility to change and become takeover targets. Nor is investment about following a recipe or legalistically following a conceptual model but a dynamic process in practice and arguably a conceptual discourse (Green et al., 2008). For example few firms in practice can be market leaders with competitive advantage. Management studies have tended to address the competitive advantage question in terms of firms seeking to secure advantage. Most firms are content to be followers, learning from the mistakes of pioneers who take greater risks (e.g. Lieberman and Montgomery, 1998). Followers typically invest less and incur fewer costs and can thus yield a higher (short-term) return for their owners. More risk-averse firms are content to be survivors in their market (cf. Skitmore and Smyth, 2007). This is particularly the case where firms have less market power (cf. Porter, 1979). All project businesses need a balance between efficient financial control and investment portfolios.

## Business development

Closely associated with market management is business development in the theoretical sense of the term (rather than the colloquial meaning of BDM). Market management addresses *how* questions, whereas business development addresses *what* questions. *Business development* is the function of growing a business through a range of activities from mergers and acquisitions, financial and performance management, and the application of particular business models with their associated earning logic, that is revenue or income in which profit is embedded. Business development includes marketing and sales as a distinct activity (Sørensen, 2012) and as one that interfaces with other activities. There is increasing pressure upon senior management to justify business development in terms of financial measures. Shareholders, finance departments and other senior management drive the need for measurement, especially where their remuneration is linked to short-term returns from existing investments and working capital, for example marketing-related investment. Measurement provides a data baseline for market planning, which develops and implements strategies to anticipate and satisfy demand in profitable ways. Marketing is an important part of this, which combines internal measures with external data, market research and identifies its ability to mobilize resources to offer value that meets demand. This is not always conducted in balanced ways. Empirical research in project businesses presented in Fact Box 1.2 and supported by the quote below finds a power imbalance between internal functions that compromise serving the interests of firms and clients: *Finance was perceived to be driving business decisions, particularly around efficiency measures, rather than serving and guiding business towards effective financial performance in relation to marketing and probably other functions too* (Smyth and Lecoeuvre, 2014).

These findings fit into a broader management picture of short-termism and power imbalance between functions. The shortcomings extend beyond those exerting power. They involve functionaries failing to engage in a dialogue around some shared values and sets of decision-making criteria. Marketing functionaries frequently fail to understand the terms on which their internal customers make assessments and thus lose opportunities for some rebalancing:

> The marketing profession is being challenged to assess and communicate the value created by its actions on shareholder value. . . . chief executives and board directors are more often disappointed in the performance of their chief marketing officers than in that of the other senior executives in the firm.
>
> (Srinivasan and Hanssens, 2009: 293)

## *Marketing*

Marketing is a value system to be owned by the chief executive and the main board. Marketing is also a management system that is linked with other functions. At the project level, marketing is about backcasting from a 'future perfect' to the present in order to configure activities to achieving the project goals (Pitsis et al., 2003), except from the marketing perspective, the goals are viewed from the being in the client's shoes as well as being in project management's shoes.

## FACT BOX 1.2 DECISION-MAKING FOR PROJECT BUSINESS DEVELOPMENT AND INVESTMENT

Large companies that are market leaders in their field, which have project business units (e.g. LVMH, PSA, Credit Lyonnais, Danone, Disneyland, Ferrero, Renault), were investigated regarding their return on marketing investment (ROMI). The underpinning decision-making for business development was assessed. The businesses had marketing budgets and the majority had dedicated marketing teams. Interviews were conducted over 6 months at several levels: President, General Managers, Marketing Directors, Directors of Communications and Marketing team members responsible for projects such as the launch new products, market development, and communication plans.

The qualitative research interviews were supplemented with some observation. Power exerted by Finance Departments was found to drive Marketing Departments to justify their recommendations for investment with ever-increasing rigor. Finance Departments used extrapolations and heuristic assessment to produce budget plans that look authoritative, yet subjectivity and uncertainty underpinned the presented data. Tangible and evidence-based hard data were being demanded from Marketing that was to serve risk-averse agendas. ROMI had to attributable to marketing in isolation from other factors to justify investment. The uneven application of rigor tended to restrict investment in marketing-related activities. In addition, the tools employed were company *specific*, having ROMI orientations without necessarily following established procedures for calculations. Intuitive objections to marketing investment from financial managers were repeatedly made on the grounds of an absence of adequate quantitative data as defined by finance rather than marketing criteria as well. Financial issues were recognized to dominating decision-making by the large majority interviewed. Some respondents evoked finance as the *cultural context*, that is, the prevailing set of shared values and underlying assumptions that render it difficult to justify proposals or challenge decisions – essentially a mobilization of bias.

In summary, the marketing–finance interface was characterized more by finance controlling inputs than upon marketing outputs and performance outcomes. This demonstrated a lack of common ground for constructive decision-making. The logic of accounting practice does not therefore accord with marketing and other management practices necessary for realistic assessment. There was a lack of a consistent business model and earning logic being applied.

*Source*: Smyth and Lecoeuvre (2014).

Marketing and the associated business strategy try to identify and set in motion the efforts to secure the right sort of work in sufficient quantity to serve the market and meet internal needs. Marketing is one of four key management areas along with the operations that provide the raison d'être, human resources so as to have people to do the work, and finance to serve other functions and account for profit and shareholder value. Marketing is about business performance. It is multi-disciplinary; there is no single source of theory, drawing upon a broad range of disciplines including economics, sociology, psychology and management (which also draws upon each of these). Theodore Levitt defined marketing in terms of:

> The purpose of a business is to create and keep a customer.
>
> (1983: 5)

More specifically two detailed academic definitions are presented:

> The central idea of marketing is to match the organization's capabilities with the needs of customers in order to achieve the objectives of both parties.
>
> (McDonald et al., 2011: 8)

> . . . a social and managerial process by which individuals and groups obtain what they need and want through creating and exchanging products and value with others.
>
> (Kotler et al., 1996: 6)

Two institutional definitions are provided. The American Marketing Association states:

> Marketing is the activity, set of institutions, and processes for creating, communicating, delivering, and exchanging offerings that have value for customers, clients, partners, and society at large.
>
> (AMA, 2007)

UK Chartered Institute of Marketing define marketing as:

> Marketing is the management process responsible for identifying, anticipating and satisfying customer requirements profitably.
>
> (CIM, 2009: 2)

Marketing helps shape capabilities (e.g. Möller, 2006) to lever value to qualify and bid for opportunities and subsequently to deliver valued solutions to clients. Supplier organizations have increasingly come to recognize the significance marketing functions make towards business operations and financial performance (Ganesan, 2012). Intensified competition has caused project businesses to reappraise their strategies, including marketing. For example, in the United States during the

1990s, construction contractors concerned with international competition recast marketing from primarily advertising and promotion to a direct contributor towards corporate performance (Kurien, 2004; cf. Narver and Slater, 1990). Understanding excellent performance from the customer perspective is seen as important for project businesses because clients seek more than meeting requirements within time, cost and quality (Butcher and Sheehan, 2010; Turkulainien et al., 2013).

Yet historically marketing was 'off the radar' and selling a rather isolated 'poor relation' in project businesses (e.g. Pinto and Covin, 1992; Turner, 1995; Smyth, 2000; Cova et al., 2002). Even amongst the reflective practitioners of professional practices, marketing has been somewhat of a taboo subject (e.g. Morgan and Morgan, 1991) of commercial disdain (Kotler and Connor, 1977). Low entry barriers compared and intense competition render many project businesses market takers rather than market makers, this being one reason for the low profile. A further reason has been a lack of language to articulate the content and benefits (cf. Lidstone, 1984), another being a consequential lack of awareness (Smyth, 2000), and management dialogue (cf. Smyth and Lecoeuvre, 2014). This has been changing slowly, marketing being in transition to a more considered and thorough set of approaches (e.g. Cova and Salle, 2005; 2007a; Smyth and Fitch, 2009; Smyth, 2013a).

Kurien (2004) found that contractors surveyed in Texas with robust marketing plans have higher levels of sales growth than those without implemented plans. She also found that those companies with a customer focus had double the growth rates compared to those largely having a task and project orientation. The rank order of factors from the survey amongst the growth firms with a customer orientation were:

1. Customer satisfaction,
2. Repeat business,
3. Making profits,
4. Increasing productivity,
5. Reducing cost.

Each of the above factors has a strategic and tactical dimension. Marketing is about strategy – *how* to do it – which includes configuring the offers and win-strategies that match generic sets of demands in the marketplace, and customized technical and tailored service offers for particular client projects. It is about sales implementation – *what* to do over project lifecycles, that is from courting and prequalification at the front-end to close out and final account. Marketing also covers market research, corporate communications, public relations (PR) and lobbying, as well as advertising. The focus here is more on the operational side of MoP. What does operations consist of in project businesses?

> Operations and operations management in project businesses is broader than the project. This is seen in two detailed ways. First is that some functions

> are located in the 'corporate centre' that inform and form part of operations such as procurement and estimating, technical services, and health and safety. Second is the operational link between the strategic front-end and project execution. These ways provide different lenses to operations management.
>
> (Smyth, 2014: 20)

Figure 1.1 sets this out, showing the interfaces between the 'corporate centre' of the project business and the operational side at the project level of the business. Projects consist of the strategic front-end to set projects up and execution through project management. Marketing and BDM is introduced into the project lifecycle at the front of the front-end, supported by project business systems and capabilities to mobilize the efforts to identify value, make commitments and develop the project-level strategies to prequalify, win bids, manage the clients, deliver added value and assess the value in use. Pan-project coordination occurs at programme management level. This in turn is supported by resource allocation through portfolio management. Marketing and BDM in concert with project management incurs

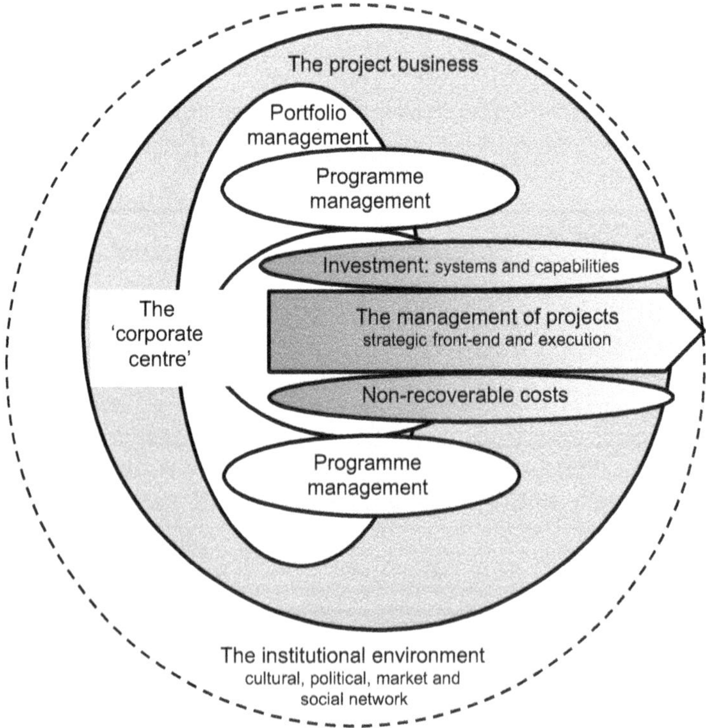


**FIGURE 1.1** The marketing interfaces in project businesses

*Source*: Adapted and developed from Smyth and Pryke (2008: 7).

non-recoverable costs to manage critical events and transgressions and undertake tactical responses excluded from project budgets (Smyth, 2000; cf. Storbacka et al., 1994; Jones et al., 2011). Marketing is less well embedded in most firms in comparison to other key functions (McDonald et al., 2011) and is particularly the case in project businesses (e.g. Cova and Salle, 2007a; Smyth and Kusuma, 2013).

### Sales and BDM

In project markets, *selling* tends to be called 'business development management', that is BDM. Business development is therefore a euphemism for sales in project businesses and is conducted by a range of people from director level to specialist BDMs. Although a conceptual subset of marketing, BDM is often disconnected from 'marketing' narrowly framed as corporate communications and promotion (Preece et al., 1998).

BDM can be defined in project businesses as the combined cross-functional and cross-departmental team effort to address and respond to all client questions to secure and retain projects (Kurien, 2004). It is managed by the marketing function, often represented by a board director with marketing responsibilities. It may also be managed at the programme level, and can include coordination through key account management (KAM) (McDonald et al., 1997; Smyth and Fitch, 2009). BDMs also undertake KAM roles. BDM is resourced through segmentation and programme management in order to mobilize a range of capabilities to secure and retain key clients, and mobilizing generic capabilities. Where a highly transactional approach is adopted, cruder categories such as procurement routes, types of contract, and track record, for example in building types are used as surrogates to imply alignment and segmentation. The scope of BDM depends upon the marketing strategy; it is essentially the implementation of the market plan (Harris and McCaffer, 2001).

## Definition and scope of marketing and BDM in theory and practice

Marketing theory and practice differ. There are substantive issues that reside between the theory and practice where concepts have yet to be fully tested. Ten *substantive issues* (SIs) are identified as key areas where there is need of conceptual development, a rebalancing of emphasis in application, and implementation rigor in practice. The source of these issues is the result of transactional practices that have been structured into the mindsets and actions on the ground. They may not have been intended consequences yet comprise many of the substantive issues that need to be addressed to induce coherence and rigor across the marketing paradigms and for the effective management of projects long-term.

**SI no. 1:** ***Market Management*** emphasizes *proactivity* in practice. Project management largely has a reactive approach to the market, and responds to trends and particular opportunities. It is a transactional approach to business and characteristic of the *marketing mix* paradigm. In crowded markets where clients make sophisticated and strategic demands of their suppliers, theory would suggest a diversity of project business approaches is healthy for the market and necessary for project businesses, yet practice has placed emphasis upon price amongst suppliers that keep investment and costs paired down to minimal levels. Academics tend to see project requirements as pre-given criteria and endorse the reactivity. Project business management and project managers have still to fully recognize the marketing contribution to operational and financial performance (cf. Ganesan, 2012).

**SI no. 2:** ***Service Management*** is part of a move towards a complementary *client* and *service focus*. Under a traditional task focus what seems 'good' from the perspective of technical and discipline-related skills and expertise, may not seem so good from a client perspective. Most customers and clients have come to expect added technical and service value from other suppliers. Projects meeting time-cost-quality/scope is merely satisfying minimum requirements or *value added*. This does not provide *added value* in technical and service content (see also **SI no. 10**). Service experience has been found to be largely 'off the radar' (Smyth, 2013a). The traditional assumption is that services reside 'downstream' (Davies, 2004). Yet the main contractor or systems integrator manages the service, indeed is the main service provider, especially if subcontracting all productive work. Service management is closely linked and is a prerequisite for the *relationship marketing* paradigm (Smyth, 2000) and for applying *project marketing* concepts (e.g. Cova et al., 2002). Client-centricity increases service management (Smyth and Fitch, 2009). It has been found that a service and client orientation benefits the supplier, for example enabling the expansion of the geographical market and the increase in market share (Kurien, 2004). It feeds into total asset management, facilities management to meet emerging 2050 sustainability criteria (Edkins et al., 2008). It facilitates service development to exceed compliance and comparative 'best' practice criteria (cf. Roberts et al., 2012; Smyth, 2013b; 2013c).

**SI no. 3:** ***Marketing Investment and Portfolio Management*** involves resource allocation to marketing that can be seen as part of overheads and expenditure and/or as *investment*. The production-orientated focus for financial management and accounting separates out investment, marketing costs and operational expenditure. Even under this conventional division, much marketing investment is dubbed as expenditure and an overhead. Attributing the return on marketing investment is difficult to predict and establish retrospectively, yet in service provision, the divisions of returns are conceptually artificial and inseparable in practice as all investment works together especially in service provision. Reducing service costs is marketing related and reduces quality (Grönroos, 2000). Theoretically, RBV allocates bundles of resources to secure competitive market positioning (Wernerfelt, 1984; Barney, 1991; 2003). A key element is marketing and BDM resources, and its linkage with other technical and service capabilities (cf. Möller, 2006; Davies and Brady, 2000; Davies et al., 2007). It is located at the level of portfolio management. Portfolio level looks for opportunities in the market and therefore links to market management (Rad and Levin, 2007). This leads to prioritization, cascading marketing-related resources down to programme and project management levels as part of $P^3M$.

**SI no. 4: *Client Management and Programme Management*** particularly emphasizes the issue between project management and complementary *coordination mechanisms for CLV*. Project businesses tend to see projects as the main unit for management. Client management and its internal interface between programme and project management are typically under-emphasized in theorization and practice. Clients are to be managed individually at programme-management level, for example by using KAM. Project businesses also have their own programmes and market segments to be managed from a marketing and BDM perspective. Here the issue is more than the value of a project and its contribution to turnover; it is the CLV over its estimated period of contribution to the project business. A client and service focus that accounts for CLV changes the criteria for informed decision-making and may change certain project decisions in the interests of client management and the supplier's long-term business performance.

**SI no. 5: *Marketing and BDM*** emphasizes the extent of functional isolation versus *integration*. Marketing operates at three levels. There is marketing as a way of thinking and attitude of mind, a way of organizing, and the set of tools and techniques from the strategic to tactical level (Grönroos, 2000). The aim is to join up thinking and action. This needs to be tackled in three ways. First, marketing and BDM are conceptually integrated activities. They are theoretically related and for integration in practice. Marketing strategy is implemented across several fronts; one of the most significant is BDM for project businesses. Second, marketing and BDM involve vertical integration, a strategy-to-tactics dimension that is implemented top-down and refined on an iterative basis from the ground. The bottom-up element is important for most project businesses because they are located near the head of the 'food chain'. Thus, much market research needs to be conducted within BDM through effective feedback loops from scanning the business environment market, identifying emergent and explicit trends, to concrete detailed evidence. Third, marketing and BDM involve horizontal integration, operating sequentially along project lifecycles in tandem with and as part of programme management. Marketing and BDM is injected at the front of the front-end, moving through the project execution stage, to the back-end of managing the *sleeping relationship* between projects (Hadjikhani, 1996) until repeat business is secured to turn the lifecycle into a loop or spiral, so starting the cycle again.

**SI no. 6: *BDM and Client Management*** particularly emphasizes the extent of the gap between discontinuity and *continuous and consistent service*. Project discontinuity is a prime feature of transactional markets (e.g. Hadjikhani, 1996). It is evident where internal resources are managed at the expense of clients and particular projects. Sensible for minimizing transaction costs, key staff are changed between projects and during projects (Smyth, 2000). Weak systems between the project business and project teams lead to non-standard practices and divergent action, compounded by leakage of understanding of client needs and tacit project knowledge. Continuity and consistency involves routinized and standardized management processes and procedures to capture consistency and retain tacit knowledge. This acts as a framework or umbrella, under which uniqueness, uncertainty, complexity and risk are managed. This is also supported from the programme level where KAM is operated (Smyth and Fitch, 2009). Resource allocation to maintain staff continuity and service consistency, enhanced from staff having scaled the learning curve of working with clients and by mobilizing tacit knowledge through project managers (e.g. Kelly et al., 2013), is thus part of a client and service focus.

**SI no. 7: *Vertical Systems and Integration*** particularly emphasizes the issues around the common attribute of weak systems at the corporate–project interface and *vertical coordination mechanisms of formal and informal routines.* It is claimed that many project businesses act as systems integrators between themselves and supply chain and cluster members (e.g. Davies et al., 2007). This external coordination is only as effective as its internal systems integration. Many project businesses have weak vertical systems with poor integration levels (e.g. Roberts et al., 2012; Smyth, 2013a). Increased significance is being attributed in research towards the relationships and linkages between the 'corporate centre' from the top level to the operational level (Morris et al., 2011) and for leveraging service content for operations and through supply chain management (cf. McIvor, 2000; Crespin-Mazet and Portier, 2010) – part of marketing as value identification and leverage (Christopher et al., 2002). Vertical integration also involves alignment of financial and human resource management (HRM) functions with a client and service management focus (cf. Bredin and Söderlund, 2011).

**SI no. 8: *Cross-functional Systems and Coordination Mechanisms*** emphasizes the issues of weak systems along project lifecycles and *systematic horizontal formal and informal routines.* BDM, through bid management, procurement, commercial management to project management functions, tends to operate in disconnected systems, based around departmental and functional expertise rather than along project lifecycles. While value chain coordination is part of the thinking towards integration (Porter, 1985), an overarching system to coordinate central departments is lacking. In contrast to Porter's value chain, marketing and sales in project businesses start before production rather than at the end. The chain model is poor at articulating the social capital and relationship management necessary for coordination, for example marketing at the front-end and towards and within TMOs (Cherns and Bryant, 1984) or broader coalitions (Winch, 2002). It describes value leverage and delivery rather than demonstrates how, which is so much more problematic where the project content is unique. The value chain planning process in the project management literature provides scant additional insight (cf. Winter et al., 2006), especially from the marketing and BDM perspective.

**SI no. 9: *Marketing and Managing the Project Lifecycle*** highlights the extent of the dissonance between linear project management and *iterative and agile management.* Reality is far removed from this 'idealized' linear conception of practices, which last planner, agile production and project management methodologies go some way to embrace. BDMs have theoretical responsibilities over project lifecycles to ensure that (non-contractual) promises made during BDM, commitments made at the front-end to add value, and specified requirements of value added are delivered through formal and informal routines during execution. Traditional feedback loops and key performance indicators are too late. Customer satisfaction measures are largely irrelevant if the expectations were inadequately articulated and captured at the outset to provide benchmarks. On top of which emergent requirements are frequently seen as deviations from project plans (Smyth, 2013b), rather than potential opportunities to add value, sometimes technical and always service value which has to be weighed up against CLV and project costs. There are also issues of continuity at the end of the project lifecycle in terms of total asset management, 2050 sustainability criteria as well as benefits derived in use (Edkins et al., 2008).

**SI no. 10: *Marketing and Value Creation*** emphasizes the issue of value added versus *added technical and service value.* Value from the marketing perspective is the realization of benefits and positive impact for the client and other stakeholders. During the project this is largely confined to service experience, upon completion value includes the project content and service in use. Value is defined by clients and by end-users. Value is more than the expertise of procurement, bid managers and commercial directors and project managers. Value creation is more than action confined to project management and execution, it is also identification and configuration at the front-end, working with supply chains and in win-strategy development. To deliver added value on a consistent basis requires in-depth understanding of the client business/operations and the motivations of the project DMU on the client side – the *deep understanding* referred to by McDonald et al. (2011). It is a function of co-creation between all parties, including the client (e.g. Vargo and Lusch, 2004; Prahalad and Ramaswamy, 2004a).

## Structure of the book

The book draws upon established theories and concepts from management and marketing and relates and 'translates' these into MoP. It draws upon empirical evidence, including case material from research published elsewhere, has been presented to limited audiences such as academic seminars and conferences, and evidence that has yet to be reported. Four main forms of representation are used: the written work, diagrammatic figures, tables and fact boxes.

The organization and brief outline of the chapters is provided next. **Chapter 2** addresses *management* at the 'corporate centre', particularly from the executive board level and portfolio management. It considers the constraints experienced in project businesses due to structuring and structures developed by management and the impact upon the conduct of market management and specifically marketing and BDM. This provides a basis for examining the marketing paradigms, lenses or approaches on offer.

**Chapter 3** commences the examination of the 'palette of paradigms' in marketing. The first approach considered is the transactional *marketing mix*. The main management literature will be briefly introduced and then the relevance to asset specific markets and project businesses in particular will be examined, especially 'place' as the delivery channel. Conceptual alignments and misalignments, hence strengths and weaknesses are evaluated and an assessment of the pertinence of this paradigm concludes the chapter. **Chapter 4** focuses upon the *relationship marketing* paradigm. The management literature will again be briefly introduced and the relevance to asset specific markets and project businesses will be examined. This is conceptually a more complex and demanding approach. More attention is therefore given to the conceptual principles and practical parameters. Scope and limitations are addressed in theory and practice. **Chapter 5** follows on from the previous chapter with consideration of the *project marketing* variant. The literature in this field is briefly reviewed and the conceptual opportunities and constraints offered by project marketing are evaluated. **Chapter 6** introduces an emergent and growing stream in marketing theory, that of *entrepreneurial marketing*. It is premature to claim it is or will become paradigmatic, but it is an insightful area for examining many current and often implicit areas of business development and marketing. An evaluation is made of its current and potential contribution to project businesses.

The marketing approaches each have implications for the way in which MoP is conducted. The next chapters begin to tease out the linkages, commencing with the execution focus, **Chapter 7** looks at market management and marketing through the lens of *project management*. The mindsets and management practice in terms the primary foci are considered, such as traditional production, project management and task foci on the one hand and customer, client and service foci on the other. The implications down the hierarchy in terms of $P^3M$ are considered. Project lifecycles are addressed as horizontal processes. The role of marketing and BDM as coordinating and integrating mechanisms are evaluated and how these relate to the extent of other horizontal mechanisms for performance improvement. The implications are considered in relation to CLV. The horizontal focus is continued in **Chapter 8**, which adopts a *management of projects* focus towards marketing and BDM. The location of marketing-related activities and the role of marketing and BDM is considered at developing project strategy and content at the front-end is examined, examining the implications in terms of $P^3M$ and along project lifecycles to post-completion.

Resources in the form of investment and commitment are needed for effective implementation. **Chapter 9** looks at resource allocation, tracing the explication to this point and interpreting the outcomes in terms of strategy and market management. This widens out the discourse into the *service-dominant logic* for **Chapter 10**, which is where the *relationship marketing* approach is currently developing and being transformed into the broader paradigm that links other aspects of management. Evaluation will be made of this emergent domain and the implications for other marketing paradigms explored in the project business context. **Chapter 11** leads on to give particular focus to value creation and delivery. Some current practices, some of the challenges and limitations are discussed for project businesses.

The *conclusion* is presented in **Chapter 12**, summing up the main issues covered, including the contribution made to the substantive issues identified in this chapter around theorization and practice. Recommendations for research and for reflective practice are made. Drawing the threads together to provide a picture of the progression of how the book develops has been attempted in Figure 1.2. This is an indicative guide and acts as a signpost as to how the book builds, showing the main marketing paradigms

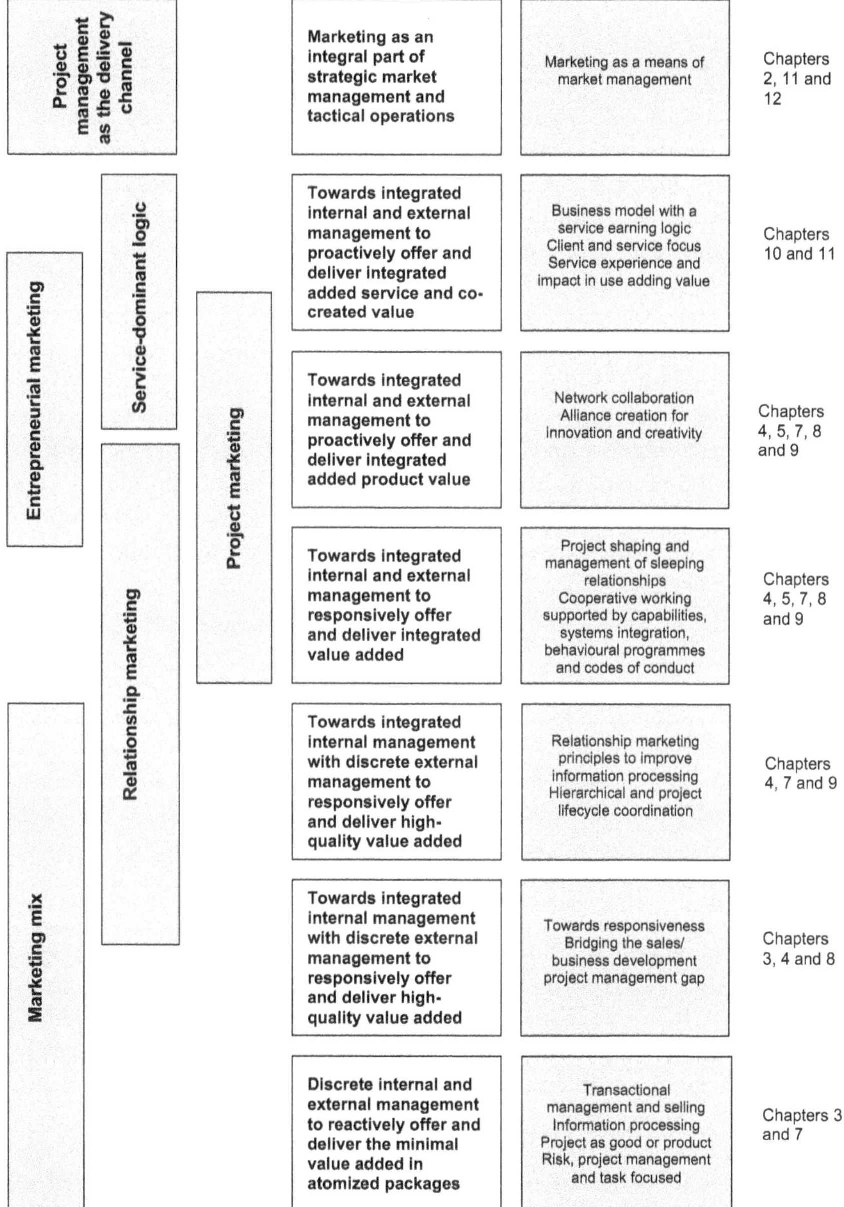


**FIGURE 1.2** Mapping marketing as a means of market management

and approaches on the left-hand side, culminating in marketing and project business development as a means of market management. Against this is mapped the shift in the integrated identification and delivery of solutions. A selection of some of the recurring issues is then presented to give a few examples of a few key and recurrent issues with a loose guide by chapter as to where threads are drawn together and progression of the arguments is made.

## Audiences and benefits

The primary audience is academic. There are two specific academic audiences. First are researchers in the field of MoP. This includes the project environment, project business and project management levels. It includes those researching areas of market management and competitive advantage, marketing and sales in project businesses. It may also be of interest to researchers in the general field of management because projects have become a major delivery channel.

The second academic audience is students, principally the doctoral researcher, master's students and to a more limited degree undergraduate students interested in the field, especially for dissertations.

The secondary audience is practitioners. Those in project businesses, especially the reflective practitioner and senior management who wish to progress their businesses will find food for thought and principals to adopt with some lessons learned from the field. There is a crossover between practice and education for those studying part-time courses, which should prove fertile ground for encouraging reflective practice.

The book is therefore *for* project management researchers, trainers and students in order to incorporate this understated yet fundamental project management set of tasks, as well as those specifically interested in market management, marketing and 'business development' research. The book is *for* management from main board and executive levels to the operations level, including those directly involved in marketing and sales as it is about management from the top-down and along project lifecycles and the CLV to project businesses.

## Conclusion

The market is undergoing fundamental changes, affecting projects and project businesses, especially around inherent complexity and sophisticated client demands. These external forces are shaping the internal structures and processes of project businesses. In turn, project businesses influence the shape of markets according to the business strategies, logic and models they adopt. It has been argued that market management and business development, marketing and selling or BDM are amongst the most influential shapers of the market. The project businesses that have most impact will be those that are most successful at so doing. They will be the ones that are satisfying their client base through identification, co-creation and delivery of value. They are therefore likely to be the ones performing best in terms of market share and profitability. The development of project capabilities, market-related and marketing capabilities to serve performance is an important part of this process. Marketing capabilities conceptually penetrate into the management of projects to influence the conduct of project management and programme management. How and the extent to which it is done depends on the quality of management and upon the choice of marketing paradigm and processes for implementation.

The chapter has introduced some key issues for research and practice, namely:

1. To what extent are markets managed by project businesses?
2. In what ways is the market managed at an operational level through marketing and BDM?
3. What is the extent of the issue between the theoretical principles applied in practice and the theory?

Ten SIs have been identified to provide detailed focus to begin to address these key issues. This is on the basis that a theoretical and applied focus upon measures of change is being developed in and across project businesses. 'Good' theory and related concepts are highly practical yet challenging, having a profound effect upon business performance. This chapter has scoped the field in order to (i) set the parameters and signpost some of the content for understanding of marketing and BDM in project businesses, (ii) select the most appropriate marketing paradigm for different businesses and client needs, (iii) approach detailed implementation from theory to practice. All management has degrees explicit or implicit marketing and BDM practice and is trying to improve market management and business development, drawing out the implications for the overall management of project businesses and performance in the core activity of MoP. At a detailed level, projects become 'skill containers' (Winch, 2013) involving the client and suppliers as relatively stable organizations and their project TMOs or coalitions as temporary organizational vehicles for the delivery. Effective market management and marketing coordinate the corporate and project levels.

Market management and business development are high-level activities setting strategic goals for implementation, largely top-down. Marketing and BDM are strategic issues for implementation through programme and project management and along project lifecycles.

# 2

# TOWARDS MANAGING THE MARKET

## Introduction

From an overview to a management view, this chapter begins to conceptually drill down to explore issues faced by management. The overview was provided in **Chapter 1**. The *aim* of this chapter is to investigate what is being done and what can be done in market management and business development, especially as it affects marketing and business development management (BDM). The issues about the extent to which project businesses are market managers begin at a senior management level in the project business hierarchy. The implications for the strategic choice of marketing approach is dealt with subsequently. This choice regards the 'palette of paradigms'. It also relates to the management of projects from the strategic front-end through project execution on to post-completion.

Market management and marketing and BDM as part of business development are changing. The picture is a dynamic one. The transitioning that is going on can be located in the three categories to gauge market management: *reactive, responsive* and *proactive* (Narver et al., 2004; Atuahene-Gima et al., 2005; Sørensen, 2012). These categories were raised in relation to some of the substantive issues raised in **Chapter 1** and are also intrinsically related to the paradigm adopted by any business, the transactional approach being most reactive (**Chapter 3**) with relationship marketing and especially the service-dominant logic being highly engaged and proactive (**Chapters 4** and **10** respectively). This can be seen as balancing the extent of being followers exploiting opportunities with greatest efficiency and exploring possibilities to maximum effect (March, 1991). The historic focus has been upon reaction in market management with responsiveness largely at the project level when requirements and briefing documents are received. Ive (1995) explains this position in his response to the Latham Report for UK construction industry in terms of a good detective story: the contractor has not the motive, means nor opportunity to drive change. This is because suppliers have largely been followers rather than market makers, having insufficient market power overall and at a detailed level, because they are working to contract where prices are 'established', at least in terms of securing a sale, ahead of production and out-turn prices.

The client is the procurer and has power, and indeed has often been the initiator of innovation, for example in procurement routes, contract types and approaches to operation (e.g. Davies et al., 2009). Adaption and innovation have largely been conducted in *reaction* to client needs and market opportunities in project businesses (e.g. Betts and Ofori, 1992; Yisa el al., 1996). The insight of Burns and Stalker (1961) is that the desire for firms in general to change has come more from a fear of losing market position to competitors than from any drive to innovate and manage the market towards competitive advantage. It can also be argued that project businesses have actively contributed to this position by educating clients to negotiate bids around lowest price, as will be examined further in **Chapter 3**. The capital cost of the project is typically small compared to the use value and cost in use, and while short-term client considerations may prevail in many instances, longer term business issues are important for many clients, and regulatory issues will increasingly feed into this picture, particularly around the environmental sustainability that affect many project sectors. There are broader institutional factors that have been identified as being of growing significance (Morris and Geraldi, 2011; Morris, 2013). The call has been made for a bigger and more ambitious paradigm for the management of projects that goes beyond the traditional tools and techniques of execution and 'soft management' issues, covering external as well as internal environments of the management context, including the interface between industrial networks, project businesses and projects (cf. Cravens and Piercy, 1994; Håkansson and Snehota, 1995). Morris et al. state we need a *broader view of the theoretical underpinnings of the subject* (2011: 2). Market management, marketing and BDM are part of this picture.

To begin to address these issues, the chapter investigates the following:

A. The management of markets, marketing and the sales process to develop the project business requires a broad theoretical view.
B. Implementation is initially top-down for structuring, governing, and therefore coordinating and integrating activities in the hierarchy and setting the parameters for horizontal integration across programmes and along project lifecycles.
C. Management recognition of constraints and barriers posed by internal organization and the need for coordination mechanisms that span organizational silos and boundaries for cross-functional working.

The next section sets out in current state of play in research and practice before examining in more detail some of the main issues around management practices in addressing issues in the hierarchy and cross-functional operations in regard to market management and marketing.

## Scoping the current state of play

Senior management holds the strategy and implementation function, which includes market management and business development and implementation at the interfaces with other functions. Care is needed addressing the call for a more ambitious paradigm to facilitate the management of project businesses and projects. Researchers can conflate management and operations, even ownership (Frame, 2002; Engwall, 2003). Organizational functions are divided into distinct groups of people and departments with their own motivations and goals (Simon, 1959; 1979). This is necessary to provide focus, be efficient and effective. When the boundaries become set and solid, rather than being pervious and perforated to enable efficient and effective integration, performance is constrained. It is the rigidity and solidity that is largely the practice problem, leading to silos, which in turn structure thinking over time to induce 'silo mentalities'. This is has been prevalent in many project businesses, with recent evidence continuing to confirm the problem amongst international construction majors in regard to marketing and BDM (Smyth, 2013a).

Management decides how to structure the business. Rigidity in structures affects the ability to adopt a broader paradigm to the management of projects (MoP). Different structures are better suited to different marketing paradigms. Structuring has management implications. The trend has been towards delayering and a reduction in hierarchical structures. The motives have been to (i) focus upon core business with the advent of portfolio management software programmes among stock market investors, (ii) reduce the opportunities for career empire building, (iii) apply more flexibly and responsive approaches to management facilitated by the introduction of IT hardware and software. The trend has also been towards being more customer and client-centric approach. The means have been (a) the introduction of just-in-time, small batch, lean and agile production, coupled to (b) the advent of alliances and partnering in industrial networks at the supplier interface and relationship marketing at the customer interface. In addition, some product and service packages of high asset specificity are characterized by complexity, demanding flexible and adaptable approaches to manage operations, and to manage the interface between the 'corporate centre' and operations. Project businesses are typically in that last category of product and service delivery of highly complex specific assets. In some countries where the state owns the project business, rigidities tend to arise from bureaucratic requirements and career empires as well as short-term issues around accountability on the one hand and corrupt practices on the other hand.

Aligning structures to operations, aligning them to interaction with suppliers and clients to provide integrated service solutions is an important role for governance (cf. Müller, 2009). Corporate and economic governance are functions that articulate the way in which business is conducted. Economic governance protects rights, enforces contracts and encourages collective action in the marketplace. Economic governance encourages the specialization of different tasks between organizations in the market and within firms to achieve efficiency. This is in line with Adam Smith's division of labour (e.g. Gibbons, 2010). Corporate governance also links to rights and contract enforcement through ethical considerations and articulates the management of diverse functions, the mechanisms of coordination and collective action (e.g. Solomon and Solomon, 2004). Governance is thus an overarching and strategic level of intervention to frame the marketing management and business development.

This raises the debate about the structuring of key functions. Marketing is conceptually a function that necessarily works with others and, as will be developed in subsequent chapters, also has an integrating role between functions in its own right (see also Smyth, 2014). There are multiple functions, although finance, human resources and marketing are essential to support and feed operational functions. Marketing and BDM functions are configured as departments or separate units of operation. Finance is typically organized departmentally or in a team. Human resource management (HRM) is typically a departmental function. Operations are structured into multiple departments, especially in project businesses.

Financial functions necessarily pervade entire project businesses in order to make investments, develop capabilities, yield profits, control costs and manage cash flow. There is a tension as to how finance views the main interests of a business. There is one view that the only interests a business serves are those of the owner or shareholders (Friedman, 1970; 2000), asserted on the basis of Adam Smith's work (Smith, 1776) although the totality of his work contradicted this assertion (Smith, 1759). There are multiple interests, for example employee interests, social and environmental responsibilities, and in this particular context the interests of *clients* being served. Interests are partly although incompletely addressed through corporate social responsibility and governance issues (Solomon and Solomon, 2004). This leads onto the other main management view, which is that is one main role of management to serve the range of stakeholder and societal interests, including the client with efficiency and effectiveness. This involves senior management strategy, governance and operational considerations, that is, from formulation to realization of diverse interests being served.

Marketing and BDM are typically organized into teams. Conceptualization and the normative position derived from the theory–practice dislocation is that this function should also pervade the configuration of value, development of capabilities, securing work, setting bid margins, satisfying clients and enhancing reputation. These functions are less integrated on the ground in project businesses. Many of the functions are split between functional teams, for example selling to prequalify, developing win-strategies in bid management, setting bid margins, are frequently undertaken by different people across a range of functions.

How has marketing and BDM emerged and evolved on project businesses in theory and practice? It is the construction literature that made much of the early running, often from the normative perspective. Marketing was sporadically adopted (Moore, 1984), and selling to a large degree conformed to the stereotype of personal networks based around entertaining and social obligations where action was totally isolated from other management activity and BDMs used personal internal networks to inform senior management and others. Contacts were not owned by the business, but vigorously guarded as the currency of BDMs (Smyth, 2000). Hillebrandt and Cannon (1990) noted the BDM emphasis upon a narrow focus of getting shortlisted for tender or bid opportunities. Bell (1981) examined prevailing attitudes within UK construction, stating distinctive services could be yet undeveloped (cf. Arditi and Davis, 1988). Hardy and Davies (1983) concluded management attitudes were indifferent. Richardson (1996) stated a cultural change was necessary, although Fisher (1986) had found more receptivity at the tactical level of BDM. Morgan and Morgan (1991) found that skepticism towards marketing still prevailed, Shearer (1990) pointing out the difficulty of translating marketing concepts into project environments. Others concurred with the lack of adoption both in specialist markets (Kotler and Connor, 1977; Morgan and Burnicle, 1991) and international markets (Pheng, 1991).

Yet management awareness of marketing was increasing in the sense that varied definitions and notions of marketing were emerging (Namo and Fellows, 1993). Pettinger (1998) stated traditional avenues for securing competitive advantages were being eroded for construction project businesses and claimed marketing offered new avenues. Yisa et al. (1996) found that more sophisticated client procurement strategies would drive contractors to adopt more strategic approaches. Partnering and supply chain management as forms of relational contracting were being advocated (Egan, 1998). Market segmentation and strategic targeting had started to be adopted by and during the early 1990s (Smyth and Fitch, 2009). A less transactional approach was emerging in general and in marketing (Smyth, 2000; Preece et al., 2003; Smyth and Fitch, 2009). The theoretical developments in marketing have proceeded apace. The slow adoption of marketing mix principles and subsequent slow transition towards the adoption of a few relationship marketing principles considerably lag conceptual developments.

Theoretical developments to aid translation and adoption of marketing into project business markets came later and from across a range of project sectors. This trend lagged yet overlapped trends in the construction literature. This literature is less normative and is more focused on what is observed 'on the ground'. Pinto and Covin (1992) pointed out the hidden marketing role of the project manager. The hidden nature arises from the historic production orientation of a task and project management focus in project businesses and temporary multi-organizational teams (TMOs) (Cherns and Bryant, 1984) rather than the complementary client and service focus (see **Chapter 1**). This strand of literature also points out the isolated position of marketing (Pinto and Covin, 1992; Turner, 1995; Themistocleous and Wearne, 2000). Discontinuity of project work and the effect upon suppliers was an early development from the management field (Hadjikhani, 1996). This was extended in project marketing management into discontinuity, uncertainty and complexity, the so-called D-U-C framework (e.g. Mandják and Veres, 1998; Skaates and Tikkanen, 2003b). This strand of work is developed under *project marketing* in **Chapter 5**. The development of project capabilities and marketing has been examined by Davies et al. (2007) (cf. Brady and Davies, 2004) to match the search for solutions with the systems integrator role that project businesses perform, especially when they are indirect producers themselves. Cooper and Budd (2007) have argued the need to integrate BDM with project management. In relation to MoP, front-end management underplays marketing (Artto, 2001), although Cova and Salle (2011) have endeavoured to establish the link. The underplaying of marketing in front-end management arises for several reasons set out below.

First, the literature on MoP pointed towards the strategic front-end prior to as well as during execution (Morris and Hough, 1987; Morris, 1994). It overlooked marketing functions. Provision of marketing-related concepts and practical guidance in MoP is subsequently light or even absent. A client perspective has primarily been adopted (e.g. Morris, 2013; Edkins et al., 2013), which is an important reason. The viewpoint is of the client meeting their own needs through its management of suppliers; it works less well for the project business trying to meet client needs from a marketing and project management perspective.

Second, marketing and BDM are located at the front of the front-end, where senior management in project businesses recognize this and the benefit of functional involvement in a sufficiently timely way.

Third, routines suggested in the literature provide direction yet do not necessarily guide content, action and behaviour. The scope and nature of the project work is open-ended, and a great deal of marketing guidance is also open-ended. There is plenty of scope for misalignment. The open-endedness may offer intellectual challenges and practical room for maneouvre in how to conduct projects. In relationship marketing terms, interfacing with multiple internal and external actors in both interpersonally and inter-organizationally is a central issue. How relationships lever value is also important, carrying high levels of uncertainty for defining of scope and requirements and responding to emergent requirements (cf. Smyth and Edkins, 2007; Edkins et al., 2013). These are necessary yet complex management issues that are less easy to resolve at a detailed level in practice for it is a purpose of management to decide how to respond and be proactive at a fine grain of implementation and that is part of the process of differentiation and hence advantage in the market. This is a management task in relation to market management and marketing.

Fourth and closely related to the previous point, implementation involves management understanding of the issues and in that sense being 'experts'. Following the concepts and principles yet having a *relatively free hand* and being less concerned with *following a script* (Edkins et al., 2013: 81; cf. Dreyfus and Dreyfus, 2005) can prove helpful in defining the precise position in which the project business is competing. At all times, the 'expert' view involves being aligned with what clients value in defining the precise market position for value creation (Vargo and Lusch, 2004).

Greater client-centricity has been noted across the literature: for example client-centricity at the front-end in pre-work and by building a customer-based approach (Pinto and Rouhiainen, 2001), and in client relationships, for example building relationships to increase the client lifetime value (CLV), that is, the worth of the customer rather than the worth of projects per se (Smyth and Fitch, 2009).

The description provided suggests that market management and especially marketing is weak in project sectors. The literature for management shows a considerable lag between theory and practice in project businesses, yet the current range of theorization is only beginning to accommodate some of the current range of practices on the ground (**Chapter 6**). Practice is also changing in line with what is conceptually understood. Looking back to the mid-1990s, it was in the United States and United Kingdom that 13 per cent of firms could be described as sophisticated marketing decision-makers (Greenley and Bayus, 1994). In a European comparison, only 50 per cent of firms had long-term and annual marketing plans in the early 2000s (Dibb et al., 2001). A later study of 750 firms confirmed a link between marketing planning and performance (Vorhies and Morgan, 2005; Brooksbank et al., 2010). It would be claiming too much to postulate that good marketing strategies always lead to better performance, but it is reasonable to conclude that good performance benefits from good marketing and perhaps excellent performance must include a degree of good marketing in the mix. It does indicate that there can be improvement in business performance where good marketing includes a comprehensive marketing strategy and sound implementation down the hierarchy and horizontally across functions and project lifecycles.

The marketing process includes all resources and activities to meet client needs and induce positive impacts for clients, society and in the environment. Marketing and BDM can be structured into a distinct function or department, but cannot be confined to a single function, department or job role. It is a set of dynamic and cross-functional activities, which are coordinated as a function and through any prescribed department to ensure all functions are aligned to these as well as other strategic and operational goals. Gummesson (2000) claims everyone is a part-time marketer. He refers to reasoning that suggests a distinct department may be unnecessary, but this is conditional on all personnel being entirely marketing as well as operationally orientated. However structured and coordinated, there are constraints to be managed.

## Constraints in coordination and from management

### *Walls and invisible walls*

Organizations have boundaries acting as both barriers and walls of protection. They also erect internal walls between functions and departments for resource allocation and management purposes. To what extent does any form of organization constrain marketing? To what extent does management in project businesses constrain BDM through silo thinking and structural solutions? Many project businesses are structured into business units (BUs). They are typically structured into BUs around *market segments* defined in terms of procurement routes and contract types, and defined at a more detailed level by project characteristics that can be promoted in terms of track record. It has the consequence that many of the early client considerations are left to the client to choose the approach by choosing the BU or division rather than the project business understand the client and help them choose from a more informed position. This is less significant for sophisticated clients with their own large programmes of project work, but it is for less frequent procurers who have large and significant projects. The point has previously been expressed this way: *Main contractors create 'walls' between themselves and the market to the extent that issues organized as processes in most industries are organized as structures.* (Smyth, 2006: 22).

These BUs allow a light touch to putting systems and processes in place. It is common in international project businesses to have a main board and BU or divisional board of directors with marketing responsibilities. The divisional board director will develop interpersonal coordination with the marketing and BDM team. There are typically few formal routines. The interpersonal dimension may evolve into informal routines that extend beyond the life of any interpersonal relationship. However, the loose nature of this type of coordinating mechanism is that it can be inconsistently applied, appear less authoritative to others and may remain underdeveloped through the iterative evolution of criteria and procedures that articulate the overall mechanism of coordination (see Fact Box 2.1). This contrasts with the finance function. The Finance Director may manage the department with strong interpersonal relationships, yet the finance team often operates with strong routines using integrated software programmes, such as ERM- and SAP-like systems, as well as spreadsheets. These feed into reporting routines that do look authoritative and have credibility with others at all management levels. This is aided by the fact that people read numerical data as authoritative, finding it difficult to challenge (Smyth and Lecoeuvre, 2014).

Interface management is significant for marketing and business development. It is stated:

> Interfaces occur between independent and semi-independent functions. Functional interfaces occur both within the project business and between the project business and project. These are hierarchical interfaces and are not especially time bound. The project business–project interface is typically poorly structured, with weak systems and relationship management for top-down management support. The main issue raised here is about the quality of management. Functional interfaces also occur horizontally along project lifecycles from the front-end, through execution to post-project stages, which includes a link back to client management and repeat business. Effective management of these functional interfaces is important for all projects and critical for complex, large projects. Interface management is one activity that is task focused.
>
> (see also Smyth, 2014: 155–6)

Gann and Salter (2000) argue that project-based organizations are only able to harness and reproduce their technological capabilities when they integrate

## FACT BOX 2.1 STRUCTURING AND COORDINATING MECHANISMS IN AN INTERNATIONAL CONTRACTOR

A large European-based engineering and construction contractor has its own structures and means of coordination, the overall strengths and weaknesses being reasonably typical of many project businesses from SME to international operators.

EuroCo has a main board in its head office, where market management and business development strategy and decisions are conducted for the project businesses as a whole. This is mirrored at national level. At national level for the operational divisions, a market strategy is developed and revised on a regular cycle.

*Customer Plans* are developed for the few key clients to define who are the key clients, what procurement routes they are expected to use, and to assess their 5- to 10-year pipeline of work. EuroCo sometimes evaluates its strengths and weaknesses in relation to key clients and in relation to competitor analysis. There was not a consistent application of this procedure. Monthly board meetings are held and discuss the key clients and progress with the current and prospective pipeline of work.

The director responsible for *customer solutions* assigns directors to counterpart client contacts in the key customers. They write reports on contact outcomes, which are for presentation to the monthly board meetings. This is monitored and scores are given. Customer drivers can be picked up at this level. The consistency of board directors making contact and writing reports and of the meeting addressing this agenda item was reported as sporadic.

BDM in EuroCo was operating without a great deal of high level market intelligence, relationship and operational knowledge from clients. Their procedures and informal routines were relatively isolated. Committing resources to clients or particular projects prior to getting through the prequalification stage is difficult because of a lack of internal awareness at senior management level of the clients, the risks, their needs and partner benefits. When a project reaches the stage with the opportunity to bid, it is referred up to the main board in its head office for risk assessment. Project risks can be informed by broader market risks and client-specific risks. The involvement of the main board at this stage is an indication of the project focus for organizing the business and the absence of a complementary customer or client focus.

As the bid proceeds and if the tender is won, there are opportunities to lever value for execution. In EuroCo, this is covered by the *preconstruction stage*, which is a recently introduced central function. BDM are not included in the preconstruction stage, although they may have an in-depth understanding of client needs and project issues. There is also an absence of coordination with *procurement*. Procurement as a functional department stated it was largely unaware of what is needed from the supply chain from the perspective of winning work and levering value to meet client needs. The marketing and BDM function were structurally isolated with underdeveloped formal and informal routines to act as mechanisms of coordination.

*Source*: Interviews conducted with directors, senior management, departmental and project managers, 1st and 2nd quarters of 2012.

non-routine project processes and routine business processes. Acha et al. (2005) argue that the challenge project-based organizations face is how to manage the interaction between temporary actions and repetitive business practices. Merrow (2011) affirms the importance of interface management (cf. Kohli and Jaworski, 1990; Slater and Narver, 1994; Biemans et al., 2010). Merrow states that each function has its own purpose and ways of interpreting conduct in task execution. Separate interpretation has been conducted on global oil and gas megaprojects with attempts to manage integrated cross-functional systems for the last 40 years, although some national petroleum companies continue to function with a lack of functional working. Oil and gas may be 'best in class'. Yet, many IT and construction companies lack necessary integration. It leads to a lack of integration in project businesses rending Market Management and BDM somewhat isolated with a consequential compromise in value configuration (Smyth, 2013a; cf. Davies et al., 2007).

How a firm coordinates its activities is a long-standing issue in economics (e.g. Coase, 1937; 1988), management structure, governance, and coordination (e.g. Ouchi, 1977; 1980; Mintzberg, 2003). The issue is echoed in market management and for marketing strategy, vertically from the corporate centre in portfolio management and at the project business–project interface, horizontally across programmes and along project lifecycles. It is more than a matter of interfacing with existing systems, but it is also about the system incorporating a marketing orientation in its design (Kohli and Jaworski, 1990; Slater and Narver, 1994).

A problem has been identified in relation to the relative isolation of marketing and BDM. The evidence presented in Fact Box 2.1 illustrates a pattern common across project businesses (Fitch and Smyth, 2009), which is broader than BDM (Smyth and Kusuma, 2013). To the extent that 'silo mentalities' prevail, an inward focus develops from a marketing perspective and from the perspective of integration a lack of systems at functional interfaces and project stages exist. Addressing these matters is a management task, perhaps *the* management task to coordinate operations. At board level integration between marketing functions and finance is necessary. To survive project businesses must keep costs and investment low. Yet selective investment is necessary to develop capacity and capabilities for performance and expansion – a part of market management and business development. There has to be the *will* to invest that is align with client *needs*. The needs are always present, but the will is not. Short-termism at the sacrifice of the medium-to-long term profitability and shareholder value (e.g. Ambler, 2005; Weissbrich et al., 2007) may threaten survival. The economic principle that investment is needed to yield a return is a truism. The return on marketing investment (ROMI) that is both marketing informed and marketing related has been argued to be a tool to aid dialogue and integration (Smyth and Lecoeuvre, 2014). Addressing this issue sets the context for management action. This interface illustrates the general need for integration between marketing and BDM with bid management, finance, procurement and supply chain management, the commercial and operations director roles, technical director and project management to cite some of the key roles and functions. To conduct this constructive evaluation to address interface management sometimes must challenge 'taken-for-granted thinking' that can be embedded or entrenched; thus, deemed change can meet internal resistance.

Returning to the isolation of market management and business development in relation to marketing and to BDM, two dimensions for integration are frequently evident:

1. Board level integrated strategic thinking and planning:
   i. Board level strategy or business plan formation for market management, especially where finance drives cost control rather than serves profit generation and long-term shareholder value;
   ii. Board level market and marketing strategy with a particular focus upon project pipelines rather than client management at the operational level.
2. Marketing and BDM level integration with other departmental functions and project lifecycle functions.

Senior management has contractual obligations to shareholders and coordinates management accordingly (Jensen and Meckling, 1976). They may emphasize survival and returning satisficing profits (cf. Skitmore and Smyth, 2007), which is a strong normative and prescriptive position. It can lead to the pursuit of explicit and implicit self-interest that falls short of the interests of the business. This may not be by active decision-making. It can be by default or passiveness. Effective management can look difficult, requiring stretch targets, including stretch targets for senior management – the paths of least management resistance and being market followers may then look attractive at least in these respects (e.g. Sen, 1987; Jordi, 2010). Survival as the first priority can include selective investment. Investment may proceed incrementally on an affordable loss basis, but so doing can cause some misalignment and confusion between the previous and new means for coordination.

Silos can look attractive. One result is that the division into separate BUs reduces the need for management supervision as formal and informal routines are established pertaining to each division. It keeps transaction costs down, minimizes training and induction needs, and tends to lead to efficiency (through input–output ratios) at the expense of effectiveness (margins and market share). Putting in place the systems and procedures for integration at the interfaces increases transaction costs (but not necessarily net operational expenditure). It increases competitiveness if conducted well.

A lack of internal integration affects the ability to lever the optimum solutions from supply chains (Davies et al., 2007) and effectively connect with the broader scope of the network economy in which marketing and BDM operates (e.g. Achrol, 1996; Achrol and Kotler, 1999; Grönroos, 2000). The network includes influencers and other stakeholders beyond immediate and potential suppliers.

## *Breaking down the walls*

What is the normative and prescriptive position? The issue in moving from theorizing about business development to a normative position can be pursued through the application of conceptual possibilities derived from that resource-based view of the firm (Wernerfelt, 1984; Barney, 1991; 2003) and behavioural theories of the firm (Cyert and March, 1992). These theories set out conceptual principles, and drilling down may suggest core competencies. At a finer grain of analysis core competencies may comprise, for example, knowledge management. Yet this type of theorization provides little conceptual guidance as to how to choose and develop competencies. The amount of research effort put into *explicit* knowledge management in management and the project management literature suggests high levels of interest in research, yet the pattern of interest and action is unsubstantiated and lacks replication in practice (e.g. Smyth, 2010b; Kelly et al., 2013).

It is necessary to drill down to a specific area of market management or business development, for example service diversification, mergers and acquisitions or marketing for research and practice prescriptions in the forms of conceptual guidance and applied options. Taking marketing, applied concepts and models help identify markets, segments and customers. They help align internal resources and capabilities with the market and configure these to deliver to requirements on time, within cost and with quality (value added) and preferably exceed this to improve competitiveness (added value) (Sørensen, 2012). Senior management is responsible for strategy approval and its coordination through formal and informal routines at operational and tactical levels for marketing and BDM. This is the strategy implementation process.

Senior management spends a great deal of time outward facing, connecting with their institutional and market networks and key clients. This has a positive effect, but it has also has limits for two reasons:

1. The senior management view is one of four market views. It is outward facing and internally top-down. The BDM is a second view that is outward facing and largely bottom-up. The client audit and feedback provide the other views. These draw in the external view bottom-up. So does market research, which is rarely used within project businesses because its position in the food chain, although networking amongst senior management and BDM, explorative and experimental sales targets (say 10 per cent of effort – see Smyth, 2000) provide indirect forms of market research. All views are needed to gain a rounded picture.
2. Competitors are typically plugged into the same networks and are privy to the same sets of information, so over-reliance on this information source leads to zero-sum outcomes, where project businesses all compete against each other based on the same or similar information.

To address the constraints and barriers faced, one way is to break down the internal boundaries and departmental walls is to have open systems and a more ecological and responsive mode of operation (McDonald et al., 2011). Another and related way is to consider other functions as internal customers of service delivery (Grönroos, 2000). If senior management fail to appreciate the role of internal marketing, money invested in internal marketing and for BDM in general will only partially pay off. Marketing investment and the form it takes is a means of differentiation in itself.

Project businesses with no differential advantage will compete largely on price. This leads to intense rivalry (Porter, 1979; 1980) and 'price wars' in many project sectors during recessive conditions (Leading Edge, 1994). Differentiation through procurement routes is marginal as these are easily replicated by competition and in many project sectors. They are structural 'solutions' to a marketing issue (Smyth, 2006), giving initiative to clients and hence stealing ground from BDMs to work with clients to develop solutions at a strategic level at the front of the front-end. The recent work of Kujala and her colleagues (2010) identifies four conceptual business models based upon market segments and find five in practice: (i) the transactional-product segment of basic installed base service as a business model, (ii) transactional-process of customer support services, (iii) the relationship-product model of Operations and Maintenance (O&M) outsourcing, and (iv) the sub-divided relationship-process segment of lifecycle solutions, which was found to be subdivided into EPC and O&M solutions. These are all closely associated with procurement routes, especially the EPC and O&M positions. These are typically structured on divisional bases to organize procurement and are thus structural marketing solutions.

BDMs can help clients formulate their project strategy and the parameters for value creation where solutions are predetermined through over-structuring. The project is always about the future (Pitsis et al., 2003). Current provision is inadequate, the client imagines something new, the decision-makers try to make sense of the need to formulate the project and possible suppliers help explore the potential. They can help identify and configure value formed around expectations and shape of requirements. The project is only the means to an end; it is the use value or benefits and impact that are required. It is probable that the most successful project businesses will be those that manage survival and go on to prioritize investment selectively. Investment to reduce the internal constraints is one important means to improve marketing as a function and provide improved performance.

How far should the project business go to overcome the constraints and barriers in order to achieve integration? There are long- and short-term answers. The long-term reply is entirely based upon how project businesses respond to each other in the marketplace. The more integrated businesses become and the extent to which this is successful in improving performance will shape what clients demand in the future and thus how project businesses behave in order to survive. The short-term reply depends upon the management strategy of project businesses and it is the success of the strategies that accumulate to affect the long term. In general a relational approach to business and to marketing will yield the greatest level of integration (see **Chapters 4**, **5** and **10**), whereas a transactional approach to business and to marketing will yield the lowest levels of integration (**Chapter 3**). Therefore, the constraints are highest under the transactional approach, yet clients are the least demanding in these exchanges, typically being concerned with time–cost–quality, and in many cases with strong cost drivers (Porter, 1980). The relational approach places more emphasis upon value, particularly added value. Added value in project businesses emphasizes value for money through additional content rather than cost reduction and the content can be both customized technical content or tailored service content.

The link between the long- and short-term views are to a large extent dependent upon how any leading project businesses in their sector, tier and geographical coverage forge increased integration and help shape the long-term trends.

## Marketing and business development management along project lifecycles

The way management addresses the market management and marketing in the hierarchy affects the way marketing and BDM perform along project lifecycles. Theorization suggests that effective BDM requires multifaceted functions, cross-functional skills and practical experience to coalesce. Marketing has a functional responsibility to enable BDM (cf. Sørensen, 2012). Other project lifecycle functions, such as estimating and procurement, technical services and project management, have dual responsibility for their realm of expertise and for marketing to ensure this occurs in order to maximize the effect of their own project inputs. Informal routines developing at interpersonal levels are typically the way this is enabled in project businesses. This is supplemented with creative activities yet creativity and problem solving may fail to correlate with performance related investment (Andrews and Smith, 1996; Slater et al., 2010) because these activities can be reactive within the project setting.

Horizontal integration along project lifecycles is far from mechanistic and is thus framed and facilitated by the management in the hierarchy. Firms with stronger marketing strategies for implementation, however, have been found to be above-average performers (Vorhies and Morgan, 2005). Investment supports lifecycle integration, (i) involving portfolio management capabilities, (ii) mobilizing the capabilities for programmes, and (iii) configuring the front of the project front-end. Organizations use generic portfolio tools, such as the Ansoff or Boston matrix, market growth and share, assessments of market risk and returns (e.g. Wheelwright and Clark, 1992; Loch and Kavadias, 2011). Portfolio measurement tools that link directly to operations, such as return on investment (ROI) and ROMI, the balanced scorecard (Kaplan and Norton, 1992) and other performance measurement systems (Deng and Smyth, 2013) provide further aids, connecting portfolio management with programme management and to an extent project management.

These generic measurement tools are important aids to decision-making and monitoring progress. They are insufficient in themselves. They indirectly underpin or support portfolio coordination and programme operations. Quite sophisticated organizations, according to Loch and Kavadias (2011), may not apply a full range of generic and specific portfolio tools. In project businesses comprehensive measures are needed to help integrate marketing and BDM where currently isolated in the hierarchy or disconnected at the front of the front-end of the management of projects. The advantage of using tools is that these are 'understood' in predominantly businesses with a task driven focus. They support analyzing project businesses in terms of portfolios and programmes, clients and service rather than primarily or solely in terms of projects.

Programme management feeds into initiating and shaping projects (Pellegrinelli, 1997). On the client side, this is about developing a project business case and defining the scope. On the demand side of project businesses, this is about engaging with clients through marketing and BDM capabilities to understand the needs and help shape the project for efficient execution while enhancing benefits of the project in use, whether the client is a project investor or end-user.

One way of integrating marketing management and BDM at the interface between projects and client management where services link projects and facilities management is part of programme management – build and operate – is to use a matrix management structure with project management and facilities management forming the two axes. Merrow (2011) advocates this approach on megaprojects despite criticisms that matrices can weaken management lines of reporting.

## Implications for the project business

Project businesses wish to do a good job for their clients, and it has been argued that it is in their interests to do so. Marketing and BDM can have direct and indirect impact upon project and business performance, however, there are barriers and mindsets that affect the ability to do so. Investment into delivering value for clients at the project business level is led by combinations of experiential judgment and intuitive assessment and has relied upon rules of thumb (cf. Kahneman et al., 1982). Increasingly project businesses require cognitive bases for decision-making. Measurement is an important means for management to gauge the state of play. ROI provides one general measure. In this context, the ROMI calculation:

$$\text{ROMI} = \frac{\text{Gross margin} - \text{Marketing investment}}{\text{Marketing investment}}$$

where the gross margin = revenue – cost of goods – incremental expenses (Lenskold, 2003)

There are two types of marketing investment. First is marketing-informed or marketing-related investment, which focus upon product and service capabilities in a project business and marketing specific investments to improve the performance of marketing and BDM itself (Smyth and Lecoeuvre, 2014). The authoritative nature of numeric data is profound yet exaggerated in decision-making. Inadequate ROMI data for investment decisions are frequently a function of financial methods as a decision-making basis than particular investment proposals. Demands for financial measurement are increasing at senior management levels, yet qualitative assessments are increasingly the key to competitiveness. Yet inter-departmental agency issues can inhibit effective working (cf. Jensen and Meckling, 1976). ROMI provides a means to induce dialogue at the marketing-financial interface and for assessing investment decisions (Smyth and Lecoeuvre, 2014), a matter that will be developed further in **Chapter 9**. As argued, the implementation of ROMI relies upon snapshot data from a transactional viewpoint, but its value for assessment and for dialogue is fundamentally long-term, based upon aggregated data sets that need to be collected over several annual cycles before becoming of much use. As it becomes useful, the viability of the dialogue and potentially increased mutual understanding across these functions is facilitated.

Where does ROMI fit in? Profit is the requirement derived from investment and the profit profile can take several forms. In other words, project business profitability depends upon several factors:

1. *Profit margin* is partly a function of bid price and costs at the bid stage, calculated as anticipated average profit margins to value of projects bid and/or won, but this is only an indicator as under contract the cost of production has yet to be incurred. Margin is mainly a function of the *final account* in relation to actual costs incurred and actual income received, calculated as actual profit margins to turnover. However, this is a set of calculations at the project rather than business level. Moving up towards the project business level, arguably more important yet under-rated is profitability as a function of the client, which starts with *repeat business*, calculated as a comparison of margins compared to new business and assessments as to whether costs are lower due to learning and effective working and/or ability to charge a premium through bidding or negotiation. The so-called 80:20 rule applies, whereby 80 per cent of turnover typically arises from 20 per cent of clients, repeat business being the critical factor (Koch, 1998). This can then be extended to the CLV, which is a calculation of the total work conducted for a key or core client and the margins achieved. CLV is also important for projecting forward to establish likely turnover and profit margin over the client lifetime, say 7–10 years.
2. *Growth* is a function of the value of bids won year-on-year, but is a poor indicator in itself as it depends on the economic cycle. Therefore, *market share* is more appropriate as it is a function of turnover in a sector and/or segment of the market. Choosing the focus or unit of analysis is important. Competition is intensive and entry barriers are low for many project businesses, however, markets are highly structured by a hierarchy of project size, geographical spread and the BU, procurement or market segment under consideration. Competition is less intense at this level, and while competitor data may be only partially available or indicative, trends in growth or decline in market share are more meaningful applied through these filters.
3. *Return on capital employed* (ROCE) is a function of managing work-in-progress and cash flow management to accelerate the circulation capital. While profit margins are typically low for project businesses compared to other sectors, ROCE is typically high because of structured stage payments and the front-loading of payments during execution. ROCE is moderated by the short-term returns from investment of 'working capital' that is not immediately in use (often defined by time-lags between payments received and payments to suppliers going out).

Marketing and BDM only has input into the first two of the three items above as part of a cross-functional responsibility for the integrated delivery of value and service experience across all project lifecycle operations.

Coordinated marketing avoids BDMs being evaluated on the bids secured alone. Narrow incentives encourage meeting targets without necessarily securing profitable work, enhancing repeat business and CLVs. Satisfying CLV and ROMI is more valuable. The value of a project business depends upon long-term factors. This goes back to some rules of thumb derived from industry experience and cited above under the 80:20 Pareto rule (Koch, 1998).

Drilling down towards the project level, any exchange does not come free. There is a transaction cost, or for projects serial transaction costs for and between each stage payment. Effective marketing along the project lifecycle can increase the costs. Investment in marketing may also have the indirect consequence of raising general operating costs. This is to be avoided under regimes of transactional efficiency rather than market growth where effectiveness supports growth. Effectiveness is more than the minimization of transaction costs. Effectiveness goes beyond immediate and short-term financial performance. Growth objectives take account of market position, value delivery, customer satisfaction and other marketing-operational issues. It takes account of network effectiveness, which feeds into effective operational and financial performance. The industrial network, especially suppliers as an important part of marketing and value delivery (e.g. Cravens and Piercy, 1994; Håkansson and Snehota, 1995; 2006).

## Conclusion

In setting out to examine the extent to which markets are managed by project businesses and how this maps out at an operational level through marketing and BDM, this chapter has sought to investigate the management of markets, marketing and the sales process to develop the project business. This involves a broad theoretical view and top-down implementation for structuring, governing, and therefore coordinating activities in the hierarchy and setting the parameters for horizontal integration across programmes and along project lifecycles. Investment has been an important theme of enablement. Constraints and barriers posed by internal organization and (lack of) coordination mechanisms across organizational silos and boundaries for cross-functional working has been the other main theme.

The strategic approach and business models, coupled with the prevailing attitude of management, inform the extent and allocation of resources, and shape the delivery of added value (Narver and Slater, 1990; Homburg and Pflesser, 2000). A transactional approach is a realistic and legitimate approach for many project businesses, although will decreasingly be viable as a dominant one if current trends persist. A market orientation and client-centric approach in particular facilitates fine-tuned market sensing and the development of capabilities to improve market responses (Day, 1994; Sørensen, 2012). It provides a relational basis for market management. Of the three categories used to gauge market management, *reactive*, *responsive* and *proactive*, project businesses are slowly and tentatively moving towards greater levels of responsiveness amongst a raft of providers in many project sectors. The most successful project businesses are likely to include those that move at a faster rate than competitors without exposing the firm to any risks around survival. It will include those with effective strategies, decision-making and tactical implementation. These will be the project businesses that are seen to differentiate their offers in general and customize technical content and tailor service provision to specific client needs ahead of rivals.

In addressing the substantive issues between the theoretical principles applied in practice and the theory, the following substantive issues have been consistently addressed in this chapter.

**SI no. 1:** ***Market Management*** has been addressed particularly in terms of strategic investment and integration – see also **SIs no. 3, 7** and **8.** The tension and choices between degrees of *reactivity* and *proactivity* have been raised in practice in relation to theorization and conceptualization. Time horizons and interests in terms of the possible positions for balancing the management, shareholders and clients have been addressed. The two main approaches to marketing and client procurement have been characterized as transactional and relational, mapping the trends from a dominant transactional towards a greater variance in practice.

**SI no. 3:** ***Marketing Investment and Portfolio Management*** has been addressed as a problematic area in conceptualization and particularly in practice in terms of balancing short-term financial interests of efficiency and long-term interests of effective growth. Resource allocation to marketing and marketing-related activities is to improve performance and enable growth. Marketing is both a source for and indirectly a contributor to investment. Tools such as calculating ROMI and CLV were introduced as key measures. CLV is more than simply client dependent but depends on how investment cascades from portfolio through programme management to project management. This touches upon **SI no. 4,** which deals with client management and programme management, although these were not major themes for the chapter.

**SI no. 5:** ***Marketing and BDM*** has provided a principle focus, emphasizing these functions as conceptual means for market management and business development. The extent of functional isolation, assimilation and integration was scoped. Potential means to join up thinking and action were considered, especially from an investment-led perspective – see **SI no. 3.** Marketing and BDM as related and integrated activities were also considered; indeed their integration provides broader opportunities for integration in the hierarchy and along project lifecycles. **SI no. 6** on BDM and client management was touched upon, yet was an indirect emphasis of this chapter.

**SI no. 7:** ***Vertical Systems and Integration*** particularly emphasizes the issues around the common attribute of weak systems at the corporate–project interface and *vertical coordination mechanisms of formal and informal routines.* This was a primary focus for the chapter and was especially considered in relation to investment. The commonplace lack of vertical integration in general and for portfolio and programme management was addressed.

**SI no. 8:** ***Cross-functional Systems and Coordination Mechanisms*** particularly emphasizes the issues around the common attribute of weak systems along project lifecycles and *systematic horizontal formal and informal routines*. Similarly, this was a primary focus for the chapter. Investment and vertical integration set the parameters, yet it is the horizontal integration that realizes performance improvement and yield a return. **SI no. 9** on marketing and managing the project lifecycle was partially considered, more in terms of providing pointers than any detailed examination or exploration of project lifecycles.

These were the five substantive issues considered. The main contribution to knowledge has been to locate marketing at the front of the front-end and provide a springboard to address this neglected issue. The chapter has confirmed and affirmed that market management and marketing and BDM as part of business development are distinct yet cross-functional activities, whereby integration occurs at the strategic and tactical levels of the project business.

There are several main recommendations for research that flow from the analysis:

A. A greater understanding as to how project businesses (explicitly and implicitly) formulate market management strategy, that is, how often reviewed, what depth, how much is assumed or challenged. Further research may help articulate the link between senior management and operations, perhaps pointing to potential improvements for practice.
B. A greater understanding as to decisions around investment, that is, the expectations, decisive issues and the extent of monitoring the evidence to evaluate the judgments made.
C. A greater understanding as to the shape and extent of constraints and barriers within project businesses, particularly the extent to which formal and informal routines manage the interfaces and what forces are necessary to overcome the constraints in project businesses.

There are several main recommendations for practice that flow from the analysis:

1. Growth is a function of investment, a need for common and mutual understanding needing to be facilitated between functions, starting with the finance and marketing functions;
2. Market management, marketing and BDM provide opportunities for direct investment to differentiate offers in the marketplace and deliver (added) value to clients;
3. Market management, marketing and BDM provide opportunities for investment into marketing-related investment through other technical and service provision to add value and render the project business attractive for selection projects;
4. Implement flexible systems to articulate the interfaces between hierarchical and horizontal boundaries and barriers in management and operations.

The chapter has raised the question as to what is the 'best' approach for marketing and BDM. There is no single answer to this and different clients will continue to want different bundles of service requirements to deliver diverse sets of project requirements. From the project business perspective, there is room in the marketplace for organizations to meet all requirements. However, there are market trends and greater opportunities for project businesses in some markets than others. To date diverse market positions of responsiveness and proactivity remain underpopulated. At a finer grain of analysis there are options within any choice of position and strategy, giving further opportunity for responsiveness. The next chapter focuses upon the relatively passive and reactive approach provided by the *marketing mix*, subsequent chapters dealing with higher degrees of proactivity.

# 3

# THE MARKETING MIX

## Introduction

The *marketing mix* is historic both conceptually and for most sectors and businesses; however, it remains a dominant or strong residual approach in many, if not most, project businesses. It therefore demands attention as a means of *market management*. The marketing mix as a particular paradigm is thus the first to be examined from the 'palette of paradigms'. As the founding conceptual basis for modern marketing, it is located with a transactional approach to the exchange process that was substantially influenced by economics, coupled with a socio-psychological lens located in production and operations management. The economic springboard was left behind in marketing as a discipline, and marketing in many ways struggles with aspects of relating to finance control, especially as financial management have also increasingly struggled to understand marketing (**Chapter 2**; see also **Chapter 9**). The focus in this chapter is more upon the business development concept than on market management. Market management implies a more active or proactive engagement with the market than the marketing mix allows, but it does help develop the business in general as well as feed the project pipeline to secure contracts.

The market is assumed as pre-given, and therefore low levels of market management are anticipated, even at the exchange level. Market forces are considered strong, and it is the responsibility of firms to be reactive in response to market demands. Effective response is assumed to yield efficient and profitable business. The marketing mix is a weak influence on the operational level during execution. Experts with specialist skills conduct operations, but marketing may have specific inputs from its expert domain. Business development management (BDM) is about selling what is produced in manufacturing, although in project businesses working to contract, sales comes ahead of production, which poses a series of issues that will be developed in the chapter.

In terms of the theory and practice, something of a paradox is explored. On the face of it, the concepts underpinning the marketing mix are simply misaligned with project businesses, yet it has been and still remains the dominant paradigm whether applied overtly or implicitly. Thus the chapter seeks to achieve the following:

A. An analysis of the theoretical and applied characteristics of the marketing mix in project businesses and an examination of how these are internally managed.
B. A description of practices and their alignment with the theoretical characteristics and other management practices.
C. An evaluation of the strengths and weaknesses of the marketing mix and its pertinence to project businesses.

The main message of the chapter is about the paradoxical role of marketing mix on its own terms and between theory and practice, but also in relation to theorization and application of other management and management of project conceptualizations.

The traditional approach to project management has been the following:

1. To meet the stated *requirements* in the request for proposal (RFP), briefing or any other form of requirements documentation.
2. To conduct the project within the framework of the so-called iron triangle of *time–cost–quality/scope*.

These can be accepted as the transactional 'ground rules' that inform how the marketing mix is applied to projects, and hence project businesses. There are a number of project sector parameters that confront project businesses that are germane to understanding the application of the marketing mix, beyond these 'ground rules'. They are the following:

- The project is the unit of conceptual analysis, and management is centred around projects; in other words, the emphasis is projects structure management, rather than management structuring projects (e.g. Smyth, 2006; Koskinen and Pihlanto, 2008).
- The project is produced after a sale is secured, which is problematic at the point of sale or securing a contract, and exchange is spread over a series of stage payments during the project execution, so in effect, the offer and 'sale' are re-negotiated at each stage for the work under consideration (e.g. Goodman, 1981; Foord et al., 1988).

## The marketing mix in theory and practice

### *The management literature*

At the general level of business management, there are three categories to gauge market management: *reactive, responsive* and *proactive* (Narver et al., 2004; Atuahene-Gima et al., 2005; Sørensen, 2012). The marketing mix is firmly located in the reactive category. There are degrees of responsiveness at the micro level of the offer in the bid, marginal customization, and market and project feedback. This position arises from some of the main principles of marketing mix. These are generally well known and so will be briefly rehearsed for the sake of thoroughness and for those less familiar with marketing. The marketing mix was developed in and for markets dominated by 'mass market consumer goods' (Borden, 1964). It expanded into a range of goods classified variously as over-the-counter (OTC) goods, packaged services, particularly from multiple outlets such as restaurant chains and from financial services. Some standardized industrial goods were suited to the marketing mix but, in general, did not fit nor were extensively addressed for specific assets in industrial markets. Projects can be services, for example aspects of management consultancy and media advertising, but are often tangible products with high levels of asset specificity, such as film production, IT hardware systems and construction projects.

An early development was the application of the so-called 4*P*s (McCarthy, 1964). This is hardly a model, more a framework of guidance in order to ensure the main ingredients are considered, namely product, price, place and promotion. Product refers to design and manufacture, and thus is in the realm of operations expertise conducted with specialist skills that excludes marketing. It occupies a marginal role to tweak project content according to market research, customer feedback and performance of the products in use as far as this is applied in project markets. Product was further facilitated through the introduction of segmentation, which organized customer into manageable groups. This permitted degrees of customization to develop specific product variations and attributes for each segment while maintaining mass production principles (Smith, 1956; Wind, 1978; Chernev, 2011).

Place refers to the delivery channel or where and how goods get to the market, which encompasses logistics and sales outlets. Thus shipping goods from factory to a distribution warehouse, where shipments are broken down and transported to retail outlets represents one channel or place. Online shopping is an entirely different channel. The project as the chosen means of delivery is a channel in its own right, with specific logistics organized around procurement route, contract types and project management. In this sense projects and project management are part of marketing as opposed to the project management perspective that tries to draw marketing into its remit. The project *is* the delivery channel. Delivery channels typically deliver what has already been produced. Projects are produced within the channel and thus the project is also bound up with producing the product and service. The project business acting in the systems integrator role is closest to the delivery channel role, while subcontractors and suppliers are closer to the production role for the 'product', but all are involved with service production, and the delivery channel involves a service. The marketing perspective of the project as a *delivery channel* brings into sharp relief service provision. Project businesses, especially those providing technical and technological content, frequently fail to perceive their occupancy of the delivery channel role. The delivery channel is manifested in two spatial forms, namely social space and locational or physical space for delivery of customized products and tailored services.

Promotion covers the realms of advertising, public relations and lobbying. Advertising is a fusion of communications and marketing (Nan and Faber, 2004). Three main approaches to advertising have been identified: (i) Janusian thinking (e.g. Rothenberg, 1971), which focuses upon bringing together different views that may seem contradictory or misaligned in creative ways; (ii) the hierarchy of effects model (Lavidge and Steiner, 1961; Palda, 1964), which focuses upon the generation of awareness, knowledge, linking, preferences, conviction and engagement amongst the targeted audiences; (iii) creative leverage (Fallon and Senn, 2006), which solicits engagement through values and benefits. In project businesses, promotion is more about reinforcing market reputation and being prominent in the industry networks.

Finally, price covers the cost plus profit, which in contract work is an estimate no matter how contractually fixed the bid or negotiated price. Price is therefore against the specification where there remain unknowns and uncertainties and incomplete contracts. Requirements change and uncertainties are manifested and thus outturn prices vary in comparison to bid prices. This is an 'old chestnut' which project businesses are the first to point out as constraining, yet they are the first to pursue price dominated strategies in transactional markets of intense competition, collectively helping educate their clients to pursue this norm and apply to their own supply chains (Smyth, 2000).

Marketing became rather obsessed with the P-framework, and thus the identification and exposition of other ingredients were forced into the development of 7*P*s (Booms and Bitner, 1981) and up to 15*P*s (Gummesson, 1994), which arguably lost the impact of the original parsimonious frame of guidance. At the same time, it was becoming more distant from its economic springboard while trying to be all encompassing from a management perspective (e.g. Kotler et al., 1996). It was failing to address some of the thorny theoretical issues. Business-to-business transactions (B2B), service transactions as asset specificity and B2B transactions, including projects as a delivery channel, were some of these and ultimately led to a paradigm shift (see **Chapter 4**). Fundamental assumptions needed to be addressed, and this is conducted below through the lens of marketing and project businesses. The marketing mix assumptions are addressed in Table 3.1.

**TABLE 3.1** The assumptions and reality of market transactions

| *Assumptions* | *Reality* |
|---|---|
| Customers know their needs | Customers and clients do not always know all their needs, and this is generally so in regard to project businesses |
| There is a perfect match in the market to meet known needs | Generic needs are served unless customization of content and tailoring of services can be achieved. Customer and client needs differ when drilling down to the product and service in use. Project businesses customize and tailor, however, this is conducted in response to selling occurring prior to production. Complexity and uncertainties in such arrangements coupled with the (in-)ability to know exactly what is wanted in advance means that many needs remain unmet |
| Supplier is proactive, the customer passive | Customers and clients are proactive and want the exchange to be interactive. In part, this is for reasons of accountability, especially within the iron triangle; it is to assess emergent requirements |
| Any one customer is insignificant; only the segment matters | Every customer and client matters whether the supplier chooses to recognize this or not. Segments help manage differentiated requirements from the client perspective, but at an insufficiently sensitive level, although niche markets, coupled for example with just-in-time, agile and small batch production techniques can achieve some sensitivity under current conditions |
| The product or service is the unit bought from the supplier | Customers and clients transact the unit, but the purchaser is interested in what the product and service does for them – they face (organizational) issues, which are looking for a solution and for the benefits to flow from resolution |
| The customer owes the supplier a favour for producing just what they need | The supplier owes the customer or client a favour for giving their patronage to the supplier, whether it be a one-off exchange or repeat business |

## *Implications from the project management literature and for practice*

Price is a contentious issue, especially for project businesses. The perceived wisdom is that the customer drives price. This might be because the marketing mix ingredients are sometimes invisible to the customer and price sensitivity is high. For example, many customers would find it hard to differentiate between the service provided by clearing banks or banks on main street. The same holds for electricity suppliers where there is competition apart from the charge levels. This is also the case from much of the technical content of project bids, especially where transactional clients have low levels of in-house capabilities to make realistic assessments (Butcher and Sheehan, 2010). Yet this is questioned where clients have a long-term purchasing strategy and greater dependence upon expert suppliers (Yeung et al., 2008). Price remains important, but value for money does too. While internal accountability within client bodies and market pressures may drive prices down, decision-making unit (DMU) members will be keen to maintain high value, especially where they also have responsibility for budgets responsible for the operation and maintenance of the project in use. Personal and social relationships are more stable than inter-organizational ones in the times of recession (Kenna, 2008) and the pursuit of value retention on the client side may appear less prominent to the transactional supplier.

The perceived wisdom is that project businesses are price-takers under the transactional approach. This simply is not the case as price is a function of costs, which include the cost of the project and profit plus an overhead cost. The overhead costs vary by client and project because of the transaction costs incurred. In sales generally, it is estimated that the costs of selling are between five to six times greater to secure a new customer than to retain an existing one (Rosenberg and Czepiel, 1984). For project businesses, this is a serious under-estimate, although by how much on average and for each project sector is something for research. However, the cost of prequalification and bid management are large. Bid costs are in the region of 3 per cent bid prices; the cost of bids lost add to overheads for deferral and spreading across contracts secured. Repeat business clients may be as expensive to bid as new clients, unless they negotiate a contract, but the strike rate is typically higher, so costs go down. Clients constitute a mix of experienced and inexperienced buyers. Experienced buyers can pose problems, particularly when procurement policy changes, for example if shifting from quality to cost drivers (cf. Porter, 1980). Inexperienced procurers tend to be more costly to administer overall. One reason is that they tend to apply conventional procurement criteria of leverage to intangible service projects, to asset specific facilities and infrastructure, where there is limited applicability. A second reason is that such clients are inexperienced in managing projects, raising the transaction costs during execution.

For complex projects, it is rare for project businesses to terminate a contract during execution. It is more common to terminate the relationship between projects, for example during a known programme. Terminating relationships with (poor) clients has to be done appropriately to avoid or minimize reputational damage in the marketplace (Reichheld and Schefter, 2000). For example, a large international concession business, which we will call FranCo, was undertaking a programme of work over several years. A change in marketing strategy led to a reassessment of working for one particular large corporate client. The margins were typically 2 per cent lower than for other clients. Three criteria led the concession business to retain the client. First was the profile of the client, which was an important part of the general sales pitch. The client was known to be both price driven and demanding, thus prospective clients perceived the concession business as one that can meet exacting demands. Second was the view that the annual turnover was sufficient, and the client helped cover a reasonable proportion of overheads and allowed the business to put in bids with higher margins for other clients. Third was concern over the reputational damage that might be done from withdrawing from this client (Interview conducted with the Customer Director of FranCo, 2008).

The project business has provided the prime focus for what has been outlined to this point, although there are clear implications for programmes and projects in particular. At this point of analyzing marketing mix theory and practice, a greater emphasis is placed upon the project level for the team within the project business, but also referring to the implication for the temporary multi-organizational team or TMO (cf. Cherns and Bryant, 1984).

Figure 3.1 sets out the sequence of stages. The marketing mix is almost solely concerned with selling to secure business, that is up to post-tender negotiations as the front-end ceases and execution proceeds. Under the marketing mix, the project business typically awaits the RFP. It is waiting because the BDM role has been to source information in project pipelines and from client programmes in order to (i) assess whether it is a prospect worth responding to, (ii) prepare for prequalification response, and (iii) add it into workload forecasting estimates (assuming a percentage will lead to RFP and hence bidding and a strike rate will help estimate the workload). Reputation and credibility are important factors at the prequalification stage. This is derived from market reputation, in order words, the result of past projects about which the business now has scant influence. It is derived from BDM activity in promoting and selling the services ahead of the RFP. This can be influenced by the project business, yet is largely confined under transactional marketing mix to information provision about track record, financial standing and project resources, and possibly the key personnel that may be involved or leading the supply-side TMO. This can be viewed as an exercise in information symmetry (Edkins and Smyth, 2013; cf. Milgrom and Roberts, 1992).

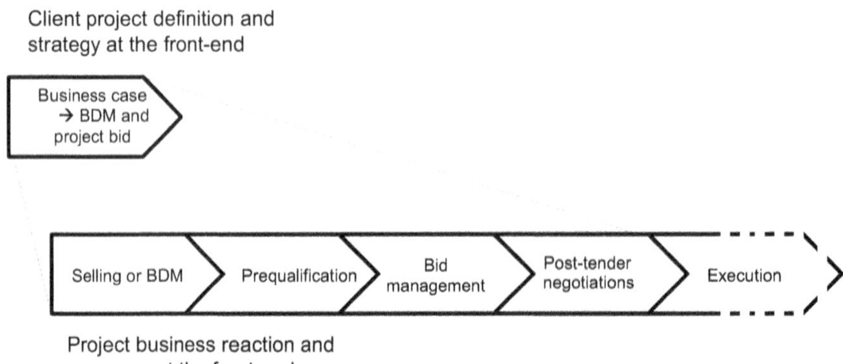


**FIGURE 3.1** The marketing mix, BDM and the management of projects

Bidding has been traditionally based around price-related competition, frequently at the expense of value (Pryke and Smyth, 2006). Price is traditionally defined as the cost plus profit margin.

It is traditionally stated that the iron triangle of time–cost–quality/scope is managed in practice through a series of trade-offs, that is, emphasizing cost has the impact of loss of quality or time and so on. Merrow (2011: 110) argues against 'misguided trade-offs' that lead to 'misconfigured projects' as the project almost certainly will fail to deliver the required benefits. The conditions are being laid for aggressive targets, which end up in adversity and high transaction costs that damage the balance sheet and may incur reputational damage for the supplier in the marketplace. From the marketing perspective, if the client is moving too far in the direction of trade-offs at the front-end, then the decision not to bid may be the optimum at the client management and project management levels of consideration. The caveat comes from the business strategy level, where survival is the first priority and in harsh market conditions, a project that helps cover overheads is beneficial, even if it may be marginally loss-making, providing security to be more selective for subsequent bids.

There are two financial views in this respect. One is to only conduct work that is at or above a margin threshold – a consistent approach regarding the profitability and the optimum to enhance market reputation. This approach is generally preferred from a marketing perspective, but more risk-averse financial departments may prefer the other approach, which is to cover overheads in any financial year first and then seek average margins on the remainder of work. This approach is akin to the transactional approach, but less so for other approaches (**Chapters 4** and **5**).

The client assumption at the project level is that driving keen prices through competitive tender provides good value for money. Project businesses are generally good at explaining to clients that selection primarily upon the lowest bid may compromise quality (cf. Kadefors, 2005). What they are less good at explaining – a great deal of re-education of clients is necessary to address this issue as suppliers have connived with this problem – is that a domination of cost drivers causes project businesses to minimize investment and overheads so that they provide poor service levels:

1. Minimize investment to carry out the development of technical and management capabilities and the resultant hollowed-out firm (Green et al., 2008; cf. **Chapter 1**);
2. Minimize overheads so there are weak systems to coordinate and integrate projects internally and with suppliers (Smyth, 2013a);
3. Cost reduction in service provision is inseparable from quality delivered (Grönroos, 2000; cf. Smyth and Lecoeuvre, 2014; cf. **Chapter 2**);
4. Minimize transaction costs from the viewpoint of firm self-interest at the expense of consistent service provision over project lifecycles, for example moving key personnel with significant tacit project knowledge between projects (Smyth, 2000; Kelly et al., 2013).

5. Incentivize or motivate BDM during selling and bid management to secure as many projects as possible, which usually results in the lowest bid with low margins, while project managers are driven to increase profit, which usually means profit clawback through claims that negates the bid price.

The net result is low-value provision that leads to high project failure rates. This is hidden at the level of any one project, yet the powerful effect is unmistakable given the extent of project failure. It needs further articulation because research has sought to identify critical factors within the project. Studies of critical success factors are conflicting and sometimes contradictory (e.g. Pinto and Slevin, 1988; Cooke-Davies, 2002). While there is value in examining success factors, the greatest source of failures reside in the project marketplace and it is at this level of exchange that research is also needed.

Developing further the second listed point, weak systems also lead to inconsistencies across projects, which is pertinent to clients with programmes. Of particular import is the prevalence of weak systems between the 'corporate centre' and the project or, to put it another way, the lack of programme management within the supply organisation. The consequence is the relative autonomy of project management at the project level with the project business team developing its own way of doing things, which compounds differences within the TMO. Project uniqueness is an inadequate excuse for failing to provide systems to coordinate a consistent service, but the lack of investment and programme support is the reason. Figure 3.2 illustrates the problem.

Are there other reasons for the emphasis upon project price from the client side? There can be but it depends upon the project industry. Where the product

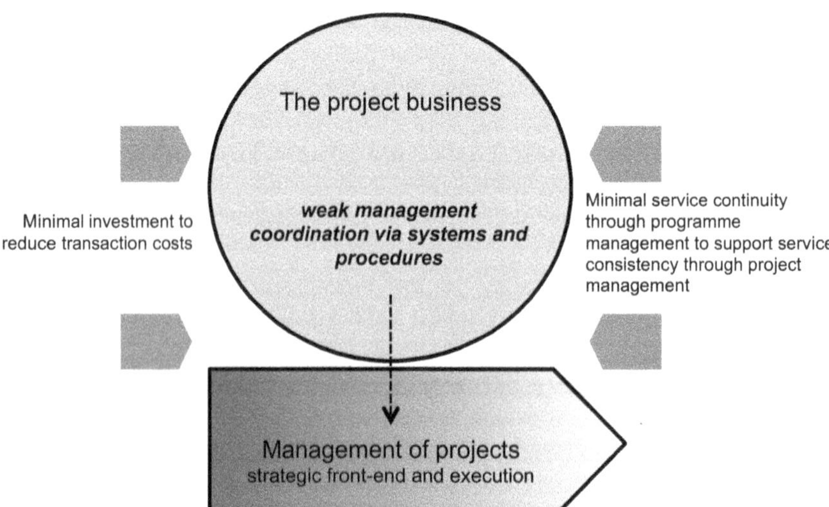


**FIGURE 3.2** Weak hierarchical systems of support and integration at the corporate–project interface

design and specification is conducted by another party, frequently employed directly by the client, such as the architect or engineer in construction, the contractor is in a marginal position to vary the ingredient. Place or delivery channel is what defines the market for projects, and even at the detailed level, clients tend to select the procurement route and contract type (**Chapter 2**). Promotion is a moderate factor, reputation being the main factor that is linked to product performance compared to, say, advertising, which is more distant. Price is therefore the main ingredient of intervention, even though the bid price is typically only indicative of outturn prices (Skitmore and Smyth, 2007). Service is ill considered as a major ingredient in this perspective.

The analysis has considered the management of projects (MoP) from the viewpoint of information about a project in the market to the bid management stage. A further transactional feature is the different functional roles that are involved at each stage. Business development managers (BDMs) are typically only centrally involved to prequalification (Hillebrandt and Cannon, 1990; Skitmore and Smyth, 2007). Bid management teams then handle bidding. There is scant handover of market intelligence. The primary assumption is that the necessary information is in the RFP and any other briefing on requirements. Estimating and procurement departments may become involved, and directors for the committing of resources and setting margins. BDMs may keep links, but mainly through individual initiative and any informal routines. Figure 3.3 shows how involvement tails off over the project lifecycle.

For many project businesses the issues described are hidden within the organizational culture, enshrining current practices as taken for granted (cf. Deal and Kennedy, 1982). These are the *silent forces* that escape the attention of managers. Marketing is a 'blind spot' due to these forces. The consequence is that project businesses experience 'capability leakage' for market management. Practices fail to be embedded in the firm and capabilities mobilized at the project front-end and for project execution (cf. Teerikangas, 2012). The marketing mix is a minimalist approach, therefore, yet aptly suited to a segment of the market defined by client type rather than procurement route, contract or type of project content.

The marketing mix raises problems for application, especially within project businesses. In addition to aspects that have been addressed above, the first general point is that the parsimonious approach is suited to businesses wanting a 'light touch' for management. Parsimony is a perceived strength of management, and certainly applies in project businesses trying to minimize investment and overheads

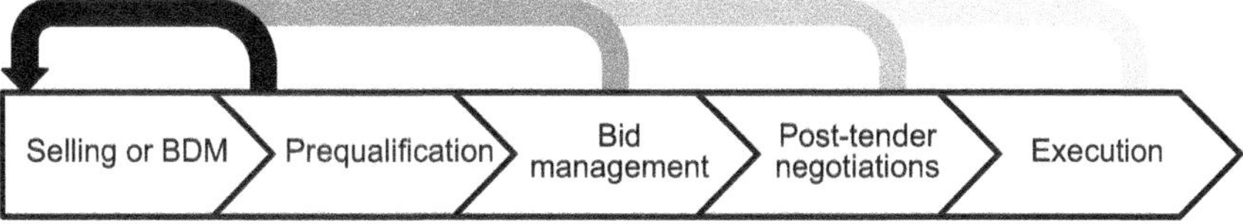


**FIGURE 3.3** The marketing mix and the BDM role

as the survival plan. At worst, it results in marketing and BDM becoming isolated in the business at two levels. It can become isolated from the business strategy, plan or model. More commonly, it becomes cut off from management systems so that the BDM processes fail to be embedded in or 'owned' by the business.

The second general point is that project businesses have tended to be characterized by a high level of subcontracting to spread risk, a trend that has increased over recent decades as most businesses have focused upon their strategic strengths of provision, sometimes described as the *core business*. The result has been that first tier suppliers or main contractors have less direct control over the 'product' ingredient, including the product design. This brings supply chain management into the mix but is outside the core remit of the marketing mix in theory and has been in project business practice. Project businesses have become systems integrators, solution and systems sellers that engineer how a diverse set of technical and service skill sets are brought together (Davies et al., 2007).

The third and more specific point is that most organizations expect added value in their marketplaces. There has been something of a fixation in project management about project failures. This is reasonable given the high level of failures, especially in IT sectors. However, it encourages an inappropriate mindset. Project management is more than about meeting time–cost–scope in service terms and delivering projects against the requirements to a quality level that is fit for purpose. Against other trends in the marketplace that still fails because added value has become the expectation. It is this factor that is decisive in terms of market management and business development. This specific point therefore leads to this important general point, and one that is closely related to the *silent forces* and blind spots for management.

Therefore the *marketing mix* is of dubious value. Where appropriate it is suited to a narrow market segment in contrast to the traditional homogenous approach. The marketing mix is transactional and is primarily driven by the financial function because all the 4*P*s are essentially organized around price and how to allocate (minimalist) financial resources, that is from the viewpoint of disciplining spend in the current budget plan rather than the strategy for growth and competitiveness (Smyth and Lecoeuvre, 2014). The marketing mix largely excludes market management and business development through the marketing function. The marketing mix does not pre-date the insights of Penrose (1959), who noted the importance of how firms allocate their resources from the viewpoint of firm growth. It does pre-date its formalization into a competitive theory, namely the resource-based view (RBV) of the firm (Wernerfelt, 1984; Barney, 1991). Yet, a greater investment-led approach can be established, but the marketing mix provides few tools of support for this and habits around the production-cum-cost control accounting mentality that see efficiency in input–output ratios are more challenging to accommodate within this view in practice. The will to invest may be lacking from the top-down (**Chapter 2**).

Looking from the general to the particular level, it is difficult to protect a model that is about assessing atomized or discrete elements – the traditional ingredients. Most sectors and businesses retaining the marketing mix have become pragmatic and graft in other applied concepts (cf. Kotler et al., 1996). Customers have become more informed and sophisticated. They always did search out their own information and were more proactive than recognized, but the choice of differentiated product propositions and diversity of demands over recent decades has driven strategic buying rather than merely acceptance of information from suppliers to make selections. They are no longer looking for packaged technical solutions (e.g. Adamson et al., 2012), but more complex bundles of tangible and intangible project content ('product') and services to meet expectation through the realization of benefits in use. Procurement has been elevated from low-level buying activities confined to purchasing departments to board level strategic issues that include strategies for supply chain management, lean and agile provision, and just-in-time deliveries. Those client organizations that are agile and are highly dependent upon service provision to guide procurement decisions for projects provide some of the most challenging, yet rewarding, projects and programmes of work for project businesses. In the marketing mix perspective where BDMs are selected and rewarded according to targets, the lines of least resistance exclude these prospects.

The degree to which frontline employees try to satisfy the needs of customers instead of trying to make an immediate sale is defined as *customer orientation* (Saxe and Weitz, 1982). *Trying to help their customers make purchase decisions that will satisfy customer needs* (Saxe and Weitz, 1982: 344) presents the challenge, and some businesses and many project businesses are unable to do so due to a lack of the required skills (Pettijohn et al., 2002). These skill sets are more than refined or enhanced threshold competencies necessary to be in a particular business sector such as installing and commissioning IT systems; they are competencies and capabilities within marketing, management and project management that add technical and service value (Hamel and Prahalad, 1994; Teece et al., 1997; Davies and Brady, 2000; Möller, 2006; Davies et al., 2007).

## Business development management in theory and practice

### *The marketing literature and its implications*

The project level has been addressed and the transactional management during project management stages has been addressed from the BDM viewpoint. The analysis will drill down to a more detailed level of sales activity within the marketing mix paradigm.

All firms have an implicit or explicit marketing strategy. They may have both and they can look somewhat different. Where largely implicit B2B firms show evidence of 'hidden marketing', practices and tactical selling proceeds on a project-by-project basis. It helps firms to *respond quickly to changing customer needs in the short-term* (Biemans et al., 2010: 188). Rapid and nimble responses are typically enabled through separate marketing and sales functions (Biemans et al., 2010), which is commonplace in transactional project businesses (e.g. Preece et al., 1998;

2003; Smyth, 2000). The separation constrains intelligence gathering and reflective sense making (cf. Schön, 1983; Weick, 1995) that would otherwise further inform sales tactics and feed into the strategic plans and programmes for operational activity (Barney, 1991; Menon and Vardarajan, 1992; Day, 1994). Therefore, marketing that echoes client procurement strategies and cascades down to the operational sales level of BDMs informs effective market sensing on the ground, mobilizes knowledge and intelligence (Day, 1994; Gill and Swann, 2004) in order to accurately identify particular client needs (Saxe and Weitz, 1982) and preferences (Kohli and Jaworski, 1990) and helps to customize technical content and tailor services accordingly (van Dolen et al., 2002; Wells and Smyth, 2011). In addition, marketing competencies (e.g. Möller, 2006) and project capabilities are needed to deliver effectively beyond meeting the minimum requirements (Brady and Davies, 2004).

These strategic capabilities provide part of the product and service ingredients. They make demands upon BDMs to act with sympathetic sophistication in selling and processing clients' needs at three levels: (i) primarily the current transaction, (ii) future transactions for that client or type of client, (iii) future strategy from the bottom-up. This is possible within the marketing mix where marketing is integrated into a wider set of business management systems and procedures. It is rare and may indicate the business has moved away from a transactional approach.

In most project businesses, BDMs work relatively autonomously from the management of their project businesses. In construction, for example, it used to be the case that BDMs were hired and fired on the basis of whom they knew and the details of the contacts. The closeness of rapport was often kept to the BDM rather than being 'owned' by the business (Smyth, 2000). CRM (customer or client relationship management) software systems have scarcely helped in project markets. Apart from the problem of engagement with CRM systems, the type of information demanded and the type recorded by BDMs shows considerable disjuncture with the sales needs of the businesses at a base level of information and certainly for customizing content and tailoring services at the programme and project levels. The isolation of BDM in project business processes and the specific lack of ownership of many contacts are surprising considering securing business is its 'lifeblood'. In media advertising, where account managers operate at a programme level and campaigns are projects, account managers tend to form personal ties with clients that are neither shaped nor owned by the firm and hence clients often move agencies as account managers move (Grabher, 2002). Across other businesses, it has been estimated that the average length of tenure of a sales person is 5.5 years, whereas the average customer lifetime is 11 years (Donay and Cannon, 1997). Ownership of BDM by the project business is therefore important. Many project businesses implicitly or explicitly seek clients with work programmes of 5- to 7-year duration and wish to have key clients with lifetimes of around 10 years.

The isolation of BDM is accompanied by an operations bias: *where operations management is a more traditional part of the organizational fabric and marketing less deeply rooted, decision-making may be skewed in favour of operations* (McDonald et al., 2011: 297). In such regimes, project management operations emphasize minimization of error and waste, efficient use of technology, simplification of tasks and standardized routines where possible. The consequence is that managers, for example the commercial management overseeing operations, tend to have narrow roles that may be unresponsive to client need.

The project business strategy under the marketing mix tends to drive BDM, including bid management operations towards meeting pipeline targets. Target drivers around workload volume encourage BDMs to pursue too many opportunities, which at times of intensive competition tend to lead to an under-resourcing of project pipeline opportunities and in times of buoyant conditions tend to lead to the overstretching of estimating and bid management functions. Under-resourced projects at bid stage require additional work during execution because they tend to be more costly than estimated, take longer to complete (Bayer and Gann, 2006), and carry high transaction costs, thus squeezing margins. The marketing mix tends to become involved once the project has been shaped (cf. Cova and Salle, 2005; 2011), that is once the scope and nature of the work are defined. The consequence is that the alignment between client needs and supplier capabilities is sub-optimal. The intellectual challenges, interfacing internal and external stakeholders both in organizational and interpersonal terms, are largely confined to the client side (e.g. Morris, 1994; 2013; Edkins et al., 2013), where BDM becomes subsequently subject to other 'expertise' upon prequalification and receipt of the RFP. Thus, the division of labour between functions over the front-end results in BDM having little or no formal involvement after prequalification (Hillebrandt and Cannon, 1990; Skitmore and Smyth, 2007 – see Figure 3.3).

A case can help illustrate the types of issues and bring to life some of the particulars. UKCo is a large international engineering project business, involved with a range of assets and infrastructure projects, predominantly based in North America and the United Kingdom. The case relates to the civil engineering division. Six interviews were conducted over 1st and 2nd quarters of 2012: one Director with BDM responsibilities, two BDMs, Head of Procurement, and two Project Managers. The marketing function comprised Corporate Communications and was separated from BDM in line with a transactional approach.

The BDM function consisted of a small team, reduced since the 2008 'credit crunch'. BDM is perceived in the business as the *provider of pipeline information* about projects for bidding. It was considered an unimportant part of the business until recently, yet some demand reduction and intensification of competition as competitors have moved into the market has brought BDM to the fore amongst those functions further along project lifecycles. However, BDM has lost capacity due to redundancies, hampering the ability to respond as opportunities arise. Overall, BDM is reactive and tactical with a short-term view.

BDM extends beyond the management of information pipelines. It uses face-to-face (F2F) contact to build relationships. Relationship building enhances information flow and quality. F2F is used to share information. It also helps prequalification through closer inter-organizational alignment. Repeat business arises for UKCo from within a tight-knit network of inter-related clients. Relationship building is focused upon this client network and has some mutually reinforcing effects between the network organizations. This takes BDM beyond the remit of mainstream marketing mix concepts and towards an alternative paradigm (see **Chapter 4**). However, the transition from the marketing mix is minimal and incremental in the case of UKCo (Smyth, 2013a). No formal guidance is provided on building relationships. Where opportunities arise outside the tight-knit network, BDM was described as being more like 'marketing on the run' (Interview conducted with a BDM).

Information on clients and other contacts is maintained on a CRM database, although keeping information current was reported as an ongoing issue. CRM was mostly used to record rather than inform action. The main way of assessing clients was through the project pipeline rather than contacts for grading prospects:

- Platinum – deemed as a 'must win';
- Gold – resources committed to investigation, but the decision to bid has yet to be taken;
- Silver – interesting prospect, but no resources committed and a decision yet to be taken;
- Bronze – too early to realistically assess the project prospect, but has potential.

Resources and resource commitment to pursue opportunities is a problem mainly because of lost capacity post-2008. BDMs are being very selective, but senior management does sometimes lack understanding of this. Targets are set for the pipeline and this conflicts with the need for selectivity.

BDM largely operates separately from other functions. Early Contractor Involvement (ECI) is critical from the project management viewpoint as it provides means to influence the project. However, there were no formal links between BDM and project management. There was a weak internal BDM–procurement relationship. Procurement perceived BDM as seeing things in terms of 'upstream and downstream'. Procurement has segmented their supply chains using a six-step procurement process and a 2x2 matrix for performance assessment in order to identify key suppliers under its strategic sourcing initiative. Part of supply chain engagement was to inform supply chain members of the project pipeline. BDMs are uninvolved with key suppliers to understand value that can be levered. Procurement takes scant account of underlying client needs but 'are having to force the issue' of functional engagement. From the BDM perspective, the segmentation is largely driven by performance against 'best practice' and compliance rather than any means to added value. Yet engagement with procurement could lead to added value identification and leverage from supply chains. BDM have left this prescription 'on the shelf'.

BDM have noticed the increase in cost drivers, partly from clients, but mainly due to increased competition. Cost reduction was described as being to the fore of thinking in UKCo. BDM is involved until prequalification, that is, the decision point to bid or not. Bid management was said to be disinterested in business development issues, although the prescriptive ideal was described as bid management being inextricably linked to sales and estimating. This is not the case, although greater integration has occurred recently with project managers being brought into the development of win-strategies. Estimating and tendering form the bid management teams under the Commercial Department.

Project briefing starts with tendering with workshops involving project managers with the bid team, post-tender briefings before starting on site. The bid strategy is not formed by nor informed by BDM as a formal process. Bid management develops tactical plans. Clients want project teams identified and thus resource intent and commitment intensifies at this stage beyond the cost of putting the bid together. It was stated to be difficult to commit resources, even though BDM keeps senior management and operations informed of the pipeline. It is a reactive process. Procurement is engaged with estimating and tendering, but they are not requested to identify added value from their supply chains. At the bid stage, the bid managers have particular ways of doing things, and therefore, there is no systematic way of managing bids; thus, this renders the interface with project managers, procurement and BDM more problematic. One consequence is that responses aim at satisficing rather than adding value. They offer what they have to and do not develop anything new at programme or project level, which was eroding the position of UKCo in relation to competitors who had entered the market and were proposing marginal improvements on added value content. UKCo were only competing on price and have experienced pressures on margins since 2008. The principal client in the tight-knit network have voiced concern to UKCo that their service is falling behind and are overtly reviewing whether UKCo should remain their largest supplier.

BDM and bid management tend to use the old traditional channels. It offers tangible features, largely consisting of value added to meet requirements rather than added value. Yet this position no longer aligns with customer perceptions or needs.

At the execution stage, project managers take the lead, but they may have had earlier involvement through ECI and in bid management. Project managers generally claimed there was no real contact with BDM, although one project manager perceived there to be regular meetings with BDMs. Handover is formally structured.

A transactional approach is taken to project management, re-allocating personnel to maximize utilization rates of project staff and sometimes improving ability to win new bids at the expense of client interest for projects underway. Relatively junior staff tend to close out projects at the time when client expectations may be at their highest. There is a formal handover, yet this was stated as not being conducted well to the detriment of client satisfaction and repeat business – analogous to dropping the baton in the relay race (Smyth, 2000).

Customer or client feedback is formally solicited at the end of projects. It is looked at by project managers, who then have an informal role of feeding this back into the bid process – an instance of tacit knowledge management being a largely unacknowledged yet key role of project managers (cf. Kelly et al., 2013). They also inform senior management of the issues that need addressing. A common message is that UKCo are very generic and lack the specificity to give 'confidence' at the prequalification and bid stages. During execution, feedback is 'quite open and loose' and is managed 'quite randomly'.

The BDM process from the front of the front-end to securing a bid is highly transactional and from the viewpoint of service delivery during execution, the pattern is replicated. There was some attempt to broaden the palette of BDM activity, and procurement is forcing change in the same direction. The marketing mix approach has worked for UKCo for a long period and will continue to work for some clients and project businesses; however, their principal client in the main client network has become more relational, and the competition is setting out to differentiate its value propositions. Therefore, this market is evidence of how the marketing mix approach is suited to a narrowing segment.

## *The changing marketplace*

The transactional marketing mix encourages a project focus rather than client-centricity. This, coupled with the semi-autonomous conduct of BDM, typically leads to BDMs becoming individualistic, which as Maister (1989) noted was characterized in the professions, such as engineers and architects, as reactiveness at the project level rather than proactivity, especially at the client level of operations. The professions have become very proactive in most developed countries, and some other project businesses have become more proactive and arguably more structured in managing the front-end, even though BDM is often poorly integrated. The reactive marketing approach in the marketing mix involves primarily focusing upon constraints from internal legal and cost factors, external client attitudes and to an extent upon competition.

The transactional sales adage is, *We sell what we produce, not produce what will sell.* Project businesses do not produce first then sell, but produce in response to contacts. The adage might be paraphrased as, *We produce what we have sold, rather than sell what we can produce.* BDMs are typically tasked with selling what has been sold – track record. Clients put store on this as they seek reassurance and low risk, and project businesses have educated them to do so. Client buying decisions are influenced by technical and technology needs. Clients vary in their ability to assess the content. Some buy in professional expertise, for example regarding many built environment projects. Other clients build significant internal capabilities. Those with in-house capabilities are less dependent upon any particular supplier and need to be more transactional. For such clients, the marketing mix approach is most suited on the supply side as their switching costs are minimal. However, recent research shows this segment only constitutes 33 per cent of the market, approximately comprising two sub-groups: clients needing reliable projects from a technical viewpoint (26 per cent) and clients sourcing from multiple project providers (7 per cent) (Smyth et al., 2010).

The reactive approach tends to be driven by turnover targets to feed the pipeline. The types of sales performance measures include the following:

1. Prospect development rate = $\dfrac{\text{Number of pre-qualification opportunities}}{\text{Number of targeted clients}} \times 100\%$

2. Pre-qualification conversion rate = $\dfrac{\text{Number of pre-qualifications}}{\text{Number of pre-qualification opportunities}} \times 100\%$

3. Strike rate = $\dfrac{\text{Number of bids won}}{\text{Number of bids/negotiations conducted}} \times 100\%$

4. Value performance = $\dfrac{\text{Value of bids won}}{\text{Estimated value of bids conducted}^{\star}} \times 100\%$

* Based upon the prices of the winning bids where known or own bid prices were not.

The value of bids accumulated into turnover provides a basis for calculating *market share*. Share is defined as the proportion of volume or value of a given market, which may be the total market or a segment: for example the share of the oil and gas platform construction market, or the top tier firms in a national IT systems installation market by contract size, or the share of facilities management (FM) contracts for PPP/PFI hospitals (where PPP stands for public private partnerships and PFI for public finance institute). Market share reflects and enables growth and as a driver for targets may compromise profitability.

The sales performance measures are used to set BDM targets. There are indicators for guidance. Other guidance should not come from simply extrapolating existing trends such as demand buoyancy and disruptive factors, which can motivate BDMs to secure an imbalance of clients and contracts for the needs of the firm within the remit of the marketing mix. *Stretch targets* applied to BDMs without investment and wider support can be problematic, even in terms of meeting the criteria of the 4*Ps* in marketing, project requirements, and project management time–cost–quality criteria.

Finance tends to view BDM as costs, indeed, part of the overheads in a downturn – see the case of UKCo above. Intensified competition at any time and especially in a downturn leads under the marketing mix to decisions to cut bid prices as the best way to survive. Generally, trimming costs and margins increases risk and can threaten survival. The ability to win work through marketing and BDM is reduced; the quality of work during execution diminishes, further hampering the ability to win work through reputation and repeat business. This begs the question as to why project businesses repeatedly pursue such action. For some, they have developed other distinguishing capabilities that will secure work and maintain reasonable margins. For others, they still retain the production-orientated mindset, whereby reductions in investment and overhead costs indirectly impinge on operations. In service markets, costs and revenues are inseparable, whereby reductions in expenditure affect quality (Grönroos, 2000; Smyth and Lecoeuvre, 2014). The drivers for cost reduction particularly come from finance directors, who frequently fail to distinguish costs that are inseparable from service provision (Srinivasan and Hanssens, 2009). The client may apply similar drivers, and thus, the consequences for project content, the service experience and associated disbenefits in use need to be teased out for all parties.

The intensity of competition in any tier of the market by project size or in any geographical area can be exaggerated. What is necessary is to have some competitive advantage in the market other than any ability to cut prices more than competitors. Restructuring and cutbacks are necessary but can also be accompanied by selective investment, coupled with critical evaluation of anticipated capabilities needed for the upturn so that human resources are configured for future expansion rather than pursuing proportional delayering (Smyth, 1998; 2010a – see Fact Box 1.1).

A lot of business is lost at the front-end of project lifecycles. From the transactional marketing mix perspective, it has been estimated that 75 per cent of all business is lost on the first contact (Harvey, 1988). There has been scant research on BDM practices, but some evidence tacitly points to it being mishandled. For example 38 per cent of management with marketing responsibilities in construction were taking initiatives to improve the ability to secure new work at the millennium turn (Smyth, 2000), yet today, BDMs exhibit varied practices within the same project business. Table 3.2 sets out a comparison between two project businesses. Both mainly employ marketing mix principles, yet both are in slow transition towards relationship marketing.

Table 3.2 indicates that contacts and relationship building were left to individual responsibility. The consequences were stated as, 'You do end up living in an area of ambiguity a lot of the time' (Interview with the Head of New Business, AntCo). Many of the differences in BDM action were justified in terms of BDM being seen in terms of 'instinct', the extreme of being reactive at the level of the individual rather than organization. Differences in action and behaviour were disguised behind business jargon, such as 'client drivers' and 'right behaviours' (Table 3.2; Smyth, 2013a). It lends a false impression of standardization and coherence of management.

**TABLE 3.2** Comparison of transactional management and behaviour in BDM

| *Project business* | *AntCo* | *EUCo* |
|---|---|---|
| **Management of contacts** | The approach is fragmented<br>The approach is project-by-project<br>BDMs had largely been made redundant post-2008, and so the management was more informal and consistent than pre-2008 | CRM database<br>Agreed potential clients to target<br>The approach is to identify key client actors and 'establish some kind of relationship with them'<br>Management of contact left to individuals |
| **Level of contact engagement for BDM** | Assessment as to whether the client values the relationship.<br>'It boils down to some trusted relationships'<br>'There's a lot of behavioural-cultural work that goes on in building relationships in this or that sector' | There is an absence of 'strict guidance' on how to develop contacts<br>Build relationships differently:<br>• some BDMs form purely transactional contacts<br>• some build relationships to improve quality of information<br>• some try to understand the client |
| **Depth of information sought** | BDM must be able to develop the 'hard' as opposed to just 'soft' issues<br>Contacts are not discrete<br>Relationships are built internally and externally in networks<br>Understand client drivers | The first step is 'information gathering'<br>The second step is to brief the BDM teams, and then ask them to find out, 'is there anything out there you think we should know'<br>The third step is regularly meeting people, having done the homework<br>Contacts should match the hierarchical positions<br>The fourth step is, stay in touch with counterparts<br>Understand client drivers |

*Sources*: Smyth (2013a); interviews conducted with directors, senior management, departmental and project managers, 1st and 2nd quarters of 2012.

A long-standing issue with project businesses has been discontinuity between projects. Discontinuity is a feature of project markets and of operations (cf. Håkansson, 1982). Discontinuity starts at the buying stage as demand is experienced as 'lumpy' compared to continuous sales from small units of output (e.g. Linder, 1994). Purchasing is said to be intermittent from any one client (Hadjikhani, 1996), although project transactions are more even due to stage payments over the lifecycle (e.g. Goodman, 1981; Foord et al., 1988). However, exchange of resources is only part of the transaction picture because contractual, technological and relational dimensions are important in exchanges. Post-completion and final account there is the period of the sleeping relationship. Even where project businesses treat each project as separate transactions, clients do not. This lesson has been increasingly taken on board even by businesses where BDM remains transactional for the *sleeping relationship* between projects (Faulkner and Anderson, 1987), which when managed improves continuity (e.g. Hadjikhani, 1996; Preece et al., 2003; Smyth and Fitch, 2009).

Discontinuity can be over-emphasized as it tends to assume the client is passive in the way transactional marketing is reactive. This is not the case. Matthyssens and Faes (1985) drew attention to the point that customer experience with previous sellers is a significant asset. Learning from previous suppliers helps clients develop purchasing capabilities. Transactional discontinuity is only in the 'mind's eye':

> The uniqueness in the content of a sleeping relationship is not only to be found in social or technological ties, but also in the strength of the ties. A sleeping relationship may only include a low degree of interdependence because of the standardized nature of the earlier project, or it may include a high interdependence and trust, due to the complex nature of the former project embedded in intensive technological, social or financial interaction.
>
> (Faulkner and Anderson, 1987: 323)

The pertinence of Hadjikhani's (1996) work is that he identified a problem and helped to shift project theorization and practice away from transactional sense making and thus the marketing mix. Most project businesses have been in transition over the last decade or two (e.g. Smyth, 2000; Cova et al., 2002; Preece et al., 2003), although the shift tends to be slow (Smyth, 2013a).

There are forms of transactional self-interest that are arguably more enduring. One is hedonic purchasing, which refers to those who gain power in career terms by appointing a project business even though they may fail to meet the project business case of the client organization (Hirschman and Holbrook, 1982). Another form of transactional cost is the bribe. Price is traditionally defined as the cost plus profit margin, yet certain costs can be hidden, including bribes. Bribes are present in all project markets, and more prevalent in some cultures and nations. As one Chinese construction contractor candidly admitted, they negotiate with each other before bidding and persuade them from bidding on a reciprocal basis if the customer cannot be bribed (cited in Liang, 2012).

This is illegal, as elsewhere, and discovery will lead to a revoked license. Yet, this practice has been an 'unwritten rule' in the Chinese construction industry and elsewhere. It has been found that strike rates can be as high as 1:2 for some project businesses. The total costs to society are higher, and it leads to a greater concentration of income in fewer hands, but purely from a cost of bidding point of view it is quite efficient. Where reduction in purchasing and bidding costs are desired, negotiation with preferred bidders is more effective and allows for open scrutiny. Behind corrupt transactions are unhealthy dependencies that represent a 'dark side' of marketing.

What are the implications of the transactional marketing mix for management and along project lifecycles? It demands little standardization of management, providing technical and technological content requirements (product) are met.

Many project businesses are seeking standardization, for example by following a project management body of knowledge (BoK), such as PMBoK® or the APM BoK. *Project management methodologies*, such as PRINCE2, Waterfall, or an agile methodology are applied. The application of these project methods have been inconsistent in practice, as shown in the IT project sector (Wells, 2011). Yet many project businesses could further standardize management practice and routines. Projects are typically unique, yet many of the 'soft' management processes need not be (Fact Box 3.1). Inconsistent and differentiated services can lead to greater transactional costs being incurred, hence lowering margins.

## FACT BOX 3.1 MARKET DEMAND FOR PROJECTS AS COORDINATED SERVICE PROGRAMMES

A firm providing elevator repair services was experiencing a loss of customers. Customers were saying the firm had the best skills and expertise to repair and maintain elevators. The customers were dissatisfied with the lack of service capabilities in the sense of how the jobs were carried out. The personnel were attentive, but did not always do the work when they said they would, the way they promised, nor seemed to understand the implications of the inconvenience and disruption to the customers' own effective operations. Nor did they seem to care about the customers' employees as people. Jobs are left unfinished with no explanation as to why and when they will be completed.

The firm thought they were offering ready-made repair 'products' that they were tasked to install, whereas the customers saw it as a process and therefore a service. It was the service quality of these mini-projects that mattered most to customers.

*Source*: Edited and adapted from Grönroos (2000).

The marketing mix inadequately distinguishes between different customers in terms of the location of provision, the extent of discrete or continuous provision and the frequency of purchase (e.g. Lovelock, 1983; Bridges et al., 2003; cf. Henisz et al., 2012), which in project businesses is frequency of purchase by project and for programmes. Discontinuity is in evidence over project lifecycles too. One of the issues of continuity relates to individuals in the absence of a strong and systematically coordinated project–project business interface. Key staff involved in the pitch and bid are absent 'from the bench' when contracts are secured. They have been allocated elsewhere to minimize transaction costs.

During execution, the transaction approach has less to say about how performance feeds into market reputation and through to corporate brand compared to other paradigms. Brand is important in business-to-business (B2B) contexts (e.g. Roberts and Dowling, 2002; Keh and Xie, 2009). Client purchasing strategy typically starts evaluation of project businesses by reputation and credibility as the first filter prior to prequalification. Reputation is strongly associated with brand where brand is the project business rather than its project 'product' (cf. Berry, 2000; Cretu and Brodie, 2010).

The problem with the marketing mix is its efficiency in accountancy terms. Input–output ratios look good. Forecasted low transaction costs tend to disguise the high hidden costs incurred, including non-recoverable project costs around disputes and legal fees. Transaction costs are high across several dimensions, including:

- High costs of soliciting new business incentivizes diluted or 'scatter gun' activity to maximize prequalification rates, rather than pursue work aligned to capabilities and long term business needs;
- High bidding costs for tenders to satisfy short-term forward workloads, rather than selective bidding with higher strike rates;
- High transaction costs in execution to deliver to time–cost–quality/scope criteria on unaligned projects to capabilities, including legal costs and shortfalls in settling final accounts.

Yet board directors and chief executives have become rather jaundiced about marketing across industries. They see the marketing function as being self-interested and resource hungry without being able to demonstrate the financial benefits according to market research on 600 chief executives (Fournaise Marketing Group, 2011). While much of the criticism is aimed at promotion in terms of brand and media, it is a reminder for marketing to be based upon business performance, defined here as more than accountancy-driven financial criteria and short-term shareholder value (Fact Box 3.2).

Client expectations and satisfaction levels play an important role in the assessment of a performance within the construction industry. Part of the satisfaction is bound up in service provision and the related experience (Maloney, 2002). Client satisfaction influences future work opportunities (e.g. Reichheld, 1996; Egemen and Mohamed, 2006). It is possible to have a dissatisfied client or partially satisfied client even though explicit time, cost and performance criteria have been met (Torbica and Stroh, 2001). Winch et al. (1998) stated that there is evidence that client perceptions of project outcomes are more important than meeting any project objectives. Further, client loyalty over the period of the sleeping relationship period is far from mechanistic and needs management. The combined process can be expressed as:

> Supplier Credibility → Project Performance → Client Satisfaction → Client Commitment → Loyalty → Repeat Business

Oliver (1997) says loyalty comprises elements of belief, affection, intention and action.

Loyalty is manifested in two ways: loyalty is related to product and/or service content, and to behaviour in delivery (Yi, 1990; Reichheld, 1996). Reichheld

**FACT BOX 3.2 MARKET MANAGEMENT, MARKETING PERCEIVED NEED DURING ECONOMIC DOWNTURN**

As cost drivers have risen and capabilities have been lost since the 2008 'credit crunch' recession, project businesses should pay some attention to the construction industry's perception of business development at the millennium turn, derived from a response of 107 managers.

- Sixty-seven per cent stated BDM needed considerable improvement, including the need for repeat business.
- Twenty-four per cent stated the stage up until prequalification needed considerable improvement.
- Eight per cent perceived the need to improve marketing in the execution stage.

Whilst these views may neither be accurate reflections of marketing and BDM across all project sectors, they are indications of some of the issues that may have resonance today.

*Source*: Smyth (2000).

(2001) argues the purpose of a business is more than making a profit; it creates value from a threshold skill set. The threshold value of meeting minimum requirements can be enhanced through core competency and dynamic capability development to add value (e.g. Hamel and Prahalad, 1994; Teece et al., 1997). These are areas of product and/or service ingredients that project business can influence and at the same time begins to shift the ground further from the 4*P*s.

Client satisfaction does not necessarily increase repeat business. One-off transactions can yield high levels of client satisfaction as expectations and requirements are low. A transactional approach on the client side will not necessarily lead to a loyalty belief that the project business will perform as well next time. The perception may be that there are equally able performers in the market (cf. Oliver, 1997). Referring to the oil and gas megaproject business, Merrow (2011) states that buyers and sellers do their best to fulfill agreements because they wish to maintain the relationships. These tended to be longer term before the 2008 'credit crunch' recession. The buyer–seller relationships were informal, conducted by informed and skilled personnel in those roles. This has broken down in part of this project sector as the specialist skills capabilities were reduced or lost:

> The coherence on the owner side disappeared . . . Owner businesspeople started referring to engineering as 'just another commodity' and in many

> cases turned the relationship management over to purchasing organizations to be procured along with office supplies.
>
> (Merrow, 2011: 132)

He refers to this change in owner–contractor relationships as *deprofessionalized* (p. 339). Aspects of the analysis towards the end of this section are pointing towards other paradigms from the marketing palette, and thus offer a critique of the transactional approach. Yet the transaction approach still dominates many project businesses, and other concepts are implicitly or explicitly applied alongside. This becomes part of the iterative and incremental transition clients appear to be driving the market towards. The transition is slow because of the first priority has been to keep overheads and investment costs under control as means of survival.

## Conclusion

In setting out to examine the extent to which the marketing mix paradigm resonates in theory and is applied in practice, the main message is that the 4*P*s category place or *delivery channel* helps understand the nature of projects, locating them intrinsically in the heart of the marketing mix as their very reason for existence. The delivery channel is thus the market to be managed.

The chapter set a series of goals for looking at the marketing mix as applied to project markets. It provided an analysis of the theoretical and applied characteristics of the conceptual approach in project businesses and an examination of how these are internally managed. The strengths and some of weaknesses were set out. The paradoxical situation that prevailed was the disjuncture between theory and the project context. In other words, the marketing mix falls short of theoretical residency in project markets but has dominated practice until recently where a slow and iterative transition away from the marketing mix is underway.

A description of practices has been undertaken supported by empirical material, which demonstrates the many transactional practices and their alignment with the characteristics of management and marketing management, yet also high degrees of misalignment. This has led to an evaluation of the strengths and weaknesses of the marketing mix and its pertinence to project businesses especially in markets of increasing client demands.

In addressing the substantive issues between the theoretical principles applied in practice and the theory, the following substantive issues have been considered in this chapter.

**SI no. 1: *Market Management*** is minimal under the marketing mix as it is reactive, and thus market management and business development have to be pursued through other strategic avenues.

**SI no. 5: *Marketing and BDM*** has provided a principal focus, emphasizing the transactional way these are conducted. The strengths are the efficiency in input–output terms as perceived at the strategic level, yet the growing transactional costs at the operational level are difficult to attribute and account for in measurement terms, except for the growth in non-recoverable costs that are excluded from project budgets. The transactional approach is frequently at the expense of client service with the consequence of constraining growth opportunities in this competitive market.

**SI no. 6: *BDM and Client Management*** has largely focused upon, first, the lack of integration with a transactional approach being echoed between functions. This leads to service inconsistency – see **SI no. 8.** Second is the discontinuity between projects. In this sense the BDM emphasis is more on serving internal interests than client management for the business and in the interests of clients. Yet practice has been making incremental improvements to continuity.

**SI no. 7: *Vertical Systems and Integration*** has drawn attention to the common attribute of weak systems at the corporate–project interface. This was a secondary focus for the chapter, linking to issues around investment (see **Chapter 2**). The lack of vertical integration in general and for portfolio and programme management was also addressed.

**SI no. 8: *Cross-functional Systems and Coordination Mechanisms*** again drew attention to the common attribute of weak systems along project lifecycles. A considerable amount of activity within BDM was left to individual responsibility rather than management, isolating marketing and BDM at the front of the front-end with scant support or resource from above (**SI no. 7**).

**SI no. 9: *Marketing and Managing the Project Lifecycle*** is considered as linear and is addressed in rigid fashion as the project passes each stage with a handover to a different functional team, especially at the front-end – see also **SI no. 7** and **8.** This constrains intervention for value creation, which is only superficially addressed in the marketing mix, that is, predominantly to satisfy minimum requirements rather than added value.

These were the six substantive issues considered. The main *contribution to knowledge* has been to locate project markets as the *delivery channel* or place in terms of the marketing mix. Management is therefore about the development of this delivery channel, not just the project as a unit of analysis and applied focus.

A further important contribution to knowledge is to locate marketing for project businesses at the *front of the front-end* and provide a springboard to address this neglected issue. The chapter has confirmed and affirmed that market management is proactive, yet marketing and BDM are conducted in a reactive and transactional way under the marketing mix. So much so that they are frequently conducted as distinct activities, and isolated ones in the hierarchy and along the project lifecycle in project business.

Consequently and in summary, the *marketing mix* fails to be a primary facilitator of investment and the allocation of resources for proactive and effective market management. In terms of the attitudes that pervade and influence organizational culture (Narver and Slater, 1990; Homburg and Pflesser, 2000; Narver et al., 2004), the transactional marketing mix is *reactive* in the marketplace, largely avoiding a market orientation to develop capabilities (Day, 1994; Sørensen, 2012). The degree of *responsiveness* is largely confined to adjusting the ingredients (whether these are 4, 7 or more Ps), many of which hold scant relevance for project businesses where the main ingredient offered up is price. Yet many project businesses are 'comfortable' with the reactive market position and justify this in the name of 'risk management', freezing decision-making and constraining responsiveness to induce perceived certainty around timeframes and costs.

Some of the most successful project business performers are amongst the most responsive and proactive. These are ones that are typically transitioning from a marketing mix paradigm towards more proactive modes of market management, and responsive marketing and BDM approaches (Smyth and Fitch, 2009; Smyth, 2010a; 2013a). They are increasingly market orientated, paying more attention to helping articulate client needs and providing added service value. These project businesses have or are moving away from the marketing mix paradigm.

Transition in practice comes in the wake of analysis showing transactional approaches to be restrictive. From a marketing perspective, inter-organizational relationships develop across several dimensions: economic bonds in the exchange, structural bonds through governance and social bonds or interpersonal relationships at the supplier-customer interface (e.g. Heide and John, 1990; Schakett et al., 2011). Economists tend to place primacy upon the economic exchange, but any exchange is socially embedded (Young-Ybarra and Wiersma, 1999), and indeed, markets themselves are socially constructed artifacts (Abolafia, 1996). For example, Schakett et al. (2011) found that service quality was only 27 per cent attributable to any economic bond, 36 per cent to a structural bond, and that 44 per cent was attributable to social bond, pointing towards the importance of relationships.

Market management nonetheless is faced with generic issues of agency theory (Jensen and Meckling, 1976) for internal governance of project businesses (Müller, 2009), whereby the marketing–finance interface, departmental silos in the hierarchy and along project lifecycles are run from a self-interest perspective that inhibits understanding, dialogue and interface coordination. Information asymmetry leads to issues of adverse selection and the moral hazard in supply chains and project governance (cf. Milgrom and Roberts, 1992; Müller, 2009). However, the proactive approach tends to lead to better resource allocation for bidding to improve selection (Bayer and Gann, 2006), and relational contracting promotes collaboration (Egan, 1998).

Marketing and BDM tend to focus upon the project level (cf. Skaates and Tikkanen, 2003a), and are confined to activity up to prequalification. A longitudinal understanding of marketing along project lifecycles has been overlooked in many project businesses until recently (Deshayes et al., 2008) and for the project in use (Turkulainien et al., 2012). The project businesses that focus most upon the 'product' or project have been found to be the most immature in service provision (Wikstrøm et al., 2009). Established relationships between project participants increases the probability of project success (Söderlund and Andersson, 1998), especially where social bonds and high levels of buyer–supplier commitment prevail (Powell, 1990; Martinsuo and Ahola, 2010; Henisz et al., 2012).

There are several main *recommendations* for research that flow from the analysis:

A. Research is needed into the project as a delivery channel within the marketing mix paradigm. This involves an analysis of the channel coupled with in-house production, outsourced to subcontractors with the project business acting as a systems integrator and the logistics represented by project management.
B. Research into transaction costs in relation to weak systems for projects viewed from the programme and market levels rather than projects per se.
C. A greater understanding as to how project businesses (explicitly and implicitly) formulate market management strategy, that is, what content and to what depth, how implemented and conducted, and how often reviewed.
D. Further detailed analysis of BDM as a function in its own right and in relation to other functions at the front-end.

There are several main *recommendations* for practice that flow from the analysis:

1. Growth is a function of investment, and as a prerequisite there is a need for common and mutual understanding at senior management level.
2. The transactional extreme evidenced as individualism, isolated activity and a lack of integration is an unnecessary function of a transactional marketing mix, which can have its main focus in the marketplace at the level of the exchange.
3. Project businesses that are more than systems integrators, and thus are involved directly in production, can be more directly involved in product adjustment and configuration with a greater client-centricity.
4. All project businesses are engaged with some level of service provision and can transactionally adjust and develop this ingredient.

The last two recommendations for practice and some of the foregoing conclusions are pointing towards increasing differentiation beyond the limits of the marketing mix, which the next chapters seek to address.

In summary, the marketing mix takes a snapshot of client needs and tries to inject the project ingredients in the offer at bid stage and for execution. The marketing mix has been said to be *myopic* in the sense of having a narrow lens (Levitt, 1960; 1983). A movie camera analogy is preferred, where the marketing mix snapshot is a 'freeze frame'. It encapsulates Zeno's Paradox. The dynamics of change in time and space cannot be captured in a snapshot. While you can take a snap of a train in two positions down the track, movement is only implied, not seen. Another approach is needed to capture dynamics – we need a movie camera as a lens to see the dynamics of marketing in projects over the entire management of projects lifecycle, indeed client lifecycles in purchasing projects. We need the movie camera to see marketing in relation to market management and to see the project as a delivery channel.

Projects are scoped and enacted on broad planes of environmental and organizational activity in relational time and space, described as project ecologies by Grabher (2002) and Ibert (2004). Market management and marketing are part of this picture and interactively affect other parts to shape the system for a project and so the marketing side of projects emerges and evolves in dynamic ways. This is to both reap the benefits of the 'economies of repetition' (Davies and Brady, 2000), and to embrace the challenge of new specific asset and service requirements.

Marketing and selling is an organized behavioural set of processes, which work to best effect when systemized, conducted amongst a set of social actors (Bagozzi, 1974; Vargo and Lusch, 2010), which goes beyond the marketing mix.

# 4

# RELATIONSHIP MARKETING

## Introduction

The second hue from the 'palette of paradigms', *relationship marketing*, is examined. A market perspective divides organizational approaches into *transactional* and *relational*. Drilling down, the three market management categories are *reactive, responsive* and *proactive* (e.g. Narver et al., 2004; see **Chapter 2**). The marketing mix is transactional and reactive in response. *Relationship marketing* is relational and proactive. It provides scope for a client and service orientation. The paradigmatic roots are in social and organizational behaviour. Relationship marketing therefore offers a distinct approach to market management and business development, enabling high degrees of differentiation between competitors for market management.

The project is conceptually a *delivery channel* for product and service provision, locating project management as the logistics that has employed outsourcing for market and project risk management, but increasingly must do so to lever specialist bundles of complex technical and service components and packages. How marketing and selling or business development management (BDM) are conducted has a significant effect on most, perhaps all, project businesses. Relationship marketing is proactive, and gives attention to the project as a delivery channel as a business-to-business (B2B) relationship within a broader network of providers and other stakeholders.

Business is based upon relationships internally and in the marketplace (cf. Grönroos, 2000). Project businesses are no exception. It is through relationships that value is added (Pryke and Smyth, 2006). Interpersonally, this starts with *who people are* rather than what role they play, or what function and power they have; we are human beings before we are human doings. Inter-organizationally, this starts at the front of the front-end where *relationship marketing* principles are incrementally guiding project businesses (e.g. Smyth and Fitch, 2009; Smyth, 2013a). As it is generally said that it costs six times more to get a new customer than retain an existing one

(Grönroos, 2000), the high costs of pre-qualification and bidding in many project sectors suggest the cost is a higher multiple in project businesses. Means to bring down these costs of securing new clients and keeping existing ones are attractive.

Relationship marketing is a way to secure business. Proactive engagement with key players at the level of the exchange shapes the market and positions the business in relation to the type of client and for each client. It is the client rather than project that is the primary unit of pursuit. Relationship marketing affects the way projects are shaped and managed to improve client satisfaction and repeat business. Relationship marketing is a way to add value during BDM and as part of project management. It does so through the client–project interface, sometimes called the *dyadic relationship*, to develop a deep understanding of the client modus operandi in order to customize the technical content and tailor the services at a detailed level. Relationship marketing also draws upon a wider network to build relationships with key suppliers to identify and lever (added) value from the supply chain.

In terms of theory and practice, relationship marketing tries to replicate close and effective relations between a sole trader and client in order to build up a long-standing market relationship and be recommended to others. For example, local builders who do a very good job and treat their clients well build their business quickly. The problem comes when the business grows and the personal touch and close client relationship is lost. The sole trader is spending less time managing the client and spends much more of their time managing the business. Relationship marketing is trying to harness and develop routines for a business that replicates the relationship building to secure work and add value for the client. Relationships are different, so how this works on the ground and what added value is identified through the relationship varies. The routines will also vary, emerging from practice (Parmigiani and Howard-Grenville, 2011). In this way, relationship marketing is pragmatic, yet can lead to organizations giving scant attention to the types and rigor of routines necessary to shape the relationships to develop the close ties or bonds (Smyth, 2013a).

How markets, market management and marketing are changing is examined. In particular, the extent to which there is a transition underway towards more proactive and relationship-based approach is examined. Whether theory suggests there is a need for greater alignment towards a relationship-based approach for certain clients and sectors is evaluated, which prepares the ground for the next chapter too. The evidence shows that currently relationship marketing principles are being adopted in partial and loosely pragmatic ways. There remains scant investment in awareness of relationship marketing concepts and principles amongst senior management. Certain relationship marketing principles also need 'translation' into the project context, which is covered in this and the next chapter. The immediate aims are to achieve the following:

A. An analysis of the theoretical and applied characteristics of relationship marketing in project businesses and an examination of how these are internally managed.

B. A description of practices and their alignment with the theoretical and applied characteristics, particularly the approaches to building and managing relationships.
C. An evaluation of the strengths and weaknesses of relationship marketing and its pertinence to project businesses, in particular performance towards client and project business benefit.

The main message of the chapter is that relationship marketing offers a variety of ways to differentiate the propositions and induce close alignment of the internal strengths with market need, and provides a means of market management and business development.

The traditional approach to project management has been to meet the stated requirements in the request for proposal (RFP), briefing or other forms of requirements documentation, and to conduct the project within the framework of the so-called iron triangle of *time–cost–quality/scope*. Relationship marketing assumes such criteria will be met and aims to improve performance by adding value over and above.

Relationships are formed at several levels: interpersonal, team level, inter-organizational level, in networks, and combinations of these. This poses challenges in project businesses, particularly at the team and network levels. Projects comprise temporary multi-organizational (TMO) teams. First, the internal relationships need establishing, then TMO relationship building, which are important in order to provide *consistent* service. Relationship marketing tries to improve internal relationship building through systems and procedures to supplement interpersonal relationships. The internal project team members require support from the functional departments and senior management. These relationships cannot be taken for granted for three reasons: (i) projects are typically dislocated in social or physical space from the 'corporate centre', and this can have the effect of diluting potential support including use of central budgets to cover non-recoverable project costs without strong relationships, (ii) there are frequently weak systems between the corporate–project interface, (iii) some key management may be hired or contracted in for the project duration and lack established interpersonal relationships and knowledge of the systems and procedures. Strong internal relationships are necessary to provide a *consistent* client service.

Second, the team members from other organizations face the same challenges with their respective organizations. The other organizations may not have a proactive and relational approach to market management and may not have adopted relationship marketing. This can pose challenges to negotiating project protocols. A high degree of alignment is needed at the market management level and mutual understanding at the marketing level with routines coordinating the internal relationships to provide *consistent* relationship marketing and management at the client interface at the project level. Further, the short-term financial driver of cost control is to maximize personnel utilization rates, which can lead to the transactional removal of key team members during a project. This practice is acceptable where service *consistency* is carefully managed through the use of robust relationship and project management systems to produce an effective 'relay team' that works together on each leg or project stage. Personnel changes otherwise tend to lead to lower performance (Parker and Skitmore, 2005). Most project businesses find this a challenge, especially on large-scale complex projects (Martinsuo and Ahola, 2010), and many clients increasingly demand personnel retention for a project and sometimes for a programme (Smyth, 2000), hence the need for personnel to be 'on the bench' at times between projects. Relationship continuity is required after the commissioning and handover stage to manage the *sleeping relationship* with the client and their representatives where a follow-up on project is lacking (Hadjikhani, 1996; Cova et al., 2002).

Project networks are highly layered, starting with the immediate network of organizations that form the TMO. Each organizational member will have its own industrial network of support and suppliers, which may have considerable overlap. Tensions can arise to protect commercially sensitive relationships around respective networks, an issue that is amplified where alliances and joint ventures are in place. Relationship building and management is important at this level to meet expectations and non-contractual promises made at the bidding stage to *add value*, both in technical content and service experience. The TMO therefore sits in a slightly broader network, initially broader than the respective decision-making units (DMU) in each organization, the subcontractors and other suppliers forming the project coalition (Winch, 2002). There is the much wider network of institutional context that is to be influenced and drawn upon for support that forms the broader industrial network (cf. Manning, 2010). Project businesses are highly reliant upon these networks, which cannot be managed top–down; they are network organizations (Pryke, 2012). Achrol and Kotler define it this way:

> A network is an independent coalition of tasks- and skill-specialized economic entities (independent firms or autonomous organizational units) that operates without hierarchical control but is embedded, by dense lateral connections, mutuality, and reciprocity, in a shared value system that defines 'membership' roles and responsibilities.
>
> (1999: 148)

Relationships and their management across these networks are essential for leveraging added value (Håkansson and Snehota, 1995; Dubois and Gadde, 2000). External relationships are only as strong as the internal relationships because there needs to be strong relationship links across the BDM–bid management–purchasing–supply chain management–project management functions. These issues are of particular significance for project businesses as the issues are magnified or unique and require translation of relationship marketing principles to fit the context. These introductory points can be accepted as relational 'ground rules' that inform how relationship marketing is applied to projects, and hence, project businesses.

## Relationship marketing in theory and practice

### *The management literature*

#### *Principles and scope*

Relationship marketing is a *relational* approach to market management and *proactive* in terms of organizational behaviour. Relationship marketing also leads onto internal and external *relationship management* (Grönroos, 2000; Gummesson, 2000). Relationship management is necessary to achieve the relationship marketing goals, especially in B2B markets for the production of asset-specific goods, and thus, across project lifecycles, programmes and for portfolio management ($P^3M$).

The term *relationship marketing* was first coined by Berry (1983). The incremental introduction of relationship marketing in theory and practice gathered momentum until a paradigm shift had occurred. As part of the momentum, Jackson (1985) used it in a B2B context. Håkansson and Snehota (1989; 1995) introduced the network dimension. Other foci emerged, such as client satisfaction (e.g. Rust and Zahorik, 1993; Berry and Parasuraman, 1991) and loyalty (e.g. Reichheld, 1996) of targeted customers in segments of one (Gummesson, 2000). Indeed, relationship marketing developed across several dimensions that are disparate at times (Coote, 1994, cited in Payne and Frow, 2006). This is because different schools emerged. Relationship marketing in North America tended to be developed as an intensification of transactional relationships (Pels and Saren, 2005) and is the most pragmatic (Smyth, 2000). The Nordic school was the most conceptual and established many of the enduring principles (e.g. Grönroos, 2000; Gummesson, 2000). The Anglo-Saxon group of researchers arose out of purchasing and a value focus (e.g. Christopher et al., 2002; Ford et al., 2003). The combination of theorization and cross-fertilization lends scope for pragmatic application to induce differentiation in practice.

Developing long-term relationships with customers and improving customer satisfaction is one key factor in survival and growth (Parasuraman et al., 1985). This is self-reinforcing with long-term relationships requiring performance improvement in order to induce satisfaction and repeat business from client programmes. It has been shown that 80 per cent of the business comes from 20 per cent of the customers (Koch, 1998). Reichheld and Sasser (1990) established a link between customer retention and profit margins. This has yet to be proven in project sectors although growth in turnover in repeat business has been established (Smyth and Fitch, 2009).

The core ideas are the following:

1. Relationships secure business for the supplier, improving profitability and market share;
2. Relationships add value for the customer or client, reducing their costs and improve their performance from the delivery of benefits.

Grönroos defines the purpose of relationship marketing as follows: . . . *to identify and establish, maintain and enhance, and when necessary to terminate relationships with customers (and other parties) so that the objectives regarding economic and other variables of all parties are met* (2000: 243).

This is a market orientation that places the customer and the service at the centre to complement the production orientation (Gummesson, 2000). Gummesson uses the following definition: *Relationship marketing is marketing based on interaction within a network of relationships* (2000: 14).

He places emphasis upon understanding customers by regularly meeting and knowing them by *training your empathy, and reflecting over your observations* (Gummesson, 2000: 87): *The emphasis is on people and adding value. This is achieved through servicing, gaining competitive advantage through more effective working relationships rooted firmly in a systematic context, and through delivering effective value. The outcome of the relationship is profit* (Smyth, 2000: 192).

Relationship marketing does inform selling or BDM, culminating with a sale, yet it is also a process that informs how production is conducted, changing the way it is configured, which is why relationship marketing leads to relationship management to achieve its objectives. Ford and his colleagues provide the following definition: *Relationship management involves analysis, investment in relationships and a clear view of the wider value that can be gained from each relationship and which extends beyond the straightforward features of the product that is exchanged* (Ford et al., 2003: 5).

The primary characteristic that relationship marketing aims to address is that production and service provision are inseparable financially and operationally (e.g. Grönroos, 2000). Requirements and consumption patterns are heterogeneous, thus clients require individual account (cf. Jackson, 1985), and services that are intangible and imperishable (Lovelock and Gummesson, 2004), although the coherence of some of these tenets have been challenged and modified (Vargo and Lusch, 2004 – see **Chapter 10**).

Key relationship marketing principals are based around senior management commitment and investment to ensure implementation (Dwyer et al., 1987; Keh and Xie, 2009). Commitments are credible where contracts are incomplete (Williamson, 1993), and the initial commitments in relationship marketing emanate from social capital. The types of commitments are set out in Table 4.1, which informs the (re)-structuring of the project businesses. This is not suited to all suppliers, nor will all clients make the corresponding effort and investment (Mende and Bolton, 2011). Some clients claim to have established relationships, formalized through partnering and framework agreements in project markets, yet their intent is to continue to use market power at the expense of the supplier. Symmetric commitment is relationally signalled by the customer or followed by resource commitments (Heide and Miner, 1992). The increasing complexity and demands for high value are driving change and amplifying expectations, although dyadic organizational behaviour may lag behind.

Management commitment underpins *relationship commitment*, which is important in industrial marketing networks (Lövblad and Bantekas, 2010). It is not driven by the market but through market management to induce psychological contracts with both cognitive and affective dimensions (cf. Rousseau, 1990). Their form

**TABLE 4.1** Relationship foci for management

| *Management commitment and investment* | *Attributes* |
|---|---|
| Developing deep relationships to improve client and stakeholder understanding | High customer service emphasis |
| Developing services that match expectations | Emphasizes customer value |
| Customization of content and tailoring of services | Focus on profitable retention |
| Delivery services to engender client and stakeholder satisfaction | Long-term timescales |
| Developing systems to engage with customers and stakeholders | High customer contact and concern with relationship quality |
| Developing procedures to manage relationships | |

varies by organizational culture (Rousseau and Schalk, 2000) and relationship type (e.g. Gummesson, 2000; Christopher et al., 2002) and only have value where resource commitments are made, helping to systematically transition interpersonal into inter-organizational relationships. This itself may take two forms: (i) customized technical and technological content and (ii) tailored services that align with client needs and added value expectations.

Investment and commitment comes top-down. Top-down internal management emphasis is upon market and customer selection, investment in relationship competencies, strategic development of corporate systems for support as well as tactical behavioural guidance and monitoring. Beyond that, relationship marketing is more egalitarian than hierarchically governed transactions and is outward facing (cf. Douglas, 1999). It is reliant upon strong horizontal relationships of collaboration where trust is present and market power is exercised with ethical responsibility leading to interdependency (cf. Gummesson, 2008; Prasad, 1998). Bottom-up internal management emphasizes systematic relationship building, initiative taking including tactical resource commitment, non-contractual promise-making and client management. Top-down and bottom-up processes meet at the corporate–project interface and through programme management. A great challenge is to get people to work together and in concurrent teams (Hartshorn, 1997) as territory and self-interest can dominate (e.g. Fishbein and Azjen, 1975; George, 1997), whereas shared vision, purpose and goals provide fertile ground for cooperation (Deming, 1993; George, 1997).

## *Coordinating relationship marketing*

There are many entry points to develop a strategic starting point, two being provided by Christopher et al. (2002) and Gummesson (2000). The six markets model provides a means to target investment, systems and procedure in comprehensive ways to facilitate relationship development, maintenance and value creation (Christopher et al., 2002):

1. *Customer or client market* – the primary market relationship between the two principals in an exchange, often referred to as a *dyadic relationship*. This requires client management linked to internal systems.
2. *Supplier market* – relationships to lever value and added value, which clients and other stakeholders want rather than what expertise might necessarily suggest. This requires value integration originating internally (cf. value chains) with supply chains.
3. *Referral markets* – clients and representatives who act as advocates to develop new business. These are prime relationships in the industrial network.
4. *Influencer markets* – similar to the above where recommendation is indirect from the industrial network.
5. *Internal market* – supplier employees and contract staff who deliver in accordance relationship marketing and are guided by relationship management principles, recognizing that everyone has an indirect marketing role.
6. *Recruitment markets* – potential employees who will maintain and support the relationship marketing strategy and tactical implementation.

Gummesson (2000) identified four categories within which were 30 relationship types, the 30Rs (Table 4.2). Each relationship is managed differently both by type and in market context. These relationships have scarcely been tested through research to evaluate applicability, although one of the few studies addresses the public private partnership (PPP) and public finance initiative (PFI) markets in construction (Fact Box 4.1).

*How* are interpersonal, team, and inter-organizational relationships built and managed? Interpersonal relationships are founded on *who people are*, rather than what they do or what (power) position they occupy. The context is the role occupied, lending a business purpose. The strengths of the individuals in terms of their character, personality, and conduct to demonstrate skills and experience should be given room to flourish. However, business relationship building extends beyond individual responsibility. Service *consistency* is needed for any one transaction and *continuity* between transactions. Therefore, there needs to be agreed procedures or behavioural codes of conduct to provide guide interpersonal B2B relationships. In this way, the supplier begins to own the relationships so that it becomes (a) effective in BDM to secure sales, (b) consistent for service provision, and (c) part of the corporate brand for delivery. On the one hand, guidance can become somewhat dictatorial, which stifles opportunities to add value; on the other hand, it can become so loose that the relationships are not owned by the organization on whose behalf they are being conducted. A balanced approach embeds relationship building at this tactical level through established procedures and norms expressed through informal routines, supported in a strategic relationship management system.

**TABLE 4.2** Thirty relationships of relationship marketing for relationship management

| *Markets by category* | *Relationships* | |
|---|---|---|
| **Classic market relationships** | R1 | The classic dyad: the relationship between the supplier and the customer |
| | R2 | The classic triad: the drama of the customer–supplier–competitor triangle. Competition is a central ingredient of the market economy. In competition, there are relationships between three parties: between the customer and current supplier |
| | R3 | The classic network: distribution channels. The traditional physical distribution and the modern channel management, including goods, services, people and information, consists of a network of relationship |
| **Special market relationships** | R4 | Relationships via full-time marketers and part-pime marketers |
| | R5 | The service encounter |
| | R6 | The many-headed customer and the many-headed supplier |
| | R7 | The relationship to the customer's customer |
| | R8 | The close versus the distant relationship |
| | R9 | The relationship to the dissatisfied customer |
| | R10 | The monopoly relationship |
| | R11 | Customer as 'member' |
| | R12 | The e-relationship |
| | R13 | Parasocial relationships |
| | R14 | The non-commercial celationship |
| | R15 | The green relationship |
| | R16 | The law-based relationship |
| | R17 | The criminal network |
| **Mega relationships** | R18 | Personal and social networks |
| | R19 | Mega marketing |
| | R20 | Alliances change the market mechanisms |
| | R21 | The knowledge relationship |
| | R22 | Mega alliances change the basic conditions for marketing |
| | R23 | The mass media relationship |
| **Nano (internal) relationships** | R24 | Market mechanisms are brought inside the company |
| | R25 | The internal customer relationship |
| | R26 | Quality and the customer orientation |
| | R27 | Internal marketing |
| | R28 | The two-dimensional matrix relationship |
| | R29 | The relationship to external providers of marketing services |
| | R30 | The owner and financier relationship |

*Source*: Adapted from Gummesson (2000).

## FACT BOX 4.1 RELATIONSHIP MANAGEMENT IN PPP AND PFI MARKETS

The primary parties are the client at a UK government ministry at central and local levels, the Special Purpose Vehicle (SPV) and constituent members comprising the contractor and operator, the financial institution and legal advisor. The facilities in question constituted a programme of both PPP and PFI projects with concession contracts ranging between 10 to 40 years and had a net present value (NPV) of about £0.5bn. Trust and confidence were used as measures of relationship strength and were mapped against 30 relationships (Table 4.1). A survey solicited over 300 relationship responses. The SPV risk manager and research team identified the critical relationships and agreed on an evaluation procedure for the operational context. The critical relationships were:

R1 The classic dyad
R4 Relationships via full-time marketers and part-time marketers
R5 The service encounter
R9 The relationship to the dissatisfied customer
R11 Customer as 'member'
R15 The green relationship
R16 The law-based relationship
R20 Alliances change the market mechanisms
R21 The knowledge relationship
R27 Internal marketing
R28 The two-dimensional matrix relationship
R30 The owner and financier relationship

Across the SPV, the relationship strength was found to be reasonable, although the main project business, the construction contractor, had the weakest relationship within the SPV. The relationships between the SPV and the client at central and local levels were found to be very weak, especially for R5, R9 and R11. In terms of the six markets model, the dyadic relationships at the client–supplier interface were poorly managed. The special and mega-market relationships essential in PPP and PFI markets were particularly weak. Some responsibility lay on the supply side; however, it was the client side that failed to address the way that relationships need managing despite being instrumental in reconfiguring the market through PPP and PFI policies. The summary relationship scores by relationship categories in the markets were the following:

| Markets by category | Relationships across SPV | SPV–public client relationships |
|---|---|---|
| Classic market relationships | 80.21 | –53.92 |
| Special market relationships | 215.88 | –574.04 |
| Mega relationships | 164.71 | –197.38 |
| Nano relationships | 322.88 | –22.29 |

Effective and consistent relationships need to be managed. They do not arise automatically or merely by good intent. Strong relationships can emerge through informal means, but if left to individual responsibility, reliance is placed upon happenstance rather than management. All the relationships between the SPV and client were negative. Responsibility rests with both sides in the exchange, but it is a lesson for project businesses that client commitment and support needs to be present as well as on the suppler side. The findings were summed up as follows:

> . . . pro-active management of relationships has yet to be instilled. This difference is essentially one between **relational contracting** and **relationship management** in conceptual terms, that is, SPVs are reacting to structural change in the market represented by PFI/PPP procurement by adjusting behaviour accordingly, rather than proactively seeking to develop and manage relationships as a matter of strategic initiative and tactical foresight. This is a significant finding given the long-term nature of PFI/PPP concessions and that projects are still in the early stages of the life cycle.
>
> (Smyth and Edkins, 2007: 239, emphasis in original)

*Source*: Adapted from Smyth and Edkins (2007).

The *purpose* of the relationship relates directly to the overall business purpose and its inter-organizational relationships. Thus interpersonal relationships support organizational purpose, which include development of strong inter-organizational relationships in its markets. Building deep inter-organizational relationships is shown in Figure 4.1. Developing serial relationships with different organizations essentially involves triangulation to gain different perspectives from different organizational actors that are mapped and profiled (Figure 4.2). This brings breadth and depth. The information needs to be captured as part of client management,

| Relationship depth | | From transactional management | Towards relationship management |
|---|---|---|---|
| | Shallow and short-term | Building relationships to get information on requirements | Understanding customer or client business solutions to be addressed |
| | Long-term and deep | Understanding motivations and considerations of the key decision-makers | Understanding the customer or client's own core business and what they perceive as valuable |

Relationship purpose

**FIGURE 4.1** Relationship purpose and depth in relationship marketing

| | Mapping | Profiling |
|---|---|---|
| **Roles** – evident through behaviour and action | Name and contact details, job title and role | Functional and team contributions, e.g. characteristics in role and context using Belbin analysis |
| **Behavioural intent** – less evident and more difficult to read and anticipate | Power and influence in relation to decision-making for purchasing and for customer or client side management of the supply side | Personal motivations:<br>• *Technocrats* – primarily legalistic and/or transactional accountability against time, cost and quality;<br>• *Power players* – primarily use positions of power to impose control and accountability;<br>• *Careerists* – primary focus upon career progression;<br>• *Approval seekers* – primary focus is to get significance from being central and popular;<br>• *Critical eventers* – overstretched or prefer an arm's length role by choice and operate on a 'need-to-know' basis |
| | From transactional management | Towards relationship management |

**FIGURE 4.2** Mapping and profiling relationships in relationship marketing

CRM (customer or client relationship management) software packages providing one means, although these are poorly used in practice, especially within project industries (Smyth, 2013a).

The depth of the relationship is about the level of engagement, leading to *relationship strength*. Frequency of contact is important but indecisive. Depth of understanding is gained through increasing strength in the relationships that leads to the formation of *relationship bonds* and *ties* (e.g. Håkansson, 1982; Ford et al., 2003; Christopher et al., 2002; cf. Granovetter, 1985). Bonds or ties can be defined as social, structural and economic. To illustrate the meaning, dyadic relationships in the travel agency business were recently explored (Schakett et al., 2011). It was found that social bonds from interpersonal aspects of the relationships were significant in regard to customer satisfaction, trust and thus potential repeat business. The social bonds accounted for 44 per cent of the perceived service quality. Structural bonds relate more to the management systems and context that affect governance criteria, comprising 36 per cent of the perceived service quality, and economic bonds are exchange criteria that only accounted for 7 per cent of service quality. Therefore building boundary spanning dyadic relationships with a business purpose and outcome are linked to effectiveness (cf. Heide and John, 1990). Industrial networks also rely upon strong relational ties and bonds in a value system of common ground and some shared norms and beliefs that define the connections with associated roles and responsibilities (Achrol and Kotler, 1999).

A stronger relationship arises from identity and identification with the other organization. This deeper level has as its starting points personal identity (cf. Mead, 1934; Erikson, 1968) and social identity (e.g. Stryker, 1968; Tajfel, 1974; Ashforth and Mael, 1989). The emotional and social aspects of relationship ties provide the basis to create interdependencies between the supplier and customer or client (cf. Campbell, 1985). Linked to business purpose, organizational identification is a strong relationship that combines cognitive and intuitive dimensions of identity (cf. Hogg et al., 1995). Organizational identity feeds several important relationship marketing functions:

1) Increases repeat business frequency (cf. Gummesson, 2000);
2) Provides a stable platform for the development of relationship and operational capabilities to add value for the customer that provide a basis for transferability (with tailoring) to other customers and clients (cf. Möller, 2006);
3) Builds social capital in the supplier organization that appreciates with use (cf. Nahapiet and Ghoshal, 1998);
4) Influences corporate brand in the marketplace (Bhattacharya et al., 1995).

Organizational identity, whether one-way or shared in the relationship, denotes a stable and potentially long-term commitment. It is difficult to recognize as it involves cognitive and experiential factors expressed through emotional attachment of the actors involved. Surrogates of intuitive assessments made of an organization, repeat business measures, interpersonal and team reliance on others are needed. Such assessments feed into the contribution of social capital to performance, reputation and corporate brand (Kim et al., 2001). One-way organizational identity with the client by the project business aids cooperation, learning and service development, providing the client respects the relationship. Moving from a transactional to a relationship marketing approach, forged and reinforced through mutual identification, is set out in Figure 4.3.

Developing deep relationships that are not merely strong but include deep understanding of the client and their organizational operations by drilling down (Turkulainien et al., 2013; Figure 4.1), routine learning and know-how for value creation. Ballantyne and Varey (2006) call this 'dialogical', where dialogue develops into mutual proactivity and responsiveness, including associated action.

| Relationship strength | From transaction-based interaction | To relationship-based interaction | To identity-based interaction |
|---|---|---|---|
| **Optimal strength** – extended to the inter-organizational and network levels | Relational contracting through (formal and informal) collaborative alliances and partnerships that are market driven with the opportunity for transitioning to proactive relationship-based interaction | Interpersonal and inter-organizational relationship building that is organizationally embedded and driven by management strategy for relationship marketing | Organizational identification that enhances the relationships, performance, the reputation and brand in the marketplace |
| **Minimal strength** – largely confined to the interpersonal and team levels | Discrete exchange in economic and information terms | Relationship building and maintenance that is largely interpersonal with spin-offs for the organization | Personal and social identification that exists between key members of the client, their representatives, suppliers and preferably the supplier with the client too |

**FIGURE 4.3** Developing relationship strength in relationship marketing

The interactive aspect has been put this way: *Dialogue means interactivity, engagement, and a propensity to act – on both sides. Dialogue is more than listening to customers: it implies shared learning and communication between two equal problem solvers. Dialogue creates and maintains a loyal community* (Prahalad and Ramaswamy, 2004a: 6–7).

Dialogue is reinforced from an ethics of care perspective. Gilligan emphasizes the role of 'voice' in a relationship whereby meaning and understanding are far more significant than open communication or information processing. A 'loss of voice' leads to a loss of relationship strength or a loss of the relationship (Gilligan, 1982).

## *Range and levels of relationships*

In relationship marketing, the relationships broadens out from the sales–procurement interface to include all those who have contact in B2B selling and operations. This inverts the traditional transactional bow-tie interface to an elongated one that needs internal relationship management to manage the dyadic relationship (Figure 4.4). As relationships are built and managed in systematic ways, both the sales and operational interface coordinate along the interface to achieve relational integration. Strong relationships, social and inter-organizational identification cause inter-organizational boundaries to become 'perforated' to complete the three-stage transition in Figure 4.4.

The interpersonal relationships to target are between those with power and influence in the decision-making units (DMUs) in the dyad. There are DMUs on both the supply and customer side, and they are broader than the TMO yet located within the project coalition (cf. Winch, 2002). The interface of exchange and operations requires horizontal management, whereas the DMU will comprise people from senior, perhaps board level down to operational levels in the hierarchy

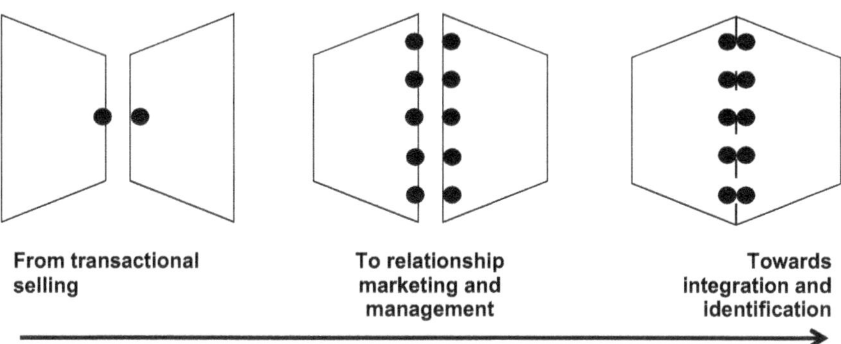


FIGURE 4.4 Towards dyadic integration through relationship marketing

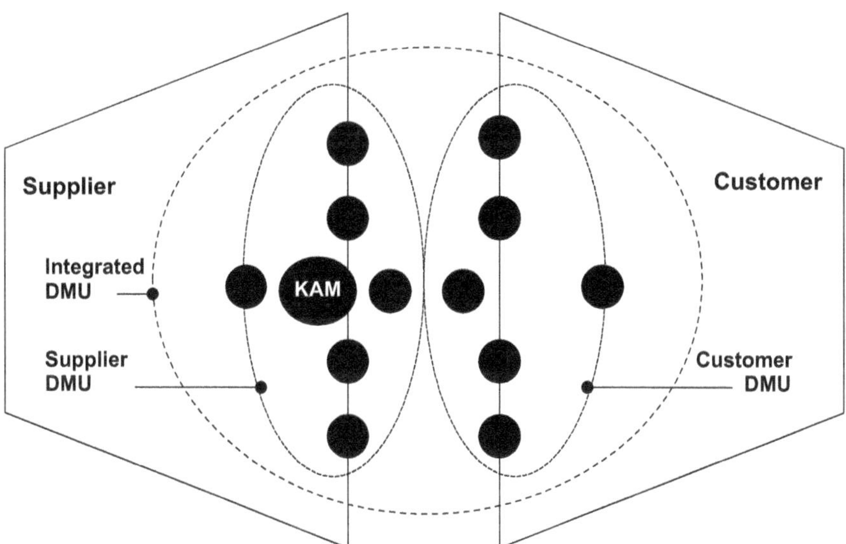


FIGURE 4.5 Inter-organizational interface

on both sides. The DMU is shown in Figure 4.5. This achieves, first, the introduction of the hierarchical element in the dyad, helping embed the commitment to the relationship at the level of client management. It also brings other vertical dimensions into play, such as portfolio and programme management. Coordinating client management is conducted purely through systems and procedures, which may include cross-functional systems integration, relationship management systems and procedures. It is aided by placing thoughtful and reflective people who value contact and responsibilities in the frontline positions (Porath et al., 2011). It may also be facilitated through key account management (KAM). A particular transaction may have a commercial, operations or sales manager in charge, yet there may be several transactions going on in parallel where continuity is needed across serial transactions of repeat business as well as consistency on a project. The KAM has the coordinating role at the programme level on the supply side (e.g. McDonald et al., 1997; see Figure 4.5).

The inter-organizational interface is therefore complex in B2B markets for the production and delivery of assets specific goods and services, such as projects. Systems are needed; hence, relationship marketing requires systems to coordinate the relationships, typically a relationship management system. There are different ways to achieve this in which the middle management option of the KAM function is located. Storbacka et al. (1994) provide an overarching system, which will be used here as it has been conceptually applied in project environments. This system is presented in Figure 4.6. The system requires investment for (a) set up in alignment with other operational systems, (b) for other systems to be reconfigured and aligned where necessary to induce integration. It also requires periodic investment for maintenance and development. Costs are incurred for running the system and for dealing with unexpected episodes and events that are linked to exchanges yet are non-recoverable cost items. In this way the system serves operational service consistency and facilitates added value opportunities to meet relationship marketing goals.

A relationship management system is necessary for embedding relationship marketing to guide the processes 'owned' by the contacts. Customer relationship management (CRM) may be a part of a system to coordinate contacts, but it is not a relationship management system internally, externally and to add value through relationships. A relationship management system coordinates BDM at the front end. It is necessary for consistent management across the project business, in the TMOs to induce shared inter-organizational routines (cf. Eccles, 1981). A system engages BDM with production and other service operational management

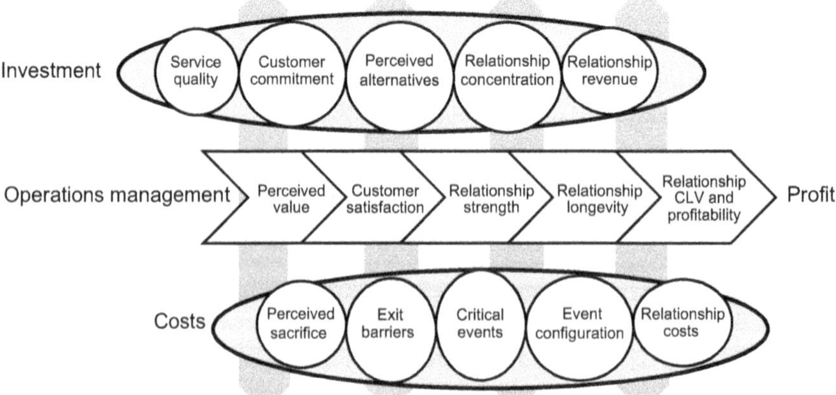


**FIGURE 4.6** Relationship marketing and management systems

*Source*: Adapted and developed from Storbacka et al. (1994).

during execution. It helps manage the sleeping relationship for repeat business, managing the client between contracts. It helps liaison across an industrial network and lever value from supply chains as networks are not automatically coordinated through either hierarchy or market mechanisms (cf. Håkansson, 1982; Powell, 1990; Håkansson and Snehota, 1995).

## *Implications from the project management literature and for practice*

### *Relationship marketing, management of projects, capabilities and investment*

Many project businesses and sectors have become familiar with relational contracting through alliances, partnering and SCM. Relational contracting is reactive to the trends in the marketplace and demands of clients, whereas relationship marketing generates *proactive* organizational behaviour (e.g. Smyth, 2006; Skitmore and Smyth, 2007). The realization of relationship marketing goals in project businesses needs support through $P^3M$ from internal and external *relationship management* (Smyth and Fitch, 2009; cf. Smyth and Edkins, 2007).

A structured approach to relationship marketing and management in project businesses is therefore needed:

1. Perforated organizational boundaries and an outward facing strategy and culture, supported by communications and relationship marketing across five markets – client, suppliers, referrers and influencers and recruitment markets. Managing perforated boundaries requires cross-functional working, especially financial and legal functions in relation to project management and marketing and BDM as these functions tend to be the most myopic and defensive.
2. Organizational structures to facilitate top-down and bottom-up relationship marketing and for cross-functional working to support integration in the internal market, addressing the socially and sometimes physically dislocated project that is further complicated by TMO project teams.
3. Formal routines form part of an integrated system, that including relationship management to connect relationship marketing cross-functionally and over project lifecycles.
4. Informal routines support the proactive development of added value including the service experience.

The core relationship marketing idea is to secure rewarding projects for the project business that are profitable and contributes to growth in market share. Relationships add project value for the customer or client, reducing costs and improving their performance. Liinamaa (2012) argues that mechanisms for technically based value creation have a social dimension in the early stages in order to enhance technical effectiveness in later stages. Relationship marketing principles are part of and support the *management of projects* (MoP). That said, the primary

MoP emphasis has been placed upon the client side and project business analysis remains under-researched for marketing (Pinto and Covin, 1992; Turner, 1995; see **Chapters 1** and **2**) and will be unpacked further in the specific context of BDM in the next subsection and in **Chapter 8**.

Relationship marketing is also conceptually connected to the resource-based view of the firm (RBV). How resources are allocated is a competitiveness factor of market management. Allocation may be into marketing capabilities (Möller, 2006) or into other core organizational competencies and capabilities, such as team emotional intelligence (e.g. Druskat and Druskat, 2006; Hobbs and Smyth, 2012), which have a marketing effect by improving service performance (cf. Davies and Brady, 2000; Davies et al., 2007). Project capabilities can be developed that are technical or management related (Brady and Davies, 2004), such as agile production and agile project management methodologies, for example SCRUM and XP, to provide further conceptual connections – agility is more suited to marketing than lean production because of the greater degree customization of technical content and tailoring of the services where the production orientation is decoupled from a client-centric view (e.g. Hoekstra and Romme, 1992; Naylor et al., 1999; Naim and Barlow, 2003). Relational contracting is a further connected concept that tries to induce governance of trust and activity based upon collaboration that elevates procurement issues to strategic ones through partnering, SCM and alliances. It is a basis for project businesses to transition from transactional relational contracting (cf. Coase, 1988; Williamson, 1975) to the more proactive relationship marketing as set out in Figure 4.7. The relational contracting tendency in project markets is for the project business to be reasonably cooperative with the client retaining

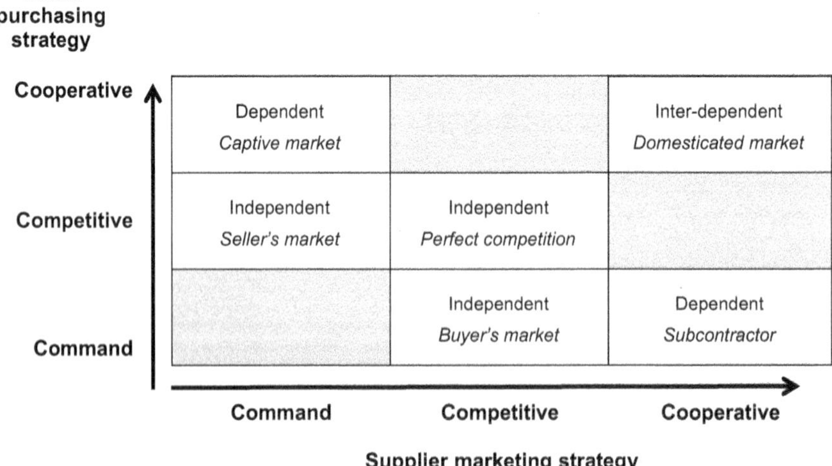


**FIGURE 4.7** Client procurement–supplier marketing interface

*Source*: Adapted and developed from Campbell (1985).

the commanding position through market power and contractual leverage, which is the subcontract market as seen in the bottom right-hand corner of Figure 4.7. Relationship marketing is interactional (Campbell, 1985), located at the top right-hand corner of mutual cooperation in Figure 4.7.

Theory posits relationship marketing increases supplier repeat business, reduces transaction costs and increases profit margins. Repeat business and lower costs are established (e.g. Smyth and Fitch, 2009), but profit margin improvement is not in project markets. Therefore effectiveness leading to improved efficiency (rather than efficiency achieved through crude input–output ratios that lower input costs, lower value and service quality – see Grönroos, 2000; Srinivasan and Hanssens, 2009; **Chapter 3**), and an increased the acceleration of working capital to improve the return on capital employed (ROCE) is the best supposition for project markets yet requires further research (Smyth and Lecoeuvre, 2014). Other indirect benefits are reputational and brand related, which help positioning in referral and influencer markets of the six markets model (Christopher et al., 2002).

Practical benefits for clients and external stakeholders are the potential for added technical and service value that improves client satisfaction and loyalty, some of which can translate into repeat business. The way to increase certainty of linkage between relationship marketing investment at the front of the front-end is to follow through with investment to reconfigure project lifecycles to integrate relationship marketing throughout, so it not only informs selling or BDM, but also is a process that informs how production is conducted. As relationship marketing is developed as much horizontally and bottom-up as it is top-down, the interpersonal level provides a good starting point for an overview.

Commitment, as a key relationship marketing concept (e.g. Dwyer et al., 1987; Keh and Xie, 2009), involves senior management rigor at a strategic level and investment for implementation top-down and horizontally across project lifecycles in project environments, reaching into the tactics of experiential and emotional commitment of interpersonal relationships. There has tended to be too much reliance upon the interpersonal level where relationships are built and developed by individuals taking responsibility (Smyth; 2013a). Overreliance upon individual responsibility leads to inconsistent services on projects and discontinuity between projects (Hadjikani, 1996; Smyth, 2000, 2013a): *Project business is characterized by a high degree of discontinuity in economic relations between the supplier and the customer* (Cova et al., 2002: 20).

Project businesses have tended to structure their organizations around projects rather than equally around clients, even where claiming application of (some) relationship marketing principles (e.g. Smyth, 2006; 2013a). The structuring of projects acts to induce organizational discontinuity whereby projects become self-contained (Koskinen and Pihlanto, 2008). This is inward facing and inhibits learning and relationship continuity to add value on projects and secure repeat business between projects.

In addition to discontinuity between projects without a relational approach (Hadjikani, 1996; see **Chapter 5**), there is a lack of integration and hence discontinuity between functions as each function in project businesses tends to operate its own sub-system without systematic integration between functions. For example, amongst the most notable from a marketing perspective at the front-end are:

i. BDM–bid management,
ii. BDM–procurement,
iii. BDM–project management,
iv. BDM–commercial management,
v. Procurement–project management.

Long-term relationships start at the interpersonal level and are inter-organizational. Mapping and profiling a range of people in the client DMU, as well as understanding the client organization from the interpersonal level, is the goal. The same applies to suppliers, referrers and influencers in the broader industrial and institutional network. Long-term dyadic relationships help to establish relationship continuity, but do not automatically produce continuity from the project business side. Key personnel change over the long term, therefore multiple long-term strong client relationships are fostered from the project business DMU at the programme level, starting with BDMs at the front of the front-end developed to cover project lifecycles, including effective handovers along any project lifecycle conveying the depth of understanding of client needs, and the value to be added at each project stage, and the project benefits in use (cf. Turkulainien et al., 2013). Continuity of people or a relay team approach from the front-end, during execution and KAM at the programme level acting as an 'account handler' is involved (cf. Figure 4.5).

Prior to examining how DMU management and KAM fits into a relationship marketing and management system for projects, the informal routines are considered. The organizational culture and climate drills down into shared norms, giving rise to shared practices that make up the informal routines (cf. Parmigiani and Howard-Grenville, 2011). These tend to be weak in project businesses for two reasons. First, the structuring of functions into discrete and non-integrated sub-systems presents one obstacle. Second, projects are executed by TMOs that may not have worked together and may not again, constraining the development of shared norms and practices (cf. Bresnen et al., 2004). Embedding informal routines during project lifecycles and pan-project, supported by formal routines – systems and procedures – forms part of effective relationship marketing in project businesses. *Temporal embeddedness* is the most important because of the temporary nature of projects, which is an extension of *social embeddedness* that guides interpersonal relations (Jones and Lichtenstein, 2008; cf. Granovetter, 1985).

Client lifetime value (CLV) or the relationship value of clients is a necessary and complementary management approach for relationship marketing. CLVs can be estimated as value of client programmes over the long term, say 7–10 years. The size of their workload and the strike rate in securing repeat business provide sound ways for estimating the volume and turnover of work, which provides one measure of CLV. Another way is to calculate the value using stock market profit/

earnings ratios for a sector, for example for different activities such as construction, concession contracting, facilities management (FM) (Smyth and Fitch, 2009). Net present value, however, may be inappropriate because it does not take into account performance along the lines of shareholder value (Ryals, 2002; cf. Cornelius and Davies, 1997). Yet, the connection between CLV and shareholder value from a relationship marketing perspective remains underdeveloped (Stahl et al., 2003; Ryals, 2005), and those in the finance function can find it difficult to decouple their thinking from shareholder value in a production rather than service mode of operation (Smyth and Lecoeuvre, 2014; see **Chapter 2**). Value is derived from two sources, the *embodied value* of the offer (technical and service content) and the *emotional value* derived from the benefits and impact (Smyth, 2000; cf. Morris, 2013; Smyth, 2014). This latter aspect is more difficult to account for in CLV calculations, but how the value of goodwill, reputation and brand are treated in the accounts may give some guidance, providing these take relationship marketing principles into account as well.

Managing supply chains along similar lines is necessary. Using social network analysis as a frame and method, Pryke (2012) identified the significance of long-term relationships for a series of development and construction projects, especially in the supply chains:

> The existence of long-term supplier relationships and the relatively intense management of these relationships were central. Major construction clients began to realise that collaborative long-term relationships provided both a threat and opportunity: the threat of escalating costs and poor performance from service providers, but the opportunity to collaborate and integrate within the context of those long-term relationships.
>
> (2012: 48)

The main contractor occupies the systems integrator role, supplied from their chain of subcontractors and suppliers that are specialist systems solutions providers. The difference between these two outcomes – the threat of cost escalation and added service value – resides in the extent to which project businesses have invested in and mobilized marketing, management and project specific capabilities to add technical and service value yet control costs.

## *Relationship building*

The *purpose* of building relationships relates to overall business goals (see Figure 1.1). Profit and growth are prime goals. Strategic pursuit tends to be guided by the equivalent of production orientated for project businesses, characterized as *task focused* (Handy, 1997; Pryke and Smyth, 2006). Inputs are controlled based upon self-interest. Relationship marketing conceptually demands a client-centric approach informed by adding technical and service value. Outputs are controlled with a greater social orientation. A client and service focus, coupled with the project and task focus, aligns project management towards a social orientation in order to serve shareholder value in the project business by growing the business.

For understanding the client, Atkin and Flanagan (1995) articulate three a priori stages: (i) identify how the client business and operations are organized by drawing upon their corporate goals, objectives, strategy and procedures; (ii) undertake client analysis to gain deep understanding of the client organization in terms of culture, values, style, behaviour in relation to their goals; (iii) conduct a technical facilities analysis of relevant (social and fixed) assets focusing upon standards. These act as a springboard for depth of understanding gained through relationship marketing and management at five levels:

1. Information on the project pipelines and requirements;
2. Understanding the motivations and considerations of the key decision-makers (clients and their professional representatives in the DMU);
3. Understanding client business solutions or organizational purposes projects are addressing (Turkulainien et al., 2012);
4. Understanding the client's core business or raison d'être to get to the bottom of what they perceive as valuable (Smyth, 2013a; Smyth and Kusuma, 2013).

This commences at the interpersonal level with the client DMU, mapping and profiling the internal decision-makers (see Figure 4.2). The DMU operates at programme and project levels. There are external representatives amongst client DMU member, for example financial, professional and others, such as stakeholders from arts councils and aid agencies. DMU members inform if they are not part of project TMOs, complicating the TMO inter-organizational interface (Figure 4.5). The DMU-TMO overlap is presented in Figure 4.8.

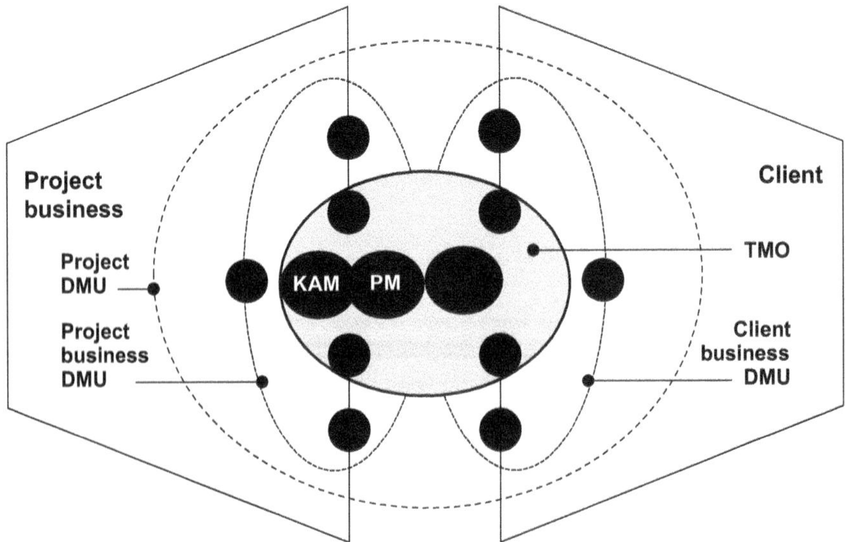


**FIGURE 4.8** Inter-organizational interface incorporating project TMOs

Relationship depth starts with high levels of project DMU-TMO engagement (Figure 4.8), building relationship *strength*. Frequency of contact is necessary, yet depth of understanding is gained through the formation of *relationship bonds* and *ties* (Granovetter, 1985; Krackhardt and Hanson, 1993). Social, structural and economic bonds or ties are developed through inter-personal and inter-organizational dialogue. Frequency and density of interaction can be measured in theory and practice using social network analysis, and this can help the mapping of the DMU identifying the relationship nodes and gatekeepers (Pryke, 2012).

Dialogue helps to understand client needs, and dialogue provides a basis to engage with client needs, but how do you know when you have a good relationship in marketing terms? Recent research has shown that those with specific and indirect BDM roles view building and recognizing a good relationship differently. In Fact Box 4.2, four international construction companies are examined. All are in the early transition towards adopting some relationship marketing principles. None of the companies claims to be using relationship marketing extensively, but there are normative implications from the evidence. The lack of integrated roles, such as KAM, and systems are two dimensions, which are subsequently developed.

## FACT BOX 4.2 PERCEPTIONS OF RELATIONSHIP STRENGTH

In four international construction majors, the *purpose* of building relationships was encapsulated in phrases such as 'understanding client drivers', yet this and similar phrases meant different things to different people in the same firm:

1. To all interviewed, 'client drivers' meant building relationships to get information on the project pipelines and requirements – *transactional* approach.
2. To some it meant understanding the motivations and considerations of the key decision-makers (clients and their professional representatives) – a responsive move away from the purely *transactional* approach.
3. To a few it meant understanding client business solutions or organizational purposes projects are addressing – towards a *relational* approach.
4. And to only one person alone, it meant understanding the client's own core business to get to the bottom of what they perceive as valuable – *relational* approach.

Relationship marketing gives all four purposes significance. The *strength* of relationships is assessed differently with widespread evidence of hiding behind business jargon to give the appearance of standardization, such as having the 'correct' or 'right behaviours' and 'understanding client drivers'.

There were a number of response types in evidence amongst those interviewed. At the extreme of intuitive individualism, it was commented that relationship building is 'just personalities', looking for mutual interests on

(*Continued*)

**FACT BOX 4.2** (Continued)

a business and personal level (Interview with a Project Manager, UKCo). UKCo was increasingly emphasizing relationship building, yet does not provide any specific guidance on relationship building. A business development director thought relationship building was guided by processes that are 'quite open and loose' and are largely about prequalification. A project manager thought, 'Behaviours are key to making this a success', and flow from core values in UKCo, whilst another project manager thought relationship building flowed from corporate governance. There were more sophisticated approaches adopted in the industrial networks. One business development manager recognized networks as a source for developing ideas and recording progress in reports. Others stated that strong interpersonal relationships are established 'when people trust you' and 'when they share confidences' and when greater collaborative working ensues. There was a lack of clarity as to what informs relationship building and the purpose of relationship building.

EuroCo displayed wide variance in relationship building. On the one hand, a business development coordinator uses the web to map the client by role, starts contact with a cold call, as prescribed in the matrix forming the Customer Plan. A good relationship is reached when the client returns a call and if they are easy to talk to: 'It is largely *instinctive'*. On the other hand, one business development manager assesses relationships by ranking their organizational and project importance, going on to say relationships are built across networks, through alliances and partnerships with key suppliers. Efficient delivery was said to be a 'given' these days, the aim being 'to shape the project' using unpublished client 'intelligence' (Interviews with a Customer Solutions Director and Technical Service Director, EuroCo). One project director sought a deep client focus, the stated aim being 'to understand what the client wants and listen to them', then, align the project strategy to the client needs. Overall, there are no guidelines on relationship building.

EUCo also were increasing the emphasis upon relationship building: 'It is all about people and relationships'. A business development manager claimed there was an approach but it is not one written down for developing opportunities and relationships. A relationship management procedure is being developed at a rudimentary level. Customers are scored by financial standing, past experience, reputational standing in the market for bids, and for the skills deemed necessary. It was stated that BDMs formed a disparate group, building relationships differently (Interview with a Regional Business Development Manager, EUCo). CRM was introduced as a procedure to fill an identified gap, yet stalled after 18 months as how the gap was to be filled and how what they wanted it to do was overlooked. Overall, building relationships remains largely intuitive. AntCo aims to build long-term relationships, focusing upon 2-year pipelines yet lacking direction from a long-term marketing strategy. They talk about the 'big picture' yet lack 'discipline' and systems to capture the information and drill down to the detailed needs, and whether the client values the relationship (Interview with a Bid Manager, AntCo).

Frequency of contact and time spent with client decision-makers is important. The first study to provide evidence for the impact of relationship length on employee knowledge of customer needs showed that high levels of customer knowledge is associated with higher levels of customer satisfaction and willingness to pay (Homburg et al., 2009a). This has been supported in a recent study amongst project businesses covering sectors including industrial engineering, power plants and shipbuilding (Liinamaa and Gustafsson, 2009). However, frequency and length of contact are not an automatic route to strong relationships. Fact Box 4.2 shows that people were acting at the interpersonal level rather than inter-organizationally, yet are looking for indicators of relationship quality, albeit in different ways; purpose was dominated by maintaining contact and soliciting information. A great deal of relationship maintenance and some relationship development is achieved through social media (Fact Box 4.3). Social media facilitates regular dialogue. Dialogue alone is one step on from information processing (cf. Winch, 2002). Dialogue gives 'voice' (cf. Gilligan, 1982). The voice of the customer conveys a hierarchy of needs, which are assigned a priority that the project business needs to glean (Griffin and Hauser, 1993). Depth of understanding can only come through face-to-face contact (F2F), through dialogue of listening and responding, supported by systems and processes constituting a dialogical process (Ballantyne and Varey, 2006).

Organizational culture and norms do provide some guidance for BDMs, but where they are rather isolated and individual responsibility pervades, there is a lack of shared meaning and action. Similarly, on the client side organizational culture provides some guidance, yet misalignments exist between stated intent and action, and note needs to be taken where dysfunctions may emanate during projects and programmes. Several conditions are helpful indicators:

1. The people in the DMU have moral integrity and behave ethically;
2. The organization has moral intent, which applies to the exercise of market power with responsibility – with market power responsibility increases;
3. The people and their support systems have an outward looking and social orientation;
4. The organization has a social orientation and behaves responsibly.

A stronger relationship still arises from identity and identification with other organizations (cf. Hogg et al., 1995) to create interdependencies at the client–project business interface (Figures 4.7 and 4.8). Organizational identification by the client with the project business is a sign of a deep relationship with a number of key DMU members. It is likely to be achieved where the project business DMU and TMO members have prior identification with the client. It has been found that those working away from their office base, such as auditors or project teams undertaking megaprojects, identify with those for and around them. Spatial dislocation is a feature of many projects, although organizational co-location for execution has been increasing. The professions and the more professional-like the working environment, the more employees are able to closely identify with

## FACT BOX 4.3 THE SOCIAL MEDIA EFFECT

A former director and a head of marketing in a major international construction company started up a specialist consultancy advising project businesses. The consultancy was organized on the project as the delivery channel. As a fledgling business, the consultancy sensed and witnessed the growing influence of social media as a means to create a network built upon their contacts and as a means to secure opportunities for work.

The brand was launched early September 2011. The business developed its website without paying for advertising. LinkedIn was used to build a high quality network. To do this, the two founding directors set targets of adding at least one connection per day. This was through a combination of invitations received and reaching out to people previously or recently met. At the same time interesting updates were posted to the timeline. These were often news articles to which a comment was added. To further extend the reach of the business cross posting to relevant groups to which the founders were members was undertaken. These posts were automatically posted to personal Twitter feeds. In particular, the founders started posting blogs to their website and then sharing these to LinkedIn and Twitter.

There were a number of measureable effects. First, the more activity on LinkedIn, the more views the profiles of the founders received. Typically posting once per day trebles the number of views, and the quality of the viewers rose correspondingly, that is, a greater number of potential customers. There was also a measureable effect on traffic to the website as measured by Google Analytics. The day after posting a blog, traffic increased by between five and tenfold. Measured over a typical month about 50 per cent of traffic came via social referral with 85 per cent of this from LinkedIn and the rest Twitter.

New business has been gained direct from LinkedIn from new customers where there was no prior contact. The profile of established contacts are thought to add credibility to the growing network of new contacts. New customers have been attracted by the profile, watching who the audiences and contacts are. Social media have become important, and the founders believe it will become more important as a source of business.

*Source*: Founders, Invennt, www.invennt.com.

both client and employer (e.g. Wallace, 1995). Identification is non-hierarchical and the project TMO is more likely to have a clan-like (e.g. Ouchi, 1980; Cameron and Quinn, 2006) or egalitarian primary or secondary organizational culture (Smyth and Kusuma, 2013; cf. Douglas, 1999; Auch and Smyth, 2010) because of the reliance on relationships and informal routines necessary to establish the

TMO and put the formal processes in place. This facilitates relationship building, yet should not be dislocated from respective organizational cultures of the respective TMO member organizations.

Interpersonal identification operates at the level of behaviour and action (Michalski and Helmig, 2008), commonly evident in activities such as innovation and joint problem solving. B2B identification changes relationships hence informal routines and decision-making. It is most likely to arise in project environments where collaborative practices are present. Anvuur and Kumaraswamy (2008) found evidence of identification derived from partnering arrangements for large infrastructure projects in Hong Kong. Smyth and Kioussi (2011b) found creative design and problem solving induces identification on the client side. As Bhattacharya and Sen state, inter-organizational identification, especially with customer or client, has a critical role in maintaining *deep, committed, and meaningful relationships* (2003: 76), building client commitment (Fullerton, 2005). An examination of five design and five project management consultants revealed they mainly followed relationship marketing, the project management firms marginally more so than the design firms. Repeat business ran at levels of over 70 per cent for all the firms, frequently at higher profit levels without clients incurring greater costs (Maheshwaran, 2012). However, solid levels of repeat business did not necessarily mean that clients are always satisfied; satisficing outcomes may provide an accurate descriptor (Emmitt, 2007). It was found that the broader design attitude was more critical than design creativity for relationship building for architects (cf. Smyth and Kioussi, 2011a).

Much of the research literature and most of the practice-orientated books focus upon the project. Projects are asserted as temporary, but the organizations undertaking them are not (Winch, 2013). There is the client organization and the supplier organization, both of which are reasonably 'permanent'. Industrial networks are reasonably stable, subject to some flux and churn, but permanent as a dynamic force. It is the project organization comprising the TMO team (Cherns and Bryant, 1984) or broader coalition (Winch, 2002) that is temporary.

### *Relationship maintenance*

Relationship discontinuity between projects, inconsistent behaviour during projects and errant behaviour on projects are the three corrosive factors. Errant behaviour erodes identification and relationships. Dialogue is curtailed and a loss of voice is felt. Yet it is not always seen as people may mask the emotional response to preserve the relationship, but the result will nonetheless be a weakened relationship (cf. Gilligan, 1982). Eroding inter-organizational relationships attacks dignity at the interpersonal level. Respect for what individual actors do in their role and dignity as a human being is challenged (Smyth, 2008a). In other words, the other party has valued the other person less through their action. Such attacks take the form of opportunism with guile or more commonly the result of arguably the fastest growing area of knowledge management, 'learned helplessness' (cf. Gummesson, 2000) based upon the policies and guidance of non-engagement with inter-organizational problem solving and relationship neglect. Relationship management systems and procedures are designed to prevent corrosion once a relationship is built. One $P^3M$ tool is KAM.

KAM is in many sectors and increasingly prevalent in project environments. One role model is the advertising and media sector. The vocabulary focuses upon accounts and campaigns rather than upon programmes and projects, but is essentially the same in another name – see Fact Box 4.4 showing how the emphasis between the programme and project level has changed over time and location.

## FACT BOX 4.4 CHANGING SIGNIFICANCE OF PROGRAMME AND PROJECT MANAGEMENT IN CLIENT MANAGEMENT

New York was the home and dominant location for the advertising industry, spawning many major agencies. This is described by Grabher (2002) as a somewhat antagonistic environment of collaborative creativity managed by account managers. A second phase was a transitional one that moved away from 'project' work dominated by personalities and moved towards more organizationally informed interpersonal relationships supported by numeric and quantitative data in business to justify and support the approach. The ascendency of London as a primary base for the ownership of global advertising agencies, including many that started in New York represented a third phase that gathered pace in the late 1980s and early 1990s. This represented the ascendency of account planning that brought programme management to the fore. Grabher describes this as:

> The prime function of the account manager is to liase *[sic]* with the client from the preparatory pre-project stages to the completion of the project.
>
> (2002: 248)

This is the KAM role, which represents the client interests in the agency. KAM is part of the account planning process or programme management, whereby the client is brought into the production process through this higher-level planning process. The approach is more qualitative than quantitative as it is relationship based. This can create tensions between the creative employees operating at the project level, but the KAM role is the mediator to link the client and project specific interests to combine the project and task focus with and client and service focus.

*Sources*: Developed from Grabher (2002); cf. McDonald et al. (1997).

The KAM can be a director, BDM, commercial director, project manager or another functionary or small team that forms a client-specific programme DMU (Figure 4.8). KAM provides relationship continuity between projects (cf. Hadjikani, 1996) and systematic coordination hence service consistency on a single project. It is implemented top-down from the portfolio level with a budget that is separate from project budgets – a mistake AntCo made when first introducing KAM (cf. Table 3.2 and Fact Box 4.2). KAM operates largely horizontally at the programme and project levels as a client management function: first, providing integration along project lifecycles to ensure the value promised during BDM and enshrined in the bid is delivered; second, coordination across the interface with the client and project DMUs (Figure 4.8). The KAM role is enabling rather than controlling, especially regarding relationships. Relationship maintenance should conform to the relationship management systems, allowing personal strengths to shine within the guidelines. The KAM role is akin to the melody or the refrain around which the jazz soloist improvises as part of the quartet of project team (cf. Barrett, 1998; Eisenhardt, 1998; Grabher, 2002).

The companies presented in Table 3.2 and Fact Box 4.2 had all introduced some form of KAM, in some cases match pairing directors with senior client managers (e.g. EuroCo), and BDMs with client project procurement, owners and sponsor roles (e.g. EUCo). In all cases insufficient time had been allocated from the portfolio level to prioritizing commitment and resources, coordination largely being isolated from marketing and BDM and confined to project execution. KAM is conceptually linked to the MoP front-end and thus integration along project lifecycles was therefore absent in all companies (Smyth, 2013a; Smyth and Kusuma, 2013; Interviews conducted with directors, senior management, departmental and project managers, 1st and 2nd quarters of 2012). Another project business, a concession contractor, had adopted a 5-year relationship marketing plan for one major division, including the KAM function. KAM was implemented via two roles. First, sector directors coordinated the strategy and sales activity. Sector meetings provided an important means for cross-functional coordination. Customer action plans had the remit to add value. Win-strategies for project opportunities were informed by these plans. Second, customer directors continued responsibility for BDM and increasingly for customer satisfaction, improving repeat business, including the cross-selling of services. For this approach, customer directors need relationship building skills, and knowledge of technical, product and service capabilities across procurement, bid management and execution. The result was an increase in net margins to 3–4 per cent (except where certain customers were identified as giving rise to other explicit strategic benefits, such as reputation, covering the base-load of overheads and being efficient payers to increase return on capital employed) (Smyth and Fitch, 2009).

## *Adding value*

Relationship marketing systems help coordinate client management in relation to organizational, marketing and project capabilities. These capabilities add value in continuous and consistent fashion at programme and project levels respectively (cf. Hamel and Prahalad, 1994; Teece et al., 1997; Miller and Lessard, 2000; Brady and Davies, 2004; Hobday et al., 2005; Möller, 2006; Davies et al., 2007). Organizational capabilities include, for example, learning and knowledge management that improve effectiveness for the project business, yet also can lever additional value for the client (Davies and Brady, 2000). Marketing capabilities have been defined as:

> . . . the integrative processes designed to apply collective knowledge, skills and resources of the firm to market-related needs of the business, enabling the business to add value to its goods and services, adapt to market conditions, take advantage of market opportunities and meet competitive threats.
>
> (Vorhies, 1998: 4)

Marketing capabilities directly improve the client service experience and indirectly lever value (Möller, 2006). The ability to learn from the market (Li and Calantone, 1998; Slater and Narver, 1995), collecting, disseminating and using market-based information, is key to the growth of organizational performance (Narver and Slater, 1990). This assumes that good use is made of these abilities to add value across the customer base. This is partial in practice and very limited attention is given to mechanisms firms use to coordinate the information and leverage (Guenzi and Troilo, 2006). Mechanisms form part of designed systems, yet often emerge from existing processes that are linked to and form part of effective capabilities (Jarzabkowski et al., 2012). The most popular two capabilities according to Day (1994) are those associated with *market sensing* and *customer-linking capabilities*. Market sensing refers to the project business capability to identify customer needs. Customer linking refers to the ability to build relationships with them. In project businesses, relationships are the means to lever value and reliance upon them is greater the weaker the other systems and procedures are as there is otherwise few internal integrating mechanisms.

Cross-functional integration is facilitated by these capabilities, but it has also been claimed necessary to have relationship marketing supported by and developed into a broader relationship management system (e.g. Storbacka et al., 1994; Gummesson, 2000), a point echoed for MoP (Smyth, 2000; Pryke and Smyth, 2006). There are several ways to develop relationship marketing and management systems. CRM software systems and products typically play a minor or minimal role, not only because there have been considerable failures and wasted expenditure in industry (e.g. Reinartz et al., 2004; King and Burgess, 2008) and ironically are as part of a bigger picture of information systems failure (e.g. Sauer, 1993), but also CRM effectiveness is dependent upon parallel human systems to utilize the software system (cf. Kale, 2004), returning the need for overarching relationship systems internally, for effective B2B relationships based upon direct and face-to-face (F2F). The relationship management systems approach proposed by Storbacka and colleagues (1994) is offered here for two reasons. First, it is sufficiently high level to offer scope to accommodate and develop or realign existing systems

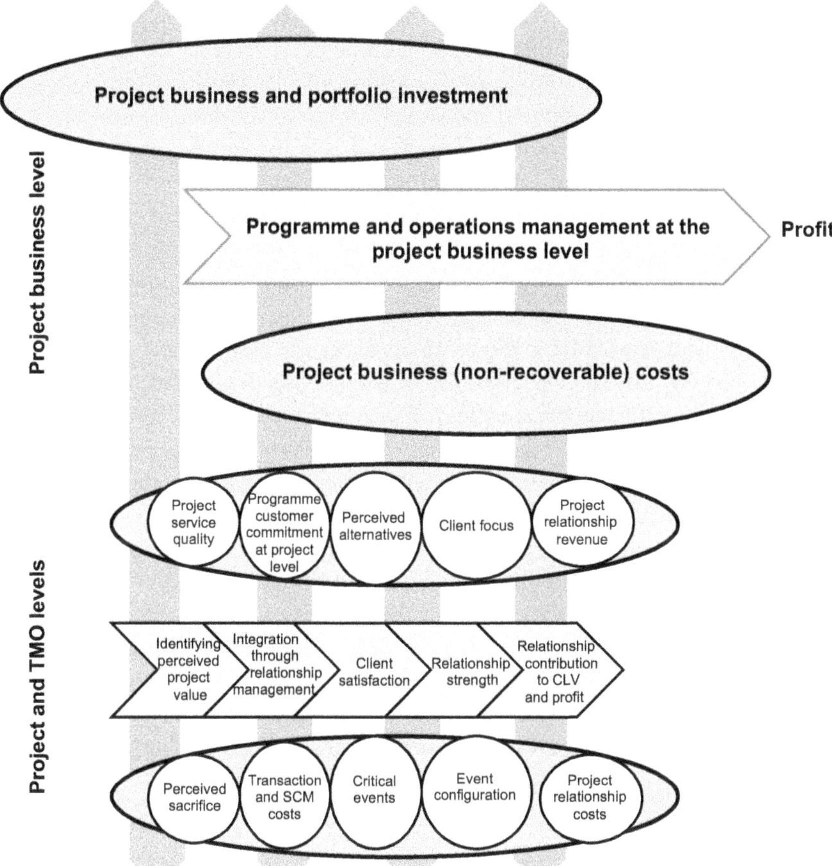


**FIGURE 4.9** Relationship marketing and management systems for project businesses

*Sources*: Adapted from Storbacka et al. (1994) and developed from Pryke and Smyth (2006).

(Figure 4.6). Second, it has previously been adapted and developed for project environments and is further developed in Figure 4.9.

Project capabilities are technical, technological and service in nature when they exceed the market norms (i.e. compared to the competition) and thus can lever added value above the stated requirements (value added) for specific projects (Brady and Davies, 2004).

A task and project management focus is linked to the temporal and event characteristics of projects, hence capabilities arise in this context. Project programming, task scheduling and sequencing are therefore linked to embedding processes (Geraldi et al., 2010). Within this frame of reference, event-based pacing provides the basis for coordination (Söderholm, 2008). Relationship marketing and relationship management conceptually shift the emphasis to a client and service focus dependent upon integrated systems that are causally linked to the daily and seasonal rhythms for organizing of the project business (cf. Clark, 1985; Ancona and Chong, 1996). This opens up scope for greater project capability development and feeding it to the programme and hence organizational level. In this context relationship management acts in the conductor role to coordinate the orchestra and bring out the best from each section (cf. Drucker, 1986).

Adding value can also be about anticipating and avoiding client error derived from deep understanding and 'deep cooperation' necessary to avoid and mitigate big mistakes made amongst the project sponsor and their senior management team (Merrow, 2011: 1). This is not an excuse for dismissing clients' inputs but is part of meeting client expectations regarding performance (Torbica and Stroh, 2001; Turkulainien et al., 2013). Client satisfaction is a function of performance indicated via size or volume of work placed with the supplier, the quality of the client in terms of ability to work with them as well as the net profit or relationship specific return on marketing investment (ROMI) made in the client (cf. Morgan and Rego, 2006; Tuli and Bharadwaj, 2009; Smyth and Lecoeuvre, 2014). It is this lack of systematic understanding that regularly leads to low client satisfaction levels and loss of repeat business opportunities (Egemen and Mohamed, 2006). Winch et al. (1998) demonstrated evidence that client perceptions of the project outcome are more important to project success than meeting any project objectives.

## Business development management in theory and practice

### *Relationships and requirements*

Merrow states in regard to oil and gas: *Successful megaprojects require an extraordinary degree of trust, cooperation, and communication between the business sponsoring the project and the technical functions developing and executing the project. Too often, we encounter the exact opposite* (2011: 82).

The result is that project teams are trying to meet objectives they partially understand. Yet this is precisely where marketing and BDM enter. It is the responsibility of the project business to help articulate the latent objectives and how these are translated into requirements. While competitors might get to hear these additional requirements, the project business applying relationship marketing principles has the pole position on three counts:

1. The project business will have gained more intimate knowledge of the client and client needs, including the process the client went through to arriving at the new and improved requirements;
2. The project business will have created a closer bond or tie at the client–supplier interface and may get some credit for help received to date in the selection process;
3. They have first mover advantage in resource mobilization to meet identified needs.

The basis is established for developing win-strategies in bid management and tender negotiations. A client-centric strategy starts with expectations rather than reliance upon RFPs and briefing documentation as the basis to proceed. Identifying client needs and expectations begins with the first contact and is built up at a generic level (drivers 2–4 in Fact Box 4.2) and then at the project-specific level (drivers 1–3 in Fact Box 4.2).

Lessons learned from past projects help inform the win-strategy for the next project. This is akin to project capabilities introduced at programme level for future roll out (Brady and Davies, 2004) and 'continuous improvement'. Most project businesses are out of kilter with this capability. If it is assumed that client satisfaction is some indication of meeting expectations, in UK construction for example at the height of the 'continuous improvement movement', clients were scoring satisfaction key performance indicators (KPIs) levels in the range of 50–55 per cent. The construction industry appeared reasonably content with 45–50 per cent failure levels, posing considerable problems with this mindset for assessing expectations and satisfaction (cf. Smyth, 2010b; Green, 2011). Lessons learned can be linked to relationship management systems, knowledge management or enhanced CRM systems that include strategy, value chain and multi-channel and cross-functional integration as well as performance assessment (cf. Payne and Frow, 2006; cf. Kaplan and Norton, 1992; Deng and Smyth, 2013). Expectations are also informed by the use value, the criteria sometimes extending beyond past achievements and lessons learned (cf. Bresnen et al., 2004; Smyth and Longbottom, 2005; Kelly et al., 2013).

BDM is typically isolated from senior management and other functions along project lifecycles. Hierarchically, the corporate strategy conceptually guides BDM through the marketing strategy, yet the level of guidance is frequently general and abstract for the tactical level of managing customers (McGovern et al., 2004). Strategy and top-down management guides relationship marketing, which then guides horizontally BDM over project lifecycles and for cross-functional working. McKean (2002) identifies eight key BDM-related principles for developing principles of engagement in supplier markets, which are adapted and developed to project businesses for dyadic application (Table 4.3). Relationship marketing is reasonably pragmatic in implementation. Selection of principles to adopt and how to implement them are a strategic responsibility. Strategic decision-making initially selects principles aligned with current strengths, systems and investment in capabilities. Contextual application and interpretation are BDM responsibilities.

The objective is to begin the process towards developing strong relationships that move from initial contact towards relationships of deep understanding and identification (Anvuur and Kumaraswamy, 2008; cf. Figures 4.3, 4.4 and 4.5). Loyalty to secure repeat business is one prime BDM objective. Reichheld (1996) found that firm profitability improves as customer retention increases, a small improvement from 85 to 90 per cent resulting in net present value and profits rise 35 per cent and 95 per cent respectively. While most firms, including many project businesses are now talking the rhetoric of relationship marketing, recent

**TABLE 4.3** Relationship development with clients and suppliers

| *Dyadic relationship building principles* | *Supplier relationship building* | |
|---|---|---|
| | *Principles* | *Selection factors* |
| Leading the 'human' firm | Internal alignment | High-quality and experienced teams |
| Client engagement | Partner selection | Relationship building capabilities |
| Client respect | Partner relationship alignment | Resources and other capabilities aligned with programmes of work |
| Trust building | Project alignment | Cultural alignment or complementarity |
| Communication listening, reflective practice and empathetic conveyance of knowledge and information | Work process alignment | |
| Consistently implementing the 'human touch' | | |
| The 'human touch' as a process applied in a relationship management system | | |
| Humanizing technology and technical processes | | |
| *Source*: McKean (2002). | *Source*: Pascale and Sanders (1998). | *Sources*: Adapted from Cook and Hancher (1990); Pryke (2012). |

research amongst 200 of the UK's largest organizations suggests that about 90 per cent of these firms are still not allocating their marketing budget appropriately (Christopher et al., 2002), which has been echoed in project businesses (Smyth, 2013a; Smyth and Lecoeuvre, 2014). Of the 200 firms, 160 tended to over-invest in customer acquisition, while 10 per cent spent too much on customer retention activities. Investment into repeat business and type of business depends upon three factors:

1. Frequency of total business opportunities (Winch, 2002; Chambers et al., 2009; Smyth and Fitch, 2009);
2. Frequency of repeat work in client programmes or types of capabilities and solutions (which is not same as project type, e.g. highway construction) (Davies and Brady, 2000; Whitley, 2006; Artto et al., 2011);
3. Frequency with which the same supply cluster or supply chain members can be used (Walker et al., 2008; Pryke, 2012).

Frequency of repeat business opportunities will determine scope for investment in key client relationships. Repeat work involves investment in technical and project capabilities. Where there is no repeat work in output terms, investment focuses upon organizational capabilities, especially relationship management to support relationship marketing over supplier programmes. The frequency with which the same supply chain members are used determines the scope for investing in the development of supply chain relationships (Christopher et al., 2002). BDM operations are therefore not simply outward facing to solicit work and feed pipelines but are inward facing to mobilize resources and integrate activities at the front-end for injection into bid management to form win-strategies and subsequently into execution. This is part of cross-functional team working at the 'corporate centre' as well as for project management.

Not all repeat business is a sign of loyalty. Loyalty is influenced by meeting expectations, which change over time (Muth, 1961; Lucas, 1973), rather than directly by KPI snapshot measurement of satisfaction. Repeat business levels affect CLV. Reputation is fairly constant, certainly medium-term; therefore, it is the quality of project service against the expectations that is particularly decisive (cf. Chiou and Droge, 2006). Relations have positive effects on repeat business and can be part of the selection criteria (Beamish and Biggart, 2012). Strong bonds based upon deep client understanding offer further potential to build repeat business. The frequency and value of repeat business feeds into CLV, ROI and ROMI, providing measures of the impact of loyalty upon the project business. Loyalty is perceptually, hence subjectively, assessed by clients and thus trends provide indicators for the supplier (cf. Jones and Sasser, 1995; Reichheld, 1996; Ganesh et al., 2000).

## *Requirements and response*

Hobday et al. (2005) posed the question as to whether companies producing high-value-specific assets, including project-based businesses and project businesses, build capabilities to provide *customer-centric solutions*. Capabilities become effective when integrated into technical project systems (Prencipe, 2003), programme management and relationship management systems (Pryke and Smyth, 2006). Liinamaa and Gustafsson (2009) argue that customer integration is part of systems integration. Client-driven performance requires both internal integration (Smyth, 2013a), the integration of external organizations such as suppliers and subcontractors (e.g. Davies et al., 2007), and integration of other organizations in the project TMO (Smyth and Kusuma, 2013). Effective BDM activity initiates the integration, linking identified customer need with internal resources and capabilities. This is proactivity in the internal market.

BDMs have to be aware of client and internal procurement strategies, essentially distinguish transactional from relational approaches (Grönroos, 2000; Hobbs and Andersen, 2001; Crespin-Mazet and Portier, 2010). Liinamaa and Gustafsson (2009) have broken this down into particular purchasing groups (see Fact Box 4.5).

Crespin-Mazet and Portier (2010) found in some national markets inexperienced clients with few in-house capabilities depend more on close co-operation such as partnering. In many the developed countries such as the United Kingdom where it has tended to be experienced clients with in-house capabilities that sought

## FACT BOX 4.5 MARKET CLUSTERS IN SHIPBUILDING AND POWER GENERATION PROJECT MARKETS

Sales survey data of over 400 customers in shipbuilding projects and the power generation fall into four clusters. The customers do not differ in their essential needs, but differ in the way they approach procurement to satisfy these needs. The four clusters are the following:

1. Customers who buy products and services, stressing supplier commitment to solving their operations problems and meeting their needs.
    a. A relational market,
    b. Reasonable sales volume: 21 per cent of the market,
    c. Size of customer base is low: 15 per cent.
2. Customers who buy products, stressing supplier commitment to providing quality.
    a. A relational or transactional market, depending upon customer preference,
    b. Very high sales volume: 53 per cent,
    c. Size of customer base is average: 26 per cent.
3. Customers who buy a small amount and see little added value.
    a. A transactional market, the customer seeing suppliers as one of many undifferentiated suppliers,
    b. Low sales volume: 7 per cent,
    c. Size of customer base is large: 47 per cent.
4. Customers who have service agreements with suppliers and have indicated they are dissatisfied with supplier performance.
    a. A relational market,
    b. Reasonable sales volume: 19 per cent,
    c. Size of customer base is low: 12 per cent.

The two relational procurement markets (clusters 1 and 4) combined constitute 40 per cent of total sales. These are the markets where relationship marketing is most suited and cluster 4 in particular offers plenty of scope for supplier improvement through understanding customer needs and responding accordingly. Interviews following the survey showed that supplier knowledge about the customer business, and their service capabilities provided opportunities for suppliers to increase their competitiveness. Suppliers needed the following capabilities to effectively satisfy these customers:

- Interest in customer business requirements and project needs;
- Prompt response and problem solving capabilities;
- Technical knowledge of the latest developments;
- Ability to listen to customers and reflect upon the information and learning to improve services;
- Taking responsibility for the project installation after handover;
- Logistics competence.

*Source*: Adapted from Liinamaa and Gustafsson (2010).

partnering to use their knowledge and experience to lever value through collaborative practices (e.g. Davies et al., 2009). BDMs therefore use relationships for different purposes in different markets in order to customize and tailor their capabilities to align with the client capabilities and fit project specificities. In order to achieve this, a more tactical understanding is also needed. A thorough understanding is needed of the everyday practices of the client and end-users (cf. Seth et al., 2000; Grönroos, 2008; Turkulainien et al., 2013).

Under relationship marketing, contacts are owned by the project business. This is typically articulated through reports on clients and projects, and some information may be lodged in a CRM database, such as Salesforce®. BDMs and those engaged with front-end project development are responsible for making commitments. Commitments take two detailed forms. One is BDM commitment to a particular relationship, which involves some resource allocation and is signalled to the other party as interest in understanding the client. The other is a direct resource commitment to the client in the form of (non-contractual) promises to clients in added technical and service value. Risk theory addresses potentially negative factors, to which contractors are attuned. Yet, risk can be conceived as opportunities as well as threats. Therefore a risk register as a commonplace tool in project management can be extended to include a promise register, which logs all added technical and service value that is identified at the front-end, which informs win-strategy development in bid management and guides project management during execution. This was found to be important; for example BDMs in the concession contractor BranCo were wary of making commitments or promises to clients even though they knew the project business had the capabilities. They lacked confidence that other functionaries would deliver against the commitments (Chambers et al., 2009). It takes skillful project managers, supply chain managers and other 'part-time marketers' who are actively engaged with BDM to deliver against promises (cf. Gummesson, 2000). Commitment is more important than time–cost–quality/scope criteria in project performance assessments upon completion (Langford and Rowland, 1995; Gustafsson et al., 2010).

In bid management, between 250 and 300 project businesses were asked to rate their bid performance (Kennedy and O'Connor, 1997). The top five factors were the following:

1. Perceived product and service quality (68.5 per cent stated this was very important)
2. Customer relationships (54.4 per cent)
3. Market position (52.2 per cent)
4. Firm's image (47.6 per cent)
5. Track record (46.5 per cent)

BDMs arguably place too much emphasis upon track record to give clients assurance and use it as a surrogate for product or technical and service quality. Track record is closely associated with market reputation, which is relatively stable, yet this does not indicate performance in meeting project specific requirements and adding value at the bid stage. The most successful firms did not perceive themselves as being very effective against these factors. Bid teams recognized the importance of relationships, yet the lack of consistent relationship marketing over the front-end stages of the project lifecycle may provide one reason for perceived poor performance.

It has been noted that MoP research tends to emphasize the client side. To redress this, it should be becoming clear that the project business side contains a different emphasis. Placing procurement and marketing from the respective organizations in parallel crystallizes this in Figure 4.10, which builds upon Figure 3.1.

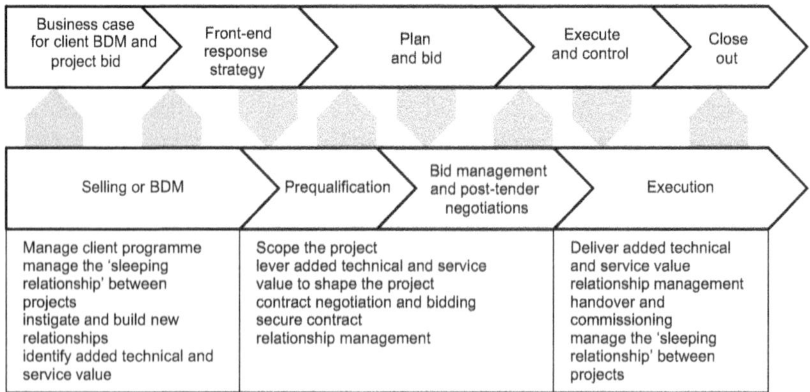


**FIGURE 4.10** The management of projects from client procurement and project business relationship marketing perspectives

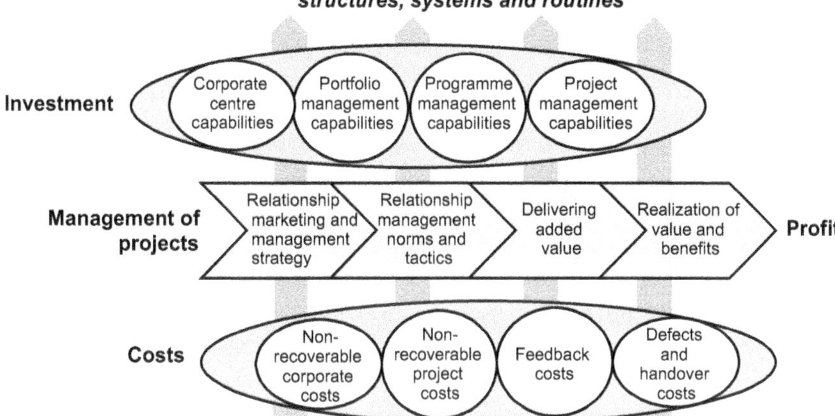


**FIGURE 4.11** A simplified model for systematic relationship marketing

*Source*: Adapted and developed from Pryke and Smyth (2006).

To reconstitute Figure 4.9 in a simplified way (along the lines of the Figure 4.6) with an emphasis upon capabilities, Figure 4.11 depicts the connection between relationship marketing and relationship management with organizational capabilities. This prepares the ground for **Chapters 7** and **8**; it also provides a basis for considering BDM in the broader context of networks.

To adequately shape projects, capabilities are required for BDM, bid management and for post-tender negotiations. Marketing capabilities are also needed to span these functions in order to achieve integration at the front-end. Part of this is provided by a relationship management system, partly by each functional system interlocking and partly by management norms and informal routines to articulate integration (Smyth, 2013a; cf. Day, 1994; Möller, 2006; Davies et al., 2007). The increasingly popular KAM function may also assist with the process (Lemaire, 1996; Smyth and Fitch, 2007; cf. McDonald et al., 1997). Aritua et al. (2009) state that the intelligent client should know their needs and be able to select the provider without any BDM assistance: *The intelligent client should also be able to maximise value from the private sector by managing the relationships and increasing the value that is added by these private sector participants* (Aritua et al., 2009: 5).

Clients may have extensive in-house capabilities (cf. Davies et al., 2009; Liinamaa and Gustafsson, 2009; Crespin-Mazet and Portier, 2010), yet this is no guarantee that they know all their needs. Some expectations need articulating cognitively and made concrete. Latent needs are to be teased out too. Emergent needs and issues attached to areas of uncertainty present unknowns at the front end. Aritua et al. (2009) advocate a client champion with analytical and conceptual skills. This may mirror the KAM function on the client side, the risk being that too much reliance is placed upon one decision-maker. The BDM role can facilitate enhanced understanding and with the technical support and supply chain, relationships collaboratively identify and lever value in response to expectations and known requirements for any project.

The picture is dynamic. In the boom market pre-2008, client–contractor relationships were managed by the *owner* function in the engineering organization. Long-term relationships were the norm and largely conducted through informally and professionally developed routines. Merrow (2011) found that post-2008 downsizing has led to increasing incoherence on the client side. Contractors bypassed the owner function and their representative, selling directly to the executive business functionaries, who are largely ill-equipped by experience or temperament to deal with these relationships because they were treating the asset specificity of projects as any other commodity in their decision-making. Price was dominant, which rendered the BDM role easier, but typically stored up problems and transactional costs for suppliers during execution. It also meant that suppliers were using the weakness to bid low and escalate disputes during execution to claw back margins shaved off from pricing low.

One project business that adopted relationship marketing is the concession contractor BranCo. Its threefold focus has been to improve customer retention, develop customer value, and improve high commitment levels to meeting customer expectations. The strategy had been in place for 4 years when a merger occurred. It is instructive to compare the marketing performance of the two firms upon merger. The two firms operated in the same markets. The firm with the 4-year relationship marketing plan behind it won over £710m worth of contracts at a strike rate of over 45 per cent by contract value. The other company that had a transactional marketing mix approach won £455m at a strike rate of just over 14 per cent by contract value. The firm employing relationship marketing was more targeted, better at developing prospects and securing repeat business through Marketing from BDM, through estimating and bid management, to post-tender negotiations. The poor performance of the transactional company is partly due to marketing, but other factors were also in play that were arguably mutually reinforcing (Chambers et al., 2009). The problem with the success rate for BranCo is that it far more difficult to manage. Targeting fewer clients and concentrating resources where quality contracts exist in the market meant that the flow of work was more uneven. Thus, the utilization rate of staff is less than optimum in efficiency terms, especially for execution. This also means that there are people on the bench at times, being retained for particular project opportunities so that the team put forward during bidding will be the team executing the project. On the other hand, this part of the business achieved better results, simply by consistently applying a limited number of relationship marketing principles. A number of project lifecycle 'blockers' were identified (Fact Box 4.6). In 2010, the business unit had 99 accounts and 80 per cent of the business was concentrated in 30 accounts, the key ones yielding repeat business and relationship continuity (Keki and Smyth, 2010a).

## FACT BOX 4.6 A CASE EXAMINATION OF RELATIONSHIP MARKETING 'BLOCKERS'

1. A lack of understanding amongst BDMs of the strategy and how to conduct their activities. The table below shows a very uneven activity focus amongst BDMs and uneven time being committed to direct client contact and client management.
2. A residual tendency for BDMs to see clients as a source of information with very uneven examination of the organizational and programme levels, although most BDMs had started or were beginning to try to solicit client expectations about projects vis-à-vis the client organization, that is, going deeper than brief and RFP requirements documentation.
3. A lack of clarity as to the purpose of relationship building and what constitutes a 'good' relationship. Descriptive phrases included 'having conversations' and 'keeping them warm' and 'knowing you have one' when a client DMU member sets 'homework' before the next meeting. All relationships need research between meetings. Some BDMs develop relationships they feel most 'comfortable' with rather than ones with greatest potential. BDMs mentally map DMUs, but few draw a map by power and motivation as well as role/job title and line management. The CRM database, Salesforce®, is used on a variable basis amongst BDM and among other staff.
4. There was difficulty making commitments or non-contractual promises to clients as the BDMs cannot be sure the commitment or promise will survive the bid management and project management process. There was a sense of a lack of management support, the fear of management 'pulling the rug', which would be damaging to relationship building.
5. The Tender Gateway Stage 1 is the handover between BDM and bid management, and continuity is poorly managed at times. Win-strategies are a major part of bid management and involve (i) identifying the most appropriate people (not necessarily the available people, which lead to lost bids or high cost projects), (ii) developing 'a bit of an angle', which particularly requires a good BDM–bid management handover, (iii) engaging directors in lobbying, interviews/presentations and key stakeholder liaison in parallel.
6. A lack of cross-functional integration and a means to lever value, especially from the supply chain. Planning and estimating are weak areas, plus the organization had recently abandoned supply chain management. There is over-reliance upon informal networks rather than management guidance. Senior management could involve marketing and BDM at the stage of setting margins rather than this being driven mainly by internal criteria.

(*Continued*)

**FACT BOX 4.6** (Continued)

7. Senior management and bid managers think in terms of project first and client second. During execution operations directors are project rather than client focused, and project managers are task focused rather than client focused.

| *Activity role* | *Weekly activity breakdown amongst on BDMs* | | | | | | | |
|---|---|---|---|---|---|---|---|---|
| | *1* | *2* | *3* | *4* | *5* | *6* | *7* | *8* |
| OJEU/generating leads | – | 1.0 | 0.5 | | | n/a | | |
| Following leads | 2.0 | 1.0 | 1.5 | | | | 0.25 | 0.5 |
| Pre-qualification | | | 1.5 | | | | 0.25 | |
| Tender stage action | | 2.5 | 0.5 | 1.0 | 1.0 | | 0.25 | |
| Watching brief on projects | 1.0 | 0.5 | | | | | 1.5 | 2.0 |
| Key account management | 1.0 | | | 1.0 | 0.5 | | 1.0 | 0.5 |
| Administration | 0.5 | | 1.0 | 2.0 | 3.0 | | 1.75 | 2.0 |
| contingency/other | 0.5 | | | | | | | |

*Sources*: Interviews conducted with Customer Director, BDMs and project managers in the 1st quarter of 2009; Chambers et al. (2009).

Inter-organizational relations are important for identifying and leveraging value in internal networks, including TMOs, vertical market networks, intermediate networks and opportunity networks where suppliers reside (Achrol, 1996). Cova and Salle (2005) explain it in terms of the multi-organizational project, buying and milieu networks (cf. Dubois and Gadde, 2000; Håkansson and Snehota, 1995). Regarding the six markets model (Christopher et al., 2006), supplier, referral and influencer markets span Achrol's categorizations and reside mainly in the project and buying networks of Cova and Salle, although the influencer market crosses into the milieu too.

In referral and influencer markets, how are stakeholders that are both influential in advocating the project business and leveraging value in the industrial network identified (cf. Jepsen and Eskerod, 2009)? At the front of the front-end, BDMs should be connected to and working the networks in conjunction with procurement and supply chain managers. At the other end of the management of projects, project managers need analytical and intuitive skills to identify actors in supplier-referral (Jepsen and Eskerod, 2009) and influencer markets and may need additional support from BDMs to facilitate and lever networks (cf. Smyth and Fitch, 2009).

Some referrers and influencers are easy to identify, including client representatives and key suppliers (Berggren et al., 2001). Berggren et al. (2001) critically argue that too much reliance upon client representatives renders the client 'absent' or more distant, which constrains development of client understanding, adaptation of offers and bid solutions, and may reduce referral opportunities. It is here that BDMs have a role in working with existing and prospective clients to tease out these expectations and needs from the level of the core business strategy and operations of the client, through the solution to the organizational problem the project addresses down to the fine level of technical content required to provide the solution.

In BranCo, the tendency had been to sideline consultants in the initial project opportunity stages. There had been an informal and *ad hoc* number of 'preferred consultants', so a detailed examination of consultants was conducted as the main players in referral and influencer markets apart from clients. CEO or MD level interviews were conducted amongst design cost consultants in the last quarter of 2009 and first quarter of 2010. From this perspective, there was a view that consultants were under-valued by the concession contractor, having 'a jobbing (transactional) attitude' (Fitch et al., 2010). It was commented by a CEO of a major multi-disciplinary consultancy:

> Contractors tend to be quite aggressive when dealing with consultants and their behaviour is not consistent but is varying enormously from project to project. The main result from their behaviour is that they treat consultants as a part of their SC (supply chain).
>
> (Fitch et al., 2010: 4–5)

There was a lack of programme management for these markets, evident in the following key ways:

- Having a policy of preferred consultants;
- Having an inconsistent behavioural approach – consultant personnel employed on a subcontract basis for one project became advisors on short listing main contractors on other contracts;
- Failing to appreciate the 'body shop' phenomenon, where consultant personnel are seconded to clients to improve capabilities and therefore report back on the contractor's approach to the consultant organization.

A programme of developing relationship marketing in referral and influencer markets was therefore instigated (Keki and Smyth, 2010a). It became appreciated that consultants, as expressed by the CEO of one of the top three cost consultants:

> . . . are looking for a strong balance sheet, scale of projects, relevant track record, etc. Once they are on that way, we are looking for the teams they have, their approach to innovation, their commercial offer and also their ability to deliver. We are also looking for the team behaviours; the organisation and the ability of the people to solve complex problems; their flexibility of approach; their ability to understand client's needs; their wish to collaborate;

> to avoid an adversarial approach in problem solving; the depth of capability and their responsiveness; depth of knowledge and skills of senior management team.
>
> (cited in Keki and Smyth, 2010b: 4–5)

Unless examined, the relationships and benefits remain tacit and unmanaged (cf. Johanson and Mattsson, 1985; Leone and Bendapudi, 2001; Artto et al., 2007; Ambler et al., 2002). Manning (2010) found network partners that came together on one project, 36 per cent were carried forward to a subsequent project and 66 per cent of had worked together on previous projects. Referral and influencer markets are powerful networks and a potential source to qualify and bid for new project opportunities.

In summary, consultants seek a close relationship with significant contractors in which they have confidence, being treated with honesty, respect, and understanding in a project team atmosphere trusting relationships (Keki and Smyth, 2010b).

Developing relationships and therefore developing relationship capabilities is a necessary part of relationship marketing. In their study of time–cost–quality and relationship factors, Butcher and Sheehan (2010) uncovered evidence that *excellent relationships* proved a clear indicator of the best performing contractors. In particular top management commitment was perceived as a significant yet intangible quality differentiator. Clients endeavoured to purchase first-tier contractors with organizational capabilities. They were perceived to add value. The client-facing staff, for example BDMs, directors and project managers, can rely upon those with specialist skills to help configure value to be delivered. The internal organizational and TMO relationships are important in this respect and supportive relationships have been found to be of particular importance when introducing new technologies and other innovations (cf. Schepers et al., 2011). However, evidence to date suggests that relationship marketing requires more integrated implementation to achieve these goals for project businesses.

### *Critical events and social capital*

Projects comprise tasks that are structured into acts, events, episodes and sequences that are sub-units found within any programme or schedule of activities. Some tasks and events become critical, often the unexpected combinations of critical events whose configuration is unrecognized in risk registers. Claims can be seen as critical events. Claims are more than a function of resolving ambiguity and uncertainty from the bidding stage during execution. Emergent project requirements are frequently part of what is known as *unknown unknowns* or 'unk unks' (Wideman, 1992; Winch, 2010; Loch and Kavadias, 2011). This is the difference between resolving incomplete contracts and new requirements outside the scope of the project definition. There is a choice as to whether to accommodate emergent requirements outside the original scope. The task-orientated approach sees all emergent requirements as problems to be minimized. A client and service orientation sees emergent requirements as one of the reasons the project mode of delivery is necessary and to be embraced in agile ways that are sources of added value to the client, turnover and profit to the supplier, an investment into repeat business and reputation as well as occasional learning opportunities to develop new competencies and capabilities (cf. Möller, 2006; Davies et al., 2007; Smyth, 2013b).

These types of actions are evidence of commitment over the project lifecycle. They incur costs but build capabilities in the form of social capital (Smyth et al., 2010; Gustafsson et al., 2010; Jones et al., 2011). Where clients recognize the commitments made, service recovery from critical events is easier to manage. Jones et al. (2011: 330) state that the *buffering* effect of relationship commitment on transgressions is consistent, clients being *more tolerant of transgressions – even to the point of accommodation or forgiveness.* The client does not tend to distinguish between the individual or the organization they represent in terms of relationship commitment (Jones et al., 2011), so the organizational relationship strength is based upon the individual or sum of individuals representing the project business, typically DMU members, including the BDM relationship on the supply side.

Managing critical events is thus *service recovery*; beyond resolving technical issues, towards *how* these are resolved. Poor handling of the critical events typically leads to poor management of the tasks and erodes relationship strength. The outcomes can be summarized as a development of social capital (Nahapiet and Ghoshal, 1998), whereby the supplier becomes an asset to the client, or a depletion of capital, whereby the supplier becomes a problem and even a liability to the client (Smyth et al., 2010). Recovery processes are types of organizational capabilities, which constitute part of the social capital of the business.

## *Towards a service orientation*

BDMs are best placed to enter client organizations at two levels. The first is amongst the least senior members of the client DMU. These are the people who will be working with the supply side TMO operationally and have the most detailed level of expectations and understanding of the project needs. Second BDMs are well placed to source the equivalent levels in the operations of the client who will be the end-users of the project and where most of the value in use resides in order to make detailed assessments of the problems and issues for which the proposed project is the solution. It is at these levels where most of the opportunities for adding value will be identified (Üstüner and Godes, 2006; cf. Schepers et al., 2011). Directors and senior management have an important strategic role in BDM. They will sell the services to their counterparts and glean understanding of the strategy of the client organization and how projects are tactical or strategic needs for the client. They will be tactical where the project is non-core to the client business, for example a management consultant carrying out a change management project or an IT system for a government ministry.

They will be strategic where projects are core to the client business, for example for a property developer, in film production, or for some parts of oil and gas exploration.

The implementation of relationship marketing in North America has tended towards an intensification of transactional relationships (Pels and Saren, 2005), whereas in Europe, a greater reconfiguration of the sales approach is more common. Project businesses typically are partial in implementing relationship marketing, particularly the four levels of service provision, that is, how the projects are delivered, and the service experienced:

1. Nature of the *service concept* – marketing competencies and management capabilities to emphasize certain distinctive strengths.
2. Resource and organize the *service menu* – a set of generic organizational and project capabilities offering configurations, mobilized and tailored to fit.
3. Develop *tailored services* – opportunities exist to 'tweak' configurations and learn from these to develop further service competencies and capabilities for future application.
4. Manage *service communication and reputation* – to generate increased internal awareness (in the project business and within TMOs), to generate increased client and stakeholder awareness of the service benefits and link to relationship building via client identification.

Relationship building involves mutual trust (cf. Kadefors, 2004; Eriksson and Pesämma, 2007; Gustafsson et al., 2010; Smyth et al., 2010; Gil et al., 2011). Chen et al. (2011) found in a study of 262 customers in 31 life insurance companies that trust was important for establishing an economic relationship, but it was less so for a social relationship, which can be interpreted in the project business context as a distinction for relationship building interpersonally and inter-organizationally. Managers in marketing and BDM cannot assume that trust established during the sales stages during BDM and perhaps up to bid submission is automatically transferred into execution. This reinforces the need for a systematic approach including relationship management. DMU-TMO membership need to take individual and collective responsibility for relationship continuity and be prepared to manage handovers between stages and functions, for example between BDM and bid management, between bid management and project management, and for any key team changes during project management. The project business interest in any project is probably lowest towards the commissioning and handover stages (Smyth, 2000). Working capital and personnel are being reduced and moved on respectively. Evidence from the industrial projects sectors, namely power generation and shipbuilding, shows that project businesses have underdeveloped relationship and technical skills for managing the commissioning and handover stages, which includes the incorporation of the customer or client into the commissioning process as a learning opportunity (Kirsilä et al., 2007; Liinamaa, 2012). As Kirsilä et al. state: . . . *there seems to be a lack of understanding and competence on how to change the behavior to become a customer-centric solution provider from previously delivering pure technical equipment* (2007: 718).

This is the difference between a production and customer orientation, and the project mode of delivery is present precisely to provide scope for service integration. BDM has a responsibility to initiate and facilitate the process to ensure that expectations are met and clients are satisfied. This leads into the extension of MoP from front-end strategy development towards becoming *back-end integrators* (Kirsilä et al., 2007).

Morris (e.g. 1994; 2013) has long advocated the need for strategic planning of the project prior to execution, while this chapter has shown the need to strategically manage Marketing BDM as part of the front-end. Leading relationship marketing theorists put it this way:

> . . . exchange relationships with many relevant stakeholders are inadequately recognized by and planned for by organisations. Attention may need to be given to a broad range of stakeholder interests because of their impact on an organisation's value creation process, and because of the systematic (or cumulative) effects of interdependencies which may not previously have been entirely understood.
>
> (Payne et al., 2005: 866)

## Benefits and impact

BDMs cannot assume clients necessarily notice all added value, especially the service components. This either means they are essentially transactional and the marketing mix approach is suited to them or that they need educating to think beyond price and have the benefits of relationship marketing pointed out at a detailed level as part of relationship building and maintenance. They can support the customer receiving a 'smooth ride'. Where service benefits are less obvious, it is a case of the supplier blowing their own trumpet at the project level. DMU members also need support communicating benefits to their own senior management who are not at and probably do not see the operational 'coal face'. Added service value to the supplier comes as an upfront cost for the supplier but is most often 'free' in the medium term as high-quality service to clients generally results in low levels of technical rework (cf. Crosby, 1979). As noted, value creation continues after handover or commissioning. It is released subsequently in use too (see **Chapter 10**). Benefits for the client organization and broader impact of the project on the organization and other stakeholders may, to use the design and construction of buildings as an example, be seen during post-occupancy evaluation (e.g. Green and Moss, 1998). Bordass (2003) cites the lack of awareness about the value of post-occupancy knowledge in real estate markets, a point general to many project markets amongst both clients and project businesses. If the clients do not have the incentive to collect and collate this, project businesses and their consultant teams can form alliances to conduct their own and offer this as a further service offer which they can recycle as feedback for learning and improving services for other clients.

Evaluation in use needs to be conducted wearing the lenses of the client. The perception of value by the client is what matters, not what the suppliers believe is valuable based upon experience and technical expertise (see also **Chapter 10**). Developing the work of Grönroos (2000) and translating it into a project context, he proposes three means of calculation for client perceived value (CPV) which correspond with hierarchical levels of application:

1. Project: *either*

$$\text{CPV} = \frac{\text{Episode benefits} + \text{Relationship benefits}}{\text{Episode sacrifice} + \text{Relationship sacrifice}}$$

*or*

$$\text{CPV} = \text{Transaction value} +/- \text{Relationship value}$$

2. Client management:

$$\text{CPV} = \frac{\text{Core solution} + \text{Added service value}}{\text{Price} + \text{Relationship costs}}$$

3. Programme:

$$\text{CPV} = \frac{\text{Client lifetime revenue} - \text{Added service value}}{\text{Lifetime expenditure} + \text{Relationship costs}}$$

These equations guide thinking, providing a means to guide qualitative assessments and produce quantitative estimates. This looks at matters from the client side and complements the supply side around marketing investment with measures such as ROMI and CLV. The emphasis is upon the qualitative rather than quantitative, for in essence relationship marketing and relationship management are concerned with a shift from efficiency drivers that usually compromise quality clients and stakeholders receive, to effectiveness from which efficiencies flow.

## Conclusion

Relationship marketing offers a variety of ways to differentiate the propositions and delivery of projects to clients aligned to internal strengths and market needs. This provides a means of managing the market and business development. Many companies believed they adopted relationship marketing. Grönroos put it this way:

> Far too often marketers state that they have turned to relationship marketing and believe that their marketing efforts are relationship-oriented, without making sure that the customers see it in the same way. In reality much of

> what marketing practitioners call relationship marketing has very little to do with creating or maintaining customer relationships.
>
> (2000: 32)

The chapter analyzed the theoretical and applied characteristics of relationship marketing in project businesses. It found that relationship marketing is being adopted partially and incrementally. The reason is the predominant concern for risk and survival, and is a function of a lack of rigorous knowledge of the relationship marketing principles. Relationship building, KAM, addressing different markets in terms of dyadic and network relationships are increasingly common, but there has been less progress at a detailed level and a lack of investment in support systems. Where relationship marketing has been implemented, the results have consistently proved beneficial. This is a function of the lack of competition from rivals; hence relationship marketing is itself a source of differentiation. First mover advantage is established and can be built upon to develop competencies and capabilities that are (i) marketing related, (ii) organizational and (iii) project based.

The main weakness of relationship marketing in project businesses has less to do with the principles so much as the lack of willingness to invest, yet market drivers may change this over the next decade or more. The other main weakness is the pragmatic nature of implementation, which is both a source of advantage because of the permutations yet a major constraint that renders implementation a more challenging and reflective process.

Simon (1969) drew attention to the need for deep knowledge to resolve operational problems and that this knowledge is held by specialists, which poses two practical issues for relationship marketing. First, deep specialist knowledge of client businesses is not demanded from BDMs nor typically held by BDMs, constraining the application of relationship marketing. Second, deep specialist knowledge of marketing and BDM is not held by other functional departments and operations: in bid management, in procurement and for SCM, amongst commercial and project managers. They are reliant upon marketing and BDM to provide this along project lifecycles and at the programme management level. Top management in most project businesses is still grappling with this issue with the current tendency to leave relationship marketing and management to individual responsibility rather than manage the processes systematically and guide behaviour accordingly. Systematic integration is needed from the 'corporate centre', that is, throughout the $P^3M$ hierarchy of portfolio investment, programme systems and project management. Integration is needed along project lifecycles from the front of the front-end to relationship management for repeat business.

Systems integration can induce dysfunction (Gadde and Snehota, 2000), setting up rigidities that inhibit flexible change for the future (cf. Gilbert, 2005). The net costs of integration may not always be positive (Gadde and Snehota, 2000; Eriksson and Pesämma, 2012). Relationship marketing is also problematic where discontinuity of demand exists, being able to respond to the complexity of technical, financial and socio-political demands and due to the number of organizational stakeholders (Skaates et al., 2002b). Iterative adjustment based upon reflective practice is necessary. There is also the tendency to use business jargon to present a perception of greater standardization and integration than exists, so obscuring the real processes that need managing. There is a further tendency to exaggerate project uniqueness as an excuse for not developing and adhering to a coherent strategy. A final weakness of project businesses is that project management round time–cost–quality/scope is frequently taken to be the end-point, whereas it is the means. Projects are preconditions for other more routinized functions (Turner, 1999; Turner and Keegan, 2000), inducing the environment for their effective operation; hence, the benefits and impact in use are the key dimensions, which relates to value created. It is important that the same conflation of means and end is avoided in marketing, lest the comment might become analogous: *A good deal of the corporate planning I have observed is like a ritual rain dance; it has no effect on the weather that follows, but those who engage in it think it does. Moreover, it seems to me that much of the advice and instruction related to corporate planning is directed at improving the dancing, not the weather* (Mintzberg, 1994: 139).

In addressing the substantive issues between the theoretical principles and practice, the following substantive issues were addressed in this chapter.

**SI no. 1:** ***Market Management*** concerns proactivity, yet is proving a stubborn issue amongst project businesses adopting relationship marketing principles, mainly due to an unwillingness to invest and a lack of management awareness and commitment at three levels. First, at board level the need for investment is poorly understood, indeed client-centric service provision is generally misunderstood. Second, senior management lack awareness of how to implement relationship marketing principles. Third, functional roles retain transactional norms and habits as implicit and sometimes explicit guidance, including among many BDMs. In sum, too much is left to individual responsibility and organizational habits.

**SI no. 2:** ***Service Management*** focuses upon the client and service needs. Predominant focus remains technical value and implementation through established project management processes. The complimentary client and service focus remains considerable (an issue to be considered further in **Chapter 10**). There is greater focus upon the client, partly a consequence of relational contracting initiatives over the last two decades, but a more concerted approach, proactively linked to service value is outstanding amongst project businesses transitioning to relationship marketing.

**SI no. 3:** ***Marketing Investment and Portfolio Management*** and **SI no. 4:** ***Client Management and Programme Management*** concern management from the 'corporate centre' and the interface with the project. Implementation of relationship marketing at the project level and support from other management levels is largely absent. The one exception is shown to be implementation of KAM albeit in very partial ways.

**SI no. 5:** ***Marketing and BDM:*** marketing and BDM are frequently configured as separate functions in project markets. One condition to implement effective relationship marketing is the integration of these functions.

**SI no. 6:** ***BDM and Client Management*** relates to discontinuity between projects consistency over project lifecycles. This is a continuing issue, and it has been shown that in consistency along project lifecycles during execution is as great and arguably greater than discontinuity between projects in terms of the 'sleeping relationship', a point which will be developed further in **Chapter 5**. Weak systems are one of the main problems in practice.

**SI no. 8:** ***Cross-functional Systems and Coordination Mechanisms*** and **SI no. 9:** ***Marketing and Managing the Project Lifecycle*** are both linked to the need for internal integration. The systems integrator role in the market, especially supply chains is an important issue that determines effectiveness of the solutions offered (Davies et al., 2007), yet this can only be as effective as internal integration. Internal integration spans functions and includes relationship management systems that provide a relationship marketing focus for integration.

**SI no. 10:** ***Marketing and Value Creation*** has been conceptually addressed from a relationship marketing viewpoint, emphasizing that marketing and BDM are more than simply a function of securing work and profitable turnover, they are a function of performance hence value creation is key. Relationships are key to delivering value, especially added value, which clients want. Value is an issue that has current theoretical resonance and is under conceptual development within the service-dominant logic, which is picked up for further consideration in **Chapter 10**. There is a gaping hole in practice.

There are several main *recommendations* for research that flow from the analysis:

A. Research into the management of projects from a relationship marketing perspective. This involves further research into relationship marketing conceptualization and application at the front of the front-end, and involves researching other project business and project management functions through relationship marketing.
B. Research into the underlying reasons for a lack of awareness of relationship marketing principles amongst management at all levels and the extent to which this relates to factors such as market and project risk assessment, and embedded habits and norms.
C. Further detailed analysis of BDM as a relationship marketing function in relation to other functions at the front-end.

There are several main *recommendations* for practice that flow from the analysis in this chapter and echo as well as progress some of the recommendations from the previous chapter:

1. Effective transition to relationship marketing requires investment.
2. Overreliance upon individuals and individualism leads to the need for a systematic approach to relationship marketing that facilitates a broader functional integration.
3. A greater client and service focus is required.

In summary, the adoption of relationship marketing has been selective. It is sometimes explicitly adopted and sometimes implicitly through following trends. Where adopted, the transition is slow and still in the early stages. There are some sound market reasons for incremental change, yet the slow transition has deeper roots than market factors of survival and corporate risk alone. Changing market demands may prompt a more considered and routinized approach that exploiting new concepts through application (cf. March, 1991; Loch et al., 2006; Loch and Kavadias, 2011).

In the broader conceptual scheme of things, relationship marketing can be located within the RBV of the firm (e.g. Wernerfelt, 1984; Barney, 1991) as part of the configuration of core competencies and dynamic capabilities that differentiate firms (e.g. Hamel and Prahalad, 1994; Teece et al., 1997). The pragmatic aspects of relationship marketing also mean it can be located in the contextual view on projects (e.g. Blomquist and Packendorff, 1998; Gann and Salter, 2000; Engwall, 2003; Brady and Davies, 2004) and project ecologies (e.g. Grabher, 2002; Ibert, 2004; Grabher and Ibert, 2011). However, this useful interpretative perspective should not be read as determinism along evolutionary lines as management are agents of change and can act within the ecological perspective to open up and close options for incremental change and occasionally for shocks to corporate systems and operations. There is nothing inevitable about relationship marketing and relationship management, and recent trends of slow transition do not mean that the transition will continue or that it will be accelerated on a wholesale basis. Relationship marketing merely offers options for differentiation in order to manage the market.

# 5

# PROJECT MARKETING

## Introduction

*Market management* is conceptually outward focused. Marketing is part of the focus. How the strategic components of market management aggregate up to influence project delivery through procurement routes and contract forms shape the market-place for projects. *Project marketing* is a development from relationship marketing that seeks to describe and conceptualize the particular features of marketing and business development management (BDM) in project markets. Project marketing is less a paradigm than a conceptual 'hue' or 'tone' of relationship marketing. **Chapter 4** on relationship marketing acts as the basis for this chapter.

Project marketing started off as a *description* of marketing in the project context. It drew attention to specific features, such as the following:

- The need to sell not just one project, but to sell a series of projects (Faulkner and Andersson, 1987).
- The link formed by technological interdependencies in after-sales service (e.g. Terry, 1992) and for the next project.
- Bonds such as social ties of trust become the basis for continuing the relationship (Blau, 1964).
- The link or means for continuity between projects cannot be ascribed to transactional exchange alone but is dependent upon the mutual interest and orientation in the buyer–seller relationship (Hadjikhani, 1996).

The chapter seeks to achieve the following:

A. An analysis of the conceptual and applied characteristics of project marketing in project businesses and an examination of how these are managed.

B. A description of practices and their alignment with the theoretical characteristics and other management approaches.
C. An evaluation of the strengths and weaknesses of project marketing and its pertinence to project businesses, as this cannot be assumed as self-evident.

The main message is about the role of project marketing in making a descriptive and conceptual contribution to this domain, yet with a caveat that there is a tendency towards exclusivity of territory and claims made around the contribution that extend beyond substantiation to date (cf. Sayer, 1992; Smyth and Morris, 2007). The elements that stand scrutiny still make important contributions to research and practice.

## Project marketing in theory and practice

The management literature on project marketing is derived from relationship marketing and develops deeper understanding beyond the project specific transaction. It started to emphasize a pre-project and pan-project approach from the marketing perspective. This, however, was not located in the management and marketing management sphere of the project as a delivery channel (cf. **Chapter 2**). This may help explain the descriptive beginnings with which project marketing began. The particular focus was on features and attributes of the sales process, derived from a relationship marketing principles applied to the project context, giving rise to the term *project marketing*. Conceptualization can be traced to the labelling provided by Holstius (1989) and developments from Hadjikhani (1996). Project marketing was defined as arising out of the nature of the project (Holstius, 1989, cited in Lemaire, 1996: 610): *Project Marketing is the marketing of complex transactions concerning discrete packages of products, services or other actions, designed specifically to create, within a designated period of time, specific assets for the buyer* (Holstius, 1989).

### *Discontinuity and the sleeping relationship*

Hadjikhani (1996) stressed the duration between projects that threatened a continuous relationship, terming this marketing problem as *discontinuity*, which has influenced much of the subsequent literature. There is discontinuity between projects, yet the full extent of it is exaggerated (cf. Turner and Keegan, 2000; Winch, 2013). Discontinuity is broadened out to include inconsistency of service within project lifecycles (cf. **Chapter 4**), a point that is developed in the light of Hadjikhani's contribution. Hadjikhani put it this way:

> Project marketing is explained not in terms of penetration into a new market, but in terms of the management of an already existing relationship wherein the formal relationship is interrupted and the ability of the buyer to change sellers is high.
>
> (1996: 320)

Intermittent purchasing that potentially breaks the existing relationship is linked to what has been termed the *sleeping relationship*. Continuity between projects is provided by maintaining relationships so as to secure repeat business, the management of the sleeping relationship.

By further way of introduction, project marketing was also claimed to be necessary because survey evidence also showed marketing is marginal for projects prior to execution (Pinto and Covin, 1992; Turner, 1995; Cova and Salle, 2005). There have been attempts to draw project management and the management of projects towards project marketing (Cova and Salle, 2007a; 2011; Cooper and Budd, 2007), but no real effort from the direction of the management of projects (MoP) and project management. Relationship marketing is now widely practiced and has strongly influenced most business-to-business (B2B) sectors and some business-to-customer (B2C) relationships as well. Yet, project marketing remains a largely normative concept for development in practice (Lecoeuvre and Patel, 2009). One reason is the client-side bias of MoP research (e.g. Morris, 1994), which Cova and Salle (2011) rightly criticize, whereby the project business sells upon demand from the client and is thus handed a pre-defined project. This can be unaligned with practice and is conceptually skewed. In the project marketing approach, a project is defined as: *A complex transaction covering a package of products, services and work, specifically designed to create capital assets that produce benefits for a buyer over an extended period of time* (Cova et al., 2002: 3).

Project marketing has been criticized by underemphasizing the customer or client and reflecting neglect of the supply-side adoption of portfolio and programme management along with project management (P$^3$M), compared to a more integrated P$^3$M in demand-side procurement strategies (Artto, 2001; Partington et al., 2005). Another general point is that focus is concentrated front-end (Cova et al., 2002; Cova and Salle, 2011) and back end (Hadjikhani, 1996) rather than linking to project management during execution, the assumption being that any shaping is delivered accordingly – a rather naive assumption. It paradoxically therefore underemphasizes execution despite attempts to functionally integrate with project management (cf. Cooper and Budd, 2007). Aside of this shortcoming, project marketing has developed by trying to be holistic (e.g. Cova and Salle, 2007a). There has been a tendency to collect all things within its remit, but there are few specific issues that have been repeatedly developed, bar (i) discontinuity and the sleeping relationship (Hadjikhani, 1996), (ii) the D-U-C framework consisting of discontinuity with uniqueness and complexity (e.g. Tikkanen, 1998; Skaates et al., 2003), (iii) project shaping (Cova and Hoskins, 1997), and (iv) the network and milieu (Cova and Salle, 2006). P$^3$M has yet to be fully addressed. There has been mixed consideration for marketing and especially BDM over the project lifecycle stages (Cova and Hoskins, 1997; Lecoeuvre-Soudain and Deshayes, 2006). Each will therefore be addressed in turn.

The seminal project marketing work of Hadjikhani (1996) brought forward the concept of *discontinuity* between projects. Exchanges are said to be intermittent for projects compared to many other markets. Discontinuity is inter-organizational and can be interpersonal too due to the length of interruption. The relationship marketing literature had already drawn attention to the potential for broken relationships due to conflict, churn and more pertinently for where key people in the decision-making unit (DMU) on the customer side leave or are replaced (Palmer et al., 1986). Cova and Salle summed it up this way: *The major implication of discontinuity in project business is a potential lack of buyer–seller bonding, interdependence and mutual orientation beyond the single project* (Cova and Salle, 2005: 356–357).

The theorization to address discontinuity has evoked concepts of the industrial or buying network that includes supply chains, the project network that includes institutional and organizational influencers, stakeholders as well as supplier chains in the project milieu and the concept of the sleeping relationship to tactically manage otherwise discontinuous relationships (see for example Håkansson, 1982; Håkansson and Snehota, 1995; Hadjikhani, 1996; Cova et al., 2002; Cova and Salle, 2006). Skaates and Tikkanen (e.g. 2003a; 2003b) and their colleagues have been major contributors to the project marketing literature. The power of B2B networks and the influx of social media influences have made much of this approach self-evident, although implicit absorption into behaviour can still constrain informed and, hence explicit, action.

### *The D-U-C framework*

Central project marketing characteristics identified in the literature are *discontinuity, uniqueness* and *complexity*, giving rise to the so-called D-U-C framework (Mandják and Veres, 1998; see also for example Tikkanen, 1998; Skaates et al., 2003). Discontinuity provides special challenges for project marketing. Discontinuity has been a perceived feature of practice that is challengeable on a number of counts:

- Intermittent project work is assumed to be worse than in the B2B and asset specific markets. The extent to which this is generally the case has yet to be fully investigated. Turner and Keegan (2000) tell us that most organizations undertake a portfolio of projects serving, client programmes, for example IT provision for health service organizations, facilities for defense clients, and infrastructure for oil and gas producers and highways agencies are sometimes (almost) continuous, sometimes with overlapping projects supplied by the same project business. Continuity can be extensive, given that 80 per cent of supplier turnover typically arises from 20 per cent of clients provided through repeat business (Koch, 1998; **Chapter 2**).
- The implementation of partnering in practice over the last two decades has shifted perception to show that many clients have programmes of work. This is an important influence on a perception of greater continuity in practice than was previously the case in project businesses because project marketing has yet to be widely adopted (relationship marketing being adopted sporadically and partially – **Chapter 4**).

- Client programmes can yield overlapping workload, and in such cases, marketing and BDM are more about the market share secured and hence the strike rate than the management of sleeping relationships.
- Programme management on the supply side is a concept that provides a client orientation. Thus, even where any one client programme does not provide continuity of work, there are conceptually bundles of projects with similar generic requirements that constitute a supplier programme (or segment) of continuity which helps increase strike rates by managing at the programme level. Where marketing, other organizational and project capabilities are mobilized, the generic capabilities can be organized into segmented business models (Kujala et al., 2010), and then they are customized and tailored into distinctive solutions of technical and service content (Davies and Brady, 2000; Möller, 2006; Davies et al., 2007). Concurring with project marketing, the incidence of effective programme management remains weak in practice amongst many project businesses, but it is in ascendency and thus increasingly challenges project marketing conceptualization of discontinuity.
- Relationship marketing proposes a customer or client-centric approach to complement the production-orientated approach (Pryke and Smyth, 2006). A client-centric lens complements the task and project management focus for project businesses. Clients are more stable than projects in duration, and thus client management provides a bridge, although managing the sleeping relationship will form a significant part of client management between projects. The description of discontinuity and the need to manage the sleeping relationship remains pertinent from this viewpoint yet poses the question as to whether a distinct marketing concept is necessary specifically for project markets.
- Discontinuity is a function of the temporary nature of projects. As with clients, project businesses are reasonably enduring (Winch, 2013), providing continuity of management, particularly when linked to client management and programme management. This provides the means for managing the sleeping relationship. The discontinuity focus can lead to the conceptual reinforcement of the project, hence a residual project focus, overlooking $P^3M$. The growth in social media can be used to help mitigate such effects alongside F2F networking.
- Project management as execution has been criticized for its limited conceptualization in favour of a more holistic and complimentary MoP that addresses the strategic front-end (e.g. Morris, 1994). MoP encourages earlier engagement with client and project (see also **Chapter 8**) and thus foreshortens the period between projects, eroding the extent of discontinuity, and thus the period for managing the sleeping relationship. While there has been attempt made to link project marketing to MoP (Cova and Salle, 2011), this has largely concerned project shaping rather than discontinuity.

*Uniqueness* is the second specific component in the D-U-C framework. Projects concern the delivery of customized products and tailored services. Uniqueness flows from project content typically satisfying a non-standard need for an organization, frequently setting up the preconditions for other activities (Turner, 1999; Turner and Keegan, 2000), for example highways for travel communication or as used to be said 'superhighways' for IT and telecommunications. This is why projects are produced to contract, and it provides some explanation as to why requirements lack full articulation in advance. The uniqueness has been categorized along the lines of technical, financial and socio-political elements (Turner, 1999; Turner and Keegan, 2000). Concerning the technical elements, content usually carries high levels of complexity, uncertainty and attendant risk (e.g. Morris and Hough, 1987; Morris, 1994; Miller and Lessard, 2000; Pich et al., 2002; Flyvbjerg et al., 2003). Financial provision is complicated for most projects, and agreed payment is based upon a bid price for an incomplete contract. Payment is structured as a series of transactions or stage payments for most projects, including one post-completion to settle the outturn cost that varies from the bid price. The socio-political elements range from the institutional level to the project level (Morris, 2013), spanning the mega, special, classical and nano or internal relationships (Gummesson, 2000). Technological and social interdependencies grow, challenging the traditional transactional discreteness; in turn, drawing attention to relationship building to form social and technological ties and the maintenance of the ties through managing the sleeping relationship between projects (Faulkner and Anderson, 1987; **Chapters 3** and **4**). These ties and interdependencies extend into a broad network of project actors and supplies (Cova et al., 1996; Cova and Salle, 2006; cf. Håkansson, 1982; Håkansson and Snehota, 1995), which although far from unique has its own complexity in project environments.

How significant is the uniqueness of projects? A number of factors have been put forward, and while the project form of delivery has its unique aspects, it shares many of the same characteristics as the production of other specific assets that are undertaken to contract. Uniqueness has been a perceived feature of practice that is also challengeable on a number of counts:

- Management in practice can hide behind the 'uniqueness' façade to rely on informal routines rather than invest in, implement and manage formal routines (cf. Nelson and Winter, 1982), because in a project environment, these are complex to coordinate at the corporate–project interface, vertically for P$^3$M and horizontally along project lifecycles. Project businesses typically have weak corporate–project interfaces, the P$^3$M levels being partially or uncoordinated. Standard management practices and formal routines provide the raw material to develop marketing and organizational capabilities for adding value and integration (Davies and Brady, 2000; Möller, 2006), and support for project capabilities (Brady and Davies, 2004; Davies et al., 2007) that can be customized and tailored to project context (see also Fact Box 3.1; Figure 3.2). In other words, the uniqueness of projects demands a strong management framework to facilitate innovation, creativity and problem solving. Increasing project complexity with high service levels requires robust coordinating mechanisms (cf. Kujala et al., 2011). Effective marketing and BDM make projects more unique by differentiating offers and adding value. It can be summed up as follows:

Uniqueness of project → Standardization of marketing → Capability development to add value and for systems integration → Uniqueness of offer and service delivered

- Programme management, organizational competencies and capabilities, integrated systems, relationship marketing and management are practical concepts to customize and tailor. The project is not therefore the sole source or explanation of uniqueness. Uniqueness arises from management, hence MoP, marketing and other management functions.
- The systems integrator concept and network theories conceptually viewed, through the lens of the industrial network (e.g. Håkansson, 1982; Dubois and Gadde, 2000), social network (e.g. Pryke, 2012) or action net (Czarniawska, 2004; Fabianski, 2014), provide means to shape and to respond to unique demands.
- The context of projects is unique in terms physical and relational space of operation. There is a tendency to conflate unique context provided by these spaces with unique management requirements. A paradox has developed whereby MoP and project management have endeavoured to standardize practices, drawing upon management concepts, while defending the uniqueness of projects and project management. There is growing consensus around the notion that there is no theory of managing projects but rather a drawing together of ideas from multiple disciplines, partly to manage the uniqueness (Morris, 2013). A parallel has been emerging in marketing, whereby project marketing is developing its own standardized terms and concepts to standardize understanding and practice, drawing upon relationship marketing and the service logic, while defending the uniqueness and conceptual distinctiveness of project marketing. There perhaps needs to be a consensus around the notion that there is no theory of marketing for projects but rather a drawing together of ideas from multiple disciplines, partly to manage the uniqueness of the project and its marketing.

*Complexity* in projects contrasts with mechanistic mainstream production, posing the problem that what happens on the ground is less easy to explain (Edkins et al., 2013). Projects have had a tendency to become more complex over recent decades with the advent of IT systems for multi-branch national and global organizations, more challenging oil and gas exploration and pipeline logistics, and large urban infrastructure projects that clash with the existing built environment as examples. New techniques and technologies help address such complex systems (e.g. Hobday, 2000; Hobday et al., 2005). Complexity of content is likely to continue to increase, especially in the top tiers of project markets by size (**Chapter 1**). It is also a matter of management complexity; for example Martinsuo and Ahola (2010) have drawn attention to issues around personnel utilization rates on large-scale projects. However, much of production is complex, and with the introduction of just-in-time and small batch production using agile techniques, there is greater opportunity to customize to limited demand or in response to orders drawn from a menu of options. Asset-specific markets for large capital goods exhibit similar features, sometimes indeed switching to project modes of delivery. Service requirements and the bundling of service attributes with products have added further complexity. Projects are not unique in these respects, and this poses problems for the complexity dimension in project markets and for project marketing:

- A transactional approach to the market and a focus upon the management, thus minimization of transaction costs is one means to keep costs under control and keep content simple, complexity coming from problem resolution, change and variation orders for which clients pay. This approach has no place for project marketing.
- Risk management is a major concern that tends towards a task and project management focus rather than a relational focus to add value. It leads to management intent to avoid shaping projects, except from a self-interest perspective.
- Risk management through extensive subcontracting to decentralize risk through large work packages to reduce perceived management complexity or to highly specialized subcontractors in order to maximize quality with a strong systems integration role (cf. Davies et al., 2007).
- Emergent requirements and problems are treated as deviations from socially constructed contracts, method statements and project plans to exclude risk and minimize complexity (Smyth, 2013b).

Complexity resonates, yet the significance could arguably be exaggerated. More credence is lent by the interplay between discontinuity, uniqueness and complexity. In particular, the features of uniqueness and complexity provide a powerful combination. The management of this combination is conceptualized in project marketing at the sales stage through the specific issue of *project shaping* (e.g. Cova and Hoskins, 1997; Cova and Salle, 2005; 2011).

## Project shaping

Miller and Lessard (2000) addressed the shaping of megaprojects on the client side, especially the role of leadership, sponsors evaluating potential project attributes against perceived needs and then allocating the value components to the organizational actors that will be contracted for delivery. On the demand-side project shaping is necessary at times (Pinto and Rouhiainen, 2001) and desirable as a fundamental means to secure competitive advantage amongst project-based industries (Miller and Olleros, 2000; Söderlund, 2011) and specifically at the bidding stage for project businesses.

Cova and Salle (2008) propose five steps: (i) identify the actors, (ii) target the actors, (iii) identify the critical factors, (iv) devise the approach towards each actor, (v) set up the co-creation of value. They also identify four levels of project shaping – see also Table 5.1:

**TABLE 5.1** Project shaping

| *Form of shaping* | *Phase of shaping* | *Scope to shape* | *Outputs* |
|---|---|---|---|
| **Macro-shaping** | Independent of any project | Strong | Creation of demand and the project, e.g. BOOT projects |
| **Joint-shaping** | Project generation and co-creation of value | Medium | Project specification and attendant services |
| **Micro-shaping** | Win-strategies and bid management | Weak | Definition and methods of execution |
| **Marginal-shaping** | Project implementation | Poor | Emergent requirements and refinements |

*Source*: Adapted and developed from Cova and Salle (2011).

1. Macro-shaping, where the ability to shape a project arises from scratch – create the project;
2. Joint-shaping, where co-creation occurs;
3. Micro-shaping, which is located at the bid level and amounts to win-strategy development to add value;
4. Marginal-shaping, where details are amended (adapted from Cova and Salle, 2011). Marginal-shaping offers opportunity to deal with emergent factors during execution too, but project marketing tends to underplay the extent of emergent requirements during execution and hence the execution stage from a marketing perspective.

In contrast to many functions, project shaping is more an 'art' according to Merrow (2011), consisting of five steps:

1. Understanding the *context* – there is an environment and a social milieu in which projects are conducted (Emery and Trist, 1965). The term *milieu* has been picked up in the project marketing literature and has been particularly developed in the context of the organizational and institutional networks in which projects are located (e.g. Cova and Salle, 2006; see below). From this viewpoint, the project business is engaged in a broad network to position the business to secure project and is using the position to intervene to shape the project to mutual advantage.
2. Assessing the potential *value* – there are the short-term, medium-term and long-term economic returns and wider sets of benefits and impact. Value management and engineering largely focus upon the short-to-medium terms

in order to justify capital expenditure in relation to budgeting and offset the costs in practice. They typically are conducted post-BDM. Return on investment (ROI) and net present value (NPV) calculations have their use but are based upon unknown capital costs and thus tend to be used to justify the subjective views of key decision-makers. Business development managers (BDMs) are conceptually positioned with the support of marketing colleagues to argue the project case, rehearse the internal challenges between client capital expenditure (CapEx) and operational expenditure (OpEx), match expectations with long- versus short-term decision-making and align with budgetary requirements (Smyth and Lecoeuvre, 2014). The role of marketing and BDM functionaries is to actively shape the project in two ways:

a. Influence the terms of the debate, especially within the client organization where short-term financial interests are overriding the interests of the business, thus what the project is trying to achieve;
b. Use this as a basis to influence the technical content of the project to enhance benefits in use and impact (cf. Morris, 2013) and minimize short-term costs where possible, that is to say, without a loss of quality.

3. Assessing the comparative *advantage* – these are complex issues and highly subjective in practice because any comparative advantage tends to be derived from a configuration of value or options of value that cannot realistically be separated for analysis and the business objectives which these meet, the business objectives also being complex bundles that are similarly inseparable (cf. Merrow, 2011; Grönroos, 2000). Assessments address client project objectives in relation to client business strategy and operations including opportunity costs.
4. Identifying and understanding *stakeholders* – recognizes the full range of interests that both project businesses and have to serve beyond their respective shareholder value (**Chapter 2**; cf. Smith, 1759) and political accountability. Shaping therefore has to meet multiple objectives, addressing conflicts and tensions which shaping helps to resolve and find compromise as well. This is more than a single event; it is part of a dynamic process that is helped by BDM taking into account the six markets of relationship marketing (Christopher et al., 2002) and the *milieu* and industrial networks of relationship marketing and project marketing (e.g. Håkansson and Snehota, 1995; Cova and Salle, 2006).
5. Thinking about *partners* – apart from a sound financial business that lends assurance to, whether in formal or informal alliances, potential partners will examine the management capabilities (e.g. Teece et al., 1997; Doz and Hamel, 1998; Davies and Brady, 2000), marketing capabilities (e.g. Möller, 2006) and project capabilities (e.g. Brady and Davies, 2004; Davies et al., 2007). There are capabilities and competencies that go beyond the threshold of what it means to be a good project business whether in IT, change management consultancy or

an infrastructure contractor (Hamel and Prahalad, 1994). These capabilities are the generic resources that can be mobilized to:

a. Help the client articulate needs;
b. Shape a project closer to those needs.

Generic resources configured into segmented business models (Kujala et al., 2010) and then customized and tailored to context are attractive to potential partners, yielding future alliance opportunities (Figure 5.1). These opportunities need to be treated with caution because alliance partners may gain unfair advantage unless the resources are recognized in the alliance negotiations, particularly the mobilization of social capital. They also need to be handled with care as capabilities can be copied. The partner gets a closer look at the capability through any alliance. This should not be of too much concern, especially as the capabilities that constitute social capital remain reasonably intangible and tangible elements are difficult to replicate from one organizational context to another. Furthermore, marketing investment should be part of the effort to drive forward capability development. By the time the alliance partner has 'played catch up', the project business has already evolved its capabilities ahead of partners.

Davies and Brady (2000) proposed the concept of 'economies of repetition'. This encapsulates the application of innovations on one project for another and the application of generic capabilities learnt and developed in one context to fit a business model with a specific earning logic to position the firm (e.g. Romme, 2003; Sawhney, 2006), for segments (Kujala et al., 2010), or a supplier or client programme of multiple projects (Figure 5.1). Shaping of a project at the front-end is, on the one hand, deterministic in anticipating the characteristics of a project and, on the other hand, constructivist in the act of shaping (Cova and Hoskins, 1997). Shaping occupies a dual position. It

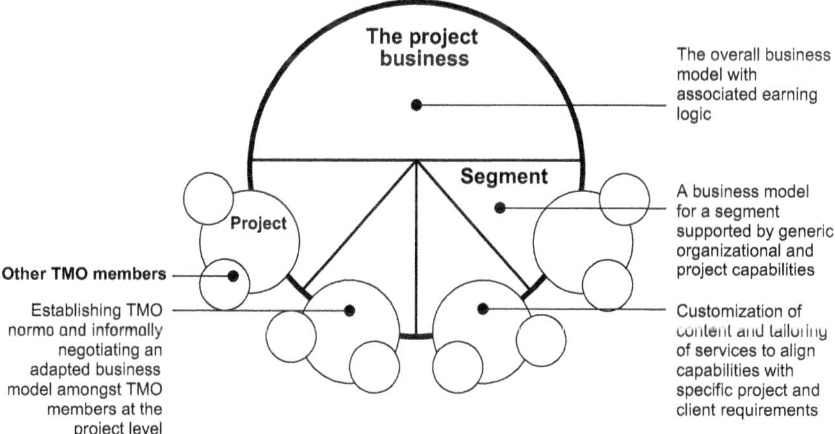


**FIGURE 5.1** A layered marketing approach to business models and capabilities

forms part of the intended or planned project strategy and is part of the emerging strategy at the front-end (Miller and Olleros, 2000; cf. Mintzberg and Waters, 1985). Reality demonstrates that projects continue to throw up emergent requirements during execution (cf. Mintzberg, 1994), which offer further opportunities for shaping, especially marginal shaping, although project marketing has less to say about this phenomenon during execution.

Shaping is easiest where relationship building has developed strong bonds or ties from BDM and perhaps identification over a series of projects. Relationships help identify and lever the value for configuration to the client and project context. Supply networks are part of the relationships.

## Milieu and networks

Industrial *networks* and the *milieu* feature extensively in project marketing (e.g. Cova et al., 1996; Cova and Salle, 2006; cf. Håkansson, 1982; Håkansson and Snehota, 1995; Cravens and Piercy, 1999). Broader than the temporary multi-organizational team or TMO (Cherns and Bryant, 1984) and broader than the project coalition (Winch, 2002), milieu is the project network in geographical and social space comprising the set of heterogeneous players. Project marketing tries to influence and shape norms around projects. The business case for each project is therefore shaped, drilling down to the project definition and hence content in alignment with the capabilities of the supplier and supply chain in the industrial network. Milieu is the relationships in a local and social network of business and non-business actors (Cova et al., 1996) that includes institutional influencers, other external stakeholders and supplier chain members.

In the territorial sphere of socio-political institutional, commercial and other organizational and individual stakeholders, general acceptance of any project is important, specifically placing a contract with a project business (Cova and Salle, 2006) and leveraging value from and in collaboration with supply chains (Håkansson and Snehota, 1995; Christopher et al., 2002). Project marketing conceives markets as networks of geographically dispersed, heterogeneous players operating through rules and norms and structured by influence from markets, contracts and interests (Cova et al., 2002; Cova and Salle, 2005). Milieu relationships are used to shape the project in ways that develop a win-strategy for the project business, taking account of the network and aligning the bid to customer requirements (e.g. Cova et al., 2002; Cova and Salle, 2011). Cova and Salle (2005) have identified three network levels. The project network consists of relationships that are largely transactional and formed on a one-off basis to satisfy minimum requirements. The buying network focuses upon a lifecycle of relationally integrated systems to shape solutions to fulfill client needs. The milieu network is the most difficult, for relationships are long-term and client-centric to lever functionally integrated relationships to provide customized services. Networks are open systems with organizational boundaries being ill-defined and flux in evidence.

### *Between the milieu and project shaping*

There are many implicit and some explicit links to programme management and a few to portfolio management. The sleeping relationship and the extent to which networks and the milieu span projects creates a link to programme management. Overall, scant attention has been directly given to P³M. The focus tends to be largely centred upon the client and project level of operation:. . . *customer-based project management sees the world through the eye of the Project Manager (PM) who is in charge of a unique project which must be developed successfully in order to achieve the highest level of customer satisfaction* (Cova and Salle, 2005: 355).

Project marketing is a broader concept than project management (Lecoeuvre and Patel, 2009; Cova and Salle, 2011), about which project marketing commentators agree, yet there is scope for development in the P³M gap. Greater conceptual attention has been given to integration with project management (Cooper and Budd, 2007; cf. Cova and Salle, 2007a). This has been unsuccessful because it narrows project marketing to fit a funnel in which project management principles and operations are used to regularize resource utilization rates and workflow from the market. The conceptualization has not been adopted in the other literature and in practice. There has been greater success linking project marketing with MoP (Cova and Salle, 2011). As previously noted, marketing and BDM are located at the front of the front-end and ought to be a comfortable fit. The way in which the link has been made is through project shaping, unpacking some nuances of MoP from marketing on the demand side (cf. Figure 3.1).

Yet, project marketing as a broader context than project management and MoP, requiring explicit linkage to portfolio and programme management levels (Tikkanen et al., 2007; Lecoeuvre and Patel, 2009; cf. Cova and Salle, 2011). Resource allocation from portfolio management for client management and developing capabilities for project shaping (cf. Davies and Brady, 2000) support searching out and prioritizing market and project opportunities (Patel et al., 2012; cf. Lecoeuvre and Patel, 2009; Rad and Levin, 2007). Programme management becomes a means of implementation, yet adoption of P³M in practice on the supply side lags both the project marketing theorization to date and the more integrated P³M in demand-side procurement strategies (Artto, 2001; Partington et al., 2005). Research has shown that practitioners perceive marketing and BDM to be already integrated with project management (Lecoeuvre and Patel, 2009), but this is more a mindset than a practice (Smyth and Kusuma, 2013). Research needs to address this issue and extend it into P³M because the practitioner perception conflicts with the reality on the ground in a number of ways:

1. Integration – the level of integration in the project business hierarchy and along project lifecycles is low, hampering project shaping in particular and to some extent the management of the sleeping relationship. It also hampers the management of uniqueness and complexity in order to further reduce their effect.
2. Execution – a lack of attention to the execution stage as project marketing largely assumes that however projects are shaped in marketing and during bid

management is how the project is executed – see Figure 5.2. Some consideration has been given to co-creation, but again, more during execution and during the sleeping relationship stage in terms of impact in use could be developed. Discontinuity has given attention between projects. It is also a factor during a project lifecycle (Hackman and Wagman, 1995; Smyth, 2000), but little or no attention has been given to discontinuity and service consistency between stage gates at the front-end and during execution where continuity is dropped, especially where personnel changes and effective handovers are lacking. Continuity is also an issue within a project lifecycle for supply chain management (e.g. Pryke, 2009), which the interaction network approach in project marketing only partially addresses. Discontinuity and loss of service consistency are important project management-cum-marketing issues that are largely ignored in project marketing with consequences for value delivery, repeat business and sleeping relationship duration.

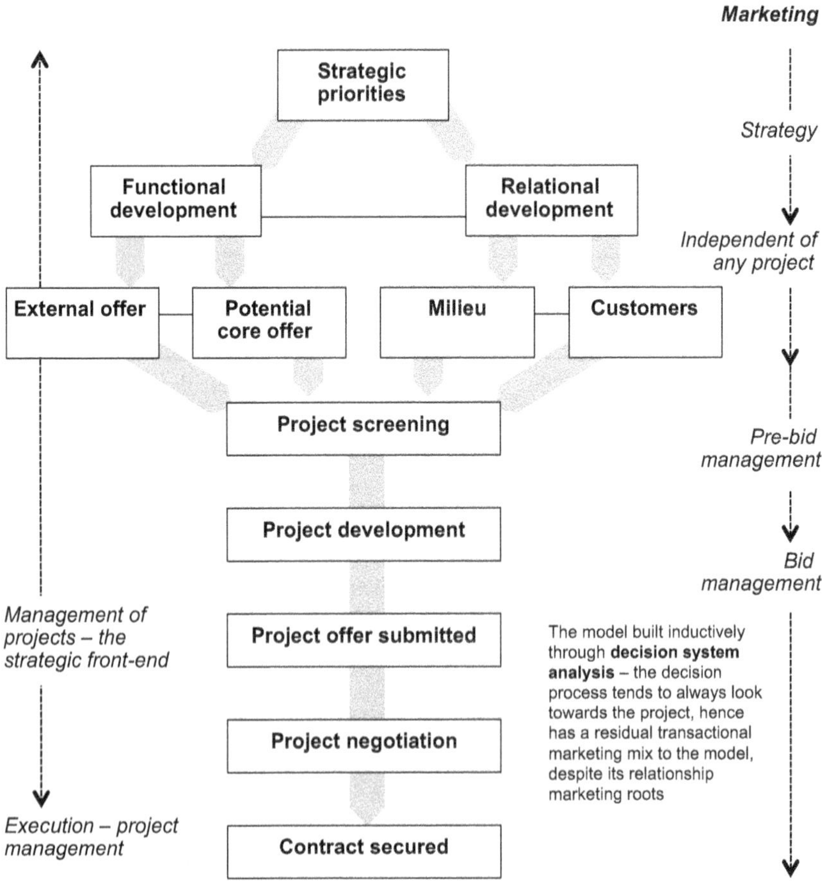


**FIGURE 5.2** The project marketing process

*Source*: Adapted and developed from Cova et al. (2002).

3. Value – means for understanding the customer or client have been underplayed. At times, project shaping has focused more upon shaping for the benefit of project management and profitability than serving the client.

## Business development management in theory and practice

A further specific issue is the selling stages. It has already been pointed out the project marketing pays scant direct attention to BDM during execution, as it is implicitly left by default to other functional roles without reference to coordinated BDM input. Project marketing is process based, focusing upon the interactions between people and projects (Leybourne, 2007) largely in the stages until the client signs the contract (Cova and Salle, 2007a; Lehtimäki et al., 2009). Thus, project marketing does have a greater and explicit contribution to the front-end role of BDM and has paid detailed attention to and up to the bidding stage (Cova et al., 2002). This section brings together these issues under a specific BDM focus over project lifecycles, linking to the corporate business and thus portfolio and programme management as necessary.

Project marketing is located at the front of the front-end. Conceptually, it has tended to reside within that stage, omitting large aspects of execution, and then comes back into play for the management of the sleeping relationship. It therefore focuses more upon activity, which is undertaken under BDM. This is a departure from relationship marketing, which gives all roles a marketing remit. Project marketing theorists would agree with this, although it is inadequately reflected in research to date. Therefore, the front of the front-end in BDM starts with the sleeping relationship because project businesses will have a series of clients providing repeat business. Around 20 per cent of clients will yield up to about 80 per cent of the project turnover (cf. Koch, 1998), and therefore, it is these few clients whose sleeping relationships will need to be managed. There will be overlapping projects and end-to-end projects, so the extent of relations that are sleeping may be quite small amongst the 20 per cent client base, but no less important.

The sleeping relationship has to be managed to enhance the opportunity to secure repeat business. This involves continuing to develop a deep understanding of the client (**Chapter 4**) by monitoring changing business and project needs, monitor personnel changes in the DMU and project team structures, personnel, and other trends and shifts in order to anticipate shaping needs that may arise for the future in client programmes, especially projects nearing the definition stage in the pipeline (Cova et al., 2002).

While there has been effort to link project marketing to MoP (Cova and Salle, 2011), explicit linkage to programme management is minimal. Connections tend to be implicit and indirect. Therefore, from the outset, BDM remains rather isolated as a function at the front-end. One way of reading the project marketing literature is that many of the activities are undertaken or could be said to undertaken by others than those with a specific BDM remit. This reading suggests that the connection comes through other functionaries that blend and combine roles and argues for the demise of the marketing and BDM specific roles, because the marketing mindset needs infusing through an organization, and marketing systems and procedures need embedding in the organization. This reading does align with some relationships marketing conceptualizations (Gummesson, 2000); however, the lack of attention to execution questions this reading. The lack of a link to programme management, integration and value delivery along project lifecycles in relation to project marketing are issues to be developed.

Project marketing is interested in what happens before and after the call for bidding on a project (Boughton, 1987). Involvement after these stages tends to wane or be moved to a more abstract level of network marketing and procurement roles, which are insufficiently grounded in BDM and project management. While conceptually there is reference to project marketing being absorbed into the project manager role (Cova and Salle, 2005) and project management (Cooper and Budd, 2007), this conceptualization is weak in relation to intent, conduct and the support process, and certainly is misaligned with most practice on the ground. Empirical investigation is needed to develop the execution dimension for project marketing.

Clients largely or solely define the project business case, frequently with related pre-work (Pinto and Rouhiainen, 2001; Figure 3.1). BDM involvement, whether through BDMs or others conducting the role, can help advise and shape the project at this stage, not only to yield client benefit but to increase the chances to secure the project by playing to their the strengths. This is the first stage of activity according project marketing. Lecoeuvre-Soudain and Deshayes (2006) developed the three-stage project marketing of Cova and Hoskins (1997) into four stages:

1. *Pre-project marketing* – the supplier, notably, anticipates rules and action range, identifying targets and keeping in touch with the client, which today incorporates B2B, F2F and social media relationship building;
2. *Marketing at the start of the project* – mobilizing the industrial network of organizational actors, including influencers, other stakeholders as well as suppliers;
3. *Ongoing project marketing* – renegotiation, modifications, and relationship exchanges until the end of the project;
4. *Marketing intended to create the conditions of a future project* – managing the sleeping relationship to prepare the project business and selling towards the future project, to which can be added programmes.

Project shaping is tactical for business development responding to specific client needs to customize the content and tailor the services. Fact Box 5.1 briefly sets out the principles employed by an international project business. How are projects shaped by marketing and BDM in low level strategic and tactical ways? There is shaping that explores different ways to meet requirements – value added – which is purely tactical. There is shaping that explores ways to exceed requirements – added value – that is tactical and strategically informed, especially from a market management and business development viewpoint. Strategic shaping to add value conceptually presents more opportunities for growth assuming that this increases the strike rate. From a marketing and BDM perspective, it also presents opportunities to improve performance.

## FACT BOX 5.1 PROJECT CREATION AND SHAPING IN AN INTERNATIONAL PROJECT BUSINESS

A well-known North American engineer and management contractor exhibits some of the features called *project shaping*, utilizing their high-level network of international, government and aid agencies, of financial institutions and commercial contacts to create and shape projects. This is their milieu and it concerns shaping at the top of the 'food chain' through network links. This is not simply a function of the quantity and quality of contacts and the relationships developed with them. This is also a function of global operations at the highest level, drawing upon institutional knowledge and having extensive organizational experience that gives leverage across the network and power in the marketplace. It constitutes organizational and marketing capabilities that frequently place them in pole position with strong political support to create projects and secure projects. This strength is reflected in the ability to bid, yet also leads to selection through being the preferred supplier and becoming the preferred supplier through negotiation.

These capabilities around network leverage and experience cascade down to the operational level, where they are frequently appointed by large national and pan-national client to manage problematic projects. They use these capabilities to impose discipline on the project, for example cost reduction, in the TMO and coalition, especially in the supply chains. This power and ability has also been exercised on occasions on the client in opportunistic and self-interested ways in predominantly transactional ways. The operational level tends towards a transactional approach in general.

*Sources*: Developed from Cova and Hoskins (1997); cf. Davies and Brady (2000); Möller (2006).

Shaping can be seen as a commitment or non-contractual promise that then has to be delivered during execution. The business development role is to investigate the extent to which clients are open to shaping. Some simply are not, but this is not always evident from those acting in the role of the sponsors or owners. However, it may reside higher up the hierarchy as it aligns with the core activities of the client organization and with their own operations management. It is the BDM function to get into position to ensure the supplier is helping to articulate the problem and project solution.

Project marketing research looks to suppliers to commit and deliver against the shaped content. In bidding and during execution, this is essentially a shift from the project network to the buying network (Cova and Salle, 2005). This second stage is where the emphasis has been put on supply chains in the network and less attention given to the operational details. There has been a lack of a grounded approach to

BDM in this transition and applied research on execution from the project marketing perspective. This is needed because many project businesses remain somewhat inept at understanding their roles and responsibilities to meet threshold requirements for the project team in order to meet time cost and quality or scope (Merrow, 2011). This is particularly the case where there is ambiguity and trade off needs to be understood. He states in regard to oil and gas: *Successful megaprojects require an extraordinary degree of trust, cooperation, and communication between the business sponsoring the project and the technical functions developing and executing the project. Too often, we encounter the exact opposite* (Merrow, 2011: 82).

In terms of project marketing, this addresses the tactical value added dimensions, whereby project teams are trying to meet objectives they do not fully understand. There is discontinuity and service inconsistency along project lifecycles, particularly in transition from the front-end to execution. The lack of integration curtails performance, thus delivery against the requirements (value added) and for exceeding the requirements (added value), whether at marginal loss for added value components, at cost or at average or premium profit. All are viable. Marginal loss can be viable where strategically linked to client management and client lifetime value (CLV) – a programme management function. Project marketing does address the growing research interest in co-created value, but mainly during the front-end stages linking this to shaping rather than delivery (Cova and Salle, 2005; cf. Pinto and Rouhiainen, 2001; Prahalad and Ramaswamy, 2004a; 2004b).

Execution has to date been downplayed, so that when the project is completed and the sleeping relationship again has to be managed, it is not simply a matter of capturing lessons learned for application generically or for repeat business. The relationship management is contingent on how well the relationship was managed during execution and upon the performance during execution. Project marketing has yet to comprehensively and extensively investigate these issues in depth, but they feed into the third phase of ongoing marketing. Ongoing marketing leads into the fourth stage of the sleeping relationship, which has been covered.

## Conclusion

Project marketing has its roots in relationship marketing. It is a development from relationship marketing, stimulated by the need to address the particularities of project environments. This aligns with the distinctive characteristics of project markets and activities. There has been a tendency to overegg the notion of projects as being special and different in research and practice (e.g. Smyth, 2000). However, there are differences, concepts transferred from the management to project environments frequently needing 'translation' for successful transfer (**Chapter 1**). This has not always been thorough in theorization and application, a notable example being knowledge management and transfer (e.g. Bresnen et al., 2004). Marketing has been shown to be rather isolated in theorization (as well as in practice), few engaging in research. There has been a trickle of research regarding marketing in construction (**Chapter 2**). For other project markets, it is project marketing that has made the major and consistent contribution. Project marketing is to be acknowledged for efforts to try to render a thorough translation to induce knowledge transfer into the project domain. This raises two questions:

1. To what extent have efforts in conceptual translation led to:
   a. Substantiated claims for and integration of project marketing into MoP conceptual developments (cf. Smyth and Morris, 2007)?
   b. Conceptual rigidities, fossilizing concepts so as to stifle research progress (cf. Gilbert, 2005)?
2. To what extent has project marketing represented actionable knowledge, which has been adopted in practice (cf. Romme, 2003; Cross and Sproull, 2004)?

Responding to these questions flows from the aims of the chapter, which has sought to analyze the conceptual and applied characteristics and management of project marketing in project businesses. It has sought to describe the alignment of project marketing theorization and practices with the theoretical characteristics of other management approaches. Some assessment has been made of particular issues as the chapter proceeded but the last aim is only satisfied through an evaluation of the strengths and weaknesses of project marketing and hence its pertinence to project businesses in this concluding section.

To reach the desired outcome, the following substantive issues between the theoretical principles applied in practice and the theory have been considered in this chapter.

**SI no. 1:** ***Market Management*** relates to project marketing in the sense that it makes a proactive contribution. The starting point is the level of the project and to the extent that project marketing remains grounded at this level. It does not make a large and direct contribution to market management and business development because of the project focus, it lacks overt linkage to corporate-level concepts, especially via portfolio management.

**SI no. 2:** ***Service Management*** is enhanced through project marketing through the greater focus upon the client. Added value, including added service value, can be realized through project shaping, although this is discretionary in context and led by management agency.

**SI no. 5:** ***Marketing and BDM*** is presented as a more coherent set of activities in project marketing although how this is conducted on the ground at a detailed level has yet to be fully explored. There is some ambiguity as to who performs these functions and the extent to which these are conducted by specialist functionaries. Marketing and BDM remains isolated yet is linked through the actors conducting multiple roles.

**SI no. 6:** ***BDM and Client Management*** is where a major contribution is made from discontinuity towards a *continuous* and, as this chapter adds, a *consistent service*. Project shaping to add value is a further aspect that is part of project-specific client management informed by relationships develop in the milieu.

**SI no. 8:** ***Cross-functional Systems and Coordination Mechanisms*** whereby project marketing considers the cross-functional and intradepartmental issues, especially in bidding and to a limited extent with execution. This supports how other systems and mechanisms provide coordination. Project marketing has left gaps as how these processes are configured on the ground, preferring to concentrate primarily upon conceptual development.

**SI no. 9:** ***Marketing and Managing the Project Lifecycle*** relates to comments about addressing the issue above. It is partial, being particularly strong at the front-end and for the sleeping relationship. Drilling down to the level of detailed conduct, especially in relation to execution, has still to be fully developed.

**SI no. 10:** ***Marketing and Value Creation*** is a strength through project shaping, providing theoretical and practical guidance on the means to add value through shaping at the front-end, albeit largely with an assumption that what is shaped front-end is delivered. There are some recent references to co-creation of value, which is potentially a fertile field for further research development.

Project marketing has seen some drift from the heart of the relationship marketing to a residual project focus. Even when considering programmes and networks, projects remain the departure point, sometimes at the expense of client management and service provision (cf. **SI no. 2** and **SI no. 6**), hence value creation. This is somewhat surprising given the relationship marketing roots, which has a greater social orientation than the traditional project or transactional marketing approaches have. Does, therefore, project marketing offer anything new?

Although there is some drift from relationship marketing, it can be argued that this is necessary to address the specifics of project markets. This has seen some broadening of coverage, for example to consider service development and logic albeit at the residual project focus (Cova and Salle, 2007b), yet retrenchment by submitting project marketing to project management as a frame of reference (Cova and Salle, 2005). This minimizes marketing compared to its analysis of delivery channels in which project management resides.

Many of the main project marketing tenets, such as managing the sleeping relationship and project shaping, are conceptualized within relationship marketing in a variety of ways. The analysis of the extent of the theory–practice interface is an important contribution with further scope for research and practice. This leads to a concluding proposition that there is development but nothing that substitutes for or renders redundant relationship marketing. Whether it constitutes a theory of marketing or is more akin to a description of activity in the same way as over-the-counter (OTC) is a moot point. Project marketing overlooks the delivery channel aspect from the client and marketing perspective.

Is project marketing justified as a theory or stand-alone theorization? Project marketing is strong in consideration of industrial networking (cf. Håkansson, 1982) as a means to shape projects in their social space. Understanding the milieu is a social concept within social and geographical space in which the project is formed and located (e.g. Cova and Salle, 2006). While this does not represent any significant departure from the tenets of relationship marketing, it has provided an enriched contribution. It arguably has further scope for development in the context of project ecologies (e.g. Grabher and Ibert, 2011).

One problem is the unjustified claims made for its research status in terms of theorization and extent of empirical evidence. Conceptual assertion and descriptive amplification appears to be the major means to identify features and patterns to form generalizations and patterns (Smyth and Morris, 2007). Relationship marketing (**Chapter 4**) and the service-dominant logic (**Chapter 10**) adequately cover the prime substantive issues. The need for a separate or distinct theorization of project marketing is probably unnecessary, but decisiveness of the evaluation on this point is dependent of how theory is viewed. Of the three main options – powers of explanation, development of understanding, identification of generalizations and patterns – only the descriptive option that identifies patterns and generalization has any justification, and it is thought that most of the authors in the project marketing domain would not ascribe to this theory definition.

A critical challenge to the theoretical approach to dyadic relations and networks (Lowe et al., 2012) is derived from the *dead mapping* concept (Derrida, 1978), which argues that theory and practice are over-rationalized. The essence of the argument is that we create maps to make the journey to the future perfect state the project promises (cf. Pitsis et al., 2003), but we end up following the map rather than seeing the territory before us. Actually this is a critique of the entirety of MoP as well as the normative aspects of marketing and project marketing. It is an unreasonable critique on several grounds. First, researchers and many practitioners would not set out unless the territory was charted, the project scoped, and tools and techniques applied. Likewise, awareness of marketing is necessary to articulate the possibilities and attempt to realize these, for example engaging with the milieu, shaping the project and managing the sleeping relationship. Second, the critique assumes a purely linear path that denies the dynamics of project management and marketing and that there is a degree of choice of concepts applied and pragmatism at a detailed level of implementation. Where the critique has bite is that maps can narrow our vision, induce the homogeneity and miss the diverse richness of experience for which Lowe et al. (2012) particularly criticize Cova, albeit not specifically for project marketing. That conflates the issues. The problem is not the map: the problem is with the user. A user can read the map and have an outward focus. In marketing, the equivalent was raised through use of the term *myopia* (Levitt, 1960). Cova and other project marketing researchers embrace diversity in content. There is nonetheless a tendency for epistemological homogeneity by arguing that all marketing about projects has to be forced through the project marketing concept, which brings the critique back to the exaggerated claims made for the concept (cf. Smyth and Morris, 2007). Marketing is about diversity and differentiation to manage the market. Conceptual pluralism provides diversity through both choice of paradigm and selection of principles and concepts applied within each paradigm.

Strengths and a number of weaknesses have been brought forward. On balance, project marketing has yet to establish coherent theorization and as a separate concept is a work in progress. While the adoption of relationship marketing has been partial and incremental amongst project businesses, adoption of project marketing has made less impact in practice. The lack of take-up can be viewed as an acid test.

In summary, the chapter scopes the role of project marketing as a descriptive and conceptual contribution to MoP. There is a tendency towards exclusivity in the conceptual territory by drawing all things to itself, which is evidence of rigidity and inflated claims of conceptual coverage (cf. Sayer, 1992; Smyth and Morris, 2007). The main contribution to knowledge is to show the valuable contribution project marketing has made to opening up the field of marketing in project environments. It has yet to make a significant contribution to practice. In the way that project management has been extended through the development of MoP, project marketing might benefit from being extended into the *marketing of projects*, so defending the concepts developed yet lending scope for further development. This may also give scope to recover lost ground in drifting away from certain aspects of relationship marketing (cf. **Chapter 4**), and giving scope for more coherent connection with other theorizations around the service-dominant logic (**Chapter 10**) and entrepreneurial marketing (**Chapter 6**).

There are several main *recommendations* for research that flow from the analysis:

A. Research needs to be rigorously linked back to relationship marketing on the one hand and developed at a more detailed grounded level on the other hand.
B. A greater understanding of market management strategy, linked to $P^3M$ and development through the broader lens of the marketing of projects.
C. Further detailed analysis of BDM as a function in its own right and in relation to other functions, especially during execution.

There are two main *recommendations* for practice that flow from the analysis:

1. Improved awareness of project marketing as an option for adoption amongst senior management level.
2. Improved awareness of marketing and project marketing amongst other managers, especially project managers.

In summary, project marketing is an important contribution to marketing in general and has helped crystallize aspects of marketing for researchers and practitioners in project markets. It has proved to be a stepping stone to understanding marketing in project environments. If the status of a theorization is insisted upon, then project marketing largely falls into the remit of pattern identification and aiding generalization; else, it has to broaden its conceptual remit as well as return to its roots.

# 6
# ENTREPRENEURIAL MARKETING

## Introduction

*Entrepreneurial marketing* is a growing area of interest in the research community. It has not reached a 'tipping point' whereby the weight of systematic evidence represents a new marketing paradigm (cf. Kuhn, 1996; Lakatos, 1970). Entrepreneurial marketing brings a new lens or approach to marketing. It is insufficiently developed to say it will become a marketing paradigm. Paradigms succeed previous worldviews; entrepreneurial marketing is emerging and may offer a different worldview in time. There are usually countertrends trying to absorb lessons from the new paradigm into the old as a means of invigoration, as occurred with the marketing mix in the face of relationship marketing (e.g. Kotler, 2003). The general market perspective adopted to address marketing in project environments is to divide organizational approaches into *relational* and *transactional* (**Chapter 2**). Drilling down, the three market management categories are *reactive, responsive* and *proactive.* The marketing mix is transactional and reactive, whilst relationship marketing is relational and proactive. Entrepreneurial marketing is fundamentally proactive, although it is less clear-cut as to whether it is relational. On balance, there is a marginal emphasis upon a relational approach, especially where alliance building is part of the entrepreneurial development.

Entrepreneurial marketing is about 'making' the market and as such is conceptually close to market management. For small enterprises, they are formed around market making, but for large project businesses, entrepreneurialism in general and for marketing specifically is located within, sometimes embedded in an organization. Markets can be made, but it is more likely to be reforming the exchange or series of exchanges. Shaping the project, the concept from project marketing (**Chapter 5**), can be undertaken with entrepreneurial 'flair' or conducted through entrepreneurial principles, but this occurs from the project perspective (cf. Cova and Holstius, 1993; Cova and Salle, 2011). Conceptually, it can occur at a higher level within the organizational hierarchy. Project businesses often leave it to clients to innovate and specify new procurement routes and contract forms that reconstitute (segments of) the market, a recent example being PPP/PFI projects in IT and construction markets. In essence, this is redefining the delivery channel because a larger load or content is being carried that requires careful monitoring based on outputs rather than inputs.

Business development in the conceptual sense (**Chapter 1**), rather than the applied sense of BDM, is in close affinity with entrepreneurial marketing. However, this does not always mean that it is market driven, accounting for many of the entrepreneurial failures that are insufficiently aligned to market or particular customer needs at a detailed level. Whilst the marketing mix and relationship marketing were primarily ways to secure business, entrepreneurial marketing is a way to make business. This does not mean there is a lack of interchange with crossover influences and activity – concepts and theorization are not always mutually exclusive – but there is a degree of emphasis that counts in the context.

In terms of conceptualizing marketing in project environments and for project businesses, the thrust developed is thus most akin to the overarching concepts of market management and business development and the interplay between them. In following chapters, project management and management of projects will be articulated in relation to marketing to enrich and deepen the connection with market management and business development. A main aim of the book is to explore how market management and marketing are changing. This chapter examines a neglected area in the sense that researchers have berated project businesses for poor understanding and implementation of marketing in project businesses. Although there is evidence for this, the claims may have been exaggerated, failing to recognize marketing that is essentially entrepreneurial. Entrepreneurial marketing may act as a normative concept as much management thinking does to guide future practice, but it also acts as a frame of reference for empirical investigation of what is present in firms and applied in the marketplace. This chapter therefore seeks to achieve the following:

A. An analysis of the theoretical and applied characteristics of entrepreneurial marketing in project businesses and an examination of how these are internally managed.
B. A description of practices and their alignment with the theoretical and applied characteristics, particularly the approach to building and managing markets.
C. An evaluation of the strengths and weaknesses of entrepreneurial marketing and its pertinence to project businesses, including performance towards client and project business benefit.

The main messages of the book are that marketing is undergoing a fundamental change in many project businesses, and therefore, it is prudent to conceptually explore entrepreneurial marketing. The transition from transactional to relational approaches has been set out. Entrepreneurial marketing offers another lens. It is one area at the cutting edge of marketing research and perhaps may be implicit in practice too. It can also help manage markets where resource constraints exist and perhaps in ways that management may not always perceive. However, a word of caution needs to enter at this point. Entrepreneurial marketing is not to be pursued with a 'light touch' from a management perspective. It is a high commitment and high engagement activity. Also, it is not a rhetorical phrase in which to rebadge current activity to lend credibility to activities that are not embedded and integrated vertically and horizontally in project businesses.

The main message is that entrepreneurial marketing offers an alternative medium to differentiate the project business in its marketplace by addressing the market at a strategic level of delivery or tactically in inventive ways to reconfigure exchanges, transactions and project content. Where successfully implemented, it increases market performance, yet carries higher risk.

In assessing how relevant entrepreneurial marketing is for project businesses, and hence its strengths and weaknesses, the extent of existing practice and prescriptive potential needs addressing, although no claim is being made as to adequately cover this within a single chapter. Scoping this field poses a challenge for researchers and practitioners for further examination and exploration respectively.

There has been a lack of direct empirical evidence to fully substantiate many entrepreneurial processes. It is simply difficult to be on the ground floor of new innovative development for research purposes, for which effectuation and effectual marketing processes as one approach to entrepreneurial marketing has been criticized (Forster and York, 2008; cf. Dew, 2003). Developing this point, Schindehutte et al. (2008) argue market advantage often starts with small acts of entrepreneurial activity overlooked in theory and by practice. It is difficult to predict when to be present to observe such acts and episodes. Even if present, the practitioner proceeds intuitively at times, making it difficult to cognitively capture the processes and turn them into actionable knowledge.

Schumpeter (1934) defined entrepreneurship as disruptive and high-risk activity that reconfigured markets, coining the term *creative destruction*. Entrepreneurial activity is a force of creative destruction that does not always accord with moving the market towards the idealized equilibrium. Idealized equilibrium is a state that asset-specific markets depart from as a matter of course over the long-term. Entrepreneurial activity can feed this dynamic flux in asset specific markets. It can also induce some stability through reconfiguring how requirements are met or exceeded at times. Entrepreneurial activity is thus a change agent for engaging with the wider forces of change, complexity, chaos and contradiction that characterize competition (Hitt and Reed, 2000). Established and mature organizations can develop entrepreneurial activity, characterized as innovative, risk-taking, proactive, competitively dynamic and forceful with a high degree of autonomy (e.g. Covin and Slevin, 1989; Sørensen, 2012). Autonomy gives individuals, business units and in-house project teams scope to explore rather than exploit opportunities (cf. March, 1991).

Porter (1980) views entrepreneurial value creation in terms of differentiation or a low cost focus. This has been developed into four types of marketing and performance practices: prospectors, analyzers, differentiated defenders and low-cost defenders (see Walker and Ruekert, 1987; Slater and Olsen, 2000; 2001; Olsen et al., 2005). Prospectors are the most entrepreneurial in creating product and service solutions to meet customer requirements. In such entrepreneurial markets, customers are not particularly price sensitive (Slater et al., 2010); however, in asset-specific markets of high complexity and uncertainty where much of the product and service remains intangible during bidding, price factors can dominate. This is the case even though customers face high risk, including variability between bid price and outturn costs. Whereas, analyzers try to trade off quality and cost (Moore, 1991; Slater et al., 2010), low cost defenders rely upon standardized practices (Walker and Ruekert, 1987) and differentiated defenders invest in quality (Walker and Ruekert, 1987; Slater and Olsen, 2001; Slater et al., 2010). Prospecting is a term most aligned to marketing and has added pertinence where the prospecting extends beyond work seeking towards identifying innovative value creation and resolution.

## Entrepreneurial marketing in theory and practice

### *The management literature*

Entrepreneurial marketing was initiated as a concept around 30 years ago and remains a developing field; indeed, the rate of expansion is increasing. From the outset, it lacked a unified conceptual approach, and with recent expansion, it is still without a unified theory (Ioniţă, 2012). There is a tension in the entrepreneurial literature as to where and when entrepreneurship and entrepreneurial marketing are possible. This is a function of conceptual diversity and definitions of application. Does its form depend upon firm size, that is, application from entrepreneurial start-ups to entrepreneurism in large corporations (Ioniţă, 2012)? The view adopted here is that individuals and groups can be entrepreneurial in principle anywhere and anytime. In practice entrepreneurship is only more difficult in groups and organizations where the systems and procedures become sufficiently rigid to constrain the necessary scope for thinking and action (cf. Gilbert, 2005). The same applies to entrepreneurial marketing. Rigidity is present in many organizations, but it is argued that with the advent of post-delayering and the focus upon core business in practice, managing emergent strategies, strategy as practice and agile management techniques developed from theory, there is more opportunity for entrepreneurism and entrepreneurial marketing in many organizations than previously has been the case.

How is entrepreneurial marketing defined? A commonly cited definition is provided by Morris et al. who state it is the: . . . *proactive identification and exploitation of opportunities for acquiring and retaining profitable customers through innovative approaches to risk management, resource leveraging and value creation* (2002: 5).

Another view places greater emphasis upon value creation in partnership: . . . *the image of the market that entrepreneurs act upon is not the battle field consisting of products and services competing on objectively based differences. Rather it is a dialogue where expectations are being created and recreated* (Gaddefors and Anderson, 2009: 33).

On the one hand, this looks back to relationship marketing and the interactive dialogue to develop understanding (cf. Gummesson, 2000; Ballantyne and Varey, 2006; **Chapter 4**) and on the other hand looks ahead to service provision through the co-creation of value (Vargo and Lusch, 2004; Kasouf et al., 2008; **Chapter 10**). The distinctive aspect is the approach to risk and innovation, frequently using relationships and partnerships as mitigating factors. The objectives are to be opportunistic in order to create value and build customer equity (Morris et al., 2002; cf. Slater and Narver, 1995). It is claimed that entrepreneurial marketing has greater application in uncertain and turbulent environments (Davis et al., 1991).

Entrepreneurial marketing requires flexibility and adaptability, placing equal or greater emphasis upon exploration over exploitation (cf. March, 1991), in turn suggesting it is less suited to large businesses and corporations with robust systems and administrative rigidities (cf. Leonard-Barton, 1992; Kotler, 2003). The two are compatible when entrepreneurship is incorporated into the strategic orientation of a large corporate business (Morris et al., 2002; Schindehutte and Morris, 2010). This is interesting where project businesses lack robust systems and operate in markets of turbulence. It creates scope for entrepreneurship, yet the outward and service focus necessary for successful entrepreneurism is oft quashed by an inward task and project management focus upon risk minimization. There is widespread agreement that the strategic pursuit of entrepreneurial marketing in large companies requires entrepreneurial actors. What constitutes such an actor is open to as much discussion and debate as to whether it is possible to pin down effective leadership traits and skill sets (Anderson and Tell, 2009; Ioniţă, 2012). There is agreement that entrepreneurs are able to intuitively anticipate market needs or create needs in the market through effectuation (Dew et al., 2009). The processes are hard to perceive and regularize, indeed, are intangible and sometimes disparate. They are hard, as noted, to observe especially in a timely way for both research and practice purposes – the small acts and episodes that build incrementally and iteratively into something more recognizable as entrepreneurism (cf. Schindehutte et al., 2008).

It requires a broad range of skills. The range includes working competitively whilst harnessing collaborative and alliance practices (O'Donnell et al., 2002) in line with relational procurement, relationship marketing mobilized through conceptual, social, and technical competencies, and skill to facilitate innovation and develop experiential learning (Carson and Gilmore, 2000; Brinckmann et al., 2007). Application demands alacrity of action and decision-making (Collinson and Shaw, 2001). Entrepreneurial marketing addresses these diverse forces to reshape and reconfigure the market and distribution channels (Day and Montgomery, 1999; Kinnear, 1999; Morris et al., 2002). Entrepreneurship extends beyond firms founded and run by entrepreneurs. It includes firms that behave with entrepreneurship across networks. Firms engaging with above average levels of entrepreneurship demonstrate evidence of higher success levels (e.g. Covin and Slevin, 1994; Morris and Sexton, 1996; Zahra and Garvis, 2000). Entrepreneurial marketers often ignore traditional marketing concepts and principles (Hills et al., 2008). This is the tension in the large organization. There needs to be adherence to the concepts and principles, even tactical behavioural codes of conduct for marketing, but specific actions may depart by agreement from established norms and formal routines.

Although entrepreneurial marketing has gained a position in the marketing canon (Morris et al., 2002), what it looks like at an operational level lacks detail. The emergence of effectual marketing has helped provide some further depth (Sarasvathy and Dew, 2005; Read et al., 2009). Effectuation is a theory of entrepreneurial activity

(Sarasvathy, 2001) that is rooted in both evolutionary economics and organizational behaviour (Cyert and March, 1992). It is located, like relationship marketing, within the resource-based view of the firm (Wernerfelt, 1984). Effectual marketing creates new markets from the bottom-up, hence from action on the ground. The context for effectual marketing is provided within marketing by the need for breakthrough strategies (Markides, 1999) and creatively reconstituting markets (Andrews and Smith 1996; Menon et al., 1999). Abernathy (1978) first questioned the extent to which it is possible to be both strategically creative and examine performance at a detailed level. This ambidexterity comprises exploration versus exploitation (March, 1991). It is an appropriate and sometimes necessary approach in asset-specific, hence project markets, in order to initially create or induce opportunities (exploration), followed by action to manage and delivery according to the opportunity (exploitation) – combining creativity and performance (cf. Morris et al., 2002; Read et al., 2009).

Where marketing and effectuation conceptually meet, the term *effectual marketing* is used as a variant of entrepreneurial marketing. Working from the bottom-up, that is, the context of operation, the following characteristics prevail:

1. A small resource base utilizing creativity and personal networks;
2. Proactivity that is at times inspirational;
3. Induction of opportunities to generate value for customers (cf. Levitt, 1983; Davis et al., 1991; Morris et al., 2002);
4. Creation of market demand at the level of the market or an exchange.

The guiding principle of much entrepreneurial marketing and certainly effectual marketing is defined in the following terms: *Effectuation starts from the position that the future is contingent upon actions by wilful agents intersubjectively seeking to reshape the world and fabricate new ones* (Sarasvathy et al., 2008: 339). *Effectuation may be called a logic because it is a coherent system of principles that are inherently interrelated, internally consistent and collectively independent . . . a clear basis for action upon the world* (Sarasvathy et al., 2008: 345).

Markets are socially constructed, shaped by skilled and specialist actors with social and moral responsibilities (Polanyi, 1944; Abolafia, 1996; Schindehutte et al., 2008; see also **Chapter 1**). Shaping is dynamic and thus subject to continual renegotiated and periodic restructuring (cf. **Chapter 5**). From the entrepreneurial marketing viewpoint, these macro-level changes are aggregated up from a series of specific exchanges and transactions that change the 'bigger picture'. At the level of the firm and exchange, new markets are created via iterative actions and transformed out of existing market configurations (Sarasvathy and Dew, 2005). Entrepreneurial transformation begins with who people are, what they know and whom they know (Sarasvathy, 2001). Those involved directly and indirectly with BDM are the agents in project sectors. New market opportunities are created with commitment, initiative and experience. Seven main characteristics and conditions for management have been identified in order to identify new products and service propositions for which demand cannot be predicted in advance (Read and Sarasvathy, 2001; Sarasvathy, 2001; Sarasvathy and Dew, 2005; Sarasvathy et al., 2008). These are set out in Table 6.1.

**TABLE 6.1** Principles of effectual marketing management

| *Principles and conditions* | *General characteristics* | *Project-related characteristics* |
|---|---|---|
| **Uncertainty, ambiguity and isotropy** | High uncertainty around levels of demand for product and service<br>Ambiguity occurs about demand *content and experience*, for example over requirements, production or service execution and functional benefits<br>Isotropy leads to a lack of clarity around goals, targets and effective decision-making | Projects are initiated from the top of the 'food chain', where greatest scope for uncertainty exists<br>Each business development opportunity and project is unique due to complex and uncertain asset specificity with customized content, choice of procurement route and tailored contracts to context<br>Uncertainty affects execution, providing the backcloth against which resources are allocated and configured, decisions are made and behaviour ensues |
| **Unpredictability** | The lack of ability to predict customer requirements from trends and market research as the past is not necessarily a good predictor for shaping the market for the next project transaction. This is especially the case in B2B and asset-specific markets | Project customers rather than suppliers tend to drive project initiation. This limits entrepreneurial marketing at the level of managing markets and their segments entrepreneurially<br>This drives suppliers to mobilize resources and spread risks by outsourcing and leveraging value in the industrial network, and this can be conducted with entrepreneurship |
| **Bounded cognition** | Information asymmetry is a boundary. It is partly a function of uncertainties, but it can also be related to market power, where withholding information yields power<br>The logic of habit and intuitive practice add stretch to and challenge bounded rationality | For projects information, asymmetry is common<br>Mobilizing tacit knowledge, hence employing problem solving and creativity, can reduce boundaries through testing what clients want<br>Most projects are in effect a 'prototype'<br>There are also self-imposed boundaries. Business developers tend to view the project as the prime focus rather than the client |

(*Continued*)

**TABLE 6.1** (Continued)

| *Principles and conditions* | *General characteristics* | *Project-related characteristics* |
|---|---|---|
| **Satisficing behaviour and affordable loss** | Entrepreneurial behaviour tends to satisfy rather than maximize returns. Satisficing behaviour has considerable value in market creation in order to manage inputs at an acceptable overall level for the range of opportunities. Thus, investment is made on an affordable loss basis because not every opportunity comes to fruition. Committed resources at the point of failure are sunk costs constituting affordable loss<br><br>A key objective is risk management and thus avoidance of overstretching resources | Project businesses are typically cash generators. Therefore, cash-flow management is critical. Profit margins are important but maximization is less important than the return on capital employed and can lead to satisfying behaviour rather than profit optimization<br><br>BDM pursuit of clients on an affordable loss basis<br><br>Project markets, project bidding and project execution are high risk. Behavioural commitments are made prior to pre-qualification. Subsequently, resource commitments are also made upon an affordable loss basis. Resource commitments are firmed up during the bid stages |
| **Locality and context** | Locality concerns geographical and physical attributes<br><br>Context includes supply chain specificity and stakeholder configurations. It includes the specificity of social and industrial networks of personal and organizational actors<br><br>Factors of locality and context increase specificity from the supplier viewpoint. Locality and context add the need to form the market for each transaction anew | Some projects are delivered in the place of inception, for example change management projects or R&D projects. Many projects are sited outside an organization's physical boundary. There are relational spaces created by the temporary multi-organizational project teams<br><br>Project markets are to a large degree negotiated from the bottom-up on an aggregated basis at the front-end |
| **Iterative commitments** | Entrepreneurial commitments and alliances are adaptive and open-ended | Commitments may not create the market, but they do help shape projects<br><br>Iterative commitments can be built during business development especially where BDMs are empowered prior to bid management |

| *Principles and conditions* | *General characteristics* | *Project-related characteristics* |
|---|---|---|
| | | The configuration of commitments contributes towards developing win-strategies. Value for each client derives from an evolving proposition and its configuration<br>Resources may be allocated procedurally bottom-up and substantively top-down according to company strategies<br>Service inconsistency and discontinuity between project stages from the front-end to completion constrain iterative commitments or their beneficial effects |
| **Alliance partners** | Alliances for entrepreneurs are predominantly structured around opportunities<br>Entrepreneurs nurture stakeholder and industrial networks to reach satisfactory outcomes<br>The resultant product-cum-service is contingent on who the partners are and how alliance partners interface<br>Formal alliances create new organizations | Outsourcing may involve coalitions, alliances or joint ventures of specialist supplier organizations |

*Source*: Developed from Sarasvathy and Dew (2005).

Morris et al. (2005) state that establishing guiding entrepreneurial principles is a matter of prioritizing and setting out some simple rules to guide the strategy (cf. Nelson and Winter, 1982; Eisenhardt and Sull, 2001), which has some resonance with strategy as practice (Whittington, 1996).

## *Implications for the project management theorization and practice*

There is little literature on entrepreneurialism in the project management domain, and entrepreneurial marketing in project markets has been almost totally overlooked in research to date. The purpose of this subsection is therefore to explore a series of points, potential links and the extent of resonance with the management of projects

(MoP) at the front-end and for execution, as well as cite the very few touch points within the existing project management literature.

Project markets are typically characterized by intense competition that can lead to defensive action to survive, which includes the defenders or leads towards differentiators and prospectors (cf. Porter, 1980). There is some indirect correspondence (but not a mechanistic link) between the transactional and relational approaches to market management. Project transactions embody unpredictable and ambiguous content (Clegg et al., 2002; Pich et al., 2002; Beech et al., 2004; see Table 6.1). New opportunities can induce new, sometimes temporary, routines requiring management flexibility to:

- Reconfigure or reshape the market, although this is uncommon in project businesses, such initiatives more frequently coming from clients (e.g. Linder, 1994; Smyth and Edkins, 2007);
- Strategically induce and shape projects at the front-end (cf. **Chapters 4** and **5**);
- Tactically respond to new or emergent project requirements (cf. Geraldi, 2008).

Routines to reconfigure or reshape the market will typically reside at board level and operate top-down and bottom-up with other senior and mid-management to create new opportunities through integrated product and service solutions, new contract types and procurement routes.

Strategic routines for projects may reside at the programme or project levels. A set of formal routines is needed, not necessarily as comprehensive as the management system for relationship marketing (Figure 4.6), but a set for BDM and bid management, for example as set out in Figure 6.1. Entrepreneurial marketing is high risk, that is, embraces risk as opportunity as means of management rather than risk mitigation. Therefore the routines and specific procedures must be carefully managed. Innovation typically requires a strong framework of controlled parameters, within which considerable room for manoeuvre is provided. The iterative and incremental approach to entrepreneurial marketing means that regular touch points within each stage at the front-end are needed to reassess the market and exchange opportunity. This is in order to effectively manage resource commitments and pursue affordable loss tactics (Figure 6.1; cf. Table 6.1).

Action and (informal) routines that release business development capacity to pursue opportunities are suited to entrepreneurial marketing. In the project context, releasing capacity is dependent upon managing the interface between BDM and those responsible for developing win-strategies, mobilizing supply chains and tendering actions. This interface is conceptually the beginning of the transition or interface between the MoP front-end and project management execution.

The project literature has referred to effectuation in regard to high-tech start-ups (Midler and Silberzahn, 2008) and ambiguity reduction in new product development (Brun and Saetre, 2008). These types of projects are typically conducted in-house. It has yet to be addressed directly in project businesses. Entrepreneurial marketing and the effectual variant have received scant attention in project markets. Bearing in mind

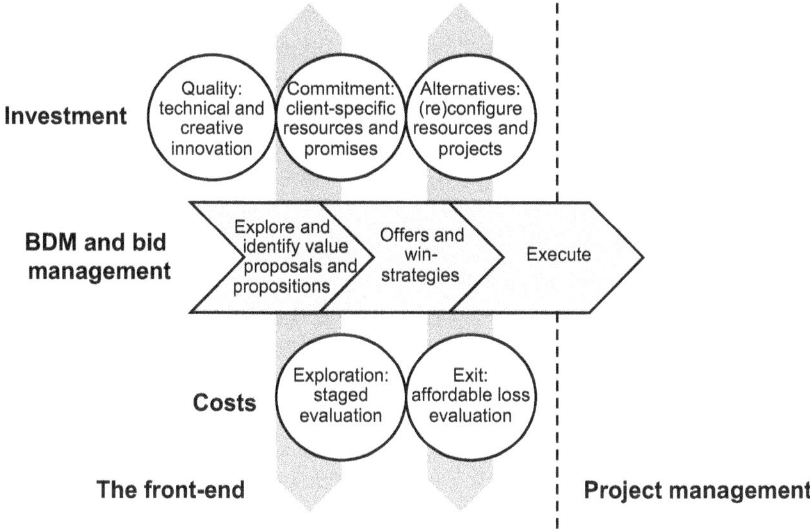


**FIGURE 6.1** Entrepreneurial marketing and management routines

marketing is frequently hidden (cf. Biemans et al., 2010) or conducted as a separate function, Marketing typically being confined to promotion with limited budgets in project organizations (cf. Workman et al., 1998; Homburg et al., 2008) and BDM historically isolated in the project lifecycle in research and practice. This is beginning to break down incrementally (**Chapter 4**). Entrepreneurial marketing offers further scope to do so, as in effectual marketing: *Organization and environment roll backwards and forwards into each other in an interactive and iterative process* (Sarasvathy et al., 2008: 345).

The entrepreneur carries out marketing and sales without necessarily recognizing this, activities being integrated in effectual mindsets, and introduced or harnessed in large organizations. This leads to the way marketing and BDM in particular are conducted and could be carried out entrepreneurially.

## Business development management in theory and practice

Can entrepreneurial marketing be linked to BDM in mainstream project businesses? Marketing and BDM have been criticized for being too scattergun in project businesses because of the lack of marketing strategy and applied rigor (e.g. Pearce, 1992; Smyth, 2000; Cova et al., 2002; Preece et al., 2003). Practices have been developing incrementally. Today, these analyses lack some substance at the client management or segment level of programme management. At the project level, a degree of tactical flexibility is needed to pursue a range of opportunities and explore shaping an exchange to tease out whether it will mature into a concrete bidding opportunity. The increased demands from many clients for detailed information at prequalification stage and for many public sector clients that fix requirements for transparency around price comparison at bid stage provide some constraints for entrepreneurial action. Most constraints are internal to the project business, including risk management processes, issues of resource commitment and project specific investment, process rigidities around being task-centric and norms of the organizational culture. These are real constraints, sometimes referred to as 'blockers' on the ground, yet tactical entrepreneurial marketing can work within the spaces left and more strategic approaches can break down and through some of the constraints (cf. Markides, 1999). Where one option does not reach fruition, the low-level investment or the sunk costs committed to date are written off. This requires a balancing act between a scattergun and highly targeted approach, in order to apply the affordable loss principle set out in Table 6.1. Therefore, effective BDM may require keeping more project opportunities live in the early pipeline stages, before prequalification or before bidding, than would be necessary in many other markets. Thus, opportunities are pursued and resources are committed until decisions on pursuit or withdrawal can be taken on an affordable loss basis. These are important assessments that strike rate calculations fail to encompass.

In entrepreneurial management, new organizations can be formed from teams or networks of individuals to undertake something that cannot be done by any one party (Birley, 1985). In project environments, this occurs at two possible levels: (i) alliances and joint ventures to undertake projects and (ii) TMOs for particular projects. New (associate or subsidiary) firms may emanate in some cases. Of course, these are only meaningful in this context if they are formed in entrepreneurial ways to secure and undertake a project that could not otherwise be undertaken.

BDM is conducted one step at a time (cf. Sarasvathy and Dew, 2005) to address the principles and market conditions (see Table 6.1 and Figure 6.1). This effectual logic dovetails with relationship marketing and management (Arndt, 1979; Dwyer et al., 1987; Morgan and Hunt, 1994). The only qualification is that effectual resource allocation tends to be procedural rather than substantive (Sarasvathy and Dew, 2005), therefore under relationship marketing, certain generic capabilities and value propositions can be mustered and tailored to fit specific client and project requirements, developing new capacity around client programmes that may add to the generic menu subsequently (**Chapter 4**; see also **Chapters 9** and **11**). This has a strong top-down element to it, whereas the formation is almost entirely bottom-up in entrepreneurial marketing around the response to (challenging and complex) client and project needs. This needs a certain amount of budget decentralization with delegated responsibility to the BDM function, specifically to BDMs and bid management teams. Commercial and operational directors, who might otherwise decide on what to spend resources upon and control the expenditure, will ensure committed resources stay within overall limits and then retrospectively evaluate the success, that is, whether particular types of commitment on an affordable loss basis have a better strike rate than others. This in turn is an assessment of the entrepreneurial capabilities.

Being entrepreneurial will primarily focus upon project content. That is the current focus amongst most project businesses. How the project is delivered, the associated services that determine the service experience during delivery, will not normally fall within the realm of entrepreneurial consideration. There may be service content bundled as part of the technical offer, for example Operations and Maintenance services in conjunction with the capital project asset. Technical and technological innovation provides opportunity for entrepreneurial activity. The technical and technological foci will suit project businesses that have strong technical departments and R&D capabilities. It will also suit those in a BDM role with entrepreneurial tendencies who have extensive networks to identify other partners and suppliers through their industrial network who can make innovative contributions to projects. On occasions, the network will be used as a bridge to identify other suppliers who offer different ways of conducting an activity or task or role models from outside the network from whom lessons can be learnt, as was done for example on supplier and transport logistics for the London Olympics 2012. Project networks contain entrepreneurs who pursue project opportunities (Manning, 2010). Indeed, networks can be described as entrepreneurial because they form 'opportunity structures' (e.g. Elfring and Hulsink, 2007; Manning, 2010), although some networks are more conducive to this potential than others. Networks are also important resources for both current and future opportunities (DeFillippi and Arthur, 1998; Grabher, 2004; Manning, 2010).

BDMs qualify their organizations and build alliances with partners to meet client demands. Between prequalification and tendering, indeed for tendering, win-strategy development can be built up using any of the marketing approaches. BDMs proceed beyond information management of project pipelines by building relationships and/or making commitments to clients both as 'soft' promises and 'hard' resources to develop win-strategies when bidding. Entrepreneurially, they evaluate potential projects based upon procedural and iterative assessments (see also Table 6.1). BDMs tend to act relatively independently of senior management (cf. Schindehutte et al., 2008), posing budgetary problems for large project businesses and continuity problems as to whether bid managers and project managers act upon commitments made. Few project firms have developed suitable capabilities at the operational level of BDM. Entrepreneurial marketing is more easily sanctioned when conducted by senior management, especially at board level.

Fact Box 6.1 sets out an example of BDM led at board level for bid management. The case involves a complex and highly novel UK public private partnership (PPP) infrastructure project. It was instigated through an imaginative proposal, which started to 'take hold' within the public sector client at strategic board level over a few weeks. It was rapidly sanctioned as technically and commercially viable. It was then fast tracked through the protocols. As a bespoke project, it created its own micro market at the level of the exchange. Client and private project intelligence are the raw marketing material for project businesses to make commitments. This was scant on the ground. The project coincided with other events that would enhance its value. Early recognition of the distinctiveness proved fundamental to the way the project was developed and bid. There was insufficient time to influence the project scoping and content. Developing win-strategies and configuring execution was organized around (i) the selection of partners, (ii) specialist technical expertise, and (iii) innovative methods for service provision. Fact Box 6.1 provides evidence as to how entrepreneurial marketing can be conducted, especially focusing on bid management.

## FACT BOX 6.1 ENTREPRENEURIAL SKILL SETS APPLIED TO AN INNOVATIVE PROJECT

Three international multi-divisional project businesses, each leading a consortium, expressed interest in the project: ProCo, BranCo and StronCo. ProCo and BranCo had secured a considerable amount of repeat business from this client. BranCo had a 5-year track record, implementing relationship marketing principles and focusing upon win-strategies that incorporated client understanding. However, the BranCo expression of interest did not arise through the usual 'traffic light' system for qualifying projects. It arose from the private network of an Operational Director who became determined to champion a bid – the entrepreneur for BranCo – yet the project was not high priority in its portfolio. StronCo was inactive in the sector, yet had a track record for delivery of innovative projects across the world and has established a strong market reputation for taking on challenging projects in terms of organizational and technical innovation. A main Board Director from StronCo led the expression of interest and bid. ProCo had worked for the client before, and it is noted for its non-traditional ways of working.

There were only three credible infrastructure manufacturer and operators (M&O) worldwide to meet a key PPP requirement. ProCo linked with the M&O having the lowest global market share. BranCo quickly moved to form an alliance with the M&O that StronCo had already worked with a decade previously on another innovative project. StronCo teamed up with the M&O, which already had an advisory input at the feasibility stage to the engineering consultants appointed by the client. StronCo perceived the steelwork component to be project-critical and elected to nominate a leading steelwork subcontractor, despite the steelwork being circa 40 per cent of the project costs. BranCo also identified a steelwork partner, which was insistent on payment in euros (€) when the project was otherwise conducted in sterling (£), potential exchange rate movements later causing significant pricing problems. They chose consultants of international standing with reputations for innovative technical capabilities.

BranCo had strong established relationships with all the key DMU members on the client CapEx side. They mobilized existing networks to strengthen their position and get responses to specific questions. They also used these questions to test ideas about how they might build a win-strategy. The project team was led by a 'grey beard' to convey solidity and safety. StronCo had to build relationships from scratch. Recognizing they were at a disadvantage, they put enormous effort into relationship building, rapidly building a team that mirrored the client decision-making unit (DMU) in numbers and responsibilities. They fielded their complete team and experts at interviews to show commitment. They worked at *being* a team to which the client could relate. ProCo now withdrew, probably due to its weaker M&O alliance.

There was little scope to shape project content. One area of innovative shaping concerned health and safety, particularly emergency evacuation as a critical service factor of the project in use. The M&Os proposed method statements and resource needs, but through dialogue with the client DMU, it was made clear that the different context and set of cultural norms on this project meant that there would need to be an alternative solution. StronCo radically revised its evacuation plan. The final solution was effective and cheap, and independent advice concluded it was sufficiently robust. This proved a decisive factor.

Project finance was not involved, the client paying the CapEx. Cost escalation was largely the contractor responsibility, and the published cost was c. £45m. The selection criteria were communicated to the bidders. During the bid, client attention increasingly focused upon the OpEx, which StronCo proved more adept at reading. OpEx was also a decisive factor in ways that were opaque in the selection criteria. StronCo paid particular attention to the post-submission stage of questions and clarifications, using their responses and submissions as a promotional initiative to help the client selection team imagine how the project might be presented to the public. This lent greater confidence to the client coupled with the innovations and integrated team presentations. At this stage the BranCo relationship strength was losing advantage and the lead BDM had been somewhat displaced by the Operations Director. StronCo appeared 'hungry' for the project, whereas it was a low priority for BranCo. As the outsider, StronCo realized they had to exhibit an above average level of entrepreneurship, applying a bottom-up iterative project commitment until they sensed they had the advantage. StrongCo secured the project, which was completed successfully.

*Source*: Edkins and Smyth (2013).

Integration and strong cross-functional coordination is needed between BDMs and bid management for effective entrepreneurial marketing. There needs to be mutual understanding of the processes in order to inject the value propositions into the offer. This is comparable with the relationship marketing approach (**Chapter 4**). There also needs to be some touch points in the bid management stage (Figure 6.1). It is unlikely that the project business will withdraw at the bid stage. The sunk costs may be quite high and thus the loss unaffordable, but this is always in proportion to the risk being incurred so it is impossible to say 'never' to unaffordable loss. More likely is that the costs are increasing along with the risk and that it is necessary to marginally reign back on the commitments and offer.

The entrepreneurial manager is creative; they are not maintainers and need to pass the management baton. Project businesses are advised to operate a relay team approach where the different functionaries perform different stages with adequate handovers for promise fulfillment and service consistency. BDM involvement is unlikely to remain throughout, except where accounts are managed in pairs whereby entrepreneurial managers are teamed up with maintainers for client relationship management. This represents the contrast between affective or experiential management based upon interpretative sense making and conviction and the rational cognitive management methods. How is continuity managed at this stage? The baton can take the form of a register. Project businesses have risk registers, which typically focus upon the potential negative manifestations. Theoretically risk can also embrace opportunities and therefore commitments and non-contractual promises made to the client and put in the offer can be recorded in the risk register or a parallel commitment register for the project management team to deliver against (see also **Chapter 4**). Entrepreneurialism, hence entrepreneurial marketing, embraces risk as opportunity and so this would be an appropriate way forward to ensure consistent delivery along project lifecycles.

Project managers are described as entrepreneurs as they bring ideas and creativity with personal strength and sometimes controversy to bear (Lindgren and Packendorff, 2003b). In this sense, they are resource investigators, bringing experience and tacit knowledge to bear on problem solving, which can at times be entrepreneurial (cf. Belbin, 1984). Entrepreneurial competencies have been cited as beneficial for successful project execution (Lampel, 2001). New ideas are exploited in everyday operations (cf. March, 1995). In this sense, entrepreneurial acts are similar to projects (Waddock and Post, 1991). Project businesses can encourage entrepreneurial strategies for action (Zahra et al., 1999). Many entrepreneurial acts can take the form of temporary organizing processes (Packendorff, 1995). As such entrepreneurial acts are temporary projects. It has been put this way:

> The project-based view of entrepreneurship proposed here instead focuses on the organising of entrepreneurial acts (action-orientation). Such entrepreneurial acts can be, but are not limited to, enterprise start-ups. . . . Saying that entrepreneurial acts are temporary projects means that people can perform several entrepreneurial acts during a lifetime – in different ways and with different results (seriality). Entrepreneurial acts are also viewed as collective ones, organised by several actors in actor networks temporarily coupled together by a somewhat common mission (collectivity).
>
> (Lindgren and Packendorff, 2003b: 86).

Lundin and Söderholm (1995) suggest that such temporary organizing involves four sub-processes over a project lifecycle, shifting in importance. These are action-based entrepreneurship, fragmentation for commitment building, planned isolation, and institutionalized termination. They see advantage in creative assembling and dissembling of organizations and structuring of activity from the entrepreneurial perspective. This is not to be conflated with fragmentation and isolated activities that are the product of incoherent systems and a lack of integration that is characteristic of many project organizations. Entrepreneurial activity tends towards holism and integration on formal and informal bases.

During execution, decisions are not always in the best long-term interests of the project business, or in the short-term interest of the client. Key project management personnel in terms of relationships and tacit knowledge held can be moved on to other projects (Smyth, 2000; cf. Baiden et al., 2006). This may look like an entrepreneurial move to secure the next project, however, it is at the expense of repeat business and programme management. This is not quite the type of 'creative destruction' that embodies the innovative entrepreneurship from the Schumpeterian perspective. It is essentially purely transactional.

Project contracts are incomplete. Requirements are seldom fully articulated by the client and conveyed in the requirements documentation. Requirements can change too. The tactical response at the project level is the only way to address these emergent requirements. Some emergent requirements are impossible to consider. Some are possible, leaving scope for a response, which can be entrepreneurial. However, new or emergent requirements are often perceived as deviations from project plans and method statements by project management teams (Smyth, 2013b; cf. Vaughan, 1999; Orr and Scott, 2008; Hällgren and Söderholm, 2010). This is a constraint to response generally and for entrepreneurial action specifically.

Whilst marketing and BDM are not directly involved in the execution stage if entrepreneurial marketing is pursued, what happens during execution is pertinent in additional ways. Entrepreneurial project managers and a more widespread project management function have a bearing on marketing once the capabilities are recognized. First, it enhances the opportunity for BDMs to sell the services with entrepreneurial content. Second, the interaction between entrepreneurial marketing and entrepreneurial project management provides what would be a rare or unique opportunity to enhance creativity and innovation through that dynamic interaction.

Entrepreneurial marketing can be linked with relationship marketing. There is opportunity for firms to develop commitment to and capabilities for entrepreneurial marketing (see Fact Box 6.1). If captured and transferred, entrepreneurial acts can be developed into capabilities that are rolled out at programme level. This is not straightforward. Project business strategies and structures do tend to support individual and team activity, yet the means to capture and systematization action and behaviour is the challenge that extends beyond the technical content, which is more transferrable. Entrepreneurial ability is also a scarce resource. Thus in many cases entrepreneurial marketing may be better suited to operating within a framework of another approach. Several options have been identified or inferred up to this point:

- Benefit can be derived from reconstituting a market (Andrews and Smith 1996; Menon et al., 1999), which might take the form of a project business working through BDM and particularly senior management with client counterparts to reconfigure a transaction or reframe the exchange. Historically, this type of initiative has largely been client driven, as was the case for the construction contracts for London Heathrow Airport Terminal 5 (Davies et al., 2009), which has been a major influence on subsequent megaproject procurement, such as the London 2012 Olympic programme and Cross Rail. Project businesses can be partnering and more proactive in this types of development – entrepreneurial shift from being predominantly market takers to market makers. This has an overarching influence within which another marketing approach exists.

- There is sometimes the need for breakthrough strategies in marketing (Markides, 1999) at a strategic level for projects, where entrepreneurial marketing can develop alternative resource configurations to shape projects. This represents adding entrepreneurial marketing into a relationship or project marketing approach to provide a creative 'shock' to those processes (**Chapters 4** and **5**).
- Nurture of customers in industrial networks and stakeholders is undertaken by initiative albeit guided by systems and procedures at times (cf. Sarasvathy, 2010). This provides scope for entrepreneurial action to identify innovative and creative solutions that fulfill specific client needs. It may result in informal alliances, partnerships and joint ventures on occasions. This helps spread risk as well as lever value. This is more than simply identifying value in an industrial network or using supply chain management techniques. The emphasis is upon the creative and innovative.
- Entrepreneurial BDMs can work alongside and with others operating another marketing approach. The relationship marketing paradigm is more conducive than the transactional marketing mix approach because relationship building can form an important part of making commitments, developing iterations and securing partners (Table 6.1). Relationship marketing requires robust systems to be effective. This can work well for entrepreneurial marketing, but as noted, more touch points for assessment are needed to progress iterative development of opportunities on an affordable loss basis. There must be room for manoeuvre within such a framework.
- Entrepreneurial project management or entrepreneurial project managers can provide increased sales opportunities for BDMs where they are using relationship or project marketing modes of operations, providing the relationship marketing commitments allow ring fencing of particular project managers or their teams for project opportunities and in a way that is not at the expense of client management and programme management for the project business. This requires rigorous portfolio and programme management decisions from the 'corporate centre' as the implications extend beyond the project level.

The ability of project businesses to align their capabilities to changing client needs poses a marketing challenge. An entrepreneurial capability can be the internal driver to induce new capabilities that can be taken into the marketplace. The advantage of this type of generation is that it is conducted from the bottom-up, that is, out of a particular client and project need, which can be captured and made available at a programme level for future projects. There is no advance top-down strategy to commit resources to develop a capability before it is known if such a capability is to be valued by clients.

The moot point is that some of these activities, particularly concerning BDM are most likely being conducted to an extent already. It is not currently recognized as marketing because practitioners have yet to articulate it in this way and arguably have been lacking the conceptual tools to do so. Researchers have paid little attention to marketing and project marketing for a project management perspective to date. Researchers concerned with the marketing of projects have not theorized nor investigated entrepreneurial marketing on the ground to date to see how prevalent practices are.

## Conclusion

Entrepreneurial marketing may be implicit in project businesses, and therefore, researchers have had a partial picture of the extent of marketing to date. Practitioners may miss opportunities because they are unaware of the potential of applying entrepreneurial marketing principles in their organizations. The analysis of entrepreneurial marketing in project markets has made several significant contributions towards addressing these issues:

1. *Nascent entrepreneurial marketing.* The conceptual analysis has reviewed the existing marketing and project management literature. The analysis and the little evidence that is available strongly suggest that there are entrepreneurial practices at work in need of understanding and articulation. To the extent that the issues become fully articulated gives rise to prescription and theorization. The point reached is one of scoping this field.
2. *Entrepreneurial marketing* and *relationship marketing.* To the extent that entrepreneurial marketing is present and could evolve, there is synergy with relationship marketing. Complementarity in practice needs careful managing with a number of management touch points required.
3. *Marketing lag.* Whilst marketing development has been founded on the theory-practice 'gap', and thus marketing implicitly and explicitly needs to be taken seriously in project businesses, the size of the gap is probably exaggerated. Entrepreneurial marketing fills some of the gap. The current lag behind other industries and the perceived lack of rigor in practice may in part be explained by the presence of entrepreneurial marketing.
4. *Actionable knowledge.* There is scope for further developments, particularly connecting tactical thinking and detailed BDM. There is also the reminder that marketing has been implemented with high degrees for partiality across most types of project business, which is characterized by a lack of management support and rigorous systems. Entrepreneurial marketing might appear to offer a 'light touch' in this respect, but requires coordinating mechanisms in a strong framework of management control to be effective. With start-up businesses, that rigor is embedded in the purpose of the individual or thinking of a small team of entrepreneurs. In large project businesses, it needs management, embedded into organizational routines.

This chapter set out to analyze the theoretical and applied characteristics of entrepreneurial marketing and how these are internally managed. The theory and alignment with actual and potential practice derived from theory has been presented, which has largely focused upon scoping this field. Theorization would suggest there is considerable scope for (i) anticipating entrepreneurial marketing to be currently implicit and made explicit through future empirical research and (ii) for entrepreneurial marketing to be used to guide practice. There are overlapping concepts with relationship marketing and the project marketing variant, which add weight to this evaluation. There are also potential interfaces between the two, further reinforcing the strength of entrepreneurial marketing as a concept for project businesses. The full scope in practice, and thus the weaknesses, has yet to be explored. One potential weakness has been inferred from the partial application of marketing principles. Entrepreneurial marketing as rhetoric is no reason to rebadge current practice and abstain from implementing management support systems. This would be a major weakness and largely render it ineffective.

There were ten substantive issues identified at the start of the book and entrepreneurial marketing contributes those commented upon below.

**SI no. 1:** ***Market Management*** and business development as a concept provide an umbrella in which marketing and BDM reside. Entrepreneurial marketing includes action and behaviour that is broader than marketing in a pure sense, although marketing can also be seen as all-encompassing itself (Kotler, 2003; Kotler et al., 1996). Entrepreneurialism is a means of market management and business development, and thus, entrepreneurial marketing is the most closely associated concept to these high-level constructs. Entrepreneurial marketing is intrinsically proactive and generative in the marketplace. The potential to address substantive issues from this concept are considerable, but have yet to be fully operationalized in research and practice.

**SI no. 3:** ***Marketing Investment and Portfolio Management*** presents an interesting challenge in project markets where there are strong market pressures to keep investment low. Entrepreneurial marketing does not particularly contribute to portfolio management, especially from a top-down perspective, but offers a bottom-up affordable loss approach to investment. This helps address the investment issue identified on a low-risk basis, although the wider context is pursuit of high-risk opportunities.

**SI no. 5:** ***Marketing and BDM*** is frequently isolated in project businesses, entrepreneurial marketing facilitating cross-functional working with bid management and coordinated handovers with project management. This is easiest, as far as the available evidence suggests, where BDM has a strong director level input or leadership (Fact Box 6.1).

**SI no. 8:** ***Cross-functional Systems and Coordination Mechanisms*** have been lacking. Whilst relationship marketing requires a steady buildup of integrated systems, entrepreneurial marketing is less demanding, cross-functional working mainly focused at the BDM–bid management–project management interfaces. However, this assumes entrepreneurial marketing is the only approach employed. Strong coordination in a controlled management framework is necessary to be effective.

**SI no. 9:** ***Marketing and Managing the Project Lifecycle*** provides a key focus. Added to what has been covered in considering the other substantive issues, entrepreneurial project management can act back to reinforce the role of BDM yielding sales strength for differentiation in the marketplace.

**SI no. 10:** ***Marketing and Value Creation*** is central to the concept and a considerable challenge to much of the project management literature that tends to think that value is either added during execution or added in the latter stages of the front-end. Entrepreneurial marketing focuses upon configuring the context and shaping the project to form value that the client wants and adding value where possible. The focus is likely to be more on technical rather than service content. Although integrating services into the offer is included, the resultant service experience around how a project is delivered is largely excluded.

The main message therefore is that entrepreneurial marketing provides fertile ground for conceptual exploration and practical application. It can help manage markets where resource constraints are an important consideration. There are several main *recommendations* for research that flow from the analysis:

A. Research needs to be conducted into entrepreneurial marketing in project businesses. This involves investigating the extent of the activity, by whom it is conducted, how it fits into the organization and what the outcomes are.
B. Research into the interface of entrepreneurial marketing with other approaches and modes of operation.
C. Further detailed theorization and conceptual development of entrepreneurial marketing in different types of project business.

There are several main *recommendations* for practice that flow from the analysis:

1. Increased management awareness to assess the current application and potential for entrepreneurial marketing.
2. Putting in place systems to capture capabilities developed on a project specific basis in order that the capability can be rolled out for future projects.
3. Personnel reviews and career paths that acknowledge entrepreneurial activity.

In summary, the adoption of entrepreneurial marketing has yet to be fully considered in theory and practice. The scoping stage is now underway. It is part of the project business storehouse from a management viewpoint in the sense that it is not 'grain to be sold, but seed to be sown' in the marketplace.

# 7

# A PROJECT MANAGEMENT FOCUS TOWARDS MANAGING MARKETS

## Introduction

This chapter takes a closer look at project management, the function responsible for delivery during execution. This is where performance is decisive. There are conceptual links between the marketing and BDM functions and the project management function. The linkage is not a simple linear process over the project lifecycle where business development managers (BDMs) position the project business for the prequalification stage with project management at the other end of the lifecycle responsible for execution, completion, commissioning and handover. From the marketing perspective, there are several factors of interplay in both directions, which can be summarized from the analysis and discussion to date as the following:

1. BDMs are aware of the technical capabilities of the project business and of the project management capabilities in order to know what to sell. Capabilities fall into two categories:

    a. *Project capabilities* that are the quality of the technical and technological skills derived from expertise and experience necessary to meet and sometimes exceed requirements, which generally are initiated at project level, but become embedded at programme and portfolio levels to spread and embed these capabilities across the relevant parts of the business;
    b. *Organizational capabilities* that have their origins in the coordinating and integrating mechanisms that are 'softer' issues to coordinate and integrate technical and service provision to add value that exceed requirements.

2. The BDM function anticipates and understands client requirements at a level of detail aligned to the marketing approach adopted and capabilities.
3. Project managers advise the BDM function and for some project businesses help configure the inputs at bid management stage.

4. Project managers ensure they are aware of what has been offered, especially added value beyond the documented requirements and deliver accordingly.
5. Project managers and the BDM function monitor delivery to ensure the value committed as non-contractual promises is delivered.
6. Project managers and the BDM function capture lessons learned for processing and applying on future projects, thus linking the project to the programme level to improve the position in the marketplace.
7. Project managers and the BDM function need to work together to provide service consistency and continuity on a project and continuity between projects, including relationship management where a relationship marketing or project marketing approach is being used.

Project managers tend to perceive the project as the unit of focus. Marketing and BDM do likewise under the transactional marketing mix. The relationship marketing approaches place similar weight upon the client as the unit of focus. Researchers tend to reflect the same picture. In most other sectors, the production orientation, product-centric or goods-dominant perspectives have added the complimentary customer-centric and service-dominant perspectives to activities and their businesses. The business models and earning logic change accordingly. Project businesses remain somewhat entrenched in the equivalent of the production orientation, which is a task-centric and project management perspective rather than complimentary customer or client-centric perspective (Handy, 1997; Pryke and Smyth, 2006). This includes project businesses transitioning to a greater client emphasis, managing the business primarily in terms of projects. The precise position adopted depends upon how comprehensively the seven issues above have been addressed. Addressing the issues involves two levels. First is direct management; second are the support systems and procedures to help articulate and encourage aligned management.

Using the above as an assessment of where project businesses are positioned applies to practitioners, yet it equally applies to researchers. While marketing and BDM are conceptually distinct functions, it is the level of integration with other functions and organizational actors that is significant for effectiveness in the marketplace. Integration certainly provides an important theme for this chapter on project management. Another theme that is picked up and developed is the delivery channel, which argues that project management is intrinsically and fundamentally located within marketing simply because the project is the marketing delivery channel for the product and service components. The two themes are related as projects of integrated elements and components. Projects provide the preconditions for another activity that is core to the client, from which they yield benefits that have impact for the client and its stakeholders.

The main *aims* of this chapter are to address:

A. The changes that projects and hence project businesses are experiencing, as a function of the changing client needs expressed through the market as demand.
B. The project as a delivery channel is fundamental to understanding how these changes are and will be manifested.

C. Marketing and BDM as being inextricably linked to project management and vice versa, the performance of the one being dependent on the performance of the other.

The main message of this chapter is that the project management is intrinsically embedded in marketing as a delivery channel. This perspective has no direct effect upon operations, but it shifts the theoretical lens and practitioner perspective as to how coordination and integration is structured and the roles of functions, particularly marketing and project management, which affects the understanding and conduct of operations. This message connects to the broader concepts of market management and business development for it will become clear that these are increasingly important concepts for managing survival, or to put it another way, keeping investment and fixed costs at low levels is unsustainable as the sole survival strategy, especially in markets of demanding clients and high complexity. Project businesses appreciating this by strategic design or post-hoc rationalization are and will be amongst the most successful, driving many other project businesses into action as followers.

## Delivery channel, systems integrators and integrated solutions

The concept of the project as a delivery channel was proposed in **Chapter 1**, and developed to an extent in **Chapter 3**. Thus, the case for arguing it as a delivery channel has been outlined briefly. A more thorough exposition is required in relation to project management as a function and with the basis of a good background in marketing of projects set out in the preceding four chapters.

The essential reasons for organizations to select a project as the mode of delivery is that its completion is usually a pre-condition for another core activity (Turner, 1999; Turner and Keegan, 2000), for example power station and power lines to generate and transmit energy, an IT system to process and deliver the appropriate information to different locations to support other operating functions, a fashion show to market designs that now need showcasing. The project is untypically the end product in itself. Perhaps a film is an end product but this is still a means to provide an instructive or entertainment experience.

A large number of projects are conducted in-house. Design and R&D functions have been and are often run as projects, although there is a trend to increasingly outsource these functions. Complex projects set apart from the core activity of an organization are very often outsourced. Realization is difficult to routinize for these projects, especially where they carry high levels of uncertainty and attendant risk. Project businesses are contracted to deliver them as specialist providers. Projects have formed a considerable part of gross domestic product (GDP) for industrializing and developing nations, especially for transportation and built environment infrastructure projects. The demand for complex solutions for non-core activities has made projects as a main means for provision. Estimates vary considerably, but the range of GDP estimates is 25–35 per cent (McKeeman, 2002; EURAM SIG, 2012).

Management has clearly recognized the significance by selecting projects as the means of delivery, even if business schools and management research have still to fully recognize this, although the initial signs of change are now in train.

Requirements are difficult to articulate from the client side. The benefits are also difficult to quantify. Articulating these needs at the front-end from the business case to the requirements specification is part of the service. Bringing these needs to the market through a contract is what makes the project a delivery channel from the client standpoint. Integration is a major part to bring the set of components to the *place* of use or consumption by the project business. The argument can be built up from a simple analogous illustration. In the marketing mix, *place* is the delivery channel (**Chapter 3**). The marketing mix was in its heyday addressing mass-market consumer goods that were produced in one place and sold in another. The delivery channel was designed to get the goods from the factory gates to the place of sale. In this crude example, it involves transport from factory to warehouse, breakdown into smaller batches for distribution, transport from warehouse to retail outlets where they are then sold. The management or *logistics* ensures the various linear components to this process are conducted effectively and efficiently. Greater emphasis is at times placed upon efficiency than effective service, for example in deliveries of supplies to a construction site at the convenience of those managing the delivery rather than in timely ways. On the other hand, ready-mix concrete has to be delivered effectively to remain usable according to the rhythm of site work. The channel is far from sacrosanct. For some goods, mail order and internet shopping provide alternative delivery channels. Different types of product demand different channels, for example a tailor-made suit is purchased prior to production, to accommodate specific requirements, hence the contract modifies the delivery channel. The project combines production and delivery through the contract.

The delivery channel is largely linear. Project management shares some similarities on linearity, for example schedules and programmes even if sophisticated developments allow departure, such as critical path and last planner techniques. Project management is linear in the development of project plans with stage gates with departure from strict linearity by applying agile project management methodologies, for example SCRUM or XP. Projects are non-linear in a broader sense. Projects are delivered with a range of organizational actors, which are directly involved, notably subcontractors who work supply components in situ and undertake bundles of the work. Some components constitute a separate project, for example design projects and many subcontracts. Series of project businesses are engaged in putting in place all the elements, which may include design in some instances, for example on turnkey and PPP-type projects (where PPP stands for public private partnerships). These aspects also have strong interactive, cross-functional and inter-organizational characteristics as well as iterative processes that are sometimes difficult to rationalize against linearity.

Delivery channels therefore primarily concern managing services, the logistics, and integrating the stages. Many of the service components are produced and consumed simultaneously. What is being sold can be described as a *system*. This logistics type of delivery channel is a system. The selling of this service means that the organization is one type of *systems seller.* Projects are more complex and the non-linear activity means that the main or prime contractor is managing overlapping systems used by a series of different providers, which needs integrating into a single system, which provides the means of delivering the project to the client. This is the project management function. What is being sold in these cases is the ability to integrate systems, and the project management organization is a type of *systems integrator* (Page and Siemplenski, 1983). The systems integrator coordinates the component externally provided by others (Galbraith, 2002). The systems integrator acts as the main or prime contractor for a project. It has been put this way: *Some of the world's leading suppliers are developing strategies to move into the provision of innovative combinations of products and services as 'high-value integrated solutions' tailored to each customer's needs* (Davies, 2004: 727).

Construction had long since been practicing systems integration although it was defense contracting that drew particular attention to the specific project management role (e.g. Page and Siemplenski, 1983; Morris and Hough, 1987).

The involvement of a range of organizations in project delivery means that other project businesses are performing other types of roles. The role performed is other than being systems integrators. Subcontractors are assemblers, and to some extent, direct producers through transforming component parts into a product. These are the *systems sellers* providing integrated and specialist solutions within the project delivery mode. The systems seller provides the total product and service package for their component in the project delivery chain. This has become less attractive to many organizations as client demands have become and continue to be more demanding. This is partly a function of organizations focusing upon core business and partly a function of growing project complexity (Azimont et al., 1998; **Chapter 1**). Therefore, systems selling is increasingly left to specialist providers who manufacture, assemble and/or integrate related services to smaller component parts that themselves are now more complex, for example cladding systems for commercial buildings. The tendency has therefore been for project supply chains to become longer and supply clusters to be more intricate and subcontractors sub-subcontract to other specialists. This can compromise the systematic integration and result in 'value leakage'. It renders the role of systems integrator more challenging yet critical.

Other specialist organizations have been described as *solutions sellers* (e.g. Mattson, 1973). They are strategic service advisors, such as engineers, cost consultants and management consultants. The solution seller offers strategic advice, because many clients do not carry all the in-house expertise necessary to inform procurement and assess product and service quality, and monitor delivery according to requirements. The service component has increased and is increasing as a function of the general complexity of projects. Some projects are mostly about service content, for example a change management programme or projects that a management consultant is advising upon or delivering.

As service content is deepening, the systems integrator role is being increasingly asked to deliver service content in one of four ways: (i) embedded services, for example maintenance services forming part of the contract; (ii) comprehensive services that includes for example finance, operation and maintenance; (iii) distribution management for another market delivery channel; and (iv) products and services integrated as solutions (Wise and Baumgartner, 1999). Integrated solutions are more than bundling through customization and tailoring for the customer. Bundling work into work packages for ease of risk management tends to constrain integration (Smyth, 2013a). Fragmented value streams are brought together for integration (Hobday, 1998).

Therefore the project business is using project management to not only integrate the different components coming from each separate organization, but at the project level is also integrating the different types of project businesses that operate with different business logics: systems integration, systems seller and solutions seller. They are either integrated as types of suppliers drawn upon as a part of a broader network (e.g. Håkansson, 1982; Håkansson and Snehota, 1995; Cova and Salle, 2005), or integrated as part of the immediate delivery temporary multi-organizational team or TMO (Cherns and Bryant, 1984), together forming part of the project coalition (Winch, 2002). In project environments, single organizations are frequently systems and solutions sellers (cf. Davies et al., 2007).

The client is using a project business to act as the systems integrator because conceptually they are specialists with capabilities for integration. This is effectively the 'buy' rather than 'make' decision. Most project businesses are more capable of reasonably successful integration compared to clients. The two are brought together at the procurement–marketing interface (cf. Penrose, 1959; Davies, 2004). Any threat to the buy decision arises from clients recruiting experts and developing in-house project management capabilities. The long-term protection against this possibility is for project businesses to strengthen their position by investing in capabilities that are mobilized in accordance with intimate understanding of the customer and detailed knowledge of their business (Penrose, 1960). New capabilities can be developed in what has been termed vanguard projects, especially at the front-end (Brady and Davies, 2004). The outcome has parallels with capability development through entrepreneurial marketing (**Chapter 6**). This lends potential for replication from learning and applying at the back-end, that is the next project if the generic attributes can be identified and focused towards client need on future projects (Davies et al., 2006). A framework for developing capabilities towards integrated solutions is shown in Figure 7.1. It shows the vertical and horizontal integration in summary form for both internal and external sources of value.

Where is the 'place' to which projects are delivered? The delivery channel is manifested in two spatial forms. The first is social space, which is typically either in the client organization to enhance effectiveness and efficiency or is linked to its own sales activity. An example of operations based is an IT system in a government department. An example of a project linked to sales activity is event management in the form of a product launch or fashion show. The second spatial form is physical space for delivery. An example is an oil and gas exploration platform or wind farm at sea or a new office for rent for a property developer.

**Scope of systems**

| | Vertical | Horizontal |
|---|---|---|
| **Internal** | Portfolio and programme management<br>Hierarchical, top-down direction through formal routines<br>Captured, bottom-up learning and capturing of informal routines | Client management and the relationship management system<br>Programme management<br>Cross-functional working<br>Project lifecycle integration<br>Co-located activities |
| **External** | Network relationship management and coordination<br>Supply chain management<br>Contract management | Network relationship management and coordination<br>Co-creation routines |

**Spread of activities**

**FIGURE 7.1** Developing systems integration for selling

*Source*: Adapted and developed from Davies (2004).

Thus, project businesses and project management are essentially structured around the market delivery channel. How does a project business address a market orientation with a client and service-centric focus in delivery? To use the transport delivery analogy, drivers can arrange the order of deliveries for their convenience or to suit customers, for example within a 2-hour window and structure their route accordingly. A system is needed to ensure action and behaviour follow the policy, for example just-in-time deliveries. Project management uses project management methodologies, but these are not inherently client-centric, and project managers tend not to adhere to them (Wells, 2011; Wells and Smyth, 2011). This persists where weak systems between the corporate–project interface exist (**Chapter 1**, **SI no. 6**; **Chapter 2**).

## Project management as delivery channel and marketing

Project management research has located marketing and business development at the periphery of the project domain (Pinto and Covin, 1992; Turner, 1995). This is echoed in a review of topics covered in the leading project management journals (Themistocleous and Wearne, 2000). The project management bodies of knowledge tend to see the marketing of projects as project-related communication in order to negotiate a fuzzy front-end, the internal linkages with project management and manage stakeholders (Lecoeuvre and Patel, 2009; cf. Cooper and Budd, 2007).

Project managers describe marketing as a project management task (Patel et al., 2012). Thus business development is present to support project management under their remit and terms (Lecoeuvre and Patel, 2009). It has been found by Patel et al. (2012) that half of the project managers they interviewed equated marketing to account management and the other half equated it to business development. Overall, project managers held the following perceptions:

- Marketing terminology is confusing,
- The best form of marketing is to do good work, to perform at the highest level and to create client satisfaction,
- Marketing communication for project promotion,
- Confusion exists between external or internal marketing.

This was far from a universal view. A vice president of a large health consulting firm stated: 'I never thought of marketing to include the management phase of the project' (cited in Patel et al., 2012: 22). At the front-end, BDM was perceived to adopt and implement the corporate approach to general management with a certain level of technical knowledge. The transfer of responsibilities comes at the proposal writing stage, which is a joint effort between BDM and project management for that firm.

Despite the practitioner view that marketing is a subset of project management and feeds project management, a conflict or tension is present where transactional approaches prevail. The project manager is encouraged to maximize profits by senior management. BDM and bid management functions are incentivized to reduce bid prices to secure contracts. The result is a disparity between bid price and profits, outturn costs and client satisfaction. At one level this can simply be seen as passive responses to intense market completion. At the strategic level, it shows a mismatch of aims and purpose over the management of projects lifecycle.

Project managers lack tactical marketing awareness, reinforcing the isolated position of marketing and BDM. There is rhetoric around coherent practices to rationalize action (cf. McDonald et al., 2011), yet the degree of incoherence is disguised by business jargon that hide the actual tensions and provide an illusion of integrated working (Smyth and Kusuma, 2013). Senior management tends to believe their organization is more customer and client orientated than others do (**Chapter 1**). There have been efforts in the project marketing literature to integrate business development with project operations (Cooper and Budd, 2007; **Chapter 5**). Using a sales funnel model, they applied project management techniques to rationalize the sales process and proposed involving project managers in qualifying bid opportunities. This does occur in some project businesses and is a positive function of engaging sales and operational staff in common effort. The funnelling is largely transactional marketing.

Cova and Salle (2005) tried to merge project marketing into project management across six dimensions. These are set out and developed as follows:

1. *The project*, secured through selling as a contract or a sales agreement as series of transactions as stage payments, conducted by temporary organizations formed

around a project to which resources are allocated. Interactions and serial transactions provide scope for relationship marketing to identify needs throughout the project lifecycle and across client programmes.

2. *Characteristics of projects* cover the discontinuity-uncertainty-complexity (D-U-C) framework, project marketing underscoring discontinuity between projects. Relationship marketing additionally emphasizes the customer and service consistency, thus feeding into client strategy, a broader approach to client management and project business P$^3$M. There has been a slow supply side adoption of P$^3$M, compared to a more integrated P$^3$M in demand side procurement strategies (Artto, 2001; Partington et al., 2005).
3. *Project lifecycles* are managed independently of project marketing which undertakes shaping at the front-end and management of the sleeping relationship at the back-end. This is a matter of sequencing rather than a lack of connection with project management. Artto (2001) has argued that front-end management underplays marketing and the customer relationship in two ways. First is the customer lifetime value: the worth of the customer rather than the worth of a project (cf. Smyth and Fitch, 2009). Second yet related is the management of the client relationship during the project lifecycle (Figure 4.6).
4. *Focus upon the approach* is essentially about having a client-centric view. Hereby is a link between marketing and project management performance to improve technical and service quality (Hackman and Wagman, 1995).
5. *Stakeholders* and management of mutual interests provide the basis for working across the network to secure projects with TMO support (project network), and secure empathetic suppliers (the buying network), aligned through the broader milieu of territorial sphere of interest any one project occupies (social and physical space).
6. *Project origin as given or jointly constructed* provides the basis front-end pre-work from a customer perspective (Pinto and Rouhiainen, 2001), innovative development, and how value is construed and co-created (Prahalad and Ramaswamy, 2004; Vargo and Lusch, 2004).

While Cooper and Budd (2007), along with practitioners have tried to subsume marketing within project management, project marketing has tried to locate project management within marketing. Project marketing researchers believe that project marketing is broader than project management (e.g. Cova and Hoskins, 1997; Cova et al., 2002; Lecoeuvre-Soudain and Deshayes, 2006; Cova and Salle, 2011), although project marketing ultimately has a residual focus on the project even when considering the sleeping relationship. Yet, this is a far more fruitful perspective. The analysis to date concurs with this broader approach. First BDM and project management are distinct functions, yet are linked through marketing, and as we shall examine in **Chapter 8** through MoP (cf. Cova and Salle, 2011). It is further been argued that project management is a function of marketing in the sense of project management being the delivery channel for the client or what the transactional marketing mix approach terms 'place'.

Project management as a function, whether conceived in terms of the various project management bodies of knowledge (BoKs), conceived through project management methodologies or through the operational tools and techniques, have yet to perceive their position in their market in terms of being a delivery channel, as being client and service-centric and to some extent, seeing project management as the means rather than an end in itself. It is suggested here that internalization of this conceptualization would change many decisions taken on the ground in practice. Some of the implications might include:

- Decisions that service client interests, especially around the benefits and impact the project will have in use, which on occasions will include a greater social interest and longer-term self-interest rather than a project-specific self-interest – project decisions that consider customer of client programmes and the client lifetime value (CLV);
- Value as technical and service value;
- Value as added value, extending beyond the cost reduction mindset;
- Risks to be evaluated as to whether they present earning opportunities;
- Problem solving as learning opportunities and the raw material for project and organizational capability development.

Tensions can emerge between inward focused, task-centric project teams and the strategy focused business with a wider view of the organization (Lycett et al., 2004). Innovation, creativity and problem solving can all be pursued with an inward focus (Bruce and Daly, 2007), borne out of performance drivers from the project business and demanded by the challenges uncertainties and complexities of the project. It can also be driven by customer or client need where the demands of solutions delivery has to be aligned with need and driven by service design in response to a service logic (Davies, 2004; Hobday et al., 2005; Davies et al., 2007; see also **Chapter 10**).

Client needs prescriptively are the drivers for integrated solutions (Davies, 2004; Hobday et al., 2005), providing a new service model with origins in technological systems on the one hand, competency and capability development (Davies and Brady, 2000; Davies et al., 2009) and, on the other hand, relational and relationship management (Bresnen et al., 2004; Smyth and Edkins, 2007; Tuli et al., 2007; Bresnen and Marshall, 2011). However, linkage requires service design (Romme, 2003; Sawhney, 2006). Service design does not occur in a vacuum, but arises out of the capabilities that the project business has, is induced from existing projects where problem solving and innovation have emerged and strategically determines development. The most pertinent capabilities in this context may be cutting-edge technical skills or hyper-expertise that no other or few competing project businesses possess, but are more likely to be capabilities that are the 'softer' issues of technical coordination and leverage internally and externally that add value and exceed the requirements. These are the project capabilities (Brady and Davies, 2004) and organizational capabilities (Davies and Brady, 2000) that add value. The organizational capabilities may include marketing capabilities (Möller, 2006), which competitors do not possess.

## Project management as delivery channel and business development management

The approach to project management is first addressed prior to execution, particularly during tender and negotiation stages of securing contracts (e.g. Powel and Young, 2004). Given that so many BDMs come from an operational background, it is worth commenting how readily a lack of engagement with the project management function ensues. There are several reasons that could be inferred inductively from the analysis, but further detailed investigation is needed. The inferred reasons in respect of BDMs include:

- Lack of support and direction from senior management;
- The sense of not excelling in project management and being moved to BDM:
    a. Rejection by the project management function;
    b. Sense of failure, affecting ability to be proactive in the BDM role;
- The transactional approach focusing on pulling information into the organization rather than pushing through responses around propositions and offers;
- Lack of resources and project lifecycle integration to shape project content under relationship marketing and project marketing;
- Lack of resource base to pursue entrepreneurial marketing in liaison with project managers.

The tendency is therefore to look solely towards the project pipeline. Bid management focuses upon compliance to requirements and bid price. Project managers focus upon the project details, especially around risk and its impact upon the contract and operational budget. The project managers are also concerned with what will practically work from their perspective and thus wish to move to specifying procedures and content at a detailed level. From the project manager perspective, early engagement with BDMs is seen as beneficial. Similarly, where clients encourage early engagement, for example early contractor involvement (ECI) in the construction sector, there are shaping opportunities. Project managers see it as a means to influence the project processes to suit implementation rather than add value for clients. Beyond that the perception is that they become drawn into meetings and protocols that are burdensome and 'impractical'. These criteria are set out in Table 7.1.

In essence Table 7.1 encapsulates divergent and convergent thinking, that is, effective BDMs are trying to open up the options in order to configure value that is best suited to meet perceived client needs, whereas project managers are trying

**TABLE 7.1** Misalignment between business development theory and project management practice

| *Conceptualizing business development management* | | | *Project management practice* | |
|---|---|---|---|---|
| *Motivation of BDMs* | *Outcome* | | *Motivation of PMs* | *Outcome* |
| Generate value propositions | Explore potential options and means to add value – need of help from project managers, other functions and suppliers to identify and lever value from generic capabilities into customized and tailored solutions | MISALIGNMENT of SCOPE | Manage risk by examining content | Proceed to a detailed level of analysis from the outset to identify and mitigate risk through elimination of options and reduction of uncertainty |
| Target margins for orders secured | Explore the balance of client drivers between quality and price; hence the value proposition and estimated margin achievable, and the extent of the competition on margin pressure | | Configure work to achieve budget | Proceed to technical solutions that are workable, easy to manage and can be value engineered or managed to reduce costs |
| Accountability based on orders secured | Incentives to secure contracts geared to the business strategy and models employed rather than meeting turnover targets that may not yield projects aligned to the business model and capabilities | | Accountability based upon successful completion | Keeping to project budget, securing good (average and preferably premium) margins on additional work and claims, acceptable KPIs |

to prematurely close down options to optimize potential content from a risk- and task-centric perspective. Effectively linking and potentially integrating BDM and project management is for the project manager to start with divergent thinking, suspending problem solving skills to mitigate risk and secure greater certainty towards exploring integrated solutions. This switch is depicted in Figure 7.2. How is this resolved? The motivation of the BDMs is to work closely with project managers to improve the value propositions, hence to guide and encourage this mindset.

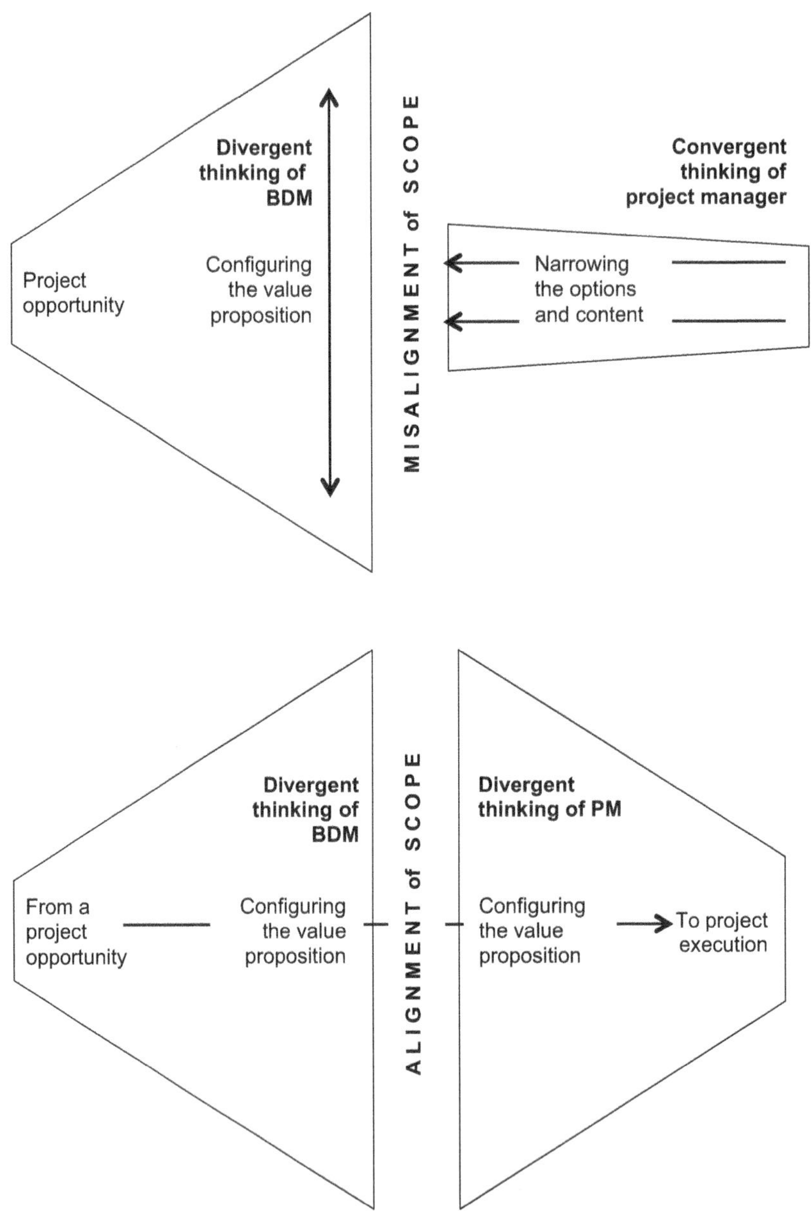


**FIGURE 7.2** Management of the BDM–project management interface

Yet, the project managers perceive the BDMs as a sub-set of, and a service to, project management and hence are unlikely to be guided by BDMs. The BDMs are the problem owner, but the responsibility lies with the project manager to demonstrate they can work with the divergent mindset. Senior management are responsible for inducting the change.

Underlying the conflicts set out above, there is a paradox or strategy contradiction between BDMs trying to secure contracts at low price and project managers trying to claw back margins in whatever way possible. It is the result of transactional market pressures but need not be the over-riding factor from a market management and business development perspective. Detailed alignment is induced for the two roles by harmonizing assessment criteria. The measures and key performance indicators for each role should be the same. Annual reviews should be also. The most important financial figure is the outturn costs and associated margin at the project level and CLV at the client level. It is a long-term business, for which assessments and financial incentives account at a general level and aligned to the earning logic at a detailed level, that is what the source and attributes of generating turnover and profit are for projects and programmes.

A project manager whose mindset was most closely aligned to client need and thus was motivated to contributing integrated solutions was responsible for a programme of work on the campus of an organization dealing with extreme toxic material. The project manager had become client-centric through having to listen and pay attention to health and safety issues, which influenced thinking as to what was needed and when (Interview conducted 2nd quarter of 2012). If project managers can acquire client-centric and service foci for health and safety, they can from an integrated approach to marketing and BDM.

The BDM–project management interface is key, yet there are other roles pertaining to integration and solutions delivery to meet client need. Procurement and cost estimating are two other roles and many of the same principles apply. Bid management of the tender process is another key interrelated function. The issue is whether the value proposition developed by BDMs up until the request for proposal is (i) translated into value and (ii) added value in the win-strategy is built into the bid. The bid management process can see its role as processing bids through the internal project pipeline to feed project management rather than adding value or finding angles for value added content. Fact Box 7.1 provides details as to how this is manifested in two development and contracting organizations in two different national locations.

The project businesses in Fact Box 7.1 operate on the basis of the marketing mix and have low levels of integration with project management, despite the presence of the project manager as the bid manager in both organizations. Higher levels of backwards integration from project management to bid management would be conceptually expected applying a different marketing approach. Strong internal relationship bonds, supported by a relationship management system working in tandem with the functional systems, provide direction for relationship marketing and may be necessary for entrepreneurial marketing at times.

## FACT BOX 7.1 BID MANAGEMENT, PROJECT MANAGEMENT AND MARKETING

Two case companies are presented. SubCo is a premises and fit-out contractor, part of a large project business providing a range of services in the solutions seller and systems integrator categories. PrimCo is a business premises provider, having a real estate development sister company. PrimCo sells integrated solutions and systems integrator roles. The two project businesses share some common features. First, they secure a proportion of their work from leads instigated inside their organization; second, there is no designated BDM role in either organization; whilst bid managers, commercial directors and operations directors can all manage this process, in both businesses it is the project managers responsible for execution who run the tenders or bid management. This forms a link with project management.

SubCo and PrimCo operate under extreme pressure in bid management, partly from a time perspective but resources are a strong contextual influence.

In SubCo, marketing has a backroom support role, an administrator 'tracking' the pipeline, progress on leads and the flow to bid management. Sourcing and collation are key tasks. There is some monitoring of client contact overlaps through the database. The flow of bids comes from the prequalification pipeline, from the estimating function, which receives some advance intelligence and from the parent company. Each project manager has 4 to 5 bids at various stages at any one time and up to 15 others at earlier stages allocated to them. Estimating and bid teams are said to work together closely as they are co-located, yet pressures mean that not all staff will have read the documents at the bid management kick off meeting. The bids comprise two main elements – technical and commercial content. They are strong on technical documentation, yet it is the commercial content that is decisive for clients. Project managers 'have a view' about how to run bids and projects, which tends to prevail. Win-strategies are simply a function of responding to the published selection criteria. Therefore the factors are selection criteria, client intelligence, price, mid-tender interview feedback. It is project focused rather than client focused. Competitors are acknowledged to know more about clients and have specialist BDMs. Project focused bids tend to be processed without a detailed focus upon project and any organizational capabilities. Value propositions are responsive to requirements rather than learning from generic lessons for customizing into added value.

In PrimCo, 50 per cent of the work is 'tender based'. They have 25 to 30 projects at any one time. Pipeline data is recorded on the CRM system, Salesforce®, which helps manage the workflow of bids – prospect, prequalification, presentation and bid management. This is coordinated by the central cost estimation function through phone calls to clients and consultants. There is minimal face-to-face (F2F) contact, except through informal networks. Their strengths are to be able to secure and successfully complete the difficult and high profile projects. These produce better margins, and there is also more variation between bid prices, which is perceived to improve the strike rate. Project managers run each bid, which are based upon an excel-type document system. Tender analysis covers client type, building type, consultants, permits, competition, deadlines, and a project SWOT (strengths, weaknesses, opportunities, threats). Once a week, they have a formal meeting with cost estimation for updates. The interfaces are informally managed through co-location. The main win-strategy is around subcontractor costs, using their international presence in regional markets, for example Latvia, Poland, and Estonia and the Czech Republic, to secure below-average prices.

The project management link needs strengthening. They can pay more attention to sequencing work on site at the bid stage. They could recognize they should think more about identifying what the client wants, especially how they can cooperate more with clients rather than fight them: 'We have to listen more'.

In both case companies, bid management is predominantly driven by time-based process criteria, rather than looking to the project management function and project capabilities to add value, as well as paying insufficient attention to client needs that lie behind the requirements documentation, which may be acceptable for a marketing mix approach, but is constraining on the project management function to effectively 'mix the ingredients'.

*Source*: Interviews conducted with directors, senior management, departmental and project managers, 2nd quarter of 2013.

## Conclusion

Consideration has been given to the extent of integration between marketing and project management. Three main views have emerged:

1. The two functions are separate in practice, which is partly a reflection of theorization and mainly a function of organizational structuring that creates boundaries;
2. To the extent that integration is recognized, marketing is largely perceived as part of project management, especially the BDM role, which is reflected in empirical evidence, while there has been tentative conceptual attempt to integrate at the strategic level;
3. Project management is located within the broader conceptual picture of marketing:
    a. Operationally as a marketing delivery channel, especially from the dominant marketing mix approach;
    b. Operationally to facilitate integration, especially from the relationship and project marketing perspectives.

The approaches from the industrial and asset specific marketing domains have been drawn upon, namely *solutions sellers* (professional and other advisors), *systems sellers* (largely subcontractor roles), *systems integrators* (main contractor roles), with an emphasis upon the provision of coordinated integrated solutions from each of the sellers. Brought together, the combined approach is therefore also looking towards integrated service design as a 'business model' with distinct earning logic depending upon how this is conducted, especially from the systems integrators. Any 'business model' is problematic in practice, divided between the *business model* for the systems integrator as a project business, which informs the project and the 'business model' of the TMO that is project specific and sometimes specific to client programmes (cf. Figure 5.1). This model and the attendant integration processes and earning logic are established at the front-end.

The complexity of project demands, including service content, is increasing. The response of project businesses is incremental change from the perspective of traditional business models around meeting minimum requirements, risk and project management within the parameters of the iron triangle. Integrated value, the service experience and delivery of benefits are beginning to show signs of receiving greater attention, yet the response is largely reactive to client demands rather than proactively driven for the benefit of the long-term business, shareholder value, clients and societal stakeholders. At the operational level, appreciation of the project as a delivery channel is fundamental to understanding how these changes are and will be manifested, changing the criteria and conduct of project decision-making. Project management and marketing and BDM are inextricably linked, the performance of the one being dependent on the performance of the other – and interdependence of equals to yield integration.

Overall, project management is intrinsically embedded in marketing as a delivery channel for clients, but this does not render project management less important and they conceptually exist together in MoP throughout and especially at the front-end. This message aligns with the broader concepts of market management and business development. It brings into focus the investment need for market protection, especially for the systems integrator role occupied by main or prime contractors. Investment also yields opportunities for competitive advantage.

There were ten substantive issues in theory and practice identified at the outset, and this chapter has contributed to a number of issues.

**SI no. 1:** ***Market Management*** requires a proactive approach not only to the market but also internally for effective market management as systems integrator, systems seller or solutions seller.

**SI no. 2:** ***Service Management*** is being driven by increasing complexity demanded by clients, which is manifested as technical and service attributes; however, the significance is the increasing integration between the two in demand terms.

**SI no. 3:** ***Marketing Investment and Portfolio Management*****,** as indicated from the foregoing comments, represent a key issue. This can be argued as normative and prescriptive. It is also a logical outcome of trends, an observed signpost for the researcher and practitioner to note, and the practitioner to be guided by depending on the basis the organization competes. Some positions may prove more successful than others. A further inference is that a pure survival strategy is itself suffering from entropy, particularly in the upper end of national and international markets.

**SI no. 4:** ***Client Management and Programme Management*** offer a mixed position. While greater awareness of client needs is central to the parameters of the chapter, client management is far from an automatic consequence, but may be a by-product. In other words, being client-centric can be achieved by knowing their needs at a deep level and providing integrated solutions on projects and across both project business and client programmes. Generic capabilities derived from investments require some customization and tailoring for each project context.

**SI no. 5:** ***Marketing and BDM*** isolation is reduced where connected to project management. The emphasis in this chapter has been on horizontal integration.

**SI no. 8:** ***Cross-functional Systems and Coordination Mechanisms*** have been considered, especially at the BDM–bid management–project management interfaces. Here BDM lacks integration over project lifecycles.

**SI no. 9:** ***Marketing and Managing the Project Lifecycle*** is covered in the issue above, whereby BDMs have theoretical responsibilities over project lifecycles to ensure that coordination occurs, particularly that commitments to provide integrated solutions are delivered in execution and promises of added value are levered in execution. Practice is intense at the front of the front-end, yet further involvement along lifecycles shows an interface issue between theory and practice.

**SI no. 10:** ***Marketing and Value Creation*** is largely bound up in the construct of integrated solutions in this chapter.

In a similar vein to the previous chapter, the analysis has opened up the marketing–project management interface to a broader sphere of debate and is thus a scoping examination. There are several main *recommendations* for research that flow from the analysis:

A. Research needs to be conducted into the inter-relationships and interplay between systems integrators, solutions and systems sellers concerning integrated solutions in terms of the organizational barriers and enablers at the interfaces.
B. Research the bid management processes and in particular the processes for win-strategy development and value leverage in relation to integrated solutions.
C. Research is needed as to how the agency motivations and structuring of organizational processes between BDM and project management affects the interface.

There are several main *recommendations* for practice that flow from the analysis in this chapter:

1. Project decision-making to be informed by project management as a market delivery channel for clients.
2. Integration of BDM as a distinct yet essential component of the execution stages.

3. Putting in place systems and capabilities for solutions integration aligned to client need.

In summary, the integration of marketing and project management has yet to be fully considered in theory and practice. The strength of solutions and of the systems integrator role is only as strong as internal horizontal integration along project life-cycles. Project management at the execution stages has been the focus of this chapter, yet the management of projects with a front-end emphasis intrinsically informs performance during execution, which provides an emphasis for the next chapter. Marketing and BDM from a management viewpoint is part of the project business storehouse in the sense that it is not 'grain to be sold, but seed to be sown' in the marketplace.

# 8

# FRONT-END FOCUS TOWARDS MANAGING MARKETS

## Introduction

The *management of projects* (MoP) is the term given to a more holistic view of project management. It includes the front-end strategy and development prior to execution, as well as execution (e.g. Morris, 1994; 2013). It is likely to increasingly involve 'back-end' issues to link in with the project in use from social, economic and environmental viewpoints (cf. Edkins et al., 2008; Turkulainen et al., 2013). Exactly where the front-end moves into execution is a moot point. While a stage gate may provide a boundary in chronology, there is a certain amount of functional interplay between the two, and that is appropriate for a more holistic conception and integrated set of practices. There is an attitudinal and mindset issue too. No matter how much time is spent at the front-end, if the thinking is tactical, the focus is always task and project-centric, with silo thinking constraining integration, rendering MoP frequently partial, rhetorical or omitted in practice.

At one level, MoP is related to market management in the sense of providing a more proactive approach to managing projects, which if conducted effectively will improve the earning logic of project management and of the business, hence indirectly contributing to development of the market for the business. MoP has tended to emphasize the client-side more than the project business side. This fails to steer client-centricity from the supply standpoint; greater consideration has been given to the actions of the client as owner, sponsor and manager for its programmes and projects (e.g. Morris, 2013; Edkins et al., 2013; see **Chapters 1** and **2**). On the supply side, marketing and BDM are located at the front of the front-end, frequently prior to a project being recognized, scoped and with a defined business case (see Figure 3.1), especially where a relationship marketing, project or entrepreneurial marketing approach is adopted (e.g. Cova and Salle, 2005). MoP acknowledges marketing (e.g. Pinto and Covin, 1992; cf. Turner, 1995), yet the research has tended to ignore marketing in practice. Given the front-end focus, this is anomalous. The conceptualization of project management as a delivery channel for the client is part of adoption of a client-centric stance, helping to lift the attitude horizon from task and project centricity to a more holistic approach. To redress this imbalance, the conceptual linkage between MoP and marketing is developed, extending further and building upon the understanding provided in **Chapter 7**.

The main *aim* is therefore to explicitly locate marketing in the MoP approach. The aim can be broken down as follows:

A. Address changing client needs that are driving project complexity, the need for holistic integration and service development that harnesses MoP with marketing and BDM.
B. Examine the connection between MoP systems and marketing implementation for programme and project success.
C. Redress a conceptual and practice-based emphasis of trying to force marketing into the execution mold of project management or as a subset of MoP.

A main message is the current lack of MoP attention to marketing reinforces the task-centric and project-centric views that are unaligned with the current trends in complex project demands from clients. A complimentary outward and client-centric focus, coupled with increasing emphasis upon service value in business-to-business (B2B) environments, links to the organization of capabilities around integrated systems and solutions in asset specific and project markets (**Chapter 7**).

MoP links with and encompasses programme and portfolio management ($P^3M$). However, portfolio and programme management largely operate in hierarchical terms in relation to project management and to some other MoP content. The prime emphasis of the MoP is horizontal, addressing project lifecycles. Some tensions exist here, and for the sake of clarity, MoP has largely been addressed as horizontal with portfolio and programme management guiding the management of projects top-down.

## The management of projects, marketing and performance

Marketing as a strategic function sets in motion the tactical plans for selling and other activities in the marketing remit. Marketing affects other functions. It is here that it engages with MoP. It reaches forward to influence performance (Andrews and Smith, 1996; Menon et al., 1999; Slater et al., 2010). Strong strategic implementation is associated with high performance (Cespedes and Piercy, 1996; Vorhies and Morgan, 2005).

MoP research shows that front-end strategic development of projects has the effect of improving performance, and indeed perceptions of project success (Morris, 1994; Cooke-Davies, 2002). The MoP focus upon the strategy for projects takes account of supplier and customer viewpoints as well as other potential stakeholders. Morris and Pinto define the aim of MoP and its challenges as:

> . . . how we set up and define the project to deliver stakeholder success – on how projects are managed. In one sense this almost makes the subject

impossibly large, for now the only thing differentiating this form of management from other sorts is 'the project'.

(Morris and Pinto, 2004: xvii–xviii).

Lowe and Leiringer define the commercial MoP as *contractual and commercial issues relating to projects, from inception to completion* (2006:11). Although inception is said to start with B2B relationships here, it is unclear whether they commence with the customer business problem or with a narrower project management perception based around pre-defined requirements. The weak links between project businesses and client-centric marketing have been repeatedly demonstrated (Smyth, 2000; Pinto and Rouhiainen, 2001; Cova et al., 2002; Cova and Salle, 2005; cf. Grönroos, 2000; Gummesson, 2000).

The model of MoP (Morris and Pinto, 2004) shows the execution stage set in the wider MoP strategic context where the initial case or justification and project definition is received by the project business from the client and further defined and configured, including potential co-creation with the client. Onto that is grafted BDM which is helping to understand the client business and project needs in order to identify and configure value propositions from the technical and service capabilities within the project business. This is conducted to secure projects on the one hand and to deliver integrated solutions to the client on the other hand. Investments and costs are incurred from client management to linkage with broader capabilities (cf. Figure 4.6). This total picture is set out in Figure 8.1.

Two important points can be drawn out from Figure 8.1. These are:

1. *Risk management* – the traditional approach is to recognize that risks are high in project management, not just in intensity but their extent too. There are those risks that are inherent to the content, those that are context related such as location and political factors, and those risks which are relational both concerning the TMO and milieu and with external actors. The extent of risks is greatest at

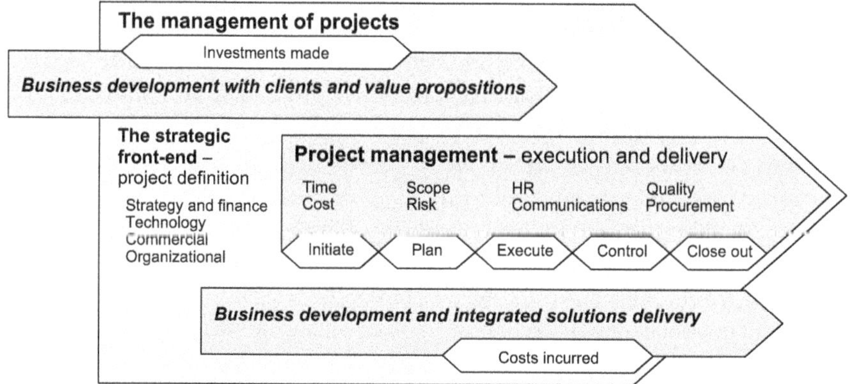


**FIGURE 8.1** The management of projects and the role of marketing and BDM

the front-end, but manifestation is most likely to occur during execution. The MoP approach sets up the project with a greater level of preparedness, taking into account a range of factors that reduces or mitigates the worst affects of many risks. Marketing and BDM mainly have an indirect impact upon risk management except where relationship marketing is applied and reduces relational risk.

2. *Added value* – the opportunity to add most value occurs at the front-end. Value is identified for prequalification through the management approach. It is manifested through win-strategy development during bid management. Value is configured through the management approach, configuration of technical and service solutions and levered through supply chain management. The process for adding value commences through BDM learning about client and project needs. BDM has a conceptual brief over this entire process to facilitate alignment of solutions to need and as the project moves towards execution to deliver the value, especially added value, to which the project business has committed. Therefore, marketing and BDM have a direct role, except under the marketing mix where ending at prequalification or bid management is an acceptable option, throughout the front-end. Value engineering and value management practices feed into the processes with equal emphasis on value and money rather than applying cost-reduction criteria, which tends to reduce value, especially service value associated with managing the consequences of technical quality reduction.

Both risk management and adding value are hindered by many project businesses own conflicting agendas. On the one hand, project businesses try to survive in the market and stay organizationally lean by minimizing investment and overheads. On the other hand, this increases project risks and constrains value optimization as they typically lack integration between functions, which then ups the ante for project risk management in other ways – a paradoxical or contradictory state of affairs.

In **Chapter 7**, the BDM–project management interface was addressed. If that is extended to include prospecting and prequalification for work at the front-end plus the corporate functions of procurement and cost estimation, then some of the implications for risk mitigation and adding value can be teased out from a marketing perspective that encourages integration to improve value propositions. The current situation is that each functional department typically operates with its own separate systems that are fragmented with a lack of formal procedures for consultation or relationship management to articulate the interfaces on a purposeful basis – see Fact Box 8.1. For example, it might reasonably be expected that marketing and BDM coordinate with procurement departments to (i) use the same criteria to segment the client and supplier markets to achieve alignment of market demands to subcontractor value propositions; (ii) qualify subcontractors, allocating them to client segments or against particular clients; and (iii) liaise over prospective clients to align specific client needs with solutions. This is part of being a systems integrator that delivers integrated solutions to their client base. The lack of integration compromises any business model and associated earning logic. How the MoP is therefore conducted is an important part of integrated business models and earning logic.

## FACT BOX 8.1 GAPS IN CROSS-FUNCTIONAL WORKING AND SYSTEMS INTEGRATION FROM A MARKETING PERSPECTIVE FOR INTERNATIONAL CONTRACTORS

Procurement in UKCo is segmenting their subcontractors, identifying key alliances and partners under a 'Strategic Sourcing' initiative. According to the Head of Procurement, BDM see things in terms of 'upstream and downstream'. The subcontractors are asking for regular updates on project pipelines, which BDM are reluctant to provide. The BDM–procurement relationship is minimal. Procurement is engaged with Estimating and Tendering, and BDM is not. Procurement have had people embedded in Estimating and Tendering to advise on suppliers over the last few years, which is already yielding benefits in securing suppliers and capturing value. Procurement operates a classic six-step procurement process, logging accreditation and assessing performance on a two-by-two matrix. There is no liaison between BDM and Procurement to lever particular value to enhance offers in the stages prior to prequalification.

In AntCo, the approach is project-by-project, bid-by-bid, whereas Procurement analyze suppliers on a programme basis as well as by project. It was thought in Procurement that the identification of value could be further helped by BDMs liaising with Procurement earlier on, rather than the occasional and informal partial liaison that is current practice.

Procurement in a large EuroCo business unit (BU) was unaware of the marketing strategy and it was not known what is needed in the supply chain from the perspective of winning work. Selection criteria of projects to bid or reject became clearer following an annual director-led 'Roadshow'. Procurement has developed structured independent systems for segmentation, improving sophistication over the last six years. All subcontractors are subject to 360° assessment or key performance indicators (KPIs), which are especially focused upon technical content of which BDMs are largely unaware. Assessment is used to inform future selection. Key and preferred suppliers are perceived to be important factors to secure complex projects, yet the decision-making for selection is conducted by Operations Directors, rather than Procurement and BDM.

An example of a segmentation matrix is provided below:

| | | |
|---|---|---|
| **Risk** | Bottleneck | Strategically critical |
| | Strategically non-critical | Leverage |
| | **Value** | |

In all cases, a reasonable liaison between Cost Estimation for the Bid Management function exists, although the balance between informal and formal systems of coordination varied across the companies. Informal systems

*(Continued)*

**FACT BOX 8.1** (Continued)

were aided by co-location in some cases. In all the cases, there was a sense that Procurement saw it the responsibility of BDM to liaise with them rather than an interaction on an equal footing with mutual and iterative initiative taking.

*Source*: Interviews conducted with directors, senior management, departmental and project managers, 1st and 2nd quarters of 2012.

The international concession contractor, BranCo, developed a twin integration strategy that is developing customer relations and developing project win-strategies. This integration has a spin-off effect of high levels of engagement with the procurement and cost estimation functions, although in a conflicting strategy decision supply chain management was withdrawn.

The identification and leverage of value links into capabilities too and how these are developed. Capabilities, particularly the core competencies and dynamic capabilities that are developed and embedded at the corporate level, or in programme management, are and can be mobilized through front-end management (cf. Prahalad and Hamel, 1990; Hamel and Prahalad, 1994; Helfat, 1997; Teece et al., 1997; Eisenhardt and Martin, 2000). This has been developed under a relationship management approach to managing complex projects (Pryke and Smyth, 2006), but has yet to be developed specifically for marketing and BDM in project businesses. Four examples are presented here:

- An *organizational capability* – for this purpose capability development has been proposed, and is illustrated in Figure 8.2. This is chosen as it relates directly to the overarching theme of the book and feeds directly into marketing. It also feeds directly into programme and project management from the portfolio level in order to improve project performance (**Chapter 7**).
- A *marketing capability* which is a subset of an organizational capability and particularly pertinent in this context – for this purpose relationship management (RM) has been depicted as shown in Figure 8.3. This is chosen as it relates to relationship marketing (**Chapter 4**) and feeds into programme management.
- A *programme capability* to show the link between the organizational and project levels – for this purpose learning and knowledge management (KM) has been chosen with an emphasis upon the problems associated with capturing, processing and embedding project knowledge at the programme level for reuse. This is illustrated in Figure 8.4.
- A *project capability* – for this purpose health and safety (H&S) has been chosen for two reasons. First, it is neither a product nor service that clients directly benefit from the delivered project in use. Second, they do not derive direct benefit from the service during execution but avoid reputational damage from avoiding H&S incidents. It also is an area that has received considerable service attention over the last 5 to 7 years, but few or no project companies have exceeded 'best practice', being largely content with compliance (Roberts et al., 2012). This is shown in Figure 8.5.

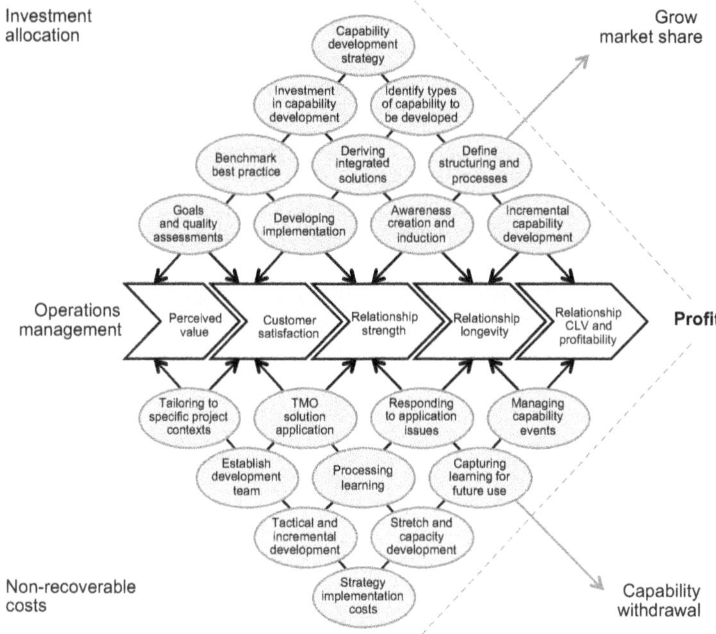


**FIGURE 8.2** Organizational capability development

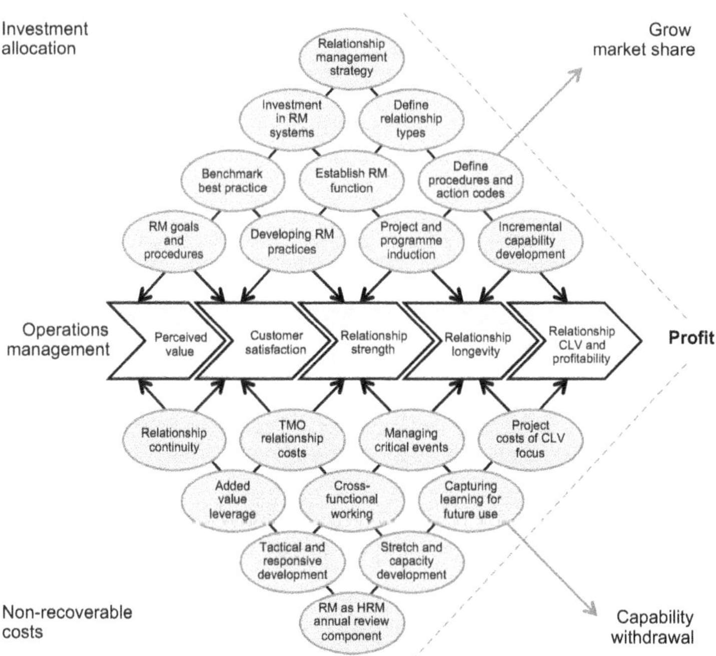


**FIGURE 8.3** Marketing capability development

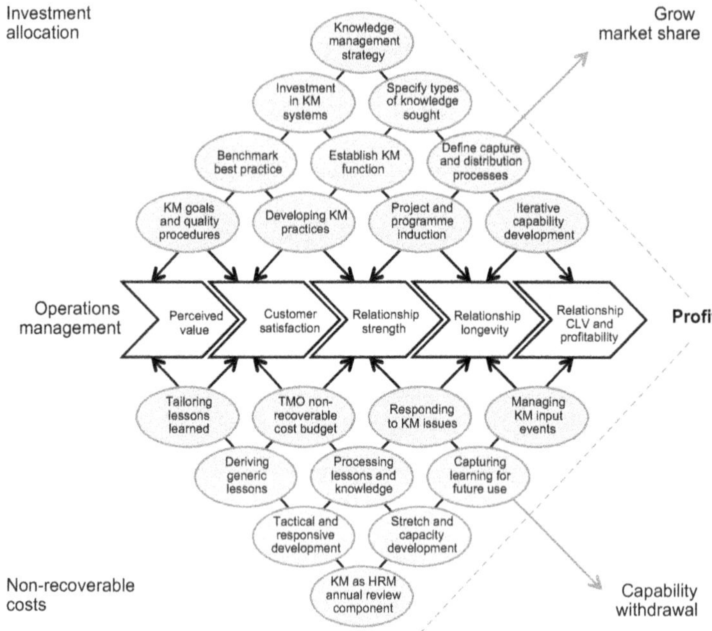


**FIGURE 8.4** Programme capability development

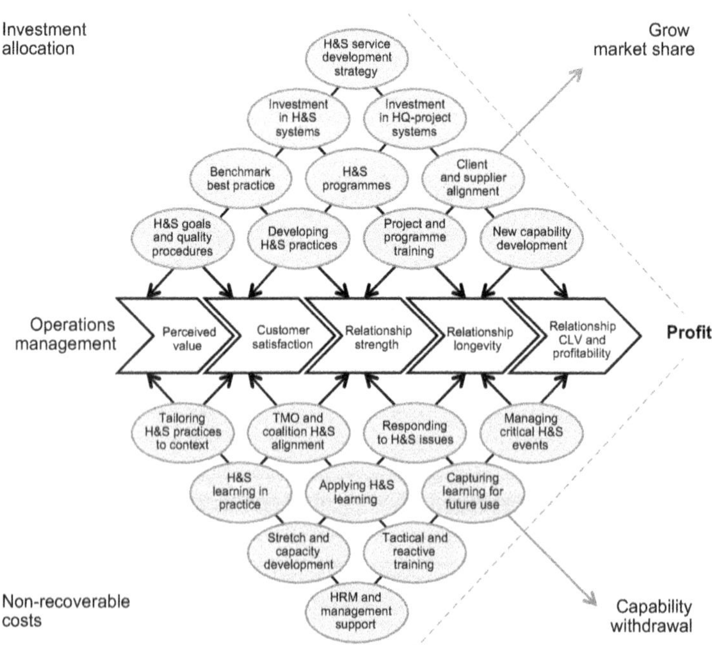


**FIGURE 8.5** Project capability development

The benefit of showing four different types of capability development is that the overall management thinking is similar for each hierarchical level, yet embedding each capability is distinctive at the appropriate level. Many businesses will start with their areas of strength or with highly problematic issues that must be addressed. They will largely have to work with the structures and processes in place for other functions (Helfat and Peteraf, 2003) unless a more fundamental restructuring or change management programme is underway. The new developments are grafted in, incremental and iterative adjustment being made to existing structures and systems. The strategy development and implementation have to align the client need with the capability content and conduct.

The argument to this point aligns with the resource-based view (RBV) of the firm. This will be developed further in the next chapter. It also is in line with service management, particularly the new service model, the heart of which is the development of a business model with a corresponding earning logic. The logic arises from identifying client and customer needs and providing integrated solutions to meet those needs, from which revenue flows. The business model is framed around the processes necessary to deliver integrated solutions and yield the revenue. This is conceptually linked to market management and business development and specifically to marketing through the work of Davies and his colleagues (2007; cf. Brady and Davies, 2004; Davies et al., 2006; cf. Kujala et al., 2010; 2011; Turkulainen et al., 2013).

What has been shown is that for MoP to be effective along the project lifecycle, it needs feeding from above. The capabilities developed are specifically configured at the front-end for delivery, first by identifying and mobilizing these resources before and at prequalification for development during bidding and leveraged during subsequent execution to ensure delivery. In this sense the MoP becomes part of the model and feeds the earning logic. The starting point had been the extensive incidence of project failure and needing to improve the range of inputs to do so (Morris and Hough, 1987; cf. Miller and Lessard, 2000). Figure 8.6 tries to capture the interconnections. If the internal integration factors around the prospecting BDM role, procurement and cost estimation are linked to capability development for systems integration, then the connection with value identification from BDM to the delivery of integrated solutions becomes apparent.

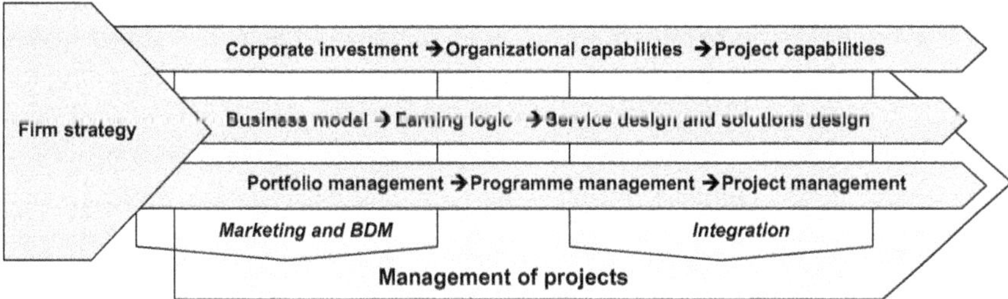


**FIGURE 8.6** Service management, marketing and the management of projects

There are two further ways in which to build upon Figure 8.6. The first way is outward facing from the project business towards the supply markets. Alliancing, and supply chain management with attendant collaborative practices can be used to improve strategic integration and project-specific integration. Previous studies have provided evidence of the positive and significant relationship between a strategic approach to supply chain management and firm performance (e.g. Min et al., 2007). It can be classified as an organizational capability that engenders organizational performance (e.g. Srivastava et al., 1999) – a supplier portfolio is an essential means of differentiating among suppliers according to their value-adding capabilities. For project businesses, it may be organized at the project business programme management level, linked to particular segments or even types of investment from the portfolio level. Supply chains can be managed as key account activities (Miocevic and Crnjak-Karanovic, 2012), hence being linked with client key account management (KAM) for the purposes of integration. Such a link has to be conducted at the programme management level. The management location where that crystallizes is MoP at the front-end, which provides the socio-economic space for setting up the strategy for subsequent delivery during execution. At one level, this is self-evident logic, but compared to the empirical evidence about the lack of integration in the tension between managing market and project risk, it is far from the case and needs management intent to make it happen.

The second way is inward facing and concerns the internal role of relationship management as a further system component for integration. As value is levered by people and through their relationships, it is important to be proactive rather than rely upon chance (**Chapter 4**; Smyth, 2014). This provides a more direct link between relationship marketing and the role of integration. It is two-way. Integration helps the value proposition and relationship marketing helps facilitate the integration for delivery.

Relationship marketing has been applied directly and aligned to MoP by BranCo, the leading concession contractor. The organization developed a hierarchy of thinking to facilitate the linkage between MoP and the relationship marketing strategy within a BU. From the recognition of the need to understand client organizations, the strategic business drivers behind projects, through to understanding the pipeline in terms of P$^3$M, project specific win-strategies were developed – a shift towards using relationships to configure technological, technical and service content around a detailed understanding of client business strategy and requirements. Relationship marketing has in turn begun to be an influence on project business performance, for example application in construction business (Smyth and Fitch, 2009). Part of the strategy has been to develop KAM. This is a coordinating mechanism operating for client management at a programme level of the project business. It is also a capability that potentially delivers higher levels of integration internally and integrated solutions for the client. Table 8.1 sets out how KAM has been shaping up across five different contracting organizations. It shows partial adoption in two main ways, hierarchically in relation to P$^3$M and at the client–project management interface.

KAM is an organizational capability located at the programme level for client management. It requires high levels of continuity from the project business

**TABLE 8.1** Variance in KAM implementation across five contracting project businesses

| *Project business* | *KAM* | | | |
|---|---|---|---|---|
| | *Corporate* | *Portfolio* | *Programme* | *Project level* |
| **Antco** | KAM recently re-introduced, set up to be proactive and supported by the 'correct behaviours'. The role is ascribed to individuals, drawn from across functions | KAM is applied to clients, consultants and principal subcontractors<br>This supports the policy to increasingly move towards branded offers | Clients like a prime or single point of contact, which aligns with KAM | Bid teams are put together project-by-project, although a more centralized resource is developing, yet is not integrated with KAMs |
| **EUCo** | Infrastructure clients demanding 'man marking' on contracts is too costly, therefore KAM is being gradually introduced as an alternative option | – | Certain clients have KAMs allocated, drawn from different roles including BDMs. The KAM role is partial with informal routines | Bids are developed on win-strategies of engineering excellence without KAM involvement |
| **EuroCo** | Director team who have to sign off project opportunities in order to make resource commitments | Customer Solutions Director assigns directors to counterpart client contacts in key client organizations – an informal KAM function Client reports are (sometimes intermittently) produced during BDM and considered at monthly board meetings | Relationships are being developed from the centre at corresponding levels in the client organization, a process of engagement amongst main board directors<br>Customer plans are produced, led by BDM until prequalification | Operations directors lead between prequalification and tender. They provide the continuity over the rest of the project lifecycle, who 'own' the projects, but they do not 'own' the clients |
| **UKCo** | Directors monitor accounts content, albeit from a limited KAM perspective | The Business Development Director coordinates KAMs | BDMs fulfil the KAM role and are paired up with client account managers, but KAMs are not involved through the project lifecycle | – |

(*Continued*)

**TABLE 8.1** (Continued)

| *Project business* | *KAM* | | | |
|---|---|---|---|---|
| | *Corporate* | *Portfolio* | *Programme* | *Project level* |
| **BranCo** | A simple system operates at senior management level with customer directors performing the KAM function<br><br>Basic behavioural codes of conduct and behavioural 'tips' were introduced to help articulate procedures | The most productive clients and relationships are identified, including whether the client is investing in order to avoid unnecessary relationship costs | KAMs assigned to clients with large programmes, and 80% of their potential pipeline being associated with the 30 largest accounts<br><br>KAM has yet to overcome problems between project lifecycle stages, especially between BDM and project management<br><br>KAM has helped bring CLV into focus | Horizontal dimension of cross-functional coordination has been instigated, yet habits and intuitively informed behaviour is a long-term issue to address |

(cf. Hadjikani, 1996; Cova and Salle, 2005). The condition of the KAM function as implemented (Table 8.1) can be assessed against capability development as presented in Figures 8.2–8.5. The project businesses have been proactive in the introduction of KAM, albeit partially. The strategic level is related on the one hand to programme management and on the other hand to the principles of relationship marketing. KAM can thus be seen through the lens of an organizational capability and specifically a marketing capability. The main focus is tentative at the front-end as well as between projects, with the exception of BranCo, and to that extent can be perceived as a project capability because of the partial implementation. BranCo is the only project business with a semblance of organizational capability at the BU-level. Therefore, the relation to the business strategy as a whole and resource allocation in particular is weak in the other project businesses. The lack of continuity of project lifecycles and between projects in practice, suggests that implementation of the strategy is either still being rolled out incrementally or is partially or poorly considered. There was recognition in the project businesses of shortcoming, and therefore, iterative developments may be forthcoming. There was also a lack of consistency in the implementation of the objectives. The source of inconsistency varied in specifics but top management proved to be amongst those who failed to prioritize their KAM-related roles. This weakens implementation and sends out a message to others about the commitment to marketing specifically and client management in general – evidence of the dominance of a task and project management orientation rather than client and service focus.

The assessment of KAM, provided above and in Table 8.1, shows that integration, as far as it pertains to marketing in the MoP context and the delivery of integrated solutions, is dependent upon organizational behaviour.

## Organizational behaviour and practice-based action

Integration partially emerges from recent and past practices (Parmigiani and Howard-Grenville, 2011; Jarzabkowski et al., 2012). The management role is to identify, nurture and develop formal and informal routines. Integration cascades down from a systems level via these and other existing routines. Specifically, it cascades into protocols, specific procedures and organizational norms, which inform action. The front-end embodies complex issues, frequently with asymmetrical and inadequate information. Present are high levels of intangibility and uncertainty that need a great deal of exploration and investigation to develop and respond to in concrete ways (Edkins et al., 2013). Relationships form an important part of the process to interpret and make sense of matters to form knowledge and information that can be acted upon. Developing understanding is predominantly managed as an instinctive process without a relationship management system (cf. Dreyfus and Dreyfus, 2005; Edkins et al., 2013), from which actors apply a sense-making approach (cf. Weick, 1995) to try to articulate some sort of order through interpretation and categorization.

In pitching for project opportunities, directors and BDMs commonly say, 'people are our biggest asset'. The truism according to Merrow is 'people do projects' (2011: 159), and therefore, it is people who add value, the tools and techniques of project management being only as good as the hands they are in (Pryke and Smyth, 2006; Smyth, 2014). The anomaly is that people do not appear much in project management theorization. Academics are more comfortable with the organizational systems and procedures, tools and techniques. 'Relationships' are linkages addressed at this indirect level. One good reason for depersonalization is that poor teamwork is seldom about poor interpersonal relationships, although effective relationships can help mitigation. It is sometimes about poor management support both directly and through the systems and procedures. It sometimes resides in the way the project was shaped at the front-end. Merrow draws upon extensive data from the oil and gas sector to make the assertion: . . . *the roots of problematic teams are almost always found in some of the fundamentals of the project itself and how it was shaped* (Merrow, 2011: 159).

The review of KAM implementation in practice at the end of the previous section demonstrated that senior management commitment is low at the front end towards understanding, managing and serving clients. The isolation of the marketing and BDM functions at the front of the front-end reinforces the specific point at a more general level. Put another way, if the same attention given to resource inputs from the financial function was given to client and service management from the marketing function, which includes senior management commitments, a different picture would emerge. The comparison is made to demonstrate the current state of play; it is not to say this is what *ought* to happen from a normative and prescriptive position. There are always options and alternative means.

Examining BDM at the front of the front-end from the MoP perspective, director-level inputs include:

a) Building contacts at a comparable level on the client side and with their consultant advisors at senior level where clients have strategic representation:

    i. In response to client demands within the marketing mix approach,
    ii. To build relationships at the most senior levels, particular in the client DMU, including the owner and sponsor roles, within the relationship marketing and project marketing approaches,
    iii. To reinforce technical and innovative alliances built by others, or even instigate alliances and lever internal technical and service capabilities under the entrepreneurial marketing remit;

b) Approving and mobilizing resources to build commitments towards clients and specific projects, based upon resources already allocated in the annual budget for such initiatives;
c) Providing support for business development efforts whether conducted by KAMs, BDMs, project managers or through any other role;
d) Facilitating cross-functional working:

    i. For post-qualification,
    ii. For win-strategy development,
    iii. During post-tender negotiations,
    iv. As part of client management.

How this is conducted sets the tone for engagement with the formal systems and procedures and the informal routines. It therefore influences trust building at the project business–client interface, the ability to make project-related commitment and non-contractual promises to add value, the management of moments of truth in the relationship prior to execution, the mobilization of capabilities as well as client and stakeholder management. Therefore marketing and BDM at the front-end at the strategic level are more than setting the strategy, its implementation and monitoring; perhaps more important is the demonstration effect through modelling the desired organizational behaviour. The support elements may also have a link to mentoring programmes if these are in place.

Director and senior management involvement in marketing and BDM increases towards the end of a project lifecycle. Actions include managing client expectations. This is particularly important where the project business captured these at the front-end and continuity has been partially maintained on the client side or the project management team assess the project for client satisfaction not only to the extent of their involvement but also in relation to the expectations from the outset. This is either an opportunity to enhance reputational capital if it went well or opportunity to capture lessons learned which senior management are monitoring. In both cases these need to be fed back to either improve existing capability or tease out the lessons to induce new capabilities. It is also time to mobilize 'after-sales service' for the defects liability period. Further and frequently neglected is monitoring how the project is used during but also beyond the defects period. This provides important feedback on (i) understanding impact for sales purposes, (ii) understanding the client operations and the project as a solution, (iii) technical feedback, that is KPI-type feedback on lessons learned, (iv) maintaining the relationship as part of management towards repeat business opportunities (cf. the sleeping relationship – see Hadjikani, 1996; **Chapters 4** and **5**). Involvement at this stage has a further demonstration effect for organizational behaviour and action.

How much attention is given depends upon the marketing paradigm employed. The marketing mix requires the lightest touch from senior management, but involvement to a degree is important for good and 'best' practice for all approaches.

One of the important routines to help support performance improvement in general and capability development in particular is the combination of reflective practice (Schön, 1983) and self-reflection (Gustafsson et al., 2010). Reflective practice is a means of learning by interacting with issues, problems and failures with an outwards focus in order to explore ways of improving performance. It is akin to professional endeavour to improve and develop performance. Self-reflection is more specific. Self-reflection encourages stepping back from the mistakes and shortcomings of other organizations, especially the client. The focus is what the project business did wrong regardless or other factors. The object is to avoid making the same mistakes and to seek ways of turning around how these mistakes were liabilities for the client on the current project into resolutions and remedies to become assets for future projects (cf. Smyth et al., 2010).

Some of the issues addressed above, earlier and from the previous chapter are drawn together in Table 8.2 to illustrate how action and behaviour can be harnessed to

**TABLE 8.2** Marketing as the stimulus for internal integration through organizational behaviour

| *Marketing and BDM stimulus* | *Internal integration* | *Client integration* | *Network integration* |
|---|---|---|---|
| Interest in client needs and expectations | ✓ | ✓ | |
| Leverage of added value | ✓ | ✓ | ✓ |
| Response to emergent requirements | ✓ | ✓ | ✓ |
| Co-creation through creativity, problem solving and innovation | ✓ | ✓ | ✓ |
| Self-reflection for performance improvement and reflective practice | ✓ | | |
| Development and maintenance of client relationships | ✓ | ✓ | ✓ |
| Focus on customer lifetime value | ✓ | | |

encourage integration and capability development. The interfaces are considered, being purely internal, dyadic with the client and in the broader network.

An implication of the foregoing analysis based upon organizational behaviour is not that marketing and BDM can somehow be absorbed into project management or MoP, but that it has distinct roles that support MoP.

## Conclusion

MoP provides the starting point as an approach to managing projects with an emphasis upon the front-end management. It has been linked to the market management and marketing. Value is an important issue for marketing and MoP alike. The implications for systems and integration, especially those that render the optimal service, have been considered. The mobilization of capabilities has constituted an important part for adding value by delivering integrated solutions. This adds up to a type of business model with an earning logic of which MoP forms part. Marketing and BDM provide strong threads running through this analysis. Marketing originates in the corporate hierarchy, yet BDM conceptually starts at the front of the front-end. A programme-cum-client management perspective is cyclical over client lifetimes and serial project lifecycles, linking vertical and horizontal management.

Project complexity is a driving force for holistic integration and service development. Complexity has been and is growing. Marketing and BDM have significant roles in proactively engaging with these issues because of its strategic position in the project lifecycle, coupled with the normative argument that the function should be involved throughout for purposes of (added) value delivery and client management. Marketing and BDM are not therefore purely part of MoP along the lifecycle but have an integrating role from investment through to earning revenue and the development of capabilities, some of which are marketing-specific. The chapter has also given redress to the conceptual and practice-based ambition of forcing marketing into the execution mold of project management and dilute it within the MoP approach. Practice has paid greater heed to marketing and BDM than researchers within project management.

A main message is that the current lack of attention to marketing within MoP serves to reinforce the task-centric approach to project management, inducing misalignment with the complex project demands from clients. A complimentary client-centric and service focus has continued to be developed, but it comes with a 'health warning' at this point. Apart from the incremental adoption, the diversity of needs and complexity means diverse approaches to marketing and BDM are required. This is not a panacea, and some clients will continue to want the marketing mix approach, either because they have considerable in-house expertise or because they are transactional. Each market segment requires service on its terms.

Ten substantive issues were introduced in **Chapter 1,** and the following contributions have been made to addressing several of these.

**SI no. 1:** ***Market Management*** is addressed to the extent that MoP forms part of a business model. While its purpose is to reduce project failures, to the extent that it induces greater success for project businesses employing it, the more the market growth is likely to be derived from improved performance. It is a proactive approach to the market. This is reinforced by the links to other functions, including marketing and BDM.

**SI no. 2:** ***Service Management*** starts with marketing and MoP. This commences with interaction prior to a project, during front-end development, in terms of the project output and application in use. How MoP is a service and how it improves the quality of the service experience during execution is germane to marketing and vice versa.

**SIs no. 3** and **4:** ***Portfolio Management and Programme Management*** are features which marketing and MoP recognize, and indeed P$^3$M is gaining traction with the project community on the supply side.

**SI no. 4:** ***Client Management*** is pertinent to the extent that MoP provides a receptive coordinating space into which clients can be managed, although it excludes CLV criteria for relational approaches. Linking MoP with programme management is important in addressing linkage between theory and practice.

**SI no. 5:** ***Marketing and BDM*** are conceptually existent prior to a project on the horizontal dimension and operates vertically too. BDM is conceptually located at the front of the front-end within the MoP approach and thus plays a strong role in the way in which projects are framed and developed at the front-end on the supply side. The involvement of marketing and BDM is continuous over the project lifecycle, including evaluation at the back-end post-completion. It extends beyond those boundaries as part of programme management through client management, whether driven by internal programme management or responding to client programme management. As has been argued, marketing and BDM occupy a *central interface function.*

**SI no. 6:** ***BDM and Client Management*** is partially addressed in terms of continuity and consistency of operation during any project lifecycle, yet is not central to managing continuity between projects as it by definition outside MoP, except through the link with programme management.

**SI no. 7:** ***Vertical Systems and Integration*** has played a secondary role to horizontal forces along project lifecycles, but the significance of the MoP lifecycle can only be fully appreciated with the inclusion of vertical systems. Coordination mechanisms for integration have been explored through organizational capabilities, including those of marketing.

**SI no. 8:** ***Cross-functional Systems and Coordination Mechanisms*** has played a significant role in this chapter, and the recognition of current weak systems in many project businesses has been identified and means to address this within the MoP frame of reference has been examined. Informal routines, especially for BDM at the front end have been addressed, assessing their coordinating contribution.

**SI no. 9:** ***Marketing and Managing the Project Lifecycle*** has provided the primary theme for the chapter with marketing and MoP intertwined in a mutually reinforcing role. While marketing is only one function within the parameters of MoP, it both precedes MoP and continues beyond its end point. Therefore, its conceptual location at the front of the front-end on the supply side mirrors the procurement function on the client side.

**SI no. 10: *Marketing and Value Creation*** are linked, in particular from the perspective of service provision, a topic to be further developed in **Chapter 10**, and from the viewpoint of delivering integrated solutions. Added technical and service value are therefore important, reinforcing the role of marketing and BDM not only as the means to secure work, but also as the gate through which client needs are served. These two issues are intrinsically linked for the quality of service, and adding value has considerable bearing on the ability to secure work.

This chapter has built upon the previous one, further opening up the marketing-project management to include the front-end and post-completion. There are several main *recommendations* for research that flow from the analysis:

A. Research into the marketing-management of projects can be developed at a finer grain of analysis and empirical research on the supply side.
B. Research needs to be conducted into the interrelationships and interplay between marketing and the development of integrated solutions.
C. Research is needed to provide more detailed analysis of organizational behaviour at the front-end, which can include marketing and BDM roles and conduct.

Several main *recommendations* can be identified for practice from the examination provided in this chapter:

1. The adoption of extensive MoP and comprehensive marketing principles is still a work in progress, and practitioners have the advantage of linking these with every new measure and principle adopted.
2. Integration of BDM as a distinct yet essential component MoP, which looks forwards along the entire lifecycle as well as back to the client and associate information, a mindset from which BDMs and those in a BDM role can benefit.
3. Putting in place systems and capabilities for solutions integration aligned to client need.

In summary, the integration of marketing and MoP has yet to be fully considered in theory and practice. The strength of solutions and the embodied value in technical and service terms is only a strong as internal horizontal integration along project lifecycles. MoP has provided the focus with a front-end emphasis. The next chapter moves back a stage and up a strategic level to locate the unfolding picture into the resource-based view of the firm.

# 9

# RESOURCES AND INVESTMENT IN THE FIRM FOR MARKET MANAGEMENT

## Introduction

The book commenced with a market management overview in the first two chapters in order to conceptually drill down to explore issues that confront management and affect marketing. One of those issues was the use of resources in general, and investment in particular. Marketing competencies and capabilities are resources for service provision according to the optimum within any paradigm, the scope being greatest under proactive relational approaches. Having analyzed several of the main marketing approaches in recent chapters and then the implications for the front-end as well as execution, it is appropriate to examine in further detail the way in which strategic investment is made in project businesses for market management, marketing and business development management (BDM). This continues to place market management and business development at the forefront of consideration. Marketing is a primary means of market management. Marketing, however, has less resonance in respect of the marketing mix than it does for relationship marketing, the project marketing variant and entrepreneurial marketing. The inductive and iterative approach of entrepreneurial marketing perhaps has fewer direct implications than relationship marketing. Nonetheless, resources have to be allocated and be ready for mobilization when called upon under the entrepreneurial marketing approach.

This chapter looks back to the strategy of the firm for market management and forward to how investment is used or can be used for the benefit of the project business and clients. The implication is that the analysis is more normative and prescriptive than in previous chapters. There is almost always some applied component in management and project management research, and its improvement can figure implicitly or explicitly. There is no apology made for a normative and prescriptive element at this point and is entirely justifiable in terms of epistemology (cf. Smyth and Morris, 2007). It is possible to distinguish between content about the current state of play and what it could or ought to be. The reporting on what *is* known from research evidence and what *is* known conceptually has been consistently applied. The normative and prescriptive aspects arise from the potential between known theory and practice on the ground, where research is either still needed or where concepts have still to be tried and tested in reality. This builds upon the analysis to examine why investment is low in project industries, which has normative implications and prescriptive ones given current trends of complexity in project requirements.

Projects, the patterns of client demand and marketing are reflexively undergoing a series of changes. These could be seen as fundamental changes in project business. Project businesses, certainly the prime or main contractor, are best placed to integrate solutions provided by others and with others. Yet, it could be argued that it is reasonably simple for clients to acquire these skills in-house for large programmes, especially if provision is at the base level of meeting minimum requirements at time–cost–quality/scope. It is possible and a case exists for project businesses to develop additional capabilities to make their position as systems integrators more compelling. This is essentially the 'make' or 'buy' issue in transaction cost economics, and as projects become more complex in terms of need profile, project businesses are unable to sufficiently grasp the complexity of client need at a transactional level. In other words, the systems integrator in the market may be insecure. Contractors in this role can be threatened with substitution from clients by their own in-house provision (cf. Porter, 1980). On the other hand, it will only take one or two significant first-tier project businesses to begin develop enhanced capabilities that prove effective in the market place. They will stimulate others to 'play catch-up'. This will start to drive resource allocation across sectors that project businesses serve towards a range of capability development, initially copying the types of capability the pioneers have already developed. Insufficient research attention has been given to how such changes work out on the ground. For example there has been a tremendous amount of interesting and useful research investigation of organizational learning and knowledge management over the last 20 years, but the actual take-up in project sectors has fallen short of the research attention it has been given. In one sense, this whole body of research work has come to have a strong normative implication, albeit indirectly, but perhaps more significantly has come to exemplify the resistance to investment in new competencies and capabilities.

This preamble begins to open up investigation into a range of issues. Resources are scarce and indeed *customers are the ultimate scarce resource* (Srinivasan and Hanssens, 2009: 293). This will continue to be the case, except in overheated markets, and thus:

A. How investments are made in project businesses will set the scope for market management, the effectiveness of marketing and the sales processes, and developing capabilities to make a positive impact on the marketplace.
B. Investment is primarily top-down, allocated through budgeting, but tactical application and the mobilization of social capital are predominantly bottom-up.
C. The extent to which resource management is characterized by practices and decision-making primarily conducted from the perspective of the discipline

of financial management or from the perspective of an integrated operational concern is an issue of tension in many project businesses.

Therefore, there are investments made top-down and resources in the form of new capabilities and social capital developed bottom-up. This raises several important theoretical issues. First, resource use has different implications for project businesses that are primarily systems integrators compared to project businesses that are primarily solutions and systems sellers, which at a general level divides the emphasis between 'soft' and technically related investment. It also raises marketing-related capabilities of sensing and relationship building, for bringing them together to deliver value that is perceived to be valuable from the client perspective rather than the supplier perspective. Finally, allocation is insufficient in itself, implementation and subsequent capability development are important and a major management challenge. This practical issue distinguishes between the act of investment and the activity (which some critics of resource-based view [RBV] fail to do). Locating theoretical issues in the content of the book, it furthers the goal of bringing together the prior emphasis upon the demand side from conceptualization of MoP with the supply-side need for the development of capabilities to deliver valuable solutions that impact client organizations.

Market management and business development, marketing and BDM are types of management capabilities that can grow the business and together provide a prime means to do so by serving clients through the delivery of high-value integrated solutions. These link with other management and project capabilities to lever and configure value through systems integration and systems production of technical and service content. This chapter provides an interesting juxtaposition to **Chapter 8**. Whereas MoP, especially at the front-end has had a research emphasis upon the demand-side factors to secure improved performance, the capabilities literature has had a greater emphasis upon the supply side. Of course, the project front-end and capabilities are relevant to both sides of the exchange. The procurement–marketing interface is a significant organizational interface for integration on the supply side. It may not always reflect practice as conducted, but theory developed poses interesting opportunities for deepening understanding for research and practice. The conceptual point of entry here is the resource issue.

## Resources, capabilities and projects

Market management and in particular marketing develops with investment and the best use of resources. There is a theoretical alliance with the RBV of the firm. According to Penrose (1959), firms are constrained by their managerial capabilities, notably how they allocate resources. The implications concern how owners and senior managers shape investment and harness resources in a competitive marketplace. Barney defines resources as: . . . *all assets, capabilities, organizational processes, firm attributes, information, knowledge etc. controlled by a firm, that enable the firm to conceive of and implement strategies that improve its efficiency and effectiveness* (1991: 101).

There are certain types of allocation that are more decisive than others in relation to the ability to compete. Few firms at any one time can have competitive advantage in their marketplace, but how they choose to compete is part of market management. In other words, the alignment of resources to serve particular sets and combinations of need means that these firms are best able to serve those markets, segments and niches. Yet they are excluding themselves from best serving other segments, although they may be able to work in those segments at an adequate level of provision. This links directly with marketing strategy as to which markets, segments and niches to occupy. However, under-investment may lead to an inability to manage the market, for example through differentiation, or low investment subjects the market to intensive competition amongst suppliers of similar base-level provision. This latter position has been the case in some project markets, for example construction.

Barney (1991; 2003) has proposed the VRIN model. The model is used to argue that the more resources are allocated to activities that are considered *valuable, rare, inimitable* and *non-substitutable*, giving the acronym VRIN, the more strongly placed the firm is in against its competitors. Integration provides an important means to organize the resource and deliver capabilities that offer differentiation (cf. Lawrence and Lorsch, 1967). VRIN can be viewed as somewhat mechanistic or static. Once investments are committed and until the next round of new investment for example from R&D or in new product development, the outcome is determined. A more dynamic picture emerged with theories of *core competencies* (e.g. Prahalad and Hamel, 1990; Hamel and Prahalad, 1994) and *dynamic capabilities* (e.g. Helfat, 1997; Teece et al., 1997; Eisenhardt and Martin, 2000; Helfat and Peteraf, 2003). Both these theories extended beyond the key activities of the firm, that is, beyond the essential requirements to be a systems integrator in the oil and gas market or a systems solution manufacturer and erector in the glass curtain wall market for office projects. Those key activities require skills and experience that comprise 'threshold competencies' to meet the minimum requirements, whereas *core competencies* are those necessary to add technical service value that create competitive advantage, typically through related activities such as organizational learning and knowledge management. These opportunities can arise from operational problem solving, for example remedying the 'wobble' on the Millennium Bridge project, London, gave engineers Arup the opportunity to turn a problem around into a competency that would be applied to tall building engineering and technology. Another example might be collaborative practices for improving performance across a programme of projects or applied to the institutional level in disaster management projects.

A core competency, according to Hamel and Prahalad (1994), must embody the following attributes:

- Create competitive advantage;
- Serve clients more effectively or efficiently, that is, yield client benefit by adding value;
- Be intangible and difficult to copy;

- Become spread across business units;
- Become embedded in the organization.

Core competencies are therefore owned and articulated by the firm through structuring and processes that are not dependent upon individuals alone, an important point not always fully appreciated by practitioners for consistent and enduring implementation. It is a moot point as to where core competencies end and dynamic capabilities begin. Dynamic capabilities can be conceived as the articulating process between functions and processes that help to improve effectiveness of operations. There is overlap and some lack of clarity across the literature. For example, organizational learning can be seen as a core competency or a capability, yet a fine distinction can be made in the sense that it is the type of learning that yields the advantage as a core competency, for example in relationship management or an area of hyper-specialization for innovation within environmental sustainability, whereas it is the process of learning that is the capability.

There is also a lack of clarity in practice, particularly around the need to invest, for example giving teams instructions to conduct an activity does not necessarily lead to the firm having the competence and capability. For example, having project key performance indicators (KPIs) and instructions to apply lessons learned do not automatically lead to capturing of the processes and actions needed to apply the lessons, nor do they lead to translation into a set of generic principles or a 'toolbox' for use, and nor do they lead to transfer to a programme level or into a knowledge management system for storage. Only awareness is created of its existence for potential roll-out and application on other projects. Implementation is dependent upon the spreading and embedding of core competencies and the dynamic capabilities, indeed spreading and embedding can be argued to be dynamic capabilities in their own right.

## Forms of capabilities and competencies

Core competencies and dynamic capabilities have taken many forms. As a heuristic or rule of thumb, the more strategic the core competency or dynamic capability, the more difficult it is to implement, but the more difficult it is to imitate, so the more sustainable it is for the competitive advantage it yields. Inversely, the more tactical it is, the easier it is to emulate and the less sustainable any advantage. They tend to develop iteratively and incrementally. This gives ample scope for the dynamic and committed firm to invest small amounts on an annual basis: step-by-step development of a competency and capability to a deeper level or an adjacent addition to a capability to keep a step ahead of the competition as they try to 'play catch up'. There is a difference as to the types of capabilities appropriate for the type of project business. The solutions seller resides in knowledge-based domains and therefore capabilities around learning and knowledge management have been on the increase of the last decade or more. The systems seller delivers specialist and integrated solutions with a considerable reliance upon technical skills and expertise. While the service content will be highly significant in order to survive, meeting threshold levels of quality is a prerequisite. Hyper-specialization in knowledge and applied technical and technological competence give the solutions and systems seller competitive advantage. Systems integrators are not direct producers and therefore their dynamic capabilities are 'softer' management issues that are underpinned by technical knowledge and expertise. These types of capabilities are less explicit and more intangible, so awareness creation of these organizational and project capabilities, including the ability to communicate them as important capability in its own right, becomes significant.

Core competencies and dynamic capabilities may be unrecognized. Frequently they develop as a consequence of other changes and bottom-up initiatives, for example from operational lessons learned, which can be harnessed through further investment, then spread and embedded across the business unit (BU) and then the business. This type of iterative and incremental development is particularly appropriate to project businesses, which avoid substantial investment programmes in markets of high risk and for undertaking high-risk projects. It is akin to the affordable loss principle applied at the level of corporate strategy. It is also relevant to marketing generally and specifically to entrepreneurial marketing at a tactical level of operation (**Chapter 6**).

One approach adopted by many firms, including project businesses, has been the recent trend to elevate tactical issues to strategy levels, building competencies and capabilities around them. For example, procurement functions have been targeted by adding partnering and supply chain management capabilities. Project businesses have emulated these initiatives, but there have been translation problems. Investment committed to intervening in the supply chain and for partnering to develop innovation can be defrayed over multiple units of manufacturing output. That is a challenge for asset specific goods and services, but it is possible to select suppliers with capabilities that are generic enough to apply to a range of clients and projects, but sufficiently specific to differentiate and add value for a range of clients to a project business. This operates at a programme or segment level (Kujala et al., 2010; Table 5.1).

Organizational behaviour and moral competencies offer scope for applicability across project businesses, for example through behavioural programmes, behavioural codes of conduct, collaborative practices, the development of trust and relationship management (Smyth, 2014). They are more difficult to monitor and develop. However, the degree of difficulty is closely associated with the potential ability to integrate. Evidence suggests that project businesses lack processes to spread and embed capabilities and managers rely upon individuals to take responsibility for implementation (e.g. Smyth, 2013a). While this may have had some beneficial outcomes, the initiative and drivers typically emanate from clients to which project businesses have reacted. There has been a lack of proactive commitment and investment amongst project businesses to develop and embed capabilities. As Yisa et al. (1996: 61) stated in a project and marketing context: *programme, controls, and commitment must breathe life into the resources provided*, and the resources must be sufficient to bring life.

For ease of discussion, I will refer to both core competencies and dynamic capabilities in terms of dynamic capabilities. There are different types of dynamic capabilities that have already been referred to throughout and especially in **Chapter 7**. Organizational, marketing and project capabilities have been raised (e.g. Davies and Brady, 2000;

Brady and Davies, 2004; Hobday et al., 2005; Davies et al., 2007). These capabilities are not always distinguished as to whether they are at the threshold level or core or dynamic levels of capabilities. Capabilities to develop and integrate solutions could be interpreted as a response to the extent of prevailing project failure and thus simply helping to improve the rate of meeting client requirements at a basic level. They can also be interpreted as merely incorporating the increasing complexity and demands of clients – keeping pace with change. These are not the same as added value, which exceeds value added or the meeting of minimum requirements. However, the rate of failure reduction and the speed of incorporating new demands could yield short-term competitive advantage.

The advantage of adopting and developing capabilities at the threshold level is less short-term advantage over competitors, but more medium and long-term protection of the systems integrator role from substitution or being downgraded by clients taking on more or all of the integration function through building up their in-house capabilities. It is around this agenda that dynamic capabilities are necessary amongst project businesses, especially those in the systems integrator role rather than solutions and systems seller roles. Clients are unlikely to want to become second-tier suppliers, such as curtain wall manufacturers and specialized software engineers, but systems integrators who lose market to clients have and may pursue a takeover strategy to acquire solutions and systems sellers if they do not otherwise develop capabilities to add value through integration.

Winch and Leiringer (2013) state that project management is a dynamic capability from the client perspective, where they can attain competitive advantage if they are better at the integration of solutions in-house than through outsourcing to a systems integrator. Currently many clients are overstretched and under-resourced, which is currently a major factor for inducing failed projects (Merrow, 2011; Winch and Leiringer, 2013). While it is easy to 'scapegoat' the supplier (cf. Flyvbjerg et al., 2003), a reversal of the outsourcing trend in the wake of general problems in supply chains, evidenced in the Deepwater Horizon oil spill of 2006 involving Macondo in the BP supply chain, will reach a tipping point and prompt a trend of reversal to the predominant outsourcing model. The reversal may induce momentum and lead to substitution and dilution of the outsourced systems integrator role.

The need to meet requirements through integrated solutions delivery, to accommodate increasingly complex demands requires investment in capabilities. Developing further capabilities constitutes dynamic capabilities and adds value as well as protects the market from clients as potential in-house providers and other competitors. This constitutes proactive market management and business development. It is intrinsically linked to marketing theory, if not always linked to marketing as practiced in project businesses. The core competencies can be based around technical and management innovation at the project level, constituting both competencies and dynamic capabilities (cf. Brady and Davies, 2004). The dynamic capabilities can be organizational, such as those that are learning based (e.g. Davies and Brady, 2000; Hobday et al., 2005). The objective is to lead to improved project performance, and for the performance to be strong enough to influence the market performance, the ability to manage the market, and hence, marketing and BDM. The dynamic capabilities can also be marketing based (Möller, 2006; Davies et al., 2007). These will have a direct impact upon marketing as well as indirect impact upon performance.

The most popular two marketing capabilities have been proposed by Day (1994), who distinguishes between market sensing and customer-linking capabilities. Market sensing refers to the ability to identify and understand customer needs. Customer-linking capabilities refer to the building relationships to add value and learn from the market (Li and Calantone, 1998; Slater and Narver, 1994, 1995). Coordinating market sensing and relationship building has received less attention (Guenzi and Troilo, 2006). This is where marketing and BDM need integrating within project businesses. Each project business has to decide how to foster capabilities, and the emphasis between sensing and relationship building is part of the differentiation. It has been argued that these two are more easily combined in project businesses occupying positions early in the food chain where market research and scanning is partly achieved through a managed element of experimental BDM, say 10 per cent of effort (Smyth, 2000). This helps anticipate and identify emergent, market trends prior to more general diffusion of market intelligence in the industrial network that induces zero sum games whereby multiple organizations have access to the same information. Market sensing is also embedded in the relationship building within relationship marketing by extracting generic information across the client base as a means to identify generic needs for which generic capabilities can be developed and from which technical and service content can be customized and tailored for specific clients and projects. The grouping of types of generic need can be used as a basis for segmenting clients and potential clients against which resources can be committed for targeting, and for starting to develop customized and tailored propositions at prequalification and subsequently bid management stages.

The types of marketing based dynamic capabilities could include a considerable range of options. Some of the issues raised to this point provide pointers as to how these can be shaped through resource commitment:

- The capability to identify project capabilities, and leverage these as a 'product' ingredient into the marketing mix approach at the level of value propositions and bid offers.
- The integration of supplier segmentation and capability assessments in procurement with marketing segmentation and BDM to align (added) value propositions between the two functions and for generically identified client needs;
- The capability to utilize relationship marketing to add value through improved client understanding of specific needs and the recording of the proposed added value propositions or solutions in a risk or promise register for delivery in execution;
- The development of behavioural codes of conduct to articulate relationship management at the client–supplier interface to promote collaboration and value creation;
- The development of relationship management as a frame of reference within which entrepreneurial marketing is encouraged and nurtured;

- The development of key account management (KAM) as a client management system interfaced with project management as part of programme management;
- Conducting post-completion evaluation at 1-, 3- and 5-year intervals of benefits in use, linked to KPIs, especially on client satisfaction, to improve technical and service content for future projects.

Marketing competencies and capabilities of relationship management are resources for a client-centric approach to service provision. These are capability inputs for the firm (cf. Barney, 1991; Peteraf, 1993). The objective has been to demonstrate how these related capabilities influence competitive advantage (e.g. Bharadwaj et al., 1993; Day, 1994; Srivastava et al., 1998; Srivastava et al., 2001). Empirical work has tested this causal chain. Results consistently corroborate the connection (Barney and Arikan, 2000).

Marketing-related capabilities link into the analysis of firm networks (e.g. Dyer and Singh, 1998; Doz and Hamel, 1989; cf. Håkansson, 1982). The demand-side perspective is better understood in this respect – the procurement perspective (e.g. Håkansson, 1982) – than the supply-side marketing perspective across project sectors. Less still is understood with regard to project businesses (cf. Dubois and Gadde, 2000), despite the fact that project markets have been heavily reliant upon outsourcing for a longer period compared to many other mainstream industrial markets. The role of the systems integrator is pivotal in this respect as a formal and informal procurer of solutions for integration. In other words, what clients are seeking is a set of operational competencies from the outsourced elements (frequently the systems sellers of integrated solutions), but in order to effectively lever these, a robust set of marketing competencies and capabilities is necessary on the supply side via the systems integrator role – the prime or main contractor as the first tier in the client supply chain. The lack of internal integration and failure to lever (added) value aligned to client need is a major issue that is being conceptualized across functions and at a detailed level (e.g. Hobday et al., 2005), yet is still largely unresolved in practice (e.g. Smyth, 2013a). Project businesses may find it less easy to continue to overlook this issue as client demands become more sophisticated and projects more complex. From the client perspective, it is not the systems and procedures that they see and observe, although these provide important means to link structures and processes, it is the action and behaviour. The actions and behaviour, expressed in relationships and through relationship management systems provide a means to convey to the client the intangible and underpinning 'soft' capabilities that are part of the service of integration and delivery. This awareness creation, as previously noted, can be a marketing capability. It is upon the basis of actions and behaviour that assessments are made as shown in Fact Box 9.1. The evidence clearly indicates the importance of social capital and how that is expressed through relationships (Nahapiet and Ghoshal, 1998; Kale et al., 2000) – a critical factor of relationship marketing (**Chapters 4** and **5**) and to an extent in entrepreneurial marketing (Sarasvathy and Dew, 2005; **Chapter 6**).

### FACT BOX 9.1 INTER-ORGANIZATIONAL SYSTEMS INTEGRATION AND THE ROLE OF RELATIONSHIPS

Senior supply management executives at a large energy company were interviewed as a potential supplier that had been assessed to have the appropriate technical capabilities. The purpose of the face-to-face interviews was to assess the potential for a strategic alliance for a large steel contract for a major facilities project that would last several years. A key issue was whether the client was able to work with the supplier at the level of organizational behaviour, which included interpersonal relationships expressed through behaviour and action. It was reported as follows:

> We first developed a short list, and then spent a day with each of the potential suppliers getting to know them and interviewing them. We recognized that the most important thing we should look for was alignment with our culture. When they walked into the room, we asked them some very general questions, such as: 'What is your business philosophy?' and 'How do you view us as a potential customer?' In some cases – we received blank looks. In other cases, we realized within five minutes that we could not work with them. We ended up selecting a supplier that we had used in the past – because they understood how we worked, and had the same values as we did. We even came up with a name for this methodology that we are now applying in other areas of the business: Value-Based Business Integration.

*Source*: Cousins et al. (2006: 859).

## Implementation and development

Customers invest time and effort to build relations with potential key suppliers (Krause et al., 2007). Conceptually, this makes a commitment of social capital to explore the potential relationship (Nahapiet and Ghoshal, 1998). The aim is to form a panel of key suppliers that achieves a balance between competition at the point of exchange and cooperation during the transaction (Fraser Johnson et al., 1999). The tangible benefits sought include reduced cost, greater quality and flexibility, and more reliable delivery. The pursuit of these benefits may require discussion and sharing of common experiences in order to develop collaborative expectations and understanding of ambiguous information (e.g. Daft and Lengel, 1984; Doz, 1996). The dialogue around benefits induces a basis from which relatively stable routines develop to lever value from suppliers. Providing the relationship is interdependent rather than dependent, problems of complacency from the supplier, groupthink between the parties and insufficient monitoring from the customer are less likely to occur (cf. Janis, 1982). This requires effort and resource commitment and capabilities for realization (Cousins et al., 2006; Winch and Leiringer, 2013; Fact Box 9.1).

Over-dependency, complacency and groupthink form part of what Villenaa et al. (2011) call the *dark side* of social capital. At this point, it is important to distinguish between how social capital can appreciate with use. While physical and fixed assets wear out and depreciate, social and ethical practices are both developed and refined through psycho-motive learning as routines, norms and habits (cf. Nelson and Winter, 1982; Helfat and Peteraf, 2003; Appiah, 2010). Working well, social capital therefore appreciates with use. If the focus stays outward and goal driven, then added value and savings increase, hence the benefits continue to accrue. Retrenching to an inward focus amongst either party invokes the risk of dysfunctional outcomes and operational rigidities.

Suppliers need to demonstrate commitment to relationship building, collaboration and having a social orientation in the way business is conducted from first contact whether they are systems integrators, solutions sellers or systems providers. A social orientation is entirely business-like, allocating resources to build relationships and manage serial customer exchanges for profit. It is merely a different earning logic to a transactional one of keeping costs low and pursuit of self-interest. The transactional approach leads to high monitoring costs, adversarial behaviour and high legal costs. Both have strengths and weaknesses, but it is the relational approach that typically induces lower transactional costs.

Transactional organizations tend to be task-centric, constraining integration in pursuit of low management costs. First, this occurs internally as each function looks at its own remit from the point of view of its expertise, designing systems and procedures without reference to other internal functions. Second, the series of internal subsystems are barriers to effective working for systems integration of external expertise and content. The summative point is the lack of an outward focus towards serving the client and typically myopia towards their own organizational shortcomings as systems integrators.

Penrose (1959) called marketing capabilities a new type of selling, which integrates functions in-house with those functions to deliver value in the industrial network of supply chain and clusters (Davies, 2004). Integration in-house combines threshold and dynamic capabilities. Figure 9.1 shows how relationship marketing and relationship management are concepts that can be dynamically linked on the ground. This is part of an increasing awareness and emphasis upon services content and experience over the years, leading to new business models each with a different earning logic for generating turnover and profit (e.g. Vandermerwe and Rada, 1988; Grönroos, 2000; Vargo and Lusch, 2004; Wikström et al., 2009; see **Chapter 10**). The environment, in particular the structure of the market, constrains marketing options. Markets where suppliers are reactive followers rather than market makers present less choice. There remain options, and the degree to which project markets provide constrained choice can be exaggerated. It is the awareness and willingness of senior management to manage the market and develop the business that is a primary bottom-up constraint (cf. McDonald et al., 2011). Management generally has

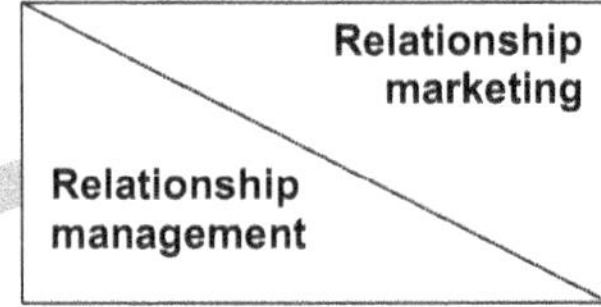


**FIGURE 9.1** The integration of relationship marketing and management capabilities

a tendency to believe they offer more in the market than customers perceive them to do (McDonald et al., 2011; **Chapter 1**), and this can lead to underinvestment in capabilities and especially service provision. This is corroborated in project markets, as the example in the roll out of phase two of a new city transport service demonstrates, where the contractors and client held different perceptions. Fact Box 9.2 provides a summary of research findings and points towards some of the issues that will also be raised in **Chapter 10**.

Clients are typically dissatisfied with completed facilities, even for projects without high complexity; for example Neap and Aysal (2004) found only 47 per cent of clients were satisfied with the facilities delivered, which is in line with client satisfaction KPIs for complex facilities in construction markets (Smyth, 2010b). There is a tendency for project businesses to shun responsibility for such issues and for their contributions to the issues faced. One line of argument presented has been that the systems integrator role is far from a secure position and investment to defend the position is needed from project businesses. Markets are made rather than pre-given, and the supply side contributes to making the market. Project businesses have been the prime educators of clients to accept upon price as the sole criteria. At the broadest level of analysis this is due to the historic dominance of the transactional approach in many project markets. It will continue to occupy an important place, but leads to price as the primary, sometimes only, criterion if dominant (**Chapter 3**). Relationship marketing, its variants, and entrepreneurial marketing lead to greater differentiation about how to compete and thus less intensive competition. The transactional approach is only one way and new strategies and segments have a place. Thus, top-down and layered strategy development for business models for service

## FACT BOX 9.2 MISALIGNMENT OF SERVICE PROVISION AT THE CLIENT–PROJECT BUSINESS INTERFACE

The new transport service revolved around a pay-as-you-go provision of bikes in a major capital city. The project involved required dispersed infrastructure provision and a project package and contracts for operation. A questionnaire survey was conducted amongst a main contractor and the client for project management. The results showed there is a misperception held by the contractor as to the quality of the service provided and the perception the client held of the service. The perception gap was considerable and during follow up interviews in the client body, the feeling was they would not have appointed the same contractor with hindsight. The contractor did not understand the client 'perceived value' and thought they understood what was valuable to the client. There were complexities and a lack of information at the outset for the project was innovative for the client, and the imposed political timescale was demanding. This provided an opportunity for the contractor to build close relationships, help the client define the benefits and articulate the requirements and co-create the project value in the early stages of execution. This could have been started during the pre-bid stage as part of prequalification on an affordable loss basis within the parameters of ethical public procurement frameworks. The contractor thought they had had proceeded on this basis but the client was reticent in sharing information.

There was agreement about the importance of collaborative relationships at the interface and deficiencies on each side. Both organizations agreed about the lack of good relationships although the client felt this more strongly than the contractor. The poor relationships are perceived to have damaged service provision and performance. The contractor believes it actively managed the client relationship. One project manager for the contractor stated:

> Yes, having strong relationships is something that we promote as being crucial to project success which is why we have many measures in place to try and achieve this. I think if we didn't have some of the challenges, which impacted the relationship then it would have continued to be a strong relationship.
>
> (p. 47)

This is not perceived to be the case on the client side. The source of the misperception is likely to have multiple dimensions, including the contractor not understanding what is valuable to the client, having a task rather than service orientation, the client being reluctant to share information, exerting

(*Continued*)

**FACT BOX 9.2** (Continued)

its market power on the contractor, and public accountability factors. As one client member stated:

> It is difficult because as a public sector organization we are cost focused to ensure value for money and throughout the procurement processes. I think there could be more emphasis placed on 'working together' and developing strong open and honest relationships as I think this will save money in the long run even though at the outset it may be more expensive. This is difficult to achieve with so many procurement restrictions.
>
> (p. 52)

There is agreement over the lack of trust and honesty. The first contractual dispute incurred considerable relational damage. The contractor is not thought to have been responsive to emergent requirements (cf. Smyth, 2013b). Some client members believe they were very transparent, but views vary on this in the client body. The contractor believes they customized and tailored to client needs, but the client has a different perception, the contractor being unresponsive to changing and emergent requirements. Despite the lack of information from the client side and the contractor claiming to manage relationships, it was the client that felt there was insufficient dialogue (cf. Ballantyne and Varey, 2006).

Although many clients under-estimate the investment needed to manage projects effectively on the client-side (Merrow, 2011; Winch and Leiringer, 2013), contractors have misperceptions that can lead to underinvestment in service capabilities.

*Source*: Data derived and analysis developed from Madhavji (2012).

development and profit generation is shown in Figure 9.2. The capability development can have an emphasis located in different parts of the primary functions, namely marketing, human resource management, finance and operations.

Service development is more discrete, configured at different levels in the hierarchy and for the integration for delivery in client and relationship management across the range of markets (Christopher et al., 2002) and over the project lifecycles from the portfolio, programme and project levels of management (Figure 9.3). The service offerings can be fed into marketing and BDM of the systems integrator from the systems seller where integrated technological and technical solutions. The systems integrator provides a service and relies upon provision of project service and systems solutions from others. To optimize provision, integration of management functions covering procurement, cost estimating, technical service departments, health and safety, legal and financial control as well as marketing directly and indirectly to configure service development and provision.

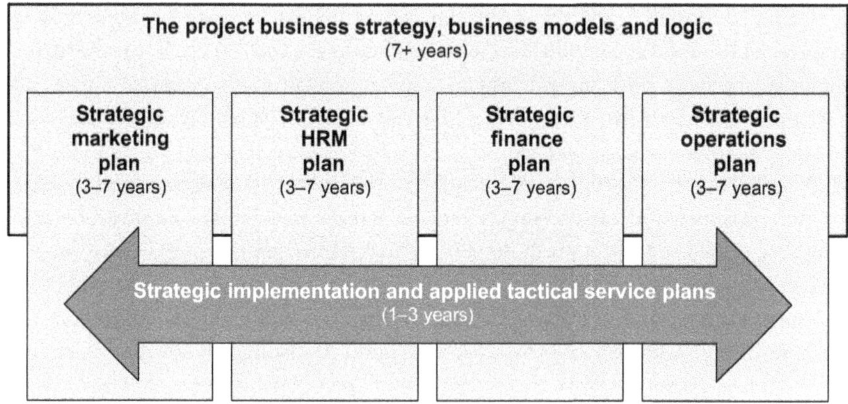


**FIGURE 9.2** Functional and cross-functional implementation

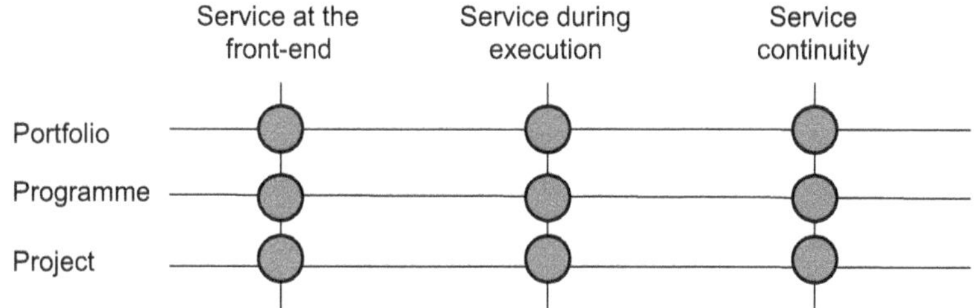


**FIGURE 9.3** A client- and service-orientated investment matrix

Two brief examples can be used as illustrations. First, environmental sustainability provides an area for service development. As a non-marketing capability it has a technological and technical focus or a service focus based upon areas of knowledge and expertise for integration. Four major international contractors were examined and all four placed considerable emphasis on their policies of environmental sustainability in their own ways. The contractors all thought they were the best in the market, although only one can be best. All placed more emphasis in practice on the office environments than site work and qualifying subcontractors, especially beyond the next tier in the supply chain. The propositions lacked distinction and were largely confined to compliance with standards and regulations and 'best practice' amongst peers. There was an absence of commitment and investment to developing services of competitive advantage or specialist knowledge areas. Rhetoric was ahead of practice, so while it is unnecessary to pursue this as an area of advantage, they were claiming to have done so. As one bid manager stated: *We are genuinely better than the competition on that . . . It's a huge differentiator.* A more candid statement was solicited from a chief executive: *. . . there is a lot of spin going on around sustainability . . . and a lot more that could be done* (Smyth, 2013c). Mature or dynamic capabilities have yet to be developed in regard to these leading contractors.

Second, customer or client relationship management has been recently addressed in project businesses at the portfolio management level (Voss, 2012), in particular the alignment between project portfolios and customer relationship portfolios. Voss had noted that increased focus was being given to customer relationship portfolios in research and practice (e.g. Tikkanen et al., 2007; Homburg et al, 2009b; Terho, 2009). Studying 174 project portfolios across different industries regarding relationship value for the customer and relationship value from the customer are significantly and positively related to project portfolio success. In other words, investing in relationship management was found to yield positive benefits for both customer and supplier.

There has been criticism of the core competencies and dynamic capabilities on the basis of tautology, which is to say it is difficult to distinguish competencies and capabilities as a resource from their existence as operational features. As Green et al. (2008: 429) argue in the project context, there is a tendency to conflate the resources with their effects, confusing the dynamic nature of the environment with the dynamic nature of the capabilities themselves. In response to this type of critique, the argument overlooks several points. Financial and other resources (or their representation in budgetary terms) are allocated into 'hard' and 'soft' artifacts and processes, which themselves become resources for mobilization in operations. The same principle holds if they are recognized from the bottom-up where committing effort into activities is distinct from the activities themselves for the effort could have been expended elsewhere or unexpended. There the effects of allocation or commitment are derived from core competencies and dynamic capabilities in use, rather than the original direct allocation. Green et al. are correct in acknowledging that they are in this sense second-order resources that affect other artifacts and processes that are threshold competencies or fundamental resources for core operations – note the different meanings for 'core' in management, whereby core business and core operations are essential to the business, yet core competencies are additional that extend beyond threshold requirements. The dynamic action 'on the ground' and the effects are different from the allocation and mobilization.

The cause-effect relationship between threshold or first-order competencies and capabilities and core competencies and dynamic capabilities or second-order inputs is non-linear and not necessarily one-directional. It is reflexive whereby they influence each other in the project business and dynamic project environment. Influence maybe within a management sphere, for example execution, or between spheres, for example between programme and project management or between marketing and procurement. This does render these capabilities hard to investigate between allocation and application, and in that respect, there is concurrence with Green et al. (2008), although the conceptual distinction remains and first- and second-order distinction in application helps yield clarification. To illustrate the point, the largest contractor in a national market was diversifying overseas operations. In terms of size, it occupied the second-tier position in the other national market. It was the most profitable amongst peers. The management believed this was due to careful sector or market segment selection. Investigation showed there were no particular sectors that yielded above-average profit rates and that the profitability in the project business was due to an effective and efficient set of routines between procurement-cum-project-management and financial operations. It was that 'dynamic capability' that needed replication regardless of market sector entered. This was not what the management wanted to hear and instead decided to select a new sector to enter – an easy decision but with hindsight proved detrimental. This also shows the intangible nature of capabilities for senior management decision-making. Replication and integration are difficult to analyze, hard to research and more difficult to manage. Further, attribution in ROI and ROMI calculations is problematic, rendering it difficult to justify (further) investment.

Less than satisfied customers are more prevalent where integration is lacking. This has been shown in research, for example, in the installation of power generating equipment and shipbuilding project markets. The cause of the lack of integration is multi-layered, yet a common starting point is the lack of customer orientation or focus. Liinamaa and Gustafsson (2009) found there is a characteristic lack of integration amongst these project businesses in three ways:

1. The integration of the technical content from both inside the project business and externally procured;
2. The increasing service component in provision of the project 'product' or technical content;
3. Integration that is customer-centric.

These three factors are interrelated. The consequence was that project businesses fail to see that services and in particular the service content as sufficiently significant. The growing service component is the product of the growing complexity of demands from clients (**Chapters 1** and **7**).

Integration is more than a simple function of joining up separate systems and aligning procedures. This is needed, but more complex integration is achieved through relationships supported from a system, which interfaces with other functional systems (Pryke and Smyth, 2006; **Chapter 4**; Figures 4.6, 8.2–8.5). This serves to emphasize that relationship marketing continues into and beyond prequalification and bid management, being involved in value creation and delivery, and vice versa as part of integration. Within the programme and project context relationships develop iteratively. Depth is aided by repeated contact, but the depth and resultant strength of relationships is more than contact frequency (Figure 4.3). Social interaction develops depth on a trial-and-error basis, cultivated and fine-tuned with effective communication (Vaagaasar, 2011). This accords with Gilligan's psychologically based ethics of care where nurture develops over time, sometimes paradoxically acceding to episodes and events that lead to a short-term loss of depth in order to preserve the relationship long-term, which is only valuable where the parties are intent upon continuing the relationship (Gilligan, 1982; Baier, 1994). Therefore, relationship capabilities are developed both top-down and bottom-up with resource allocation and iterative refinement being conducted. It is difficult, or else, everyone would already be doing it. That is why the relational aspects are the 'softest' and least tangible of the resource issues. Managed relationships are amongst the most difficult to develop, monitor and refine in ways that are simple enough for people to follow, powerful enough to support integration and flexible enough to evolve in changing markets.

## Conclusion

This chapter has sought to examine how resources are allocated in project businesses at a detailed level. The types of investment to deliver value to the client-base have been considered. Organizational, marketing-specific and project resources have provided a way to conceptually categorize investments. Threshold competencies and capabilities as categories and dynamic capabilities and core competencies as other categories provided another way. A further applied consideration has been the 'soft' management capabilities versus the harder edged technical and technological capabilities. This relates back to the type of project businesses conceptualized as systems integrators solutions and systems sellers of integrated technical and service provision. System sellers frequently occupy the second tier and below in supply chains as suppliers and subcontractors. The systems integrator and solutions seller are indirect producers of components but facilitators to bring together the components as the first-tier provider for the client.

These capabilities are typically pre-existing any one project, even though some of them may have emerged out of problem solving and innovation on previous projects. They are therefore injected into the sales activity to show the capability for adding value, into the bid management as win-strategies and into the execution stage for delivery. The process starts with investment allocation through portfolio management with detailed development either in specific functional roles, directly in client and programme management and implementation for or at the project level. The integration of the capabilities is tested at the front-end of each project for the injection at the front-end and for delivery during execution. The extent or lack of integration is partly evident during the front-end stages. The final test is integrated delivery, which is a function of the continuity between the front-end and execution as well as the integrated delivery during execution.

This entire process forms an important part of market management. The overarching concepts of market management are highly practical, although a major challenge for implementation on the ground. The effectiveness of marketing and the sales processes at the front of the front-end are critical to help establish the needs of clients. The fullness of client needs are seldom articulated in the requirements documentation or clarified in thought. Marketing and BDM functions help facilitate articulation. This is what brings together the previous demand-side emphasis upon MoP in a complimentary supply-side emphasis with the current supply-side emphasis upon capabilities for integrated solutions. As marketing and BDM are critical to this role, they become the locus for some capabilities, for example relationship management systems and procedures.

Investment is top-down, allocated through budgeting. However, tactical application and the mobilization of social capital are predominantly bottom-up. Top-down implementation currently poses challenges around financial management where issues of service provision are partly comprehended (**Chapter 2**). Senior management has an optimism bias of the value of the capabilities of their organization, believing they are performing better than they are perceived to be by clients and other stakeholders. This leads to underinvestment. Investment is necessary to yield returns for the long run. Market management and business development, marketing and BDM are types of management capabilities that can grow the business and together provide a prime means to do so by serving clients through the delivery of high-value integrated solutions. Marketing and BDM are a source of capabilities, enablers to identify the need for capabilities and facilitators to help support integration of other capabilities. They are not unique in this role, but prior research on MoP has paid this little attention to date, to the detriment of both research and practice. Project management can be considered a dynamic capability, particularly on the client side where it is separate from the core operations and provides options to grow their own capabilities for systems integration rather than outsource projects.

The theoretical issue of bringing together MoP and integrated capabilities on the supply side has been addressed. This has implications for practice in general and business development in particular. A series of substantive issues were identified in **Chapter 1** and progress on addressing these has been assessed chapter-by-chapter. The assessment for this chapter is presented next.

**SI no. 1:** ***Market Management*** is covered by the bringing together MoP with investment and the mobilization of capabilities at the front-end. This is a conceptual key to market management and business development. It is fundamentally *proactive* regarding investment prior to injection into any specific project opportunity or value proposition.

**SI no. 2:** ***Service Management*** conceptually assumes service content, whereas practitioners report service content as 'off the radar' of many project businesses. Services are of growing importance bundled attributes with technical content. Leverage occurs through organizational capabilities and systems integration. Services are also important in terms of the service experience, which leads to how project content is delivered and the impact this has on the client organization and other stakeholders. Further attention to addressing this issue is given in the next chapter.

**SI no. 3:** ***Marketing Investment and Portfolio Management*** are both central to firm performance. Resources are scarce, and foci for investment need to be aligned, whether marketing and BDM provide one potential foci. The function is typically isolated, so in terms of this chapter, there is a need to integrate marketing into mainstream project business activity in the same way that it needs incorporating into mainstream project management research. This does not involve subjugation but integration.

**SI no. 4:** ***Client Management and Programme Management*** are closely linked or integrated as functions and have been mentioned in that context, although not developed further in this chapter. Structuring of and investment in these functions is part of staking out the ground of competitiveness.

**SI no. 5:** ***Marketing and BDM*** take up position as a *central interface function* in this chapter. Three levels were identified as part of the issue. As an attitude and mindset, the issue has been addressed at senior management level for projects and corporate management in terms of the aligning investment to create value with how clients perceive value and performance. As a way of organizing, integration has provided the main focus to address investment and solutions delivery. Some attention has also been given to marketing capabilities as sets of tools and techniques, from market sensing to KAM.

**SI no. 10: *Marketing and Value Creation*** are inextricably linked, and this helps to link marketing to other functions too for *adding technical and service value*. This has been a general and underlying theme in the chapter, albeit not one pursued at a high level of detailed application. This issue and indeed the others on systems integration and coordination are important but may form detailed content of certain capabilities on the ground. However, this has been abstract consideration to link to investment and resource use.

There are several *recommendations* that flow from the analysis for the research communities:

A. Research into marketing as a pivotal point for integrating MoP and capability development at the front-end and tracing that through programmes and projects.
B. Research, as recommended in the last chapter and reinforced here, needs to be conducted into the interrelationships and interplay between marketing and the development of integrated solutions.
C. MoP has emphasized the demand side in many ways, yet there is greater need to examine investment in capabilities on the client side to both adequately manage projects and also as a dynamic capability for client organizations.

Several main *recommendations* can be identified for practice from the examination:

1. A more considered analysis of what investment is needed to ensure survival and develop the project business, which may be anchored in judgment and qualitative assessments as much, if not more, than quantitative measures.
2. Realistic assessments by senior management of what the capabilities are in their project businesses and the extent to which clients perceive them as valuable.
3. Putting in place systems and capabilities for solutions integration aligned to client need, as previously recommended and reinforced here.

This chapter has set up the conditions for what follows concerning an increasingly explicit and detailed focus upon services and service content from the client perspective. The service logic is an extension of a number of conceptual and theoretical developments in other management domains, although relationship marketing is a key source that provides a thread of continuity through what has come to be known as the *service-dominant logic*.

# 10

# THE SERVICE-DOMINANT LOGIC AND MARKET MANAGEMENT

## Introduction

Services account for over 70 per cent of gross national product (GNP) in advanced countries (Ostrom et al., 2010). Services are processes or process-led activities and artifacts. They are often time bound, for example projects and consultant services (Bitner et al., 2007). Service content is on the increase, and frequently bundled with the technical product content (e.g. Matthyssens and Vandenbempt, 1998; Normann, 2001; Vargo and Lusch, 2004; Edvardsson et al., 2008). The fastest growth is from the increase in business-to-business (B2B) transactions (e.g. Axelsson and Wynstra, 2002; Wölfl, 2005). To say that service content is on the increase within the content of projects arises from the growing complexity of projects and demands from clients. Further and fundamentally, projects require management and the management of projects *is* a service. This is the case in general, but even more so is it the case for the systems integrator role in project business. The systems integrator does not produce anything directly. Therefore, the systems integrator *is* a service provider. When the service issue is considered through the marketing lens of the project as a delivery channel, then service provision is evident: indeed, it should be self-evident.

The technical and engineering mindset that is dominant in so many sectors, from IT projects to oil and gas projects, is largely framed around the notion that they are producers. The production focus has long since been complimented with an attendant customer focus and service orientation across most industries. In the project domain, the task focus as the production equivalent prevails (Handy, 1997; Pryke and Smyth, 2006; **Chapters 1**, **4**, **7** and **8**). Projects are less about production, even amongst systems sellers producing and delivering integrated solutions; they are about tasks that are integrated to render the service, to deliver the project to the client, as owner and sponsor, and for other stakeholders.

How does this fit into the unfolding theorization on services and service provision? The conceptual and practice challenge is that project management provides a service, indeed sets of detailed services. Further, the management of production and other productive operations is being reconceived as service provision. In other words, the old product-service divide is breaking down. Products render services. Thus, the project management challenge becomes twofold. Under the inherited understanding, project management has been largely conceived as a producer role and under the current reconsideration is additionally seen as a service bundle.

This chapter is about that second shift in thinking. The challenge is provided by the theorized worldview or developing paradigm of service logic, usually termed the *service-dominant logic* (Vargo and Lusch, 2004). The shift is from a goods-dominant logic or inward looking production orientation to a service one. The service-dominant logic (S-DL) is still a work in progress (Vargo and Lusch, 2008a; Gummesson et al., 2010). It is grounded and has emerged from a number of applied and theoretical fields, but the main roots are in marketing, specifically relationship marketing and can be seen as an evolution of this paradigm.

The main shift in thinking offered by S-DL is that service and services are less a category of offer in the marketplace, but a perspective that informs how management is conducted (Vargo and Lusch, 2004; Edvardsson et al., 2005; Grönroos and Ravald, 2010). From a marketing viewpoint services, unlike goods, do not necessarily involve any transfer of ownership (Fitzsimmons and Fitzsimmons, 2011). This can be the case for some projects, for example a management consultancy involved with a change management project. Even where there is content that is transferred, project services account for around 80 per cent of the impact made, whereas goods or the 'product' content account for about 20 per cent of the project impact (Smyth, 2000). The logic of a service focus places the customer in a different position – an evolution of customers from 'passive audiences' to 'active players' (Prahalad and Ramaswamy, 2000). This is a reinforcement of the reactive to proactive argument in the transition from the marketing mix to relationship marketing.

The changing face of market management and marketing is bound up with the current shift to S-DL and how this impacts business models, the earning logic and service design. While project businesses are and claim to be transitioning towards a relationship marketing approach (**Chapter 4**), making incremental improvements towards a client orientation, a corresponding service orientation has still to get underway. While S-DL can be used to measure a theory–practice divide, S-DL is already present in practice, yet unacknowledged, managed or enhanced due to the lack of awareness. Certain authors place greater emphasis on current conditions and others place greater emphasis upon normative aspects. Vargo and Lusch (e.g. 2004; 2008; 2008b) place more emphasis upon the reinterpretation of what is currently conducted, while Prahalad and Ramaswamy (2004; 2004b) put more emphasis upon enhancement and prescriptive potential. Any difference is a matter of degree rather than a conceptual chasm. This chapter will examine the scope for reinterpreting current practices and for normative development and seeks to provide:

A. An analysis of the theoretical and applied characteristics of S-DL in project businesses and an examination of how these are internally managed.

B. A description of practices and their alignment with the theoretical and applied characteristics, particularly as a development of approaches to relationship marketing.
C. An evaluation of the strengths and weaknesses of S-DL and its pertinence to project businesses, in particular performance towards client and project business benefit.

The main message is that S-DL offers a way of understanding project delivery, pointing towards further ways to conceive of value propositions for clients, indeed for evaluating projects from a client perspective.

## The service-dominant logic in theory and practice

Services are said to be intangible (e.g. Berry and Parasuraman, 1991; Ballantyne, 1997), although more tangible than sometimes assumed (Vargo and Lusch, 2004). Figure 10.1 divides services into three categories. The tangibility of services ranges along a continuum from services that can largely be cognitively assessed in advance, for example an insurance policy, to a service that cannot be assessed in advance, except from reputation, such as some legal services or design services, to those that are highly intangible. In case of intangible services, you may not know exactly what you have got for a long time afterwards, for example the value of an education. Project management resides in the middle ground in terms of the way the service is delivered. Some of the benefits delivered can only be assessed long after the content is put to use.

S-DL has its primary roots in marketing, plus other influences, in particular the rise of *co-production* (Ramírez, 1999). Agile production, customization that harnesses small-batch production, and just-in-time techniques have been additional influences. Service development in what has come to be known as the *experience economy* (Pine and Gilmore, 1999; Payne and Frow, 2006), derived from the performing arts and activities where producing and consuming the service are simultaneous, is another source: for example a fairground ride or a concert has fed into the S-DL concept. The service encounter (e.g. Bitner, 1992; Gummesson, 2000) is another feeder that is closely associated with marketing. All challenge to some degree the

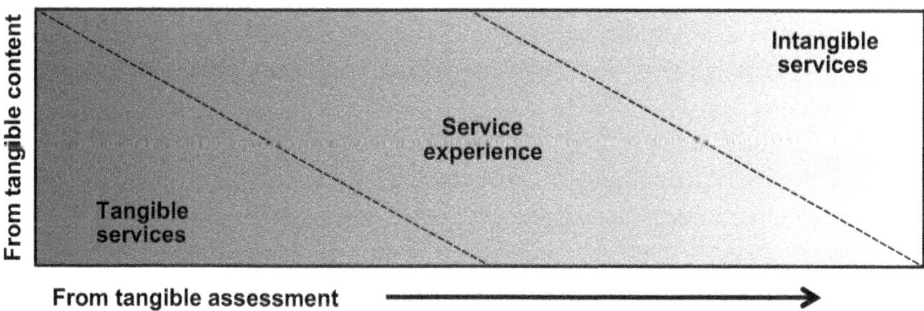


**FIGURE 10.1** The service continuum

goods–service split by blurring boundaries through production and through how and where profits are earned. For example, producing aero-engines and desktop printers do not make profits, but maintenance services and selling ink cartridges do. The car is a consumer product, and although some people are interested in cars as artifacts, such as collectors and enthusiasts, most people are interested in the service enabled of getting from 'A' to 'B'. Being a collector also derives an indirect service rendered. The goods-dominant logic is concerned with delivering outputs, the cars from the production line, and S-DL is concerned with doing something for others as a process or enabling others to do something for themselves. As such, S-DL does not supersede a production focus, but it complements it. Similarly, S-DL does not supersede a task focus in projects, but it supplements the task and project management focus. Vargo and Lusch put it this way:

> Whereas goods-dominant logic sees services as (somewhat inferior to goods) units of output, service-dominant logic sees service as a process – doing something for another party. The locus of value creation, then, moves from the 'producer' to a collaborative process of co-creation between parties.
>
> (2008b: 255)

The marketing influence becomes more apparent in the implications of this perspective, whereby the goal is:

> . . . to customize offerings, to recognize that the consumer is always a co-producer, and to strive to maximize consumer involvement in the customization to better fit his or her needs. It suggests that for many offerings, tangibility may be a limiting factor, one that increases costs and that may hinder marketability.
>
> (Vargo and Lusch, 2006: 21)

The consequence is that the perceived customer value assessments are better predictors of loyalty and repeat business than measures of satisfaction (Rust et al., 1995).

Services are complex and need careful consideration in conception and configuration. Building upon Figure 10.1, service attributes are highly variable at the level of standardization versus customization, perishability and durability, their short-term and long-term impact in use, but most of all, between the provider and consumer. Providers tend to ignore several attributes which S-DL particularly draw attention towards, namely:

- Providers tend to misperceive what the customers or clients really need and want, focusing upon the surface appearance of market demand;
- Providers tend to overvalue tangible contents, which are the most easily measured attributes;
- Providers tend to undervalue to service content as transitory and temporary, whereas service productivity does increase and social capital appreciates with use;

- Providers tend to view themselves as producers or providers, rather than co-creators of value;
- Providers tend to undervalue the customer or client perception of value, looking at short-term key performance indicators rather than long-term (mutual) benefits.

Vargo and Lusch argue that supplier can only make value propositions for it is the customer that determines the realized value in use. Therefore, profit is obtained through the dynamic application and exchange of specialized knowledge and skills used to enable and facilitate value creation (Vargo and Lusch, 2004; Lusch and Vargo, 2006). They have established ten foundational principles, set out in Table 10.1.

**TABLE 10.1** The ten foundational principles of the service-dominant logic

| *Foundational principle* | *Foundational premise* | *Comment and explanation* |
|---|---|---|
| **FP1** The application of specialized skills and knowledge is the fundamental unit of exchange | Service is the fundamental basis of exchange | The application of dynamic resources of knowledge and skills provides the service and is the basis for all exchange – service is exchanged for service |
| **FP2** Indirect exchange masks the fundamental *unit* of exchange | Indirect exchange masks the fundamental *basis* of exchange | The complex combinations of goods, money, organizations and institutions, mean the service is not always apparent |
| **FP3** Goods are a means for service provision | Goods and services are a means to yield service benefits | Goods derive their value through receipt and use – the service experienced and the service rendered |
| **FP4** Knowledge and skills are the fundamental sources of competitive advantage | Dynamic and intangible resources are the fundamental source of competitive advantage | The comparative ability to cause desired change drives competition |
| **FP5** All economies are services economies | All economies are *service* economies | Service is only now becoming more apparent with increased specialization and outsourcing |
| **FP6** The customer is always a co-producer | The customer is always a co-creator of value | Value creation is interactional and perceptual |
| **FP7** The enterprise can only make value propositions | The provider only facilitates value creation | Enterprises can offer their applied resources and collaboratively create value, but cannot create or deliver value per se |

(*Continued*)

**TABLE 10.1** (Continued)

| *Foundational principle* | *Foundational premise* | *Comment and explanation* |
|---|---|---|
| **FP8** A service-centred view is customer orientated and relational | Service provision is customer orientated and created relationally | Customer-determined service benefits are inherently relational and perceptual |
| **FP9** Organizations transform specialised competences into complex services | All social and economic actors are resource integrators | The context of value creation is network-based inside and across organizational boundaries |
| **FP10** Value perceived as objective | Value is unique and perceptually decided by beneficiaries | Value is idiosyncratic, experiential, contextual and meaning laden |

*Source*: Developed and adapted from Vargo and Lusch (2008).

There have been attempts to add further principles (e.g. Williams and Aitkin, 2011), however, and to be consistent with the 4*P*s (**Chapter 3**). Focusing upon the initial ten is sufficient for drawing out the main implications for marketing in project businesses. The implications can be summarized as:

- From producing something expertly towards using expertise to secure and execute projects in order to assist clients in value creation;
- From value as something produced and bought towards value delivered through co-creation and against a broader set of criteria than time–cost–quality/scope;
- From applying tangible and static (operand) resources towards applying less tangible and intangible, dynamic (operant) resources and capabilities;
- From treating customers as targets towards collaborating with them as resources;
- From marketing and business development management (BDM) as pre-given towards initiation, and an interactive and holistic approach within the project business and for the client;
- From predominantly efficiency drivers of cost control towards effectiveness drivers from which efficiency and (premium) profits flow.

It is claimed that S-DL creates superior value, although the capabilities to execute this are still being articulated. Organizational behaviours to include environmental scanning abilities, collaboration, and learning, founded upon a client and service focus are important organizational components (Karpen et al., 2012). This provides a baseline from which solutions are developed (cf. Davies et al., 2007). Interpersonal behaviours of interaction, relational and ethical collaboration based upon delegation and empowerment with management support for development and coordination of interactions are important contributions individuals provide (Karpen et al., 2012).

A great deal of the recent S-DL literature has focused upon the co-creation of value. This is probably for two reasons. First, many of the other foundational principles give a new perspective to what is currently conducted where relationship marketing practices are rigorously applied. Second, the co-creation of value as a foundation principle (Table 10.1) as a logical extension of co-production and the experience economy, but as a foundational principle is a concept that offers new areas for activity and new processes to develop beyond current practice. Co-creation is therefore worth further focus. It can be divided into two distinct categories:

1. *Direct involvement in joint activities to create value that neither organization could create on its own.* This involves engagement around processes and practices (Payne et al., 2008) that may arise from or induce technological breakthroughs (Payne et al., 2008), product and service development and joint problem solving as the goods or services are produced and delivered. The joint experience combines cognitive, emotional and behavioural practices, some of which can be planned for or anticipated in advance, some of which are creative responses to the demands of the activities and arise from how the relationships map out. The joint activities and the processes of co-creation are themselves part of the service experience.
2. *Perception of the value in use and context.* It involves cognitive reflection and emotional response of the service rendered. This is divided into two components:
   a. The service experience during delivery, which is particularly important in B2B transactions and remains underdeveloped in much of the S-DL research to date. It is a key aspect of asset specific markets including project markets. It links back to the joint activities in the first point above.
   b. The product and service as used post-production and delivery. This is the use value based around benefits and impact. The same product will render different service benefits for different customers as will the same service. Therefore the inputs do provide a scant basis for measuring this type of value – added value is only valuable if perceived to be so by the customer or client. An objective measure of outputs, that is, the benefits and impact in use are hard to assess. Individual customers act at the perceptual level, and their judgment will inform their next purchasing decision regardless of how reasonable (or unreasonable) their assessment is perceived to be by the supplier or suppliers.

Perception is always difficult to assess and often impossible to measure quantitatively, yet this is what S-DL relies upon because co-creation in use is always present. The Sydney Opera House provides a good example of the type of problem faced. It has been a failure by any traditional attributable accounting and project management measure, but its value for tourism, culture and the national economy of Australia cannot be accurately quantified, nor can the emotional pleasure and broader cultural contribution be assessed to those that have seen it and used it. Perceptually, most would agree it has provided a service of immense value at multiple levels. This would immediately become palpable if anyone were to suggest imminent demolition. A more tangible example might be a new warehouse replacing an old one of the same size in order to reduce running costs, introducing new heavy equipment and a more efficient layout for modern needs. Some comparable measures could be made in monetary terms, but nonetheless the improved working environment may increase worker productivity or attract better quality staff in ways that are difficult to anticipate and directly attribute.

It is the variance in benefits and impact expected that gives rise to variance in customer need, hence providing the driver for suppliers to design and configure their offers as customized products and tailored services. Design, configuration and delivery are necessarily incomplete. Customers or clients typically inadequately forecast and specify the benefits required. Even where specified, many customers find it difficult to 'backcast' from the benefits and impact in order to frame their needs. This provides a role for marketing and BDM to help the articulation of these needs. In this way the (potential) supplier is co-creating demand during the sales process and providing a service. This only indirectly yields income, yet helps position the supplier to secure a contract. Co-creation to this point frames the value proposition and then the offer in the bid for a supply contract. Co-creation continues after a contract is secured to improve or maximize the value through joint activities.

A model of co-created value has been proposed by Prahalad and Ramaswamy (2004a). A further model has been proposed by Vargo and Lusch (2008a). Both are briefly introduced. The Prahalad and Ramaswamy process model is based upon activities, their implications and manifestations (Figure 10.2). This was developed from research into IT and internet interactions with customers. They went on to propose the DART acronym as a means to scope some of the key ingredients to facilitate the model in practice. DART stands for dialogue, access, risk assessment and transparency. Dialogue concerns *interactivity, engagement, and a propensity to act* together on both the supply and demand side (Prahalad and Ramaswamy, 2004a: 6). It is closely related to

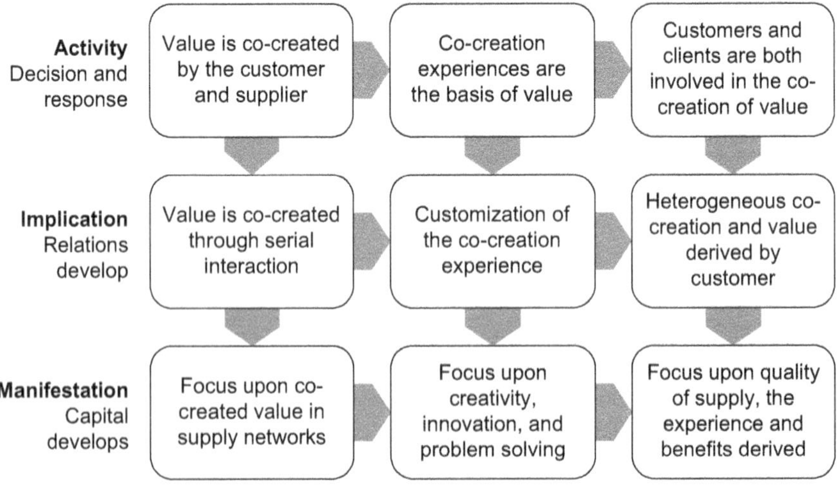


**FIGURE 10.2** A model for the co-creation of value

*Source*: Adapted and developed from Prahalad and Ramaswamy (2004a).

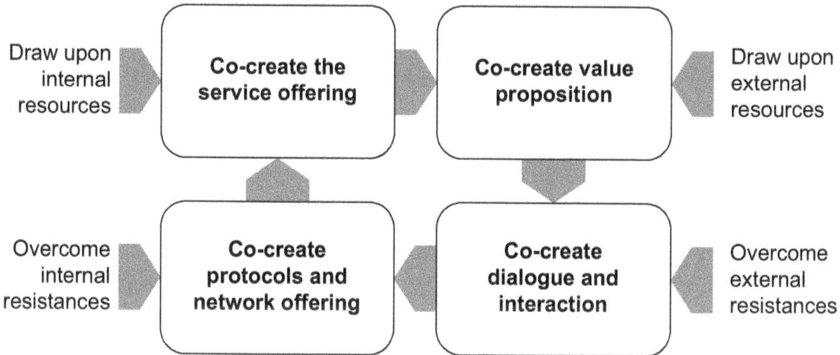


**FIGURE 10.3** A model for developing the co-creation of value

*Source*: Adapted and developed from Vargo and Lusch (2008a).

the dialogical approach of Ballantyne and Varey (2006). Access is about effective communication and tools. Dialogue and access are closely linked, involving listening on both sides. This is less about market power in the sense of clients commanding and suppliers listening and responding. It is a dialogue on a more equal footing of mutual respect. It is part of an inclusive approach to the third element, risk assessment and how this is apportioned (cf. Davies et al., 2009; Gil et al., 2011). Transparency concerns the reduction of asymmetry of information and power, including openness about prices and costs on both sides. Transparency also facilitates the use of shared technology platforms, for example the ways that project portals, intranets and building information modelling (BIM) have been developing.

The Vargo and Lusch (2008a) model has some similarities and so is presented in a way to facilitate visual comparison (Figure 10.3). The model gives awareness to the rigidities and path dependencies present in organizations that act as barriers to implementation (cf. Gilbert, 2005). Lusch and Vargo (2006) argue that effective co-creation is dependent upon improving the deep understanding of customer needs and wants at the front-end. Payne et al. (2008) argue that mechanisms for co-creation are less well understood, interactions and dialogue needing to be mapped and means needing to identify co-creation opportunities (Payne et al., 2009), which is one interface where entrepreneurial marketing can have an impact (**Chapter 6**).

Theorization is somewhat bound by conceptual paths previously trodden. The production–consumption divide is essentially grounded in economics (Smith, 1776). S-DL breaks down the divide, and the methodology for practice as well as research is far more interpretative, using sense making for understanding, sense giving to promote direction and heuristics to guide actions and assessments (cf. Kahneman et al., 1982; Weick, 1995). Philosophically, there is an existential dimension to S-DL with buying being a way to bring an object and what it can render into the realm of (organizational) action (Sartre, 1943; cf. Belk, 1988). We therefore have to distinguish between production, management, acquisition and consumption (cf. Perry, 1916). Acquisition is predicated upon exchange, but production is not. It used to be thought that production occurred prior to exchange or on demand under contract as with projects, and thus prior to consumption. S-DL challenges the idea that consumption is a post-production activity alone as service provision, and its management on the client side is part of the service experience, hence consumption. In addition, production is also a function of the use value that is induced during consumption. Therefore, management extends beyond (i) managing production and (ii) managing the transaction hence exchange process. Management is engaged in consumption to understand what needs to take place to improve value during the production and delivery of products and services (including co-creation activity), and in the case of projects, their production and delivery. Thus production and value creation are distinct rather than synonymous activities.

This concludes the overview of S-DL. Research has also tried to drill down to frame the specifics at an operational level of S-DL, which is influenced by a broader conceptualization of services in management or business studies. Service and service design are considered next. The business model provides the starting point. S-DL implies a range of capabilities, which form a business model (Storbacka and Nenonen, 2009). Therefore, capabilities developed as part of an explicit strategy or evolving incrementally to form a business model, some being more successful than others at securing a market position. To put it another way, each explicit or implicit business model has its own earning logic from which profits are generated. This has been traced to some degree in the preceding chapters. The relevance to S-DL is that most organizations exert resistances to adopting relationship marketing and to S-DL. To this extent, a consciously designed, and thus explicit, strategy is needed. Marketing plays an important part strategically. At the operational level, service provision needs to be designed at a generic level around the capabilities and then customized and tailored to customer and client needs for each exchange. This is particularly important for project businesses largely operating in asset specific markets, whether these are product assets rendering a service or whether these are service assets or social capital rendering services or some combination.

Zott and Amit (2008) suggest that business models provide a conceptual context for viewing the co-creation of value. Business models are externally orientated to address issues of how to compete by aligning types of value propositions with customer and client needs. The conceptual origin is located in supply chain interaction (Zott and Amit, 2003), but it becomes client facing and coupled with earning logic under S-DL. This is more specific than market position and segmentation, which tend to be applied at a higher and general level. There is a place for generic capabilities and differentiation, but the customization of the content and service tailoring is client-specific.

The findings of Mäkinen and Seppänen (2007) suggest there is considerable scope for further conceptual development of the business model construct. A business model can be defined as combining key resources, key processes, customer value propositions, and profitability derived from the ways in which income is earned. Added to this are the types of processes and expertise that form decisive and dynamic competencies and capabilities (**Chapter 8**). Research to date shows that multiple business models can be successful in the marketplace, as the evolution or development of the model is part of differentiation and thus the reduction of direct competition in entrepreneurial markets and international markets (Zott and Amit, 2003; Baldwin and Clark, 2006). From this, basis services are designed (Romme, 2003). Design means developing instructions and guidance to turn financial resources, knowledge and expertise and other social capital into goods and services that other organizations use and value (Baldwin and Clark, 2006). It also has to yield a return, hence the earning logic to do so. Developing and evaluating the earning logic also involves *backcasting* rather than forecasting. Forecasting looks at the inputs and sees what profit can be generated through sales. The business case is based upon a sufficient return, for example being in line with the industry average. *Backcasting* assesses client expectations of benefits as the starting point, then assesses how these are shaped into the types of client need and whether meeting these needs can yield a profit for the supplier.

Co-creation in this respect poses particular problems as to how the financial benefits are divided up. In this respect, the B2B customer or client poses the biggest threat where market power is not applied with ethical responsibility. The jury is out at the time of writing as to whether many businesses and the financial sector in particular have learnt the lessons of the 2008 downturn or 'credit crunch', in other words, recognizing that the *moral economy* is as important and as fragile as the financial economy. The two are conceptually distinct yet interdependent on the ground. At the micro level, this affects whether customers and clients get what they want and need – the core justification of the market system if businesses are to make reasonable profits. How this maps out will determine to a large extent the take-up of S-DL, which might prove to be an engine of growth for the next stages of economic development.

The application of backcasting suggests that what is needed is less a value chain model driven from the supply side and more of a *demand chain of value creation* in order to configure value from the demand side on the supply side and through co-creation. This provides a conceptual contribution to the emergent S-DL body of thinking. A tentative depiction is provided in Figure 10.4. In contrast to Porter's value chain, marketing and sales are prior to other activities in Figure 10.4, as

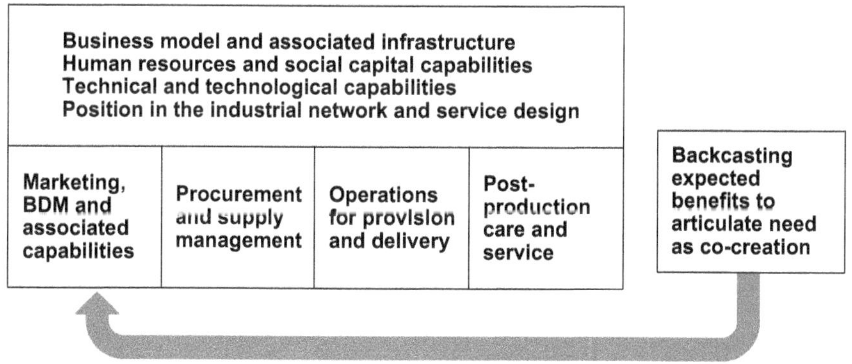


**FIGURE 10.4** Towards a demand value chain

provision is undertaken to contract in many B2B markets rather than production taking place ahead of sale. This reversal is an increasing feature in many consumer markets too where goods are customized and produced to order, which is in line with S-DL principles.

The service concept has been defined as the way in which an organization serves its customers, employees, shareholders and lenders (Heskett, 1986). S-DL has been coupled with the concept of *new service development*, defined as developing new service offerings from conception to implementation and launch (e.g. Johnson et al., 2008; Edvardsson et al., 2000). *Service design* has been more narrowly defined in terms of specifying an idea by developing drawings, flowcharts and other tools to ground service design in concrete ways (e.g. Gummesson, 1991; Romme, 2003; Bitner et al., 2007). Romme (2003) proposes several levels for service design, which have been developed below:

1. *Blueprinting*, which is a flow-chart technique or mapping technique for visualization of the service to be provided (Shostack, 1987);
2. *Mapping processes and logistics*, which provides a detailed breakdown of activities (Kingman-Brundage, 1992);
3. *Visualization of the intangible service*, which helps to articulate the need in forms that permit assessment of the alignment between need and provision, scope and gaps where co-creation is necessary, opportunity for emergent requirements to be anticipated at an early stage;
4. *Configuration of the service*, bringing internal and external propositions together, and including setting out the anticipated relationship contact points during execution to add to the visualization (see also Figure 4.5).

The above can be used in marketing and BDM to help guide and delve into the understanding of the customer or client business. Service design within S-DL is not therefore about completeness, but it harks back to the discussion on capabilities where these are framed generically the customized and tailored to client context and need. This therefore has to be conducted at two levels in project businesses. One level is the corporate level of portfolio-programme management to design generic capabilities and the second is at project level to customize and tailor the generic into the specific offer.

## Business development management in theory and practice

What is the shape of the goods-dominant logic in project businesses? In project businesses, the primary unit of analysis by most senior management is the project, not the client, nor the benefits provided. At the project level, the tendency is to analyze the constituent components and activities for realization, for example using work breakdown structures, where the interdependence with clients and the network is peripherally acknowledged. Risk is often *the* major factor of consideration, largely managed through a narrow aperture of self-interest involving risk spreading via subcontracting. New initiatives, such as procurement routes and partnering, tend to emanate from clients. Project businesses tend to be reactive recipients of what the market demands of them.

What is and might be the shape of S-DL in project businesses? The S-DL implications for project businesses are that the primary units of consideration are no longer the project per se: they are (i) the client and (ii) MoP applying project, programme and portfolio management ($P^3M$). Projects are analyzed in holistic ways and the configured to maximize value through both direct provision and the co-creation of value. The combined client and service focus means that the services rendered from the client and stakeholder perspective occupy the central position, from the concept, down to capability development and mobilization, associated service design, the long term benefits and impact derived by the client.

Interdependencies already lead to collaborative practices and the co-creation of value through joint working (see Figure 4.7), innovation, and creative problem solving, which can be enhanced with greater awareness, especially in project business supply chains. Boundary spanning activities and the perforation of organizational boundaries are more pertinent to market needs than individual firms as accounting units. The market is too complex to be served by a firm or firms per se. Markets increasingly require a considerable outward focus and a social orientation. New initiatives and innovations can arise from the inter-organizational dialogue and interaction. The focus becomes an increasingly client and service one.

In terms of marketing and BDM, S-DL challenges assumptions that value is solely or largely created during project execution by the project management team. Value creation through the S-DL lens is an extended process across project lifecycles from the front-end, reaching beyond completion into the useful life of projects. Therefore, business development managers (BDMs) would be expected to assist understanding needs, backcasting to help configure the service and assess use value post-completion. BDMs are therefore expected to be identifying and leveraging value opportunities across the six markets, building relationships in customized ways by relationship type (cf. Table 4.2), and mobilizing resources and making commitments accordingly for future projects (**Chapters 4, 8** and **9**). S-DL brings a broader definition of systems integration. It includes marketing as a function and further draws the client into the systematic approach on the supply side. S-DL is holistic and multi-disciplinary, combining interpersonal and team skills and other facets of organizational behaviour, including the interface with the tangible technical and technological components for creativity, innovation and problem solving.

BDM is a function that covers a broad range of activities and thus can engage with others under entrepreneurial marketing as well as relationship marketing. BDM is conceptually a team effort drawing in a range of skill sets. This is amplified further under S-DL. For example, identifying client needs in terms of the benefits of a project in use, whether a new set of process arising from a change management project, a new corporate headquarters or IT system, can help anticipate the types of co-creation required during execution and allow the project business time to muster and configure the internal resources and external actors. This is already commonly done through joint ventures in order to spread risks and together deliver something neither party can on their own, but this is normally conceived on the basis of known technical capability rather than what combined capabilities can achieve as added value. Informal collaboration does and can lead to extensive co-creation. Co-creation can be used to spread the risks and/or costs related to the development and production of complex projects.

Service design includes a considerable role for marketing and BDM in the identification of client needs and configuring the value to put forward as propositions during the sales process and firmed up as a detailed offer during bid management. The staged process proposed (Romme, 2003) can be used to guide capability configuration into tailored services. This involves blueprinting in flow-chart format for a service perspective, rather than a project management tools and techniques perspective that is task driven, in order to envisage the client experience and benefits in use. It can also combine with backcasting from the desired benefits to provide a detailed breakdown of service activities. This acts as a bridge to project management tools and techniques and, finally, visualization to depict the service arising from the generic capabilities in an accessible way using testimonies and track record illustrations and the specific customization and tailoring. Project businesses and their BDMs tend to rely heavily on presenting track record, but this is traditionally conducted to provide reassurance of the experience and ability to undertake different types of work rather than using track record to say how they conduct the projects from a service perspective.

S-DL proceeds in several directions. An increase in innovation, creativity and enhanced problem solving abilities as part of a more proactive engagement in value creation is a further direction. This requires higher levels of specialization and could lead to higher levels of outsourcing, including adding to the trend to outsource front-end functions that help frame the service proposition, complicating the integration task at an early stage (Balakrishnan et al., 2008).

Collaboration involves the pooling of firm and project resources, which is a precondition for innovative co-creation (cf. Clegg et al., 2011). Higher levels of engagement with supply chains is another direction in order to understand and leverage member capability in creative ways, joint working being cascaded down the tiers as a requirement of participation on projects (cf. Pryke, 2009; 2012). Helkkula et al. (2012) propose narrative as a means of intensive engagement, one way being to use an *action net* perspective that focuses upon processes between actors (Czarniawska, 2004). Action net is suitable for research purposes yet is possibly too intensive for practitioners to cognitively apply, except as part of the BDM function of dialogue to gain a deep understanding of the client. Social network analysis (cf. Pryke, 2012) is another approach that can be applied for research and in practice, arguably in more economical ways.

Outsourcing at the front-end and outsourcing to project subcontractors and suppliers raises the stakes of service consistency on a project. Managing the sleeping relationship between projects, not only regarding the client (Hadjikhani, 1996; Cova et al., 2002; Skaates and Tikkanen, 2003a; 2003b; Cova and Salle, 2005) but also suppliers too, supports continuity. It has been found that maintaining the relationship at sufficient depth to embody trust and commitment is problematic (Eloranta, 2007; Keh and Xie, 2009; Martinsuo and Ahola, 2010), and enhancement of internal and external relationship management is a further direction implied by S-DL.

An increase in the application of agile production and project management methodologies, such as SCRUM and XP, provides another direction. Agile methods improve responsiveness to client needs. Projects require modification from the client not only at the front-end (Pinto and Rouhiainen, 2001; cf. Cova and Salle, 2005), but also during execution with change orders and variations. An increase in the treatment of emergent requirements as opportunities is a further direction, rather than perceptions of changes as negative risks that are deviations from plan and task (Smyth, 2013b). In terms of organizational and project team behaviour, there is likely to be further development along the collaborative and cooperative practices towards a greater emphasis upon nurture from an ethics of care perspective (Gilligan, 1982; Smyth, 2008a; 2008b) and social identification as stronger bonds and ties develop (Anvuur and Kumaraswamy, 2008; cf. Appiah, 2005; 2010).

Knowledge management as a dynamic capability or core competence has rarely featured, but is relevant at this point and provides a further direction. Payne et al. (2008) found in their research that suppliers hold a lot of tacit knowledge about customers, which is not always put to use, the need being to organize tacit and explicit knowledge management around customers rather than around IT capabilities. Sharing tacit knowledge facilities co-creation. It feeds into joint problem solving as one of the two main means of co-creation. IBM, which organizes a great deal of its consultancy on a project basis as a systems solution seller, has tried to address these issues by developing 'T-shaped people', which means people with a depth of expertise and the ability to manage a broad range of service issues including relational attributes and knowledge that links the technical and the relational for service provision (Bitner et al., 2007). IBM with its 'service science' agenda has been an influence in grounding S-DL from a practice perspective (Gummesson et al., 2010).

Co-location has been a growing feature of project execution with the aim of facilitating understanding and knowledge sharing, relationship development for collaboration and joint problem solving on TMO teams. It has received little attention in the S-DL literature as a facilitative mechanism for the enhanced co-creation of value, yet it provides another avenue for pursuit that builds upon current practices. The quality of the associated experience may be low yet is a service aspect to develop.

Butcher and Sheehan (2010) found that hiring people with collaborative behaviour was more important than technical or disciplinary competency on occasions in order to meet client requirements. This provides a final direction for S-DL regarding human resource management (HRM) policies and practices employed to select future staff.

There will be different implications for project businesses that are systems integrators and those that are systems sellers and integrated solution providers. Taking the systems seller first, there is a greater emphasis upon technical and tangible content whether in physical form or expertise associated with a discipline or professional service. The project business as systems seller will develop services with more direct involvement through joint activities to induce innovation around the technical content. The integrated solutions provider acting as subcontractors or suppliers are second tier or further down the chain. The project business as systems integrator provides value by drawing together the constituent elements and organizational actors to deliver integrated solutions. This is beyond meeting minimal requirements and risk management; it is about service provision and will place greater emphasis upon the service experience along project lifecycles from the way the front-end is approached, integration and service experience during execution, and the post-project realization of benefits and impact. Input into scope management and project definition through the thoroughness of applying backcasting and service design and detailed configuration are critical. *Backcasting* and *demand chain* analysis provide important means to apply S-DL in concrete ways in project environments, coupled with the marketing and BDM processes derived from relationship marketing as a key component of service design.

Relationship marketing and management offers further traction under S-DL, reinforcing the ability to engender affinity at the project business-client interface through emotional attachment (Dainty et al., 2005). This is what Nicolini (2002) calls 'project chemistry', but at a heightened level of intensity and client identification for S-DL. It starts with marketing and BDM, builds upon interdependencies induced across TMOs and particularly across client DMUs. Strong relationship ties initiated through BDM are a precondition to generate effective cooperation on a project. Strong relationship ties are also a product of cooperation especially for intense co-creation. It is therefore a self-reinforcing process, whereby the project business becomes an asset to the client (Gustafsson et al., 2010; Smyth et al., 2010). Capabilities, some of which may be configured into generic service packages, are also derived both from collaborative and co-created activities (see **Chapter 8**), as well as feeding their further development. Service and capability development under S-DL are virtuous self-reinforcing mechanisms underpinned by social capital.

This is not to say that S-DL is a panacea or that management for service design and capability development is intrinsically good. S-DL will only suit certain sorts of clients in project markets in the same way that any of the marketing approaches from the marketing mix, through relationship and entrepreneurial marketing do. Nor is there anything intrinsically good about relationships. It depends how they are used. Mutual identification can lead to 'in-group' favouritism, a mobilization of bias, normalization of deviant behaviour, and ultimately illegitimate or criminal action involving negligence or fraud (see Liu et al., 1999; Bachrach and Baratz, 1973; Vaughan, 1999; Smyth, 2013b; Gummesson, 2000 respectively). The remedy is to keep an outward focus, but also in the sense of a social orientation in economic interaction (e.g. Baier, 1994; Lyons and Mehta, 1997; Smyth, 2008).

Client interactions at the front-end are where an outward focus starts – not only what work will they provide us, but also what can we do for them. The front-end is part of the service experience from the client perspective. This in turn adds to the increase in service offerings seen in project businesses (cf. Davies, 2004; Wikström et al., 2009). The increased complexity and service content gives rise to a need for a new model. In terms of drivers, Wikström et al. (2009) produced a model of business logic. Figure 10.5 shows the combination of innovative working and a service orientation that leads towards developing business drivers to serve complexity in mature ways. This may be more appropriate for the systems seller than the systems

| Project complexity | | |
|---|---|---|
| | Technology and innovation drivers | Business drivers |
| | Product drivers | Service drivers |
| | Project business maturity | |

**FIGURE 10.5** A model of project business logic

*Source*: Adapted from Wikström et al. (2009).

integrator for delivering integrated solutions to clients. However, the thrust of change is clear, markets are evolving as demands and the understanding of how to manage such demands develop. This is impacting project businesses, and those most adept at managing the market are likely to be amongst the most successful.

The benefits of increased service offerings to the project business are improved market entry, added value to clients that enhances profit levels and turnover, resultant competitive advantage, more efficient delivery, learning and innovation, and new services as discrete projects.

The misperception among project businesses about their service provision amongst senior management has been raised in **Chapter 9**. The problem is endemic in many project businesses as Fact Box 10.1 sets out. The analytical point to draw out is that S-DL exists in project businesses, but that does mean project businesses are fully aware of their service provision, its pertinence or lack of it. This is important, particularly from project businesses that might benefit from enhancing their service offering using the S-DL approach.

Project management methodologies are applied with high degrees of discretion in project businesses. They are frequently applied with myopia. It has been stated about a hybrid method PRINCE that is required for government contracts in the United Kingdom and carries certification:

> Most companies who adopt a PRINCE approach to project management adapt the methodology to their commercial environment and use those parts of PRINCE that work for them. This is quite acceptable as the puritanical days of sticking rigidly to a method are seen now as undesirable and unnecessary.
>
> (Haughey, 2009: 2)

But how are project management methodologies being adapted in practice? From the S-DL perspective, tailoring would accord with a client and service orientation, preferably with opportunities for the co-creation of value by configuring the applied project management methodology to the needs of the client and other

## FACT BOX 10.1 SERVICE PROVISION AND TOWARDS A SERVICE-DOMINANT LOGIC

A survey of BranCo showed that 91 per cent of staff thought they provided their customers with a good or very good service. Fifty-eight per cent of staff believed customer engagement procedures to be effective. In particular, the technological support given to projects by a specialist division was considered significant amongst staff.

Yet clients took this aspect for granted, believing this is what a large international project business should automatically be doing. A series of client interviews demonstrated that this service was not considered to provide added value. Further enhancement and differentiation was needed to add value above minimal expectations. The project business was unaware of this issue and therefore in what direction it could develop its service offer for its client base and particular clients.

One client had organized innovation 'beauty parades' amongst those on its partnering panel to solicit added value that could be shared across the panel of first-tier project businesses (BranCo client interviews and internal survey conducted in 2009; Chambers et al., 2009).

This is a type of co-creation, however the trend continues the established pattern of clients managing what project businesses should be proactively instigating. The example of the 'beauty parade' demonstrates the distinction between the service logic from the client perspective and the project business failing to appreciate use value in context for its clients. This observation needs to be placed in the context of this project business being at the forefront of relationship marketing practices in the division in question.

stakeholders. This has yet to be found in the IT sector, as set out in Fact Box 10.2. In sum, tailoring was not necessarily conducted for either the satisfaction of client needs or for the needs of the project business. The project management methodologies were largely aligned to the 'comfort zones' and self-interest of the project manager. This may have served the plan and task of project execution well on many occasions, however, it was not necessarily servicing the employer or client interests to optimal levels. It strongly suggests that the IT sector is unaligned to S-DL and that this might be a more general pattern across many project sectors. The implication is that there are weak systems between project management and the 'corporate centre'; thus, stronger management intervention is needed to implement S-DL (Wells and Smyth, 2011). Further, Milin and Morača (2013) found project businesses applying project management methodologies generally had higher levels of performance than those that did not. They found that the application of project management methodologies was significant and sometimes more than employing trained project managers, even though they too make decisive contributions to performance improvement compared to uncertified project managers. It would therefore appear that project management methodologies provide a generic set of capabilities of value.

## FACT BOX 10.2 PROJECT MANAGEMENT METHODOLOGIES AND THE SERVICE-DOMINANT LOGIC

The Head of Best Practices from a responsible UK government department lacked confidence in project business responsiveness in applying project management methodologies, stating, *PRINCE2 doesn't consider benefit realisation, an old fashion method of delivering product. The realisation of benefit is assigned to the owner.*

One IT company required the application of consistent and proven project management practice. Yet project managers conveyed mix messages, for example one senior consultant stated that the methods employed satisfied contractual conditions but not necessarily client needs. This situation was largely accepted as the norm.

In another large IT company, there was a suggestion that project management methodologies were not fit for purpose, and project management was conducted in a reactive response mode rather than investigating and helping to articulate client needs:

> We heavily rely on business people to tell us what they need; this makes our development team's job very difficult. Also business people define requirements differently to systems analysts, which adds to the complexity of the requirement definition phase.
>
> (Portfolio Manager)

> Traditional methods fall apart and the only thing you can rely on is the personal relationship and the rapport with the customer.
>
> (Project Manager)

> The monitoring is mainly against time and money. Quality is not measured as a priority.
>
> (Project Manager)

In a further case, the IT division of a telecommunications business employing an agile project management methodology, there is a vision *to help customers to thrive in a changing environment* according to the Head of Tools and Methodologies. Yet there was *no system in place to evaluate how to satisfy our*

(*Continued*)

**FACT BOX 10.2** (Continued)

*customers from the beginning to the end experience* according to one project manager. It was further said:

> One of the biggest problems that we had is that we do not involve our customers enough in our new product launches. It often begins with a separate requirement from marketing and is not tested with the customer.
>
> (Product Manager)

> For instance initially after the changeover from Waterfall to agile, it became apparent that 80 per cent of the work we were doing wasn't going to add any value to the user. It had been defined by a manager who was not actually a user.
>
> (Project Manager)

> The reaction on modifying and tailoring was 'over our dead body', so ultimately we had to backtrack; we had to stick with a six-stage process and incorporate [agile] in the six-phase process.
>
> (Product Manager)

In none of the cases did the project management methodologies support success in terms of adding value and pursuing S-DL. Understanding the customer and end-user was a common omission in addressing formal requirements. There was repeated evidence of decision-makers being passive towards the customer or frustrating efforts to improve customer service. The pattern of attitudes appeared to subdivide into several categories. First were the inexperienced project managers who valued project methodologies as a guiding tool. Second, where hierarchical accountability was strong, the methodologies were followed. Third, the experienced project managers were the least likely to use the project management methodologies. Success levels did not seem to be significantly greater where experienced managers were key decision-makers. Experienced project managers largely shunned a customer focus. They rhetorically used 'client needs' as a justification for tailoring, yet they followed predispositions and managed projects according to their 'comfort zones', rather than serving employer or client interests.

*Source*: Adapted from Wells and Smyth (2011).

The overall lesson to be derived is that flexible service response needs firm guidelines. In other words, the generic service and capabilities need to be designed and firmed up at corporate level and consistently implemented at project level through portfolio and programme management, with agreed tailoring that is adhered to at project level. Thus, a more standard and routine service provides a strong organizational and team basis for consistency and continuity of service within one

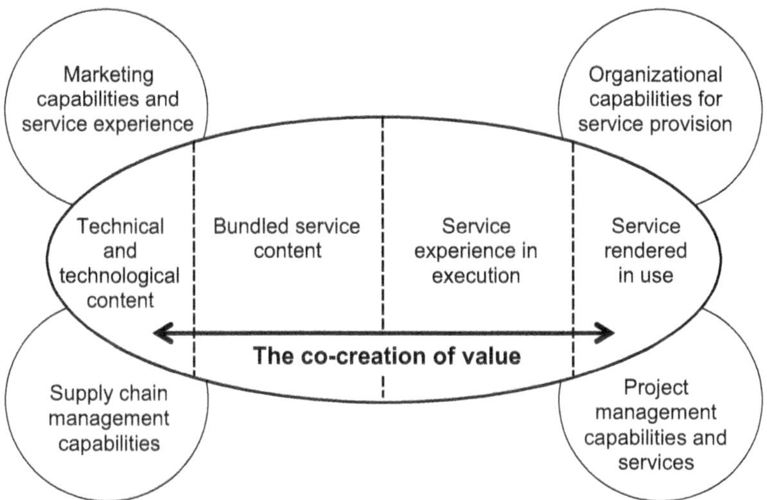


**FIGURE 10.6** Developing the project offer under the service-dominant logic

project and across a programme. It also provides a point of departure where service provision can be tailored to add value and improve the service experience from the client and stakeholder viewpoint.

Kujala et al. (2011) develop ideas for a service model with S-DL influence; however, their focus is primarily upon the content or solutions delivered rather than also including the surrounding services experienced during delivery. It can be built upon to develop a scheme for service tailoring and therefore is shown in Figure 10.6.

Developing effective S-DL depends upon current awareness and practices. As has been seen, senior management and project managers are frequently unaware of how their services are perceived by clients (for example Fact Boxes 9.1, 9.2 and 10.1). Misperception is a widespread problem covering IT, energy and transport infrastructure provision, to which can be added design disciplines. Further evidence comes from research into architects in Thailand who are restricted from soliciting work. Potential clients assess practices by identifying good service practices and design from the architectural peer press. Research showed the architects were unaware of this type and breadth of assessment (Tejavanija, 2010). This echoes the findings of clients in the Netherlands, United Kingdom and Greece being concerned with service and relationship content, implicitly or explicitly. These practices contrasted with the view of the architects, which believed that design merit was sufficient (Smyth and Kioussi, 2011a).

Adoption of S-DL has pointed towards the importance of client behaviour several times. This begs the question as to whether S-DL is a realistic proposition for project businesses to develop further. There are issues over the exertion of power, how the benefits will be divided up and therefore whether project businesses will earn a reasonable rate of return. It could be argued that this is already adequately managed in current practices of collaborative joint working. There are also potential problems over commercial confidentiality and intellectual property rights for co-created value.

BIM arguably raises some of these issues. On the client side, capabilities are needed to drive through the service agendas. Economic downturns tend to see clients run down their in-house capabilities (Merrow, 2011; Winch and Leiringer, 2013). Intelligent clients with dependencies upon successful projects for their own performance will have motivation to engage with capability development. As argued in previous chapters, the development of in-house client capabilities is a potential threat to the systems integrator project business. The project business needs to counter the move. Therefore, the systems integrator project business that develops capabilities *and* clients who develop such capabilities provide the most fertile market conditions in which S-DL will be adopted and survive.

## Conclusion

An exploration of the service-dominant logic or S-DL has been undertaken. This has included an analysis of the theoretical and applied characteristics of S-DL for project businesses and an examination of how these characteristics are and can be internally managed. The bridge between what is currently conducted and what could be conducted is dependent upon awareness levels in project businesses and the research community, to which the chapter contributes. Relational aspects and perceptions of value have been addressed. An evaluation of the strengths and weaknesses of S-DL has been undertaken. While current activity includes creative and innovative collaboration and problem solving, the underdeveloped position of marketing and BDM at the front of the front-end and the lack of integrated activities across project lifecycles (**Chapters 7** and **8**) pose major constraints to further adoption of S-DL principles. Market power, profit attribution from co-created value and commercial sensitivity over intellectual property pose additional challenges. These are surmountable, especially project markets and exchanges where both clients and the project businesses are actively developing project management related capabilities that facilitate collaboration and co-created value opportunities.

S-DL offers a new and additional way of understanding and articulating project delivery. It can act as a stimulus to driving innovation, creativity and inventiveness in both technical and service content. It combines a client and service orientation. It offers diverse ways of proceeding in heterogeneous markets and market segments and differentiation at the project business level. 'Copy-cat' or 'one-size-fits-all' notions in practice are unsuitable and singular, linear solutions towards notional 'maturity' are inapplicable in a research context for S-DL.

While the emphasis upon service content is to be encouraged generally in project business and for project management, in the long run, this new norm should increasingly be taken for granted, diminishing overt consideration. It has been stated this way: *. . . at some point one would expect no such thing as service marketing or service management but merely marketing and management with the service-focus implicitly understood* (Gummesson et al., 2010: 11).

Project businesses are barely at the starting line, especially where the project content is largely technical or engineering led. Society has never commissioned as many projects outside and within market parameters. Consequently, never have so many projects failed against time–cost–quality, and never have so many projects failed to meet user needs, fallen short of providing much societal benefit, caused environmental damage and continue to ignore 2050 agendas. These are all service problems beyond the immediate service experience. There lies the challenge and S-DL offers a set of principles to help deal with these issues. At present and for the short-term, it is only appropriate for part of the market.

This chapter therefore addresses a number of substantive issues identified at the outset of this book. The relevant ones are cited below.

**SI no. 1:** ***Market Management*** and S-DL are highly connected and overlap. The conscious application of S-DL in research and practice can be considered a form of market management that perforates firm boundaries in proactive ways, in particular to facilitate the co-creation of value.

**SI no. 2:** ***Service Management*** is a *client* and *service focus* and lies at the heart of S-DL. The task and project management focus driven by socially constructed disciplinary sets of expertise and experience are supplemented by concentrating upon the purpose of projects rather than means – the use value embodied in benefits and impact that flow from the project. This is far more significant than the maintenance, facilities management and whole life cost issues of a project but is about what the project achieves in use for users and other stakeholders. Further, service management has been shown to be a source of added value in its own right and an opportunity for intensive collaboration to add value through joint activities.

**SI no. 4:** ***Client Management and Programme Management*** incorporates the *coordination mechanisms for customer lifetime value* (CLV). This has indirectly been touched upon, attention being drawn to the implications at this point and in preparation for the next chapter.

**SI no. 5:** ***Marketing and BDM*** moves from an isolated position towards a *central interface function* under S-DL, taking the arguments embedded in relationship marketing a step further (see **Chapter 4**). To put it another way, marketing and BDM become functions to be integrated into other operations as well as facilitators of integration whether for the systems seller project business or the systems integrator project business.

**SI no. 6:** ***BDM and Client Management*** are inherently consistent and continuous under S-DL, encouraging other functions to operate in accordance throughout project lifecycles and over project business programmes.

**SIs no. 7** and **8:** ***Vertical Systems, Cross-functional Systems and Coordination Mechanisms*** are important under S-DL in order to achieve a key service component, namely *integration* on the supply side internally and for its supply chains, configured to meet demand need and for co-creation.

**SI no. 9:** ***Marketing and Managing the Project Lifecycle*** is insufficient because the whole project lifecycle in use is incorporated through S-DL, especially the co-created value derived from the perceptual benefits and impact in use.

**SI no. 10:** ***Marketing and Value Creation*** is pivotal in S-DL. Added value and co-created value are central propositions, S-DL emphasizing effectiveness to drive efficiency rather than input–output ratios of production-orientated thinking and the lack of service consideration.

There are several main *recommendations* for research that flow from the analysis for academic communities:

A. Research into S-DL has been scant to date, much of the applied work being in management around service design and the linkage to strategic business logic for the supplier and customer. Asset specific markets have been largely overlooked and projects only beginning to be considered at the time of writing. S-DL is a highly pertinent area for research in project businesses, linking to MoP, capability development and the role of marketing over project lifecycles.
B. Research into generic service design and the customization and tailoring mechanisms is recommended from the strategic level, through programme management to project management methodologies to delivery at the project level.
C. Research into clients and project businesses that adopt S-DL implicitly and explicitly is recommended as little is currently understood about current practices in relation to strategies for prescriptive adoption in industry.

Several main *recommendations* can be identified for practice from the examination provided:

1. Realistic assessments by senior management of what service capabilities currently are delivered in their project businesses and the extent to which clients perceive them as valuable.
2. A more considered approach to service provision is recommended for project businesses, and this could embrace the provocation of S-DL as part of formulating service development.
3. The adoption of multiple S-DL practices amongst a selection of project businesses as a means of differentiation, of which awareness creation and education of clients is incorporated to align strategies and develop capabilities.

The service-dominant logic or S-DL has introduced a comprehensive client and service approach to project businesses in general and for marketing. It combines an analysis of current practice with a normative and prescriptive dimension for development and enhancement, in line with a much of the management research on S-DL. The conceptual potential and limits have been set out from a marketing perspective. The appropriateness of the potential for project businesses has yet to be tested in practice.

S-DL has introduced a broader and more inclusive approach to the consideration of value. This adds complexity and challenges to some of the main conceptions of value in both mainstream economics and management. It will prove helpful to take stock of where this brings the analysis and provides a main theme for further consideration.

# 11

# MARKET MANAGEMENT, BUSINESS DEVELOPMENT AND VALUE CREATION

## Introduction

A considerable body of knowledge has arisen from looking at production and at the project as a locus for production and assembly. In particular, new strategies for innovation to improve the delivery of solutions have emanated from such research. Davies puts it this way: *Some of the world's leading suppliers are developing strategies to move into the provision of innovative combinations of products and service as 'high-value integrated solutions' tailored to each customer's needs* (2004: 727).

Less attention has been given to the role of market management as a driver for developing value strategies and solutions to production and project-related issues. This is particularly the case in project businesses where market management has received little attention as both academe and practice have a largely passive view of the project business, being content to retain a narrow focus of reacting at the project level, initially through project management and the management of projects (MoP). A proactive approach is central to market management. This applies for marketing as a market management function. Marketing has two main and related tenets – securing new work and delivering value to customers and clients. Effective value delivery secures work directly by demonstrating ability, and indirectly through reputation and track record. Value delivery is therefore important to expansion and profit growth.

Having introduced marketing paradigms and approaches, **Chapters 7** and **8** were closely related to value configuration and delivery during project execution and in the broader frame of MoP respectively. **Chapter 9** focused in particular on resources and investment necessary for delivering value, especially added value propositions. This led to an enhanced client and service focus through an analysis of the service-dominant logic (S-DL). Value is a central S-DL tenet, particularly the notion of the co-creation of value (**Chapter 10**). It is therefore appropriate to consider the role of value and how it is changing in conceptualization and application.

Therefore, the following agenda provides:

A. An examination of the different views and definitions of value and how these apply in market management and marketing for the project.
B. An exploration of the implications for the management of project businesses.
C. An exploration of the implications for the management of marketing and business development management (BDM) for project businesses taking into account the different approaches to marketing.

Within this agenda are located three main types of project business, namely the solution seller, which comprises of consultants and other advisors, the systems seller of integrated solutions, which tend to be second-tier suppliers and below, and the systems integrator, which brings together the other suppliers in the delivery of holistic solutions and the value is the service in so doing. The main message is that value delivery is the means to realize a profit and is proportional to a large degree. It is also the case that value delivery in the long term is contingent upon investment. While short-term profits can be squeezed from cost cutting, value is compromised squeezing resources long-term. Indeed, in service provision, resources are largely inseparable from short-term expenditure and long-term investment in the sense that one affects the other at an operational level, an issue poorly understood from a production-orientated mindset in boardrooms and from a task focus in project operations (see **Chapter 2**).

## Value in management, economics and project management

*Value* is one of those words with multiple meanings. At the most general level, there is the distinction between value created of worth and a value as a belief and something of moral import. It is the former usage that provides the main focus. Even within this realm, value is highly problematic. As noted in **Chapter 10**, the production–consumption divide in economics (e.g. Smith, 1776) gives rise to two different perceptions of value, the difference narrowing around negotiations and an exchange. One general definition of value is *what something is perceived to be worth (to society or and individual decision maker)* (Fellows, 2009: 54). Value can be ethically measured as a fair equivalent in project exchange (Dell'Isola, 1982).

Taking an economics perspective, the predominant view is that value is driven by the market, with the supply side having the creative position of dominance, determining the inputs as to what is produced. The raw value of the inputs is an important factor. The production process results in *value added* and is expressed as follows:

Value added = Value of output – Value of factor inputs

(Bowles et al., 2005)

Value added meets the minimum requirements for an exchange and has been the level at which most project businesses have tended to operate. Of course, it depends where clients pitch their minimum requirements, but in many sectors, competition has encouraged producers to go further to secure sales and grow their businesses. The additional element is termed added value and exceeds the minimum requirements of value added. There are three main issues around added value, namely its recognition, its worth and its durability at the point of exchange. First, value has to be recognized by the client. Added value is only of value if the client wants the extra value, perceives it as valuable to them or their organization. This links back to the production–consumption divide, and there has been evidence produced to show that there is a strong tendency for suppliers to overestimate the value of proposition delivered (for example Fact Boxes 9.2 and 10.1). This issue is always present yet is most prevalent where project businesses have a task and project management focus without the complimentary client and service focus. Second and from the supplier perspective, worth is whether there is a return on added value. There are a number of options. The project business may not charge for the added value, and thus the payback comes through the hope of repeat business or referrals. The project business may charge at cost to recover the additional expenditure. It increases turnover and thus shows market growth on each occasion and may spur further growth through repeat business. Another option is to charge at the same rate of profit as for the main contract. In this case, both parties must fully acknowledge the additional value is beneficial to the client. The yield may be a function of the project business being one of only a few suppliers with the dynamic capability or core competency for delivery. Yet another option is to charge at a premium rate of profit on the added value component, which usually requires two conditions to be present to be able to consistently do so. The added value must yield significant benefits for the client against which a 'rent' can be charged, and the project business is the only one that can deliver the added value component. In addition, there is the durability of the value. There is the technical content comprising the product and/or service, for example an oil platform or a change management process. There is the service experience during delivery, for example how the platform or process was delivered. Finally, there is the project service in use, for example whether the platform is performing effectively and efficiently and whether the change management process is proving to be successful. Project value continues to be released beyond the completion date as it is used (as in the platform) or acted upon (as with the outcome of a change process) (Alderman et al., 2003).

Another traditional definition of value that is more management orientated is as follows:

$$\text{Value} = \frac{\textit{Function}}{\text{Cost}} \quad \text{or} \quad \frac{\textit{Quality}}{\text{Cost}}$$

The Association of Project Management (APM) uses a modified definition:

$$\text{Value} = \frac{\textit{Satisfaction of needs}}{\text{Use of resources}}$$

The engineers Arup have a broader definition still that begins to embrace other stakeholder needs and expectations – the wider set of impacts that a project delivers:

$$\text{Value} = \text{Efficiency or Excellence} = \frac{\textit{Commodity specified in brief} + \textit{Excess beyond brief} + \textit{Delight or Artistic quality}}{\text{Price} + \text{Social price}}$$

Professional practices as project businesses are more overtly knowledge based, which has been used as a basis by Dunn and Baker (2003) for a further definition with a particular emphasis upon the additional component:

Value = Value added + Added value,

where . . . Added value = Knowledge + Expertise + Relationship value

The above definition of added value points towards the relational dimension, while the Arup definition points towards the benefits and impact in use. Together, these two definitions begin to link back to the client and service approach embodied in S-DL. Value is embedded in relationships. The technical expertise, technologies, tools and techniques are merely the means to extract the value that relationships harbour and generate through collaboration and the co-creation of value. The outcome of a relationship is profit (Smyth, 2000: 192).

One of the challenges facing the market in general and firms in particular is that the creation and production of value are no longer confined within the walls of any one organization. Indeed, organizational boundaries are frequently barriers to effective value identification and leverage. The global spread and reach of organizations may help expansion of markets yet can impose considerable problems for value creation too. Firms no longer act *autonomously* in designing, developing production and delivering products and services. Nor they do so in ways that are separate from the customer or client (cf. Prahalad and Ramaswamy, 2000; 2004b).

How does this affect the way in which project businesses configure their value propositions? In addressing this issue, the assumption is that the project business does have a thorough understanding of the client needs beyond the documented requirements (**Chapter 4**) and has developed a set of generic capabilities that are distinctive in the marketplace (**Chapters 7** and **8**). Lanning (1998) defines a value proposition as the resulting experiences the client will receive, including the charges to cover costs. Anderson et al. (2006) suggest that is useful to divide the value proposition into three, covering parity of performance and functionality, differences between options and alternatives, and areas of dyadic contention as to what constitutes value.

Grounding value in practice proves problematic. Adding value and value for money frequently are perceived as taking cost out. This cost-cutting view fits well within project businesses that are highly transactional and try to minimize expenditure, as it accords with definitions of efficiency around managing inputs.

There is a role for cost reduction. Lean production and budget control procedures more appropriately reduce waste and costs. On projects value engineering and value management tend to focus upon cost cutting rather than raising value propositions. In the value for money equation, a 'value' emphasis focuses primarily upon product and service outputs to increase *effectiveness*, whereas a 'money' emphasis focuses upon controlling product and service inputs to increase *efficiency*. The latter almost always reduces the benefits and impact of the project in use. The perceived value of the project content is reduced, especially in use. The client decision-making unit (DMU) may exclude operational users and asset managers; therefore, the perceived value from the user perspective of the project content is absent in cost reduction considerations and the functional boundaries on the client side inhibit integrated working. In addition, the DMU is frequently incentivized to address and held accountable for the cost of the means – delivery of requirements against time–cost–quality/scope – rather the costs and liabilities of the project in use. Understanding the client on the supply side is to understand the criteria of the DMU to find where the boundaries of value added exist and thus where there is scope for added value. In addition to responsible suppliers, this includes assessing the scope to influence DMU criteria for perceived value, where:

Perceived value = Affordable needs + Affordable desires = Anticipated benefits and impact in use

This is particularly important where the project business has adopted S-DL and where value perception includes co-creation. S-DL builds upon and develops many existing lines of thinking, drawing them together. This is true of value, where it has long been recognized as being created through the eyes of the customer (Womack and Jones, 1996; Wise and Baumgartner, 1999; Galbraith, 2002). Value in use can be for the client, it can be cultural and for society at large or the environment (Macmillan, 2006). Shenhar et al. (2001) draw attention to project success being in terms of impact upon the customer, the business success and preparation for the future, and therefore, this broader consideration is far from new for projects. Pertinently, it is a view that is less frequently acted upon through research and in practice.

The usage of the constructs 'value proposition' and 'offering' are key parts of marketing and BDM. The definitions are overlapping in the literature, indicating that there is a need for accommodation and further clarification of the differences. The value proposition can be viewed as an idea or promise. This is what BDMs (conceptually) develop at the front of the front-end in close cooperation with clients and suppliers with procurement. The value offer is what is put forward in the bid. This is a more granular configuration and has the opportunity to identify value, configured as additional options and priced at cost, average or premium profit margins depending upon context. Figure 11.1 provides a template in the form of a matrix to strategically guide how value propositions may be developed. Developing generic propositions at a more detailed level will depend upon a range of investment, marketing and operational factors in any project business.

| Client buyer strategy | **Added value over programmes** | Build in-house capabilities and shift to in-house provision | Strategic partnering and relationship marketing upon the supply side | Service-dominant logic for client programme management |
|---|---|---|---|---|
| | **Value added per exchange** | Perceived underperformance hence drives prices down | Mutual advantage of benefits and profits using relationship marketing and entrepreneurial marketing | Relationship marketing to increase profitability as well as repeat business |
| | **Value added per exchange** | Purely transactional marketing mix approach | Supplier competitiveness to secure repeat business | Either exit from relationship after single transaction or evaluate scope for influencing client strategy |
| | | **Value added per exchange** | **Added value per exchange** | **Added value over client lifetime** |

**Project business BDM (sales) strategy**

**FIGURE 11.1** The development of value propositions

Project businesses tend to price all bid elements as a bundle using a single percentage markup (cf. Stremersch and Tellis, 2002). While a total price has to be presented, the bid can be broken down and the price offered for each component being internally calculated utilizing different profit margins based upon sensitivity in comparison to need and market conditions. This is done irregularly. The measurement of value creation in buyer–seller relationships is still in its infancy (Ulaga, 2003), and therefore the ability to effectively price, especially against need, has considerable potential for development amongst project businesses. One area that requires development is the responsiveness to and pricing of emergent requirements. Current practice is based upon the propensity to reject emergent requirements as deviations (Smyth, 2013b) rather than to see these are value opportunities that can enhance benefits for the client and enhance client lifetime value (CLV) for the supplier.

Eggert et al. (2006) conclude that marketing metrics are generally shifting away from aggregated measures such as turnover targets, profit, and market share towards more emphasis upon performance indicators at the customer or client management level. Therefore, more careful consideration of programme and project margins, and CLV take on increased significance in order to assess which types of project are most profitable and assess which clients are profitable. An apparently low-margin client at the project bid stage may yield an above-average profit because of the effectiveness of relationships, the learning undertaken over serial projects, and the profitability of responding to change orders and other emergent requirements. Certain clients may yield an average profit, but certain types of project may yield above average projects. The profit yielded needs to be based upon outturn or final account costs rather than the bid price, despite the delay in getting 'hard facts' on final accounts. Project businesses require discernment concerning the types of client and types of project for which they bid. This proves useful for identifying where the strengths lie and thus where dynamic capabilities and core competencies can be developed at organizational and project levels.

Pareto-type rules of thumb prevail. It is usual for around 20 per cent of the clients to yield 80 per cent of the turnover (Smyth, 2000). Therefore, nurturing a few clients and the capabilities to serve these clients yield substantial benefits to the supplier and hence profitable micro-level market management. It has also been found that 26 per cent of the project managers contribute 80 per cent of the profits in one major international construction company. The successful project managers in this respect are the proactive planners. Many of these go unnoticed whereas the reactive 'troubleshooters' are seen as capable problem solvers under pressure. It is this latter troubleshooting group that tend to be promoted above the proactive ones (Eiken, 2013). It is unknown whether the percentage split is typical, but this is an area for further examination in research and within individual project businesses. It has considerable implication for profitability. It is probably the case that the proactive project managers are the better client and relationship managers.

This analysis of value creation and derived profit is rather different from the traditional transactional and price driven criteria. Value defined as a currency measure for an item or service is unsupported, for example as proposed by Kelly and Male (1993). While value for money is an optimum to combine the whole lifecycle cost and expected quality (Connaughton and Green, 1996), the short term and silo mentality associated with enactment have poor rationale. For project businesses to capture value, there is a prescriptive need to structure their resource portfolio, bundle resources to build capabilities, and leverage capabilities to exploit market opportunities. There is abundant opportunity for business model differentiation by choice of marketing paradigm (**Chapters 3** to **6**), business models (**Chapter 10**) and developing performance improvement by delivering integrated solutions (e.g. Brady et al., 2005) and moving from emphasizing products towards a service emphasis (Oliva and Kallenberg, 2003). Whatever the differentiation logic is, redefining the content, processes and management of interaction and exchange in customer relationships will be the outcome.

These normative and prescriptive points arise out of a solid examination of the current practices of many project businesses. Wikström et al. state: *Most of the firms are still strongly focusing on products and their organizational structures, processes and culture are not to give a high priority to the customer or the business benefits* (2009: 118).

Helkkula et al. (2012) echo the call of Woodruff (1997: 150) to develop *richer customer value theory that delves into the customer's world.* They put forward a series of propositions that can be turned into interrogative tools for practitioners as well as for research:

- How is the experience of value organizationally assessed objectively and subjectively?
- How is value an experience imagined in advance to inform expectations for the next project?
- How is value constructed from previous and current experiences to inform the expectations for the next project?
- How is value related to context?

This may begin at a single point, but is ongoing. Karpen et al. (2012) suggest value needs to be scoped in different ways, in particular around interaction capabilities, which provides a more dynamic dimension adapted as follows:

- Individual interaction to understanding customer needs;
- Relational interaction in response to product and service provision to solicit social and emotional responses to improve understanding;
- Ethical interaction to improve fairness in business-like ways;
- Developmental interaction to assist customers to develop their own knowledge and capability;
- Concerted interaction to provide co-created value.

Beyond profit realization in operations, what is the value to the project business? It is declared profit, which translates into shareholder value. The appropriate value can be assessed as the discounted present value of future cash flows. CLV is a helpful measure in this respect and can feed into qualitative evaluations of the return on marketing investment (ROMI). Quantitative calculations are more difficult to attribute (see **Chapter 2**; Smyth and Lecoeuvre, 2014). This is more than a disaggregation of complex data, being derived from interaction within integrated activities on the ground. Nonetheless, managers are increasingly challenging market managers and marketers to demonstrate how marketing fits into financial metrics (Ganesan, 2012). Investors are risk averse, being more concerned about potential losses than gains (Tuli et al., 2007). Reconfiguring or increasing value propositions across a portfolio of customers may increase customer satisfaction; however, a series of studies have shown that increasing customer satisfaction does not reduce risk to the supplier, although recent evidence has shown contrary results (Tuli et al., 2009).

Discrepancy has emerged between ROI in aggregate and at the disaggregate levels. The aggregate levels show higher returns (Manchanda et al., 2005), suggesting some type of presentational categorization from an accountancy perspective. This would suggest the need to consider ROI and ROMI at project, programme and portfolio levels ($P^3M$). It would be expected that ROI would be higher at the corporate level due to the reinvestment of working capital as it circulates through the system in periods of lower utilization rates due to less operational demand and positive cashflow management. At the $P^3M$ levels, some explicable and comparative ROI analysis would show returns in operations and from capability development.

At the portfolio level, the issue of (lack of) capital investment and the reasons for this have been analyzed (**Chapters 1** and **2**). At whatever level set, investment and expenditure resources have to be judiciously dispersed. This is a critical component of portfolio management (Lecoeuvre and Patel, 2009). It is far from straightforward in project businesses. Increased investment and expenditure on fixed costs reduce profit margins unless they yield an adequate return, that is, ROI and ROMI, to increase margins and/or market share. Investment and expenditure on fixed costs can help accelerate projects through their lifecycles, for example through more effective BDM to increase bid strike rates and the negotiation of contracts, effective project management, and effective client management. Such measures improve the return on capital employed (ROCE). Positive cash flow in buoyant market conditions and improved ROCE overall can both generate surpluses to support investment to develop capability and capabilities to undertake market diversification or investment on financial markets.

Marketing and BDM provide an avenue for market management and business development by investing in services and capabilities that add value over and above the competition, for example health and safety beyond compliance and 'best' practice (Roberts et al., 2012), knowledge management, environmental capabilities (e.g. Smyth, 2010b; 2013c; Kelly et al., 2013), marketing capabilities (Möller, 2006) or technological adoption and innovation (cf. Davies and Brady, 2000) and other project capabilities (Brady and Davies, 2004; Davies et al., 2007). A few core objectives for investment are claimed to be the optimum for competitive advantage (Chatterjee, 2005; McDonald et al., 2011). These types of issues have been set out in **Chapters 7** and **8**, but can be developed in collaboration for the co-creation of this value based upon what the clients perceive to be of use (Vargo and Lusch, 2010; **Chapter 10**). Such value formed between suppliers and clients provided added value implemented as 'soft' social and psychological contracts. They may be recorded in risk registers or promise-cum-commitment registers as a means to account for delivery over the project lifecycle (**Chapter 4**) and even beyond where KPIs are conducted on benefits, say, 1, 3 and 5 years post-completion.

Value creation can be led bottom-up through entrepreneurial marketing to induce a market for an exchange (cf. Sarasvathy and Dew, 2005), to be innovative in configuring the project in response to a set of demands and requirements (e.g. Kraus et al., 2010; Ioniţă, 2011). This can be linked to co-creation and thus lowers the risk and may improve the affordable loss equation (**Chapter 6**). A disincentive to pursue innovation amongst systems integrator project businesses are the network costs. Leveraging from systems sellers and the impact upon other suppliers is disruptive to the established norms and routines of work (Beamish and Biggart, 2012). It also incurs higher risks. Entrepreneurial marketing can be one means to break such habits and effectuate alternative routines for working. Routines are only relatively stable and robust revision and iterative renegotiation will occur, management steering these to fulfill goals and business purpose (cf. Parmigiani and Howard-Grenville, 2011).

Value creation from a marketing perspective not only feeds into market reputation, but it also feeds into the brand presence of the project business in the market, extending beyond the client base to reach shareholders, investors and other project stakeholders (Merz et al., 2009). Brand profile acts back to positively reinforce shareholder value. Firms increasingly recognize brand as a valuable asset (e.g. Madden et al., 2006; Merz et al., 2009). Differentiation is therefore needed to secure valuable brand recognition. Brand is created by their perception of the business and services. It is the functional benefits and impact that have the greatest long-term impact upon the generation of brand value emanating from a firm. Supplier capability and therefore careful selection of supply chains are further important factors in generating brand value (de Chernatony, 1999).

## Conclusion

The different views on value and its creation show some tensions and conflicts between the views, but more significantly, highlight the trend towards a broadening of the concept of value. The chapter started by showing the differences in meaning, especially between the worth in terms of creating something and worth in moral terms. The prime focus was on the meaning of value creation, yet the two come together through the perceptual lens of the co-creation of value in use terms. At macro-level, how value is created and profit generated feed into the moral economy upon which the financial or wealth creating economy depends (Smyth, 2014).

Value is a key component of securing work, survival in the marketplace, and a key dimension of differentiation. It is central to market management and business development, and should be central to marketing and BDM, especially for project businesses employing relationship and entrepreneurial marketing. The transactional view does tend towards keeping value propositions to a minimum, in practice necessary for competing in predominantly price-driven project markets. This minimalist approach is insufficient for other marketing approaches and, where the demands of clients become more complex, requiring specialist outsourced provision (see also **Chapter 9**). This raises the question on the extent to which project businesses wish to keep clients in the *zone of indifference* or differentiate their value propositions and offers to serve certain markets and particular clients to great effect (Grönroos, 2000).

The chapter has brought together several threads woven into other chapters concerning value and its creation. The examination of views on and definitions of value is far from exhaustive. The exploration of value commenced with value propositions and offers in market management and marketing. Measurement of the benefits of value delivery, especially added value, has been brought into this discussion (see also **Chapter 2**), especially the difficulty of making realistic assessments. In sum, while it is difficult to justify investment, the implications of no investment leaves cost drivers as the dominant factor to the extent that it can increase market risk. Value as lowest cost may prove to be a business model confined to smaller market segments in future.

The management implications largely focus upon the benefits of delivering added value. Selecting the propositions and developing offers effectively requires integrated processes, most of which are outside mainstream project management. Market management, client management, relationship management, capability management are decisive management factors. The marketing paradigm selected guides value creation. The granular level of strategy and tactics provide key differentiators, as different project businesses will choose to respond in different ways.

The main message has been that value directly affects turnover and profitability of the project business derived from the benefits delivered to clients and experienced in use. It is also the case that value delivery over the long term is contingent upon investment. While short-term profits can be squeezed from cost cutting, value is compromised by squeezing resources in the long-term. The focus on cost control can absorb 75 per cent of portfolio spending, while expenditure geared to growing the market is single figures. Costs must be controlled, yet with recognition, expenditure is intrinsically linked to value in service sectors. The two problems for the project business are that it is not perceived as a service sector and the market driver that provides powerful counterforces. Indeed, project businesses have educated clients to adopt price as the primary driver through a lack of differentiation and being the first actors to resort to price competition against each other (Smyth, 2000). Clients need education and awareness creation to look at the broader sets of criteria as part of the marketing effort. This is proactive management, which brings the examination to the substantive issues identified in **Chapter 1**.

**SI no. 1:** ***Market Management*** engages directly with proactive value creation as part of recognizing and enhancing co-creation activities on projects, but also operating more strategically at a programme management level to generate and deliver value. Greater engagement post-completion can also influence, as well as monitor, the co-creation of value in use.

**SI no. 3:** ***Marketing Investment and Portfolio Management*** underpins value creation, especially in the medium-to-long term. The capacity to generate value, especially the knowledge and expertise, and other organizational and project capabilities, is dependent upon investment and effective portfolio management.

**SI no. 4:** ***Client Management and Programme Management*** in terms of inputs depends upon understanding the richness and diverse needs, especially those that are not encapsulated in requirements documentation, and assessing outputs in terms of value derived in use of the project and attendant processes.

**SIs no. 5** and **6:** ***Marketing, BDM and Client Management*** have tended to focus upon securing work rather than value creation. This excludes seeing how the one helps the other – they are mutually reinforcing, and therefore, value is a *central interface function*. The aim is to facilitate cross-functional working and integration for value identification and delivery in ways that grow the market and profitability for the project business. More detailed analysis of clients and P$^3$M is necessary to understand, which clients, programmes and types of project are most profitable – the earning logic in business model terms.

**SI no. 9: *Marketing and Managing the Project Lifecycle*** pertains to value too as it conceptually starts at the front of the front-end when the (unpaid) service of relationship building, sense giving to a project, advice giving for a project commences, and conceptually continues over the project lifecycle into post-completion to evaluate the project in use.

**SI no. 10: *Marketing and Value Creation*** has been the central theme. Value and *added technical and service value* from the market perspective are key to the success of project businesses as well as clients. The points raised all feed into addressing this issue.

There are several main *recommendations* for research that flow from the analysis for the research communities:

A. Understanding value and value creation from the broader perspective presented have yet to be adequately researched and are pivotal for MoP development and necessary for the evaluation of capability development.
B. Detailed research into value creation and the realization of profits for the project business is urgently needed, including evaluation of how different profit profiles relate back to past investment and inform future investment decisions.
C. Research into the benefits and impact of project in use post-completion has yet to be adequately examined, especially beyond total asset management and whole life cost criteria, which only form a small, yet important, and under-researched part of the picture of projects in use.

The main *recommendations* for practice are set out as follows:

1. A more considered approach of what value is needed to serve the client base and individual clients, especially added value, and the financial benefits for the project business.
2. Realistic assessments by senior management of what the value creation capacity and capabilities are in their project businesses and detailed knowledge of the extent to which clients perceive these as valuable.
3. Putting in systems through relationship marketing to solicit detailed information and a rich understanding of value amongst each key or core client over project lifecycles and for their programmes.

Completing the exploration and examination of the topics with a focus upon value provides a basis for summing up and drawing out the primary conclusions in the next and final chapter from conceptual and applied viewpoints.

# 12

# LIFE LIVED FORWARDS

## Introduction

'Life lived forwards' is derived from the work of Karl Weick (2003) in management research, which in turn evokes the philosopher Søren Kirkegaard (1843) who said that life can be understood backwards, and yet it must be lived forwards. Weick (2003) distinguishes between life understood backwards and life lived forwards in terms of theory and practice. There is a difference between describing and explaining 'what is' and designing and evaluating 'what can be' (Simon, 1969). In management, it is important not only to be able to learn from the *shadows of the past*, but it is also important to induce a strong creative element and embed change towards better application for researchers and practitioners. The bridge to the imagination is normative research, and prescription can be derived from research. There are always obstacles and boundaries. Overcoming obstacles is less to do with project management theorization and market management concepts; it is the underpinning ideas of our imagination – the future perfect project (Pitsis et al., 2003) and the plan for preparing the project rather than the 'rationality' of project management (Kreiner, 2012). The 'rationality' is derived from the logic of socially constructed plans rather than some 'natural order'. The plans are only as good as their ability to accommodate the reality of unfolding events. This is not a risk management problem. Risks are also perceived social constructions, which have profiles of possibilities and probabilities that rarely match the reality. This does not mean there is a need to throw out the rational. It provides a starting point, but not an end point. Rather, we use the borders of rationality as the basis for moving forward. Amy Purdy recently put it this way in *Living Beyond Limits*:

> Our imagination can be used as tools for breaking through borders. . . . Innovation has only been possible because of my borders. I've learned that borders

> are where the actual ends, but also where the imagination and the story begins . . . It's not about breaking down borders; it's about pushing off of them.
> (2011)

This applies to theorization and application, indeed theory and practice are related in this way. Theory is also practical, and concepts get applied. Theory can be generated inductively from applying imagination in practice and analyzing the outcomes. Theory is also generated deductively by applying imagination to form testable conceptual ideas in practice. Practices are adopted and embedded through systems and procedures and can become norms and part of the taken-for-granted thinking that no longer need formal routines (e.g. Bresnen and Marshall, 2011; Morris and Geraldi, 2011; Morris, 2013). However, these can become rigidities (Gilbert, 2005), and hence the need for new concepts and models. Life lived forwards is both experiential and conceptual, the two coming together at various points to improve understanding and inform action.

This book has argued that one new way of looking at project management is that the project is a *delivery channel* and thus a service for clients. The application of this marketing concept can change thinking. It places the project within marketing rather than seeing marketing as a peripheral activity to be linked to project management. Marketing and business development management (BDM) are one of the most important conceptual tools of market management and business development, especially in project businesses. Market management starts at the front of the front-end with marketing and BDM. It sets the tone for service delivery according to the focus adopted, the paradigm chosen and the implementation in the hierarchy and along project lifecycles. But marketing and BDM are not just part of the management of projects (MoP). They inform all activities in the same way that finance and people do.

The chapters have tried to progressively draw together market management with an emphasis upon project business development from a transactional approach of discrete internal and external management to reactively offer and deliver the minimal value added in atomized packages towards integrated internal and external management to proactively offer and deliver integrated added service and co-created value – see Figure 1.2. A distillation of some of the main objectives across the chapters and hence the issues covered are set out below:

- A broad theoretical approach to market management, marketing and the sales process to develop the project business, which is necessarily based upon a solid and improved understanding of the role of marketing and BDM in project businesses in theory and practice.
- Part of the understanding is to have informed views of the marketing approaches and paradigms available, including their strengths and weaknesses:

    a. An analysis of the theoretical and applied characteristics of the marketing mix in project businesses and an examination of how these are aligned and internally managed;

b. An analysis of the theoretical and applied characteristics of relationship marketing in project businesses and an examination of how to build and manage relationships;
c. An analysis of the conceptual and applied characteristics of project marketing in project businesses and an examination of how these are aligned and are managed;
d. An analysis of the theoretical and applied characteristics of entrepreneurial marketing in project businesses and an examination of how these are aligned and internally managed.

- Changing client needs are driving project complexity experienced by project businesses, which is arguably bringing to the fore a growing imperative to examine the connection between MoP systems and marketing implementation for programme and project success. Meeting the challenge requires redress of the conceptual and practice-based emphasis to try to force marketing into the execution mould of project management.
- Analysis of resource allocation in project businesses in relation to top-down and bottom-up financial management, market management, the effectiveness of marketing and the sales processes, and developing capabilities to make a positive impact on the marketplace is necessary, including an analysis of the theoretical and applied characteristics of the service-dominant logic (S-DL) in project businesses and an examination of how these are internally managed, and aligned with relationship marketing. An examination of the different views and definitions of value in relation to market management and marketing, and the implications for projects and the management of project businesses flows from this.
- Application of theory and concepts in practical ways for business performance, including the alignment of functions and processes. A theoretical and applied focus on performance measurement in rigorous and balanced ways is needed.
- Structuring, governing, coordinating and integrating activities in the hierarchy and setting the parameters for horizontal integration across programmes and along project lifecycles.
- Management recognition of constraints and barriers posed by internal organization and the development of management coordination mechanisms across organizational silos and to span boundaries for cross-functional working.
- Improve understanding of the implications of BDM practices for the overall management of project businesses.

These are interlinked and complex issues that the chapters have woven together. Practitioners tend to make commitments and invest in initiatives incrementally with iterative refinement, although the management risk is loss of rigor and inconsistent implementation over time.

## Contributions to knowledge

In exploring and examining the objectives, a number of theoretical and conceptual contributions to knowledge have been developed. The book has addressed several overarching theoretical issues:

1. *Projects are a delivery channel* – conceptually, the project is a choice in the ways a bundle of product and service attributes reach the customer or client in the marketplace, which in marketing terms is called 'place' within the marketing mix and more generally termed the *delivery channel*. On the one hand, this has huge implications in the sense that it firmly places the project within marketing. This is in contradiction to the current perceptions that marketing is located at the periphery of projects and conceptual attempts to link marketing and BDM to project management. On the other hand, it provokes a 'so what' type of question as to how this might change research and practice on the ground. The challenge is more at the level of changing mindsets in research and practice. What flows from a change in mindset is that research and practice are informed by market management and by marketing and BDM as a key and integrating ingredient for MoP, including execution. The contribution to knowledge is to make the connection between projects and delivery channels explicit.
2. *Market management and marketing are integral to portfolio, programme and project management ($P^3M$)* – marketing is a key component of market management and arguably the key concept in project businesses. Market and marketing management operate in the hierarchy from the 'corporate centre' into all $P^3M$ levels through resource allocation, client management and value creation and delivery along project lifecycles. Marketing and BDM also provide a fine grain of understanding of the marketplace, which feeds into market management and business development from the bottom-up. The contribution to knowledge is the articulation of marketing and market management across $P^3M$.
3. *Integrating the management of projects (MoP) and capability development* – to date, MoP research has had a client-side bias in general and has specifically overlooked marketing and BDM, while capability development on the supply side has yet to be completely integrated with MoP. Indeed, many project businesses have had difficulties developing capabilities and competencies that are dynamic and add value. There are multiple factors for improving integration, yet a fully developed marketing and BDM function, especially using non-transactional marketing mix approach, provides a major driver for integration in practice. The contribution has been to develop the conceptual integration.
4. *Marketing and business development management (BDM) is located at the front of the front-end in the project lifecycle* – selling or BDM emanates from the marketing strategy as part of the project business model or strategic plan, and BDM contact with clients typically pre-dates project definition of the client side. Once a project is in the client investment plan, BDM can focus upon the project level, and therefore, on the supply side, marketing and BDM are located

at the *front of the front-end*. This has been neglected in most MoP research. It also leads to overlooking value identification that conceptually takes place at this stage from the project management perspective of execution. The marketing and BDM role is not confined to BDMs, but conceptually continues through bid management, project management and post-completion for the maintenance of relationships under relationship marketing approaches (**Chapters 4** and **5**) and for monitoring co-created value in use within S-DL (**Chapter 10**). The contribution is to locate marketing as a central and continuous function along project and programme lifecycles.

5. *The systems integrator, solutions and systems seller for integrated provision as three marketing categories of project business* – these terms categorize types of activity. The *systems integrator* in its purest form does not produce anything. It brings together other organizational actors from supply chains in integrated ways to make the sum total of value greater than otherwise would be the case. Indeed, their role depends upon their ability to do so. Systems integrators require internal integration in order to facilitate effective external integration. The *systems seller* is a producer of products and services, which works with the systems integrators and sometimes directly with client sponsors or owners to develop high-value product and service bundles. Systems sellers tend to be second-tier subcontractors and below. The contribution is to have further developed the concepts of the systems integrator, solutions and systems seller role in the marketplace. It is also to have linked this with *internal integration* within the project business and the role of marketing and BDM as important facilitators and a driving force for internal integration.

Bringing together MoP and capability development with the two main conceptual roles of project businesses enables some initial scoping of the marketing paradigms and approaches against these factors. This is set out in Figure 12.1. The figure

| **Marketing, organizational and project capabilities** | | | |
|---|---|---|---|
| **Systems integrator** | From the marketing mix through entrepreneurial marketing and relationship marketing towards the service-dominant logic | From the marketing mix through relationship marketing towards the service-dominant logic | From relationship marketing for continuity (cf. project marketing) to the service-dominant logic |
| **Systems seller** | From selling using the marketing mix to entrepreneurial marketing for innovation and relationship marketing | From selling using the transactional marketing mix towards the service-dominant logic | From transactional maintenance to the service-dominant logic around use value |
| | **Front-end** | **Execution** | **Back-end** |
| | | **The management of projects** | |

**FIGURE 12.1** Marketing, the management of projects and capabilities

shows that the transactional marketing mix approach offers the least scope for effective marketing by the type of project business and role and in relation to MoP. The marketing mix is the easier and least demanding marketing paradigm to employ, yet is the least relevant conceptually. As argued, client needs, and hence their demands, are becoming ever more complex. It therefore appears less likely that the path of least resistance regarding investment and management is sustainable as the dominant marketing approach for the long-term.

**Chapter 1** introduced some key issues for research and practice:

- To what extent are markets managed by project businesses?
- In what ways is the market managed at an operational level through marketing and BDM?
- What is the extent of the issue between the theoretical principles applied in practice and the theory?

Drilling down to a finer grain of analysis, a number of substantive issues were identified in the chapter, ten in total. Each subsequent chapter has reviewed the extent to which these substantive issues have been filled. A map of the outcome is presented in Figure 12.2. All the substantive issues have been addressed in more than one chapter. **SI no. 7** on vertical systems and integration was addressed the least, yet top-down systems are present in most organizations and the main issue is to ensure that strategies, systems and procedures are implemented from a market management and marketing perspective. The marketing mix was covered in **Chapter 3,** and the evidence from the map shows this paradigm is least able to tackle the substantive issues through theorization and for practice.

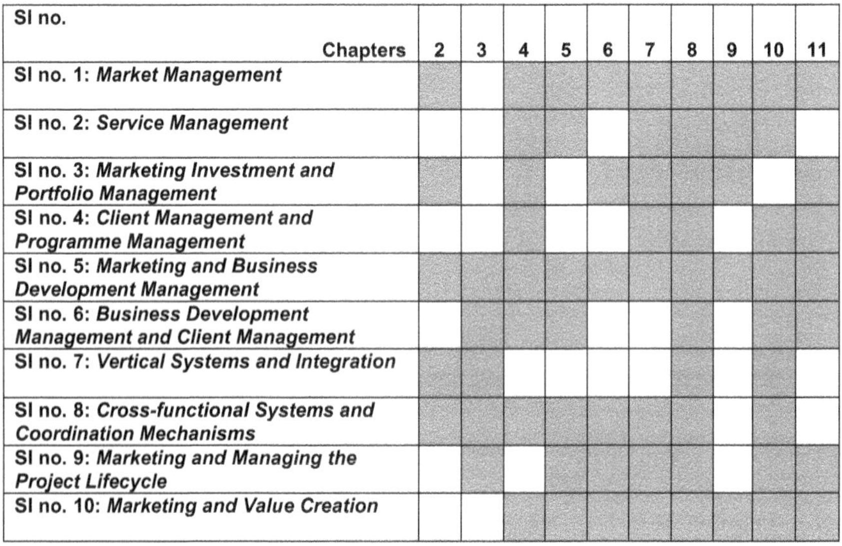

| **SI no.** Chapters | 2 | 3 | 4 | 5 | 6 | 7 | 8 | 9 | 10 | 11 |
|---|---|---|---|---|---|---|---|---|---|---|
| **SI no. 1:** ***Market Management*** | | | | | | | | | | |
| **SI no. 2:** ***Service Management*** | | | | | | | | | | |
| **SI no. 3:** ***Marketing Investment and Portfolio Management*** | | | | | | | | | | |
| **SI no. 4:** ***Client Management and Programme Management*** | | | | | | | | | | |
| **SI no. 5:** ***Marketing and Business Development Management*** | | | | | | | | | | |
| **SI no. 6:** ***Business Development Management and Client Management*** | | | | | | | | | | |
| **SI no. 7:** ***Vertical Systems and Integration*** | | | | | | | | | | |
| **SI no. 8:** ***Cross-functional Systems and Coordination Mechanisms*** | | | | | | | | | | |
| **SI no. 9:** ***Marketing and Managing the Project Lifecycle*** | | | | | | | | | | |
| **SI no. 10:** ***Marketing and Value Creation*** | | | | | | | | | | |

**FIGURE 12.2** A map of the ten key substantive issues of research

The contribution to addressing each research issue is consolidated in the commentary provided next.

**SI no. 1:** ***Market Management*** – provides the overarching construct for growing a project business. It includes business development through diversification of products and service lines, mergers and acquisitions and marketing. In project businesses marketing and BDM play a considerable role because other means of market management are less favourable under most circumstances. Market management is a proactive construct. It is not always adopted by project businesses, because many project businesses choose to minimize investment and expenditure. The contributions made to addressing this substantive issue are the following:

- Strategic investment and integration in market management with operations and (transactional and/or relational) marketing (**Chapter 2**).
- The proactive focus of relationship marketing and related developments of project marketing and S-DL (**Chapters 4**, **5** and **10**).
- There is a need for further research into this area to facilitate management awareness of the relevance of market management and investment issues to project businesses (**Chapter 4**).
- Proactive management was found to be needed on the ground in order to align behavioural norms and habits with marketing approaches; too much tends to be left to individual responsibility for effective practice (**Chapter 4**).
- Entrepreneurialism is a means of market management and business development, and thus, entrepreneurial marketing is the most closely associated concept to broader and higher level entrepreneurship (**Chapter 6**).
- Effective and proactive market management in terms of the systems integrator, solutions and systems seller roles (**Chapter 7**).
- The development of project business models inclusive of the management of projects, (MoP) and marketing and BDM (**Chapter 8**).
- Bringing together of MoP and investment with the mobilization of capabilities at the front-end aligned to and guided by a strategic marketing (**Chapter 9**).
- The application of S-DL in research and practice is a form of market management that perforates firm boundaries in proactive ways, in particular to facilitate the co-creation of value (**Chapter 10**).
- Assessing value, value leverage and generation, especially co-creation in programme and project management with increased emphasis upon post-completion assessments of value in use (**Chapter 11**).

**SI no. 2:** ***Service Management*** – a *client* and *service focus* with an emphasis upon added value to include the service experience, areas of total asset management, facilities management, and 2050 sustainability agendas, including the performance benefits and impact in use. The contributions made to addressing this substantive issue are:

- Foci upon client and service needs, particularly through the application of relationship marketing and management, and S-DL (**Chapters 4**, **5** and **10**).

- Added service value is realized through project shaping in marketing (**Chapters 4** and **5**).
- Increasing complexity of demand, manifested as technical and service attributes, is driving the need for increased integration (**Chapters 7** and **9**).
- MoP makes an important contribution to service experience at the front-end and for setting up the service experience during execution (**Chapters 8** and **9**).
- Service management focus on the purpose of projects in terms of the services rendered, that is benefits and impact in use, rather than project management as an end in itself (**Chapter 10**).

**SI no. 3:** ***Marketing Investment and Portfolio Management*** – business requirements in order to yield a return. Different investment approaches are needed to cover both service- and production-orientated financial management. The resource-based view of the firm allocates bundles of resources to secure competitive positioning, and marketing and BDM is a key bundle of resources on its terms and as resources to be linked with other technical and service capabilities. This is part of portfolio management, and cascades marketing-related resources to programme and project management. Working towards addressing this substantive issue has included:

- Investment from the 'corporate centre', cascading through portfolio and programme management to the project level ($P^3M$), to resource and functionally integrate marketing and BDM, especially relationship marketing and S-DL (**Chapters 4**, **5** and **10**).
- Entrepreneurial marketing requires resource availability on a bottom-up affordable loss basis (**Chapter 6**).
- Complex demands in markets of intense competition involve differentiation, and this is achieved through investment (**Chapter 7**). MoP and $P^3M$ are likely to increase investment yield (**Chapter 8**).
- Resources are scarce, and investments involve alignment with marketing and BDM, as well as allocated to marketing and BDM (**Chapter 9**).
- Investment and portfolio management underpin effective value creation in the medium-to-long term (**Chapter 11**).

**SI no. 4:** ***Client Management and Programme Management*** – coordination mechanisms for customer lifetime value (CLV) at the interface between client management, project business programme management and project management. The contributions made to this research issue are the following:

- Awareness of client needs with a depth of rigor is central to client management. Integrated solutions to fulfill the needs are generically developed at programme level and subsequently customized and tailored for each project (**Chapters 4**, **7** and **9**).
- Client and programme management are gaining traction with the project community, MoP providing space to coordinate client management over

project lifecycles, client lifetime value (CLV) criteria being central for relational approaches (**Chapters 8** and **10**).

- Both functions enhance opportunities to add value and grow the market (**Chapter 11**).

**SI no. 5:** ***Marketing and Business Development Management*** – recognizing effective interface functions in theory and practice through ways of thinking and attitude of mind, ways of organizing, and the sets of tools and techniques applied. The contributions made to examining this research field are the following:

- Marketing and BDM are functions for market management and business development. Functional integration is necessary between these two and other functional interfaces, especially BDMs with bid management and operations/project management, and BDMs with procurement and technical services (**Chapters 2**, **4**, **6** and **7**).
- The conceptual limitations or the marketing mix paradigm and the dominance in application pose tensions during exchange and execution, which is increasingly being challenged by demand (**Chapters 3** and **4**).
- Marketing and BDM involvement is conceptually continuous over project lifecycles, including evaluation post-completion (**Chapters 8** and **9**). Marketing and BDM are functions not only to be integrated into other operations but also facilitators of integration for the systems seller and the systems integrator project business (**Chapters 9** and **10**).
- Cross-functional working and integration are important for profitable value identification and delivery to align BDM with capabilities (**Chapter 11**).

**SI no. 6:** ***Business Development Management and Client Management*** – highlights the prevalence of weak systems between the project business and project teams, inhibiting continuity and consistency of service. Analysis plugging this research gap includes:

- Service consistency over project lifecycles and in supplier programmes is an unresolved issue in many project businesses (**Chapters 3** and **5**). It is consistent and continuous under S-DL over projects and programmes (**Chapter 10**).
- Project shaping to add value is underdeveloped (**Chapter 5**).
- Managing programme continuity partly lies outside MoP and is a marketing function (**Chapters 5** and **8**).
- BDM has tended to focus upon securing work rather than value creation. Value creation and securing work are mutually reinforcing. Detailed analysis of clients and $P^3M$ is necessary to understand, which clients, programmes and types of project are most profitable (**Chapter 11**).

**SI no. 7:** ***Vertical Systems and Integration*** – vertical coordination mechanisms of formal and informal routines for implementing marketing and BDM, and for supporting BDM along project lifecycles to secure work and deliver value. Alignment with financial and human resource management (HRM) functions, as well as operational functions, is important. Working towards addressing this research issue has included:

- The extent of the systems gap at the corporate–project interface towards and the relation to investment from portfolio and programme management to the project level remains overlooked in research and practice (**Chapters 2** and **3**).
- Coordination mechanisms for capability integration and development are necessary internally and for leveraging value in supply chains (**Chapters 8** and **10**).

**SI no. 8:** ***Cross-functional Systems and Coordination Mechanisms*** – horizontal coordination mechanisms of formal and informal routines for implementing marketing and BDM, including relationship management to coordinate temporary multi-organizational teams (TMOs) in value leverage, delivery and project risk. The contributions made to addressing this research area are the following:

- The extent of the systems gap along project lifecycles and the relation to investment for systematic coordination. Performance improvement, using for example performance measurement systems and return on marketing investment assessments (ROMI), provides guidance (**Chapter 2**).
- Senior management defers multiple coordination tasks to individual responsibility and informal routines (**Chapter 3**).
- The systems integrator role in relation to supply chains is only as effective as internal integration. Internal integration spans functions and includes relationship management systems that provide a relationship marketing focus for integration (**Chapter 4**).
- Project marketing addresses the cross-functional and intradepartmental issues, especially in bidding and, to a limited extent, with execution. This supports how other systems and mechanisms provide coordination. Project marketing has left gaps as how these processes are configured on the ground, preferring to concentrate primarily upon conceptual development.
- Relationship marketing requires comprehensive integrated systems (**Chapters 4** and **5**); entrepreneurial marketing requires cross-functional working mainly at the sales-bid management–project management interfaces (**Chapter 6**).
- BDM covers sales (conducted by BDMs), bid management and client management and monitoring value delivery during execution, but traditional project management excludes recognition of the remit (**Chapter 7**). MoP offers scope for incorporation, yet consistently overlooks the marketing and BDM role in research and practice (**Chapter 8**).
- Coordination and integration are integral to S-DL to meet demand need and for the co-creation of value (**Chapter 10**).

**SI no. 9:** ***Marketing and Managing the Project Lifecycle*** – iterative and agile management to deliver non-contractual promises and commitments made at the front-end to add value and responding to emergent requirements. Added value has to be weighed against CLV and project costs. Working towards addressing this substantive issue has included:

- Management working to linear socially constructed plans in rigid fashion is frequently found to be dysfunctional to value creation and profit making (**Chapters 3** and **11**).
- Managing relationships during projects and between projects is beneficial to client and the project business in relational approaches to marketing. Drilling down to the level of detailed conduct has still to be fully developed (**Chapters 4** and **5**).
- Entrepreneurial project management can act back to reinforce the role of BDM yielding sales strength for differentiation in the marketplace (**Chapter 6**).
- BDMs have responsibilities over project lifecycles to ensure coordination, deliver integrated solutions, and lever added value in execution (**Chapter 7**).
- Marketing and MoP are intertwined. BDM is conceptually located at the front of the front-end on the supply side, mirroring the procurement function on the client side (**Chapter 8**).
- Technical and service content, the service experience and benefits of the completed project in use are part of S-DL (**Chapter 10**). Value identification conceptually starts at the front of the front-end and continues over the project lifecycle into post-completion to evaluate the project in use (**Chapter 11**).

**SI no. 10:** ***Marketing and Value Creation*** – technical and service value added satisfies minimum requirements, while added value includes a broader range of value definitions, the broadest being found in S-DL. Value is more than simply a function of supplier creation; it is a function of co-creation between parties. Analysis to address this substantive issue includes:

- Relationship marketing is a function of operational performance and value creation (**Chapter 4**). Value has current theoretical resonance and is under conceptual development within S-DL (**Chapter 10**).
- Project shaping adds value at the front-end (**Chapter 5**). Entrepreneurial marketing focuses upon configuring the context and shaping the project to form value propositions (**Chapter 6**). Value realization depends upon the delivery of integrated solutions (**Chapters 7** and **8**).
- Gaps between client need, project business capability and delivery of integrated solutions are ultimately a function of investment and resource allocation (**Chapter 9**). Marketing needs indicators and measures to justify investments.
- Value, added value and co-created value are central to S-DL, emphasizing effectiveness to drive efficiency (rather than input–output ratios as and efficiency measures) (**Chapter 10**). Value and added technical and service value from the market perspective is central to the success of project businesses (**Chapter 11**).

## Future directions

*You gotta fight every day to keep mediocrity at bay* is the first line from *Mediocrity at Bay*, performed by Van Morrison on *Magic Time*. The *shadows of the past* comprise mediocrity because they comprise established practice, many of which become routinized, standardized and have induced rigidities. The new developments of yesterday become the common practice of tomorrow, or the added value of yesterday becomes the value added of tomorrow. Everyday pressures in management and organizational pressures are enormous, hence the understandable desire to stay with what we know and with what we feel comfortable; thus the need to fight. This applies as much to those engaged in project management research as project management practice. The next innovation may arise from a major investment (cf. **Chapters 2** and **9**) or it may develop incrementally and iteratively on an affordable loss basis (**Chapter 6**). Some will prove more successful than others, and some will simply fail. A major investment can be phased in over a programme and thus incrementally built up, for example implementing relationship marketing and developing S-DL (**Chapters 4** and **10**). There will be tensions and misalignments, but typically, major investments need adjustment and refinement so there is always a degree of iteration. It has been an argument that project markets are undergoing fundamental change. The implication is that the old models will not work, and at the time of writing, the same could be argued at the macro-economic level; that is another story, but one that may induce further changes. Project management as a domain is more holistic than researchers necessarily embrace and the bodies of knowledge currently accommodate (cf. Smyth and Morris, 2007).

Added to this picture, managers and researchers alike tend to choose approaches that suit their own worldviews (Starbuck, 1982), and in response, they frame the reality around them (Morgan, 1986; cf. Weick, 1995). There is a tendency to reach for the familiar and to pursue satisficing routes as these are paths of least resistance and carry less risk, on top of which, there are constraints and restraints including the availability of resources. This does not mean it is all about trade-offs as many claim (e.g. Coase, 1988; Hart and Holmstrom, 2010). Research and management environments are more akin to ecologies than linear mechanisms. This is not to use ecology in the deterministic sense as human agency has a structuring effect (cf. Giddens, 1981). Both research and practice around project management are embedded in and are a part of social and moral capital rather that fixed capital.

In accordance with Morris (2013), the analysis presented has highlighted value, context and impact as continuing issues for the future. This book has demonstrated that marketing and BDM are a means but also an end in themselves to the extent that they deliver services as well as lever service value. This point has yet to be fully appreciated and acted upon in project businesses and in project management research. This point provides direction for the future. It links to the importance of projects in terms of benefits delivered and impact made, where the means of project management serves the end.

## Recommendations for research and practice

A number of recommendations have been proposed for each chapter, and a consolidated list is presented at this point. First, recommendations are presented for further research.

A. Research into the project business.

   a. Research is needed into the project as a delivery channel, coupled in the context of in-house production, outsourcing and the logistics represented by project management. In addition, research into transaction costs and weak systems at programme level.
   b. Research needs to be conducted into the inter-relationships and interplay between systems integrators, systems and solutions sellers in terms of the organizational barriers and enablers at the interfaces.
   c. Research into S-DL has been scant to date, much of the applied work being in management around service design and the linkage to strategic business logic for the supplier and customer. Asset specific markets have been largely overlooked.
   d. S-DL is a highly pertinent area for research in project businesses due to asset specificity, linking to the management of projects, capability development and the role of marketing over project lifecycles.
   e. Research into generic service design and the customization and tailoring mechanisms is recommended from the strategic level, through programme management to project management methodologies to delivery at the project level ($P^3M$).
   f. Research into clients and project businesses that adopt S-DL implicitly and explicitly is recommended as little is understood at the moment about current practices in relation to strategies for prescriptive adoption in industry.

B. A greater understanding as to how project businesses (explicitly and implicitly) formulate market management strategy, how strategy is reviewed, implemented from senior management to operations level.

   a. A greater understanding on investment decisions, and the use of measures and evaluation to inform judgments made.
   b. A greater understanding of market management strategy, and development through the broader lens of the marketing of projects.
   c. Research into marketing as pivotal for integrating the management of projects and capability development at the front-end and tracing that through $P^3M$.
   d. A greater understanding as to the constraints and barriers within project businesses, between formal and informal routines, and at functional interfaces.

C. Research into marketing.

a. Conceptualization and application of marketing at the front of the front-end: relationship, project, entrepreneurial and service logic marketing.
b. Linked to $P^3M$.
c. Research into the lack of awareness of relationship marketing principles amongst management.
d. Detailed analysis of BDM in relation to other functions at the front-end and in relation to other front-end functions.
e. Research into the interrelationships and interplay between marketing and the development of integrated solutions.
f. Research the bid management processes and in particular the processes for win-strategy development and value leverage in relation to integrated solutions.

D. Research into the management of projects from a marketing perspective.

a. Marketing interface with other project business and project management functions through a relationship marketing lens.
b. Research analyzing organizational behavioural conduct at the front-end, including marketing and BDM roles.
c. Research conducted into entrepreneurial marketing, the extent of the activity, how it is conducted, alignment to the organization and outcomes.
d. Research into the interface of entrepreneurial marketing with other approaches and modes of operation.
e. Further detailed theorization and conceptual development of entrepreneurial marketing in different types of project business.

E. Research into project management from a marketing perspective.

a. Further detailed analysis of BDM as a function in its own right and in relation to other functions, especially during execution.
b. Research is needed as to how the agency motivations and structuring of organizational processes between BDM and project management affect the interface.

Second, recommendations for practice are presented.

1. Investment:

a. Growth is a function of investment, facilitated by mutual understanding between functions, where informed consideration can be undertaken, starting with the finance–marketing interface.
b. A considered approach to the transition from marketing approach to another requires investment.

   c. A considered analysis of investment to ensure survival and develop the project business, anchored in judgment, qualitative assessments and quantitative measures.

2. Market management:

   a. A greater client and service focus is required.
   b. Market management, marketing and BDM, and marketing-related investment to differentiate offers and deliver (added) technical and service value.

3. Systems and procedure:

   a. Implement flexible systems to articulate the interfaces between hierarchical and horizontal boundaries and barriers in management and operations.
   b. Align systems and capabilities for solutions integration to a rigorous understanding of client needs (as opposed to requirements).
   c. Capture capabilities developed on specific projects for roll out on future projects.
   d. Form systems through relationship marketing to solicit detailed information and a rich understanding of value amongst each key client programmes and projects.
   e. Aligning MoP with comprehensive marketing principles, BDM practices along the project lifecycle for systems integrator and systems seller roles.
   f. Personnel reviews and career paths that acknowledge entrepreneurial activity.

4. Marketing paradigms and approaches:

   a. Project decision-making to be informed by the project as a market delivery channel.
   b. Address individualism, isolated activity and a lack of integration within the marketing mix. Overreliance upon individuals leads to the need for functional integration for all approaches.
   c. Improved awareness of relationship, project and entrepreneurial marketing principles amongst senior management and project managers.
   d. Increased attention to be given to service elements and service experience, and consider S-DL as part of service development.
   e. Integration of BDM as a distinct yet essential component of execution stages.
   f. Realistic assessments by senior management of capabilities and the extent to which clients perceive them as valuable and (potential) financial benefits.

## Conclusion

The book has considered market management and business development. It has addressed marketing and selling as functions. It has linked these functions with strategy and management implementation top-down from the 'corporate centre' through portfolio, programme and project management. It has considered the marketing role along project lifecycles, linking the management of projects and capability development with marketing. The current conceptual state of play has been presented. This has been supported by evidence-based research from a range of sources and substantive issues mapped between the current state of knowledge through theorization and practice. The resultant theoretical potential identified between research and practice has led to a degree of normative and prescriptive conceptualization for research and practice.

Several main messages have been carried throughout. First, marketing is undergoing a fundamental change in many project businesses. There are market forces and resultant resource constraints to the rapid development of marketing, which are surmountable, yet most senior, commercial and project managers have poor awareness of marketing. Second, many large project businesses are in a slow transition to relationship marketing, the pace partly being dictated by balancing the perceived need for change with investment restraint and partly due to a lack of awareness particularly amongst senior management, including those responsible for marketing and financial management. Third, there is choice over the selection of theoretical approaches, marketing paradigms and the tools and tactics of implementation. Fourth, caution is needed in research and practice to translate and transfer mainstream management concepts into project businesses and for projects.

Project practice and project research are extremely exciting. The pan-industry take up of projects as a delivery channel and the expansion of research in project management provide new insights into and ways of understanding projects. The increasing awareness of management researchers of the management of projects as a complex and significant activity bodes well for inducing new developments in the research field and in practice. Developing the project business–project interface is a major challenge. Market management and project business development have significant contributions to make to the broad and challenging issues. It is hoped this book has made a contribution in these directions. The challenge is to take the market management and business development of project business beyond current limits.

# REFERENCES

W.J. Abernathy, *The Productivity Dilemma: roadblock to innovation in the automotive industry*, Baltimore, MD: Johns Hopkins University, 1978.

M.Y. Abolafia, *Making Markets: opportunism and restraint on Wall Street*, Cambridge, MA: Harvard Business Press, 1996.

V. Acha, D.M. Gann and A.J. Salter, 'Episodic innovation: R&D strategies for project-based environments', *Industry and Innovation*, 12, 2005, 255–281.

R.S. Achrol, 'Changes in the theory of interorganizational relations in marketing: toward a network paradigm', *Journal of the Academy of Marketing Services*, 25 (1), 1996, 56–71.

R.S. Achrol and P. Kotler, 'Marketing in the network economy', *Journal of Marketing*, 63, 1999, 146–163.

B. Adamson, M. Dixon and N. Toman, 'The end of solution sales', *Harvard Business Review*, 4, 2012, 61–68.

N. Alderman, C.J. Ivory, R. Vaughan, A. Thwaites and I.P. McLoughlin, 'The project management implications of new service-led projects: new issues and directions for research', *Paper presented at* EURAM 2003, 3rd–5th April, Milan, 2003.

T. Ambler, 'Maximizing profitability and return on investment: a short clarification on Reinartz, Thomas, and Kumar', *Journal of Marketing*, 69, 2005, 153–154.

T. Ambler, C.B. Bhattacharya, J. Edell, K.L. Keller, K.N. Lemon and V. Mittal, 'Relating brand and customer perspectives on marketing management', *Journal of Service Research*, 5 (13), 2002, 13–25.

American Marketing Association (AMA), 'About AMA: definition of marketing', www.marketingpower.com/aboutama/pages/definitionofmarketing.aspx, American Marketing Association, 2007. Accessed April 2013.

D. Ancona and C-L. Chong, 'Entrainment: pace, cycle, and rhythm in organizational behavior', *Research in Organizational Behavior*, 18, 1996, 251–284.

J.C. Anderson, J.A. Narus and W. van Rossum, 'Customer value propositions in business markets', *Harvard Business Review*, March, 2006, 91–99.

S. Anderson and J. Tell, 'The relationship between the manager and growth in small firms', *Journal of Small Business and Enterprise Development*, 16 (4), 2009, 586–598.

J. Andrews and D.C. Smith, 'In search of the marketing imagination: factors affecting the creativity of marketing programs for mature products', *Journal of Marketing Research*, 33, 1996, 174–187.

A. Anvuur and M. Kumaraswamy, 'Better collaboration through cooperation', *Collaborative Relationships in Construction*, H.J. Smyth and S.D. Pryke (eds.), Oxford: Wiley-Blackwell, 2008, pp. 107–128.

K.A. Appiah, *The Ethics of Identity*, Princeton, NJ: Princeton University Press, 2005.

K.A. Appiah, *The Honor Code: how moral revolutions happen*, London: W. W. Norton and Co., 2010.

D. Arditi and L. Davis, 'Marketing of construction services', *Journal of Management in Engineering*, 4, 1988, 297–315.

B. Aritua, S. Male and D.A Bower, 'Defining the intelligent public sector construction procurement client', *Management, Procurement and Law*, 162 (MP0), 2009, 75–82.

J. Arndt, 'Towards a concept of domesticated markets', *Journal of Marketing*, 42, October, 1979, 69–75.

K. Artto, 'Management of projects as portfolios', *Project Management*, 7, 2001, 4–5.

K. Artto, K. Eloranta and J. Kujala, 'Subcontractors' business relationships as risk sources in project networks', *International Journal of Managing Projects in Business*, 1 (1), 2007, 88–105.

K. Artto, A. Davies, J. Kujala and A. Prencipe, 'The project business: analytical framework and research opportunities', *The Oxford Handbook of Project Management*, P.W.G. Morris, J.K. Pinto and J. Söderlund (eds.), Oxford: Oxford University Press, 2011, pp. 133–153.

B.E. Ashforth and F. Mael, 'Social identity theory and the organization', *Academy of Management Review*, 14 (1), 1989, 20–39.

B. Atkin and R. Flanagan, *Improving Value for Money in Construction: guidance for chartered surveyors and their clients*, London: Royal Institution of Chartered Surveyors, 1995.

K. Atuahene-Gima, S.F. Slater and E.M. Olsen, 'The contingent value of responsive and proactive market orientations for new product program performance', *Journal of Product Innovation Management*, 22 (6), 2005, 464–482.

F. Auch and H.J. Smyth, 'Cultural divergence in project firms: the case of a leading main contractor operating from multiple offices', *International Journal of Managing Projects in Business*, 3 (3), 2010, 443–461.

B. Axelsson and F. Wynstra, *Buying Business Services*, Chichester: Wiley, 2002.

F. Azimont, B. Cova and R. Salle, 'Solution selling and project marketing: a convergence towards customer intimacy for joint construction of offer and demand', *Proceedings of the 14th IMP Annual Conference*, Turku, Finland, 3rd–5th September, 1, 1998, 113–132.

P. Bachrach and M.S. Baratz, *Power and Poverty: theory and practice*, Oxford: Oxford University Press, 1973.

R.P. Bagozzi, 'Marketing as an organized behavioral system of exchange', *Journal of Marketing*, 38, 1974, 77–81.

B. Baiden, A. Price and A. Dainty, 'The extent of team integration within construction projects', *International Journal of Project Management*, 24, 2006, 13–23.

A.C. Baier, *Moral Prejudices: essays on ethics*, Cambridge, MA: Harvard Business Press, 1994.

K. Balakrishnan, U. Mohan and S. Seshadri, 'Outsourcing of front-end business processes: quality, information, and customer contact', *Journal of Operations Management*, 26 (2), 2008, 288–302.

C.Y. Baldwin and K.B. Clark, 'Between "knowledge" and "the economy": notes on the scientific study of designs', *Advancing Knowledge and the Knowledge Economy*, B. Kahin and D. Foray (eds.), Cambridge, MA: MIT Press, 2006.

D. Ballantyne, 'Internal networks for internal marketing', *Journal of Marketing*, 13, 1997, 343–366.

D. Ballantyne and R.J. Varey, 'Introducing a dialogical orientation to the service-dominant logic of marketing', *The Service-Dominant Logic of Marketing: dialog, debate and directions*, R.F. Lusch and S.L Vargo (eds.), Armonk: M.E. Sharpe, 2006, pp. 224–235.

J.B. Barney, 'Firm resources and sustained competitive advantage', *Journal of Management*, 17, 1991, 99–120.

J.B. Barney, *Gaining and Sustaining Competitive Advantage*, Upper Saddle River, NJ: Prentice Hall, 2003.

J.B. Barney and A. Arikan, 'The resource-based view: origins and implications', Ohio: Ohio State University Working Paper, 2000.

F.J. Barrett, 'Creativity and improvisation in jazz and organization: implications for organizational learning', *Organization Science*, 9 (5), 1998, 605–622.

S. Bayer and D. Gann, 'Balancing work: bidding strategies and workload dynamics in a project-based professional service organisation', *System Dynamics Review*, 22 (3), 2006, 185–211.

T.D. Beamish and N.W. Biggart, 'The role of heuristics in project-centred production networks: insights from the commercial construction industry', *Engineering Project Organization Journal*, 2, 2012, 57–70.

B. Bechky, 'Gaffers, goffers, and grips: role-based coordination in temporary organizations', *Organization Science*, 17, 2006, 3–21.

N. Beech, H. Burns, L. de Caestecker, R. MacIntosh and D. MacLean, 'Paradox as invitation to act in problematic change situations', *Human Relations*, 57 (1), 2004, 1313–1332.

R.M. Belbin, *Management Teams: why they succeed or fail*, Oxford: Butterworth-Heinemann, 1984.

R.W. Belk, 'Possessions and the extended self', *Journal of Consumer Research*, 15, 1988, 139–168.

R. Bell, 'Marketing and larger construction firm', *Occasional Paper 22*, Chartered Institute of Building, Englemere, 1981.

C. Berggren, J. Söderlund and C. Anderson, 'Clients, contractors and consultants: the consequences of organizational fragmentation in contemporary project environments', *Project Management Journal*, 32 (3), 2001, 39–48.

L.L. Berry, 'Relationship marketing', *Emerging Perspectives on Service Marketing*, L.L. Berry, G. Shostack and G. Upah (eds.), Chicago: American Marketing Association, 1983, pp. 25–28.

L.L. Berry, 'Cultivating service brand equity', *Journal of the Academy of Marketing Science*, 28 (1), 2000, 128–137.

L.L. Berry and A. Parasuraman, *Marketing Services*, New York: Free Press, 1991.

R. Bessom, 'Marketing's role in construction firms', *Journal of Construction Engineering and Management*, 9, 1975, 647–659.

M. Betts and G.O. Ofori, 'Strategic planning for competitive advantage in construction industry', *Construction Management and Economics*, 10, 1992, 511–532.

S.G. Bharadwaj, P.R. Varandarajan and J. Fahy, 'Sustainable competitive advantage in service industries: a conceptual model and research propositions', *Journal of Marketing*, 57, 1993, 83–99.

C.B. Bhattacharya and S. Sen, 'Consumer-company identification: a framework for understanding consumers' relationships with companies', *Journal of Marketing*, 67 (2), 2003, 76–88.

C.B. Bhattacharya, H. Rao and M.A. Glynn, 'Understanding the bond of identification: an investigation of its correlates among art museum members', *Journal of Marketing*, 59, 1995, 46–57.

W.G. Biemans, M.M. Brenčič and A. Malshe, 'Marketing–sales interface configurations in B2B firms', *Industrial Marketing Management*, 39, 2010, 183–194.

S. Birley, 'Encouraging entrepreneurship: Britain's new enterprise program', *Journal of Small Business Management*, 23 (4), 1985, 6–12.

M.J. Bitner, 'Servicescapes: the impact of physical surroundings on customers and employees', *Journal of Marketing*, 56, 1992, 57–71.

M.J. Bitner, A.L. Ostrom and F.N. Morgan, 'Service blueprinting: a practical technique for service innovation', Phoenix: Center for Services Leadership, Arizona State University Working Paper, 2007.

P. Blau, *Exchange and Power in Social Life*, New York: Wiley, 1964.

T. Blomquist and J. Packendorff, 'Learning from renewal projects: content, context and embeddedness', *Projects as Arenas for Renewal and Learning Processes*, R.A. Lundin and C. Midler (eds.), Boston: Kluwer Academic, 1998, pp. 37–46.

B.H. Booms and M.J. Bitner, 'Marketing strategies and organization structures for service firms', *Marketing of Services*, J. Donnelly and W.R. George (eds.), Chicago: American Marketing Association, 1981, pp. 47–51.

B. Bordass, 'Learning more from our buildings – or just forgetting less', *Building Research & Innovation*, 31 (5), 2003, 406–411.

N. Borden, 'The concept of the marketing mix', *Journal of Advertising Research*, June, 1964, 2–7.

P.D. Boughton, 'The competitive bidding process: beyond probability models', *Industrial Marketing Management*, 16 (2), 1987, 87–94.

S. Bowles, R. Edwards and F. Roosevelt, *Understanding Capitalism*, New York: Oxford University Press, 2005.

T. Brady and A. Davies, 'Building project capabilities: from exploratory to exploitative learning', *Organization Studies*, 25 (9), 2004, 1601–1621.

T. Brady, A. Davies and D.M. Gann, 'Creating value by delivering integrated solutions', *International Journal of Project Management*, 23 (5), 2005, 360–365.

K. Bredin and J. Söderlund, *Human Resource Management in Project-Based Organizations: the HR quadriad framework*, Basingstoke: Palgrave Macmillan, 2011.

M. Bresnen and N. Marshall, 'Projects and partnerships: institutional processes and emergent practices', *The Oxford Handbook of Project Management*, P.W.G. Morris, J.K. Pinto and J. Söderlund (eds.), Oxford: Oxford University Press, 2011, pp. 154–174.

M. Bresnen, A. Goussevskaia and J. Swan, 'Embedding new management knowledge in project-based organizations', *Organization Studies*, 25 (9), 2004, 1535–1555.

P.J. Brews and M.R. Hunt, 'Learning to plan and planning to learn: resolving the planning school/learning school debate', *Strategic Management Journal*, 20, 1999, 889–913.

E. Bridges, K.B. Ensor and K. Raman, 'The impact of need frequency on service marketing strategy', *Services Industry Journal*, 23 (3), 2003, 40–60.

J. Brinckmann, S. Salomo and H.G. Gemuenden, 'Start-up conditions and development paths of new technology-based firms', *Frontiers of Entrepreneurship Research*, 27 (13), 2007, 16.

R. Brooksbank, R. Garland and D. Taylor, 'Strategic marketing in New Zealand companies', *Journal of Global Marketing*, 23, 2010, 33–44.

M. Bruce and L. Daly, 'Design and marketing connections: creating added value', *Journal of Marketing Management*, 23, 2007, 929–953.

E. Brun and A.F. Saetre, 'Ambiguity reduction in new product development projects', *International Journal of Innovation Management*, 12 (4), 2008, 573–596.

*Building Magazine* (2009) 23 January.

T. Burns and G.M. Stalker, *The Management of Innovation*, London: Tavistock, 1961.

D.C.A. Butcher and M.J. Sheehan, 'Excellent contractor performance in the UK construction industry', *Engineering, Construction and Architectural Management*, 17, 2010, 35–45.

K.S. Cameron and R.E. Quinn, *Diagnosing and Changing Organisational Culture: based on the competing values framework*, San Francisco: Jossey-Bass, 2006.

N. Campbell, 'An interaction approach to organizational buying behavior', *Journal of Business Research*, 13 (1), 1985, 35–48.

D. Carson and A. Gilmore, 'SME marketing management competencies', *International Business Review*, 9 (3), 2000, 363–382.

F. Cespedes and N. Piercy, 'Implementing marketing strategy', *Journal of Marketing Management*, 12, 1996, 135–160.

M. Chambers, T. Fitch, I. Keki and H.J. Smyth, 'Differences between customer experience and business development propositions: the case of a major contractor in the infrastructure market, *Proceedings of the ARCOM 2009*, 7th–9th September, Nottingham, 2009.

S. Chatterjee, 'Core objectives: clarity in designing strategy', *California Management Review*, 47 (2), 2005, 33–47.

T-Y. Chen, Tser-Yieth, T-L. Yeh and H-C. Yeh, 'Trust-building mechanisms and relationship capital', *Journal of Relationship Marketing*, 10 (3), 2011, 113–144.

A. Chernev, *Strategic Marketing Management*, 6th edition, Chicago: Cerebellum Press, 2011.

A.B. Cherns and D.T. Bryant, 'Studying the client's role in construction management', *Construction Management and Economics*, 2, 1984, 177–184.

J-S. Chiou and C. Droge, 'Service quality, trust, specific asset investment, and expertise: direct and indirect effects in a satisfaction-loyalty framework', *Journal of the Academy of Marketing Science*, 34 (4), 2006, 613–627.

S. Christensen and K. Kreiner, *Projektledning: att leda och lära i en ofullkomlig värld*, Lund: Academia Adacta, 1997.

M. Christopher, A. Payne and D. Ballantyne, *Relationship Marketing: creating stakeholder value*, Oxford: Butterworth-Heinemann, 2002.

CIM, *Marketing and the 7Ps: a brief summary of marketing and how it works*, Maidenhead: Chartered Institute of Marketing, 2009.

P. Clark, 'A review of the theories of time and structure for organizational sociology', *Research in the Sociology of Organizations*, 4, 1985, 35–79.

S.R. Clegg, J.V. Cunha and M.P. Cunha, 'Management paradoxes: a relational view', *Human Relations*, 55 (5), 2002, 483–503.

S.R. Clegg, K. Bjørkeng and T. Pitsis, 'Innovating the practice of normative control in project management contractual relations', *The Oxford Handbook of Project Management*, P.W.G. Morris, J.K. Pinto and J. Söderlund (eds.), Oxford: Oxford University Press, 2011, pp. 410–437.

R.H. Coase, 'The nature of the firm', *Economica*, 4, 1937, 386–405.

R.H. Coase, 'Industrial organization: a proposal for research', *The Firm, the Market and the Law*, R.H. Coase (ed.), Chicago, IL: University of Chicago Press, 1988, pp. 57–74.

E. Collinson and E. Shaw, 'Entrepreneurial marketing: a historical perspective on development and practice', *Management Decision*, 39 (9), 2001, 761–766.

J.A. Connaughton and S.D. Green, *Value Management in Construction: a clients guide*, Special Publication 129, London: Construction Industry Research and Information Association, 1996.

E.L. Cook and D.E. Hancher, 'Partnering: contracting for the future', *Journal of Management in Engineering*, 6 (4), 1990, 431–446.

T. Cooke-Davies, 'The "real" success factors on projects', *International Journal of Project Management*, 20 (3), 2002, 185–190.

M.J. Cooper and C.S. Budd, 'Tying the pieces together: a normative framework for integrating sales and project operations', *Industrial Marketing Management*, 36, 2007, 173–182.

L. Coote, 'Implementation of relationship marketing in an accounting practice', *Research Conference Proceedings, Relationship Marketing: theory, methods and applications*, J.N. Seth, A. Patel and A. Parvatiyar (eds.), Atlanta: Emory University, 1994, pp. 1–9.

I. Cornelius and M. Davies, *Shareholder Value*, London: Financial Times, 1997.

P.D. Cousins, R.B. Handfield, B. Lawson and K.J. Petersen, 'Creating supply chain relational capital: the impact of formal and informal socialization processes', *Journal of Operations Management*, 24 (6), 2006, 851–863.

B. Cova and K. Holstius, 'How to create competitive advantage in project business', *Journal of Marketing Management*, 9, 1993, 105–121.

B. Cova and S. Hoskins, 'A twin track networking approach to project marketing', *European Management Journal*, 15 (5), 1997, 546–556.

B. Cova and R. Salle, 'Six points to merge project marketing into project management', *International Journal of Project Management*, 23, 2005, 354–359.

B. Cova and R. Salle, 'Communications and stakeholders', *Management of Complex Projects: a relationship approach*, S.D. Pryke and H.J. Smyth (eds.), Oxford: Blackwell, 2006, pp. 131–146.

B. Cova and R. Salle, 'Introduction to the *Industrial Marketing Management* special issue on "Project marketing and marketing solutions": a comprehensive approach to project marketing and the marketing of solutions', *Industrial Marketing Management*, 36, 2007a, 138–146.

B. Cova and R. Salle, 'Marketing solutions in accordance with the S-D logic: co-creating value with customer network actors', *Industrial Marketing Management*, 37, 2007b, 270–277.

B. Cova and R. Salle, 'Creating superior value through network offerings', *Advances in Business Marketing and Purchasing*, 14, 2008, 317–342.

B. Cova and R. Salle, 'Shaping projects, building networks', *The Oxford Handbook of Project Management*, P.W.G. Morris, J.K. Pinto and J. Söderlund (eds.), Oxford: Oxford University Press, 2011, pp. 391–409.

B. Cova, F. Mazet and R. Salle, 'Milieu as a pertinent unit of analysis in project marketing', *International Business Review*, 5 (6), 1996, 647–664.

B. Cova, P.N. Ghauri and R. Salle, *Project Marketing: beyond competitive bidding*, Chichester: John Wiley, 2002.

J.G. Covin and D.P. Slevin, 'Strategic management of small firms in hostile and benign environments', *Strategic Management Journal*, 10 (1), 1989, 75–87.

J.G. Covin and D.P. Slevin, 'Corporate entrepreneurship in high and low technology industries: a comparison of strategic variables, strategy patterns and performance in global markets', *Journal of Euromarketing*, 3 (3–4), 1994, 99–127.

D.W. Cravens and N.F. Piercy, 'Relationship marketing and collaborative networks in service organizations', *International Journal of Service Industry Management*, 5, 1994, 39–53.

F. Crespin-Mazet and P. Portier, 'The reluctance of construction purchasers towards project partnering', *Journal of Purchasing & Supply Management*, 16, 2010, 230–238.

A.E. Cretu and R.J. Brodie, 'The influence of brand image and company reputation where manufacturers market to small firms: a customer value perspective', *Industrial Marketing Management*, 36 (2), 2010, 230–240.

P.B. Crosby, *Quality is Free*, New York: McGraw-Hill, 1979.

R. Cross and L. Sproull, 'More than an answer: information relationships for actionable knowledge', *Organization Science*, 15 (4), 2004, 446–462.

R.M. Cyert and J.G. March, *A Behavioral Theory of the Firm*, Oxford: Blackwell, 1992.

B. Czarniawska, *Narratives in Social Science Research*, New York: Sage, 2004.

R.L. Daft and R.H. Lengel, 'Information richness: a new approach to managerial behavior and organization design', *Research in Organization Behavior*, B.M. Staw and L.L. Cummings (eds.), 6, Greenwich, CT: JAI Press, 1984, pp. 191–233.

A.R.J. Dainty, A. Bryman, A.D.F. Price, K. Greasley, R. Soetanto and N. King, 'Project affinity: the role of emotional attachment in construction projects', *Construction Management and Economics*, 23 (3), 2005, 241–244.

A. Davies, 'Moving base into high-value integrated solutions: a value stream approach', *Industrial Corporate Change*, 13 (5), 2004, 727–756.

A. Davies and T. Brady, 'Organizational capabilities and learning in complex product systems: towards repeatable solutions', *Research Policy*, 29 (7–8), 2000, 931–953.

A. Davies, T. Brady and M. Hobday, 'Charting a path toward integrated solutions', *MIT Sloan Management Review*, 47 (3), 2006, 39–48.

A. Davies, T. Brady and M. Hobday, 'Organizing for solutions: systems seller vs. systems integrator', *Industrial Marketing Management*, 36, 2007, 183–193.

A. Davies, D. Gann and T. Douglas, 'Innovation in megaprojects: systems integration at London Heathrow Terminal 5', *California Management Review*, 51, 2009, 101–125.

D. Davis, M.H. Morris and J. Allen, 'Perceived environmental turbulence and its effect on selected entrepreneurial, marketing and organizational characteristics in industrial firms', *Journal of Academy of Marketing Science*, 19, 1991, 43–51.

G.S. Day, 'The capabilities of market-driven organizations', *Journal of Marketing*, 58 (4), 1994, 37–52.

G.S. Day and D.B. Montgomery, 'Charting new directions for marketing', *Journal of Marketing*, 63, 1999, 3–13.

T.E. Deal and A.A. Kennedy, *Corporate Culture: the rites and rituals of corporate life*, Reading, MA: Addison-Wesley, 1982.

L. de Chernatony, 'Brand management through narrowing the gap between brand identity and brand reputation', *Journal of Marketing Management*, 15, 1999, 157–179.

R.J. DeFillippi and M.B. Arthur, 'Paradox in project-based enterprises: the case of film-making', *California Management Review*, 40 (2), 1998, 1–15.

A.J. Dell'Isola, *Value Engineering in the Construction Industry*, New York: Van Nostrand Reinhold, 1982.

W.E. Deming, *The New Economics*, Cambridge, MA: MIT Center for Advanced Engineering Study, 1993.

F. Deng and H.J. Smyth, 'Contingency-based approach of firm performance in construction: a critical review of the empirical research', *ASCE Journal of Construction Engineering and Management*, 139 (10), 2013, http:/doi.org/10.1061(ASCE)CO.1943–7862.0000778.

J. Derrida, *Writing and Difference*, London: Routledge and Kegan Paul, 1978.

P. Deshayes, L. Lecoeuvre and H. Tikkanen, 'Interactions and congruencies between project marketing and project management: dynamics of project marketing and project management in a co-constructed industrial project', *7th International Marketing Trends Congress*, 17th–19th January, Venice, 2008.

N. Dew, *Lipsticks and Razorblades: How the Auto Id Center Used Pre-Commitments to Build the Internet of Things*, 2003, available at SSRN: http://ssrn.com/abstract = 964507. Accessed 15th November 2010.

N. Dew, S. Read, S.D. Sarasvathy and R. Wiltbank, 'Effectual versus predictive logics in entrepreneurial decision-making: differences between experts and novices', *Journal of Business Venturing*, 24 (4), 2009, 287–309.

S. Dibb, M. Farhangmehr and L. Simkin, 'The marketing planning experience: a UK and Portuguese comparison', *Marketing Intelligence and Planning*, 1, 2001, 409–417.

W. van Dolen, J. Lemmink, K. de Ruyter and A. de Jong, 'Customer–sales employee encounters: a dyadic perspective', *Journal of Retailing*, 78 (4), 2002, 265–279.

P.M. Donay and J.P. Cannon, 'An examination of the nature of trust in buyer–seller relationships', *Journal of Marketing*, 61, 1997, 35–51.

M. Douglas, 'Four cultures: the evolution of a parsimonious model', *GeoJournal*, 47, 1999, 411–415.

Y.L. Doz, 'The evolution of cooperation in strategic alliances: initial conditions or learning processes', *Strategic Management Journal*, 17, 1996, 55–83.

Y.L. Doz and G. Hamel, *Alliance Advantage: the art of creating value through partnering*, Boston, MA: Harvard Business School Press, 1998.

H.L. Dreyfus and S.E. Dreyfus, 'Peripheral vision in real world contexts', *Organization Studies*, 26 (5), 2005, 779–792.

P.F. Drucker, *The Frontiers of Management*, London: Heinemann, 1986.

V.U. Druskat and P. Druskat, 'Emotional intelligence in project working', *Management of Complex Projects: a relationship approach*, S.D. Pryke and H.J. Smyth (eds.), Oxford: Blackwell, 2006, pp. 78–96.

A. Dubois and L-E. Gadde, 'Supply strategy and network effects-purchasing behaviour in the construction industry', *European Journal of Purchasing and Supply Management*, 6, 2000, 207–215.

P. Dunn and R. Baker, *The Firm of the Future: a guide for accountants, lawyers, and other professional services*, Hoboken, NJ: Wiley, 2003.

F.R. Dwyer, P.H. Schurr and S. Oh, 'Developing buyer–seller relationships', *Journal of Marketing*, 51 (2), 1987, 11–27.

J.H. Dyer and H. Singh, 'The relational view: cooperative strategy and sources of interorganizational competitive advantage', *Academy of Management Review*, 23, 1998, 660–679.

R. Eccles, 'The quasifirm in the construction industry', *Journal of Economic Behavior and Organization*, 2, 1981, 335–357.

A.J. Edkins, J. Geraldi, P.W.G. Morris and A. Smith, 'Exploring the front-end of project management', *Engineering Project Organization Journal*, 3 (2), 2013, 71–85.

A.J. Edkins and H.J. Smyth, 'Winning a novel Public Private Partnership project: strategy and serendipity', *Proceedings of EPOC 2013 – International Community*, 9th–11th July, Colorado: Winter Park, 2013.

A.J. Edkins, H.J. Smyth and P.W.G. Morris, *Building a Client-Orientated, Knowledge-Based, Value-Driven Industry*, National Platform, www.nationalplatform.org.uk, 2008. Accessed April 2013.

B. Edvardsson, A. Gustavsson, M.D. Johnson and B. Sandén, *New Service Development and Innovation in the New Economy*, Lund: Studentlitteratur, 2000.

B. Edvardsson, A. Gustafsson and I. Roos, 'Service portraits in service research: a critical review', *International Journal of Service Industry Management*, 16 (1), 2005, 107–121.

B. Edvardsson, M. Holmund and T. Strandvik, 'Initiation of business relationships in service-dominant settings', *Industrial Marketing Management*, 37 (3), 2008, 339–250.

Sir John Egan, *Rethinking Construction*, www.constructingexcellence.org.uk/pdf/rethinking%20construction/rethinking_construction_report.pdf, Department of the Environments Transport and Regions, London, 1998. Accessed 7th August 2013.

M. Egeman and A.N. Mohamed, 'Clients' needs, wants and expectations from contractors and approach to the concept of repetitive works in the Northern Cyprus construction market', *Building and Environment*, 41 (5), 2006, 602–614.

A. Eggert, W. Ulaga and S. Hollman, *Linking Customer Share to Relationship Performance: the customer perspective*, Working Paper, ISBM Report 10–2006, Pennsylvania: Institute for the Study of Business Markets, The Pennsylvania State University, University Park, 2006.

P. Eiken, 'Bygg 21: a Norwegian initiative to change the building and construction future', *Keynote presentation at the 7th Nordic Conference on Construction Economics and Organisation 2013*, 12th–14th June, Trondheim: Norwegian University of Science and Technology, 2013.

K.M. Eisenhardt, 'Strategic decision making as improvisation', *Strategic Decisions*, V. Papadakis and P. Barwise (eds.), Boston, MA: Kluwer Academic, 1998, pp. 251–257.

K.M. Eisenhardt and J.K. Martin, 'Dynamic capabilities: what are they?' *Strategic Management Journal*, 21, 2000, 1105–1121.

K.M. Eisenhardt and D. Sull, 'Strategy as simple rules', *Harvard Business Review*, 79 (1), 2001, 107–116.

T. Elfring and W. Hulsink, 'Networking by entrepreneurs: patterns of ties formation in emerging organizations', *Organization Studies*, 2 (4), 2007, 1849–1872.

K. Eloranta, *Supplier Relationship Management in Networked Project Business*, Licentiate Thesis, Helsinki: Helsinki University of Technology, 2007.

F.E. Emery and E.L. Trist, 'The causal texture of organizational environments', *Human Relations*, 18, 1965, 21–32.

S. Emmitt, *Design Management for Architects*, Oxford: Blackwell, 2007.

M. Engwall, 'No project is an island: linking projects to history and context', *Research Policy*, 32, 2003, 789–808.

E.H. Erikson, *Identity: youth and crisis*, New York: Faber & Faber, 1968.

P.E. Eriksson and O. Pesämma, 'Modelling procurement effects on cooperation', *Construction Management and Economics*, 25, 2007, 893–901.

P.E. Eriksson and O. Pesämma, 'Buyer–supplier integration in project-based industries', *Journal of Business and Industrial Marketing*, 28 (1), 2012, 29–40.

EURAM SIG, *Special Interest Group on Project Organizing*, http://euram2012.nl/userfiles/file/61%20%20Project%20Organising%20General%20Track%20bis.pdf. Accessed 5th April, 2012.

C. Fabianski, *Complex Partnership for the Delivery of Urban Rail Infrastructure Project (URIP): how culture matters for the treatment of risk and uncertainty?* PhD Thesis, London: UCL, 2014.

P. Fallon and F. Senn, *Juicing the Orange: how to turn creativity into a powerful business advantage*, Cambridge, MA: Harvard Business Review Press, 2006.

R. Faulkner and A. Anderson, 'Short-term projects and emergent careers: evidence from Hollywood', *American Journal of Science*, 92 (4), 1987, 879–909.

R. Fellows, 'Culture in supply chains', *Construction Supply Chain Management*, S.D. Pryke (ed.), Chichester: Wiley-Blackwell, 2009.

M. Fishbein and I. Azjen, *Belief, Attitude, Intention and Behavior*, Reading, MA: Addison Wesley, 1975.

N. Fisher, *Marketing for the Construction Industry*, London: Longman, 1986.

T. Fitch, I. Keki and H.J. Smyth, 'Power and perceptions in business development: the case of a major contractor and design consultancies in civil engineering influencer and referral markets', *Proceedings of ARCOM 2010*, 6th–8th September, Leeds, 2010.

J.A. Fitzsimmons and M.J. Fitzsimmons, *Service Management: operations, strategy, information technology*, New York: McGraw-Hill, 2011.

B. Flyvbjerg, N. Bruzelius and W. Rothengatter, *Mega Projects and Risk: an anatomy of ambition*, Cambridge: Cambridge University Press, 2003.

R. Foord, B. Armandi and C. Heaton, *Organization Theory: an interactive approach*, New York: Harper & Row, 1988.

D. Ford, L-E. Gadde, H. Håkansson and I. Snehota, *Managing Business Relationships*, Chichester: Wiley, 2003.

W. Forster and J. York, 'The effects of effectual logic: nascent entrepreneurial performance and effectuation (interactive paper)', *Frontiers of Entrepreneurship Research*, 28 (10), 2008, Article 4, digitalknowledge.babson.edu/fer/vol28/iss10/4. Accessed 14th August 2014.

Fournaise Marketing Group, *73 per cent of CEOs Think Marketers Lack Business Credibility: They Can't Prove They Generate Business Growth*, www.fournaisegroup.com/

Marketers-Lack-Credibility.asp?_fwaHound=15127937_12185_15127937_0_0_0_0, 2011. Accessed March 2013.

J.D. Frame, *The New Project Management: tools for an age of rapid change, complexity, and other business realities*, Chichester: Wiley, 2002.

P. Fraser Johnson, M.R. Leenders and H.E. Fearon, 'The chief purchasing officer: previous background and experience', *European Journal of Purchasing & Supply Management*, 5 (2), 1999, 95–101.

M. Friedman, 'The social responsibility of business is to increase its profits', *The New York Times Magazine*, September 13, 1970.

M. Friedman, *Capitalism and Freedom*, Chicago, IL: University of Chicago Press, 2000.

G. Fullerton, 'How commitment both enables and undermines marketing relationships', *European Journal of Marketing*, 39 (11/12), 2005, 1372–1388.

L-E. Gadde and I. Snehota, 'Making the most of supplier relationships', *Industrial Marketing Management*, 29 (4), 2000, 305–316.

J. Gaddefors and A.R. Anderson, 'Market creation: the epitome of entrepreneurial marketing practices', *Journal of Research in Marketing and Entrepreneurship*, 10 (1), 2009, 19–39.

J.R. Galbraith, *Designing Organizations: an executive guide to strategy, structure, and process*, San Francisco, CA: Jossey-Bass, 2002.

S. Ganesan, *Handbook of Marketing and Finance*, Cheltenham: Edward Elgar, 2012.

J. Ganesh, M.J. Arnold and K.E. Reynolds, 'Understanding the customer base of service providers: an examination of the differences between switchers and stayers', *Journal of Marketing*, 64, 2000, 65–87.

D.M. Gann and A.J. Salter, 'Innovation in project-based, service-enhanced firms: the construction of complex products and systems', *Research Policy*, 29 (7), 2000, 955–972.

S. George, 'Focus through shared vision', *National Productivity Review*, 16 (3), 1997, 65–74.

J.G. Geraldi, 'The balance between order and chaos in multi-project firms: a conceptual model', *International Journal of Project Management*, 26, 2008, 348–356.

J.G. Geraldi, L. Lee-Kelley and E. Kutsch, 'The Titanic sunk, so what? Project manager response to unexpected events', *International Journal of Project Management*, 28, 2010, 547–558.

R. Gibbons, 'Transaction cost economics: past, present, and future?' *Scandinavian Journal of Economics*, 112, 2010, 263–288.

A. Giddens, 'Agency, institution, and time-space analysis', *Advances in Social Theory and Methodology*, K. Knorr-Cetina and A.V. Cicourel (eds.), London: Routledge & Kegan Paul, 1981, pp. 161–174.

N. Gil, J.K. Pinto and H.J. Smyth, 'Trust in relational contracting as a critical organizational attribute', *Oxford Handbook on the Management of Projects*, P.W.G. Morris, J.K. Pinto and J. Söderlund (eds.), Oxford: Oxford University Press, 2011, pp. 438–460.

C.G. Gilbert, 'Unbundling the structure of inertia: resource versus routine rigidity', *Academy of Management Journal*, 48, 2005, 741–763.

M.J. Gill and W.B. Swann, Jr., 'On what it means to know someone: a matter of pragmatics', *Journal of Personality and Social Psychology*, 86 (3), 2004, 405–418.

C. Gilligan, *A Different Voice*, Boston: Harvard University Press, 1982.

R.A. Goodman, *Temporary Systems: professional development, manpower utilization, task effectiveness and innovation*, New York: Praeger, 1981.

G. Grabher, 'The project ecology of advertising tasks, talents and teams', *Regional Studies*, 36 (3), 2002, 245–262.

G. Grabher, 'Architecture of project-based learning: creating and sedimenting knowledge in project ecologies', *Organization Studies*, 25 (9), 2004, 1491–1514.

G. Grabher and O. Ibert, 'Project ecologies: a contextual view on temporary organizations', *Oxford Handbook on the Management of Projects*, P.W.G. Morris, J.K. Pinto and J. Söderlund (eds.), Oxford: Oxford University Press, 2011, pp. 175–198.

M. Granovetter, 'Economic action and social structure: the problem of embeddedness', *American Journal of Sociology*, 91 (3), 1985, 481–510.

S.D. Green, *Making Sense of Construction Improvement: a critical review*, Chichester: Wiley-Blackwell, 2011.

S.D. Green and G.W. Moss, 'Value management and post-occupancy evaluation: closing the loop', *Facilities*, 16 (1/2), 1998, 34–39.

S.D. Green, C. Harty, A.A. Elmualim, G. Larsen and C.C. Kao, 'On the discourse of construction competitiveness', *Building Research & Information*, 36, 2008, 426–435.

G. Greenley and B. Bayus, 'Marketing planning processes in the UK and US companies', *Journal of Strategic Marketing*, 2, 1994, 140–154.

A. Griffin and J.R. Hauser, 'The voice of the customer', *Marketing Science*, 12 (1), 1993, 1–27.

C. Grönroos, *Service Management and Marketing: customer management in service competition*, 2nd edition, Chichester: Wiley, 2000.

C. Grönroos, 'Service logic revisited: who creates value? And who co-creates?' *European Business Review*, 20 (4), 2008, 298–314.

C. Grönroos and A. Ravald, 'Service as business logic: implications for value creation and marketing', *Journal of Service Management*, 22 (1), 2010, 5–22.

P. Guenzi and G. Troilo, 'Developing marketing capabilities for customer value creation through marketing–sales integration', *Industrial Marketing Management*, 35, 2006, 974–988.

E. Gummesson, *Qualitative Methods in Management Research*, Newbury, CA: Sage, 1991.

E. Gummesson, 'Making relationship marketing operational', *International Journal of Service Industry Management*, 5 (5), 1994, 5–20.

E. Gummesson, *Total Relationship Marketing*, Oxford: Butterworth-Heinemann, 2000.

E. Gummesson, 'Extending the service-dominant logic: from customer centricity to balanced centricity', *Journal of the Academy of Marketing Science*, 36 (1), 2008, 15–17.

E. Gummesson, R.F. Lusch and S.L. Vargo, 'Transitioning from service management to service-dominant logic: observations and recommendations', *International Journal of Quality and Service Sciences*, 2 (1), 2010, 8–22.

M. Gustafsson, H.J. Smyth, E. Ganskau and T. Arhippainen, 'Bridging strategic and operational issues for project business through managing trust', *International Journal of Managing Projects in Business*, 3 (3), 2010, 422–442.

R.J. Hackman and R. Wagman, 'Total quality management: empirical, conceptual, and practical issues', *Administrative Science Quarterly*, 40, 1995, 309–342.

A. Hadjikhani, 'Project marketing and the management of discontinuity', *International Business Review*, 5 (3), 1996, 319–336.

H. Håkansson, *International Marketing and Purchasing of Industrial Goods*, London: Wiley, 1982.

H. Håkansson and I. Snehota, 'No business is an island: the network concept of business strategy', *Scandinavian Journal of Management*, 5 (3), 1989, 187–200.

H. Håkansson and I. Snehota, *Developing Relationships in Business Networks*, Boston, MA: International Thomson Press, 1995.

H. Håkansson and I. Snehota, 'No business is an island: the network concept of business strategy', *Scandinavian Journal of Management*, 22 (3), 2006, 256–270.

M. Hällgren and A. Söderholm, 'Orchestrating deviations in global projects: projects-as-practice observations', *Scandinavian Journal of Management*, 26, 2010, 352–367.

G. Hamel and C.K. Prahalad, *Competing for the Future*, Boston, MA: Harvard Business School Press, 1994.

C.B. Handy, *Understanding Organizations*, London: Penguin, 1997.

L.W. Hardy and E. Davies, 'Marketing services in the UK construction industry', *European Journal of Marketing*, 17 (4), 1983, 5–17.

F. Harris and R. McCaffer, *Modern Construction Management*, London: Blackwell Science, 2001.

O. Hart and B. Holmstrom, 'A theory of firm scope', *Quarterly Journal of Economics*, CXXV (2), 2010, 483–512.

K. Hartshorn, 'A humane workplace is a productive workplace', *National Productivity Review*, 16 (2), 1997, 1–8.

C. Harvey, *Secrets of the World's Top Sales Performers*, London: Century Random, 1988.

D. Haughey, *The History of PRINCE2*, www.projectsmart.co.uk/history-of-prince2.php, 2009. Accessed 16 June 2014.

J.B. Heide and G. John, 'Alliances in industrial purchasing: the determinants of joint action in buyer–seller relationships', *Journal of Marketing Research*, 27 (1), 1990, 24–36.

J.B. Heide and A. Miner, 'The shadow of the future: effects of anticipated interaction and frequency of contact on buyer–seller cooperation', *Academy of Management Journal*, 35 (2), 1992, 265–291.

C.E. Helfat, 'Know-how and asset complementarity and dynamic capability accumulation', *Strategic Management Journal*, 18 (5), 1997, 339–360.

C.E. Helfat and M.A. Peteraf, 'The dynamic resource-based view: capability lifecycles', *Strategic Management Journal*, 2003, 997–1010.

A. Helkkula, C. Kelleher and M. Pihlström, 'Characterizing value as an experience: implications for service researchers and managers', *Journal of Service Research*, 15 (1), 2012, 59–75.

W.J. Henisz, R.E. Levitt and W.R. Scott, 'Towards a unified theory of project governance: economic sociological and psychological supports for relational contracting', *Engineering Project Organization Journal*, 2, 2012, 37–55.

J.L. Heskett, *Managing in the Service Economy*, Boston, MA: Harvard Business School Press, 1986.

P.M. Hillebrandt and J. Cannon, *The Modern Construction Firm*, London: Macmillan, 1990.

G.E. Hills, C.M. Hultman and M.P. Miles, 'The evolution and development of entrepreneurial marketing', *Journal of Small Business Management*, 46 (1), 2008, 99–112.

E.C. Hirschman and M.B. Holbrook, 'Hedonic consumption: emerging concepts, methods and propositions', *Journal of Marketing*, 46, 1982, 92–101.

M.A. Hitt and T.S. Reed, 'Entrepreneurship in the new competitive landscape', *Entrepreneurship as Strategy*, G.D. Meyer and K.A. Heppard (eds.), Thousand Oaks, CA: Sage, 2000.

B. Hobbs and B. Andersen, 'Different alliance relationships for product design and execution', *International Journal of Project Management*, 20, 2001, 465–469.

S. Hobbs and H.J. Smyth, 'Emotional intelligence in engineering project teams', *Proceedings of the CIB Research to Practice Conference*, 26th–29th June, Montreal, 2012.

M. Hobday, 'Product complexity, innovation and industrial organisation', *Research Policy*, 29, 1998, 871–893.

M. Hobday, 'The project-based organisation: an ideal form for managing complex products and systems?' *Research Policy*, 26, 2000, 689–710.

M. Hobday, A. Davies and A. Prencipe, 'Systems integration: a core capability of the modern corporation', *Industrial and Corporate Change*, 14 (6), 2005, 1109–1143.

G.M. Hodgson, *Economics and Institutions*, Cambridge: Polity, 1988.

S. Hoekstra and J. Romme, *Internal Logistics Structures*, London: McGraw-Hill, 1992.

M. Hogg, D. Terry and K. White, 'A tale of two theories: a critical comparison of identity theory', *Social Psychology Quarterly*, 58, 1995, 225–269.

K. Holstius, 'Project business as a strategic choice', *Research Report 12*, Lappeenranta: Lappeenranta University of Technology, 1989.

C. Homburg and C. Pflesser, 'A multiple-layer model of market-oriented organizational culture: measurement issues and performance outcomes', *Journal of Marketing Research*, 37 (4), 2000, 449–462.

C. Homburg, O. Jensen and H. Krohmer, 'Configuration of marketing and sales: a taxonomy', *Journal of Marketing*, 72 (2), 2008, 133–154.

C. Homburg, J. Wieseke and T. Bornemann, 'Implementing the marketing concept at the employee–customer interface: the role of customer need knowledge', *Journal of Marketing*, 73 (4), 2009a, 64–81.

C. Homburg, V.V. Steiner and D. Totzek, 'Managing dynamics in customer portfolio', *Journal of Marketing*, 73, 2009b, 70–89.

O. Ibert, 'Projects and firms as discordant complements: organizational learning in the Munich software ecology', *Research Policy*, 33 (10), 2004, 1529–1546.

D. Ioniţă, 'Entrepreneurial marketing: a new approach for challenging times', *Management & Marketing Challenges for the Knowledge Society*, 7 (1), 2012, 131–150.

G.J. Ive, 'Innovation and the Latham Report', S.L. Gruneberg (ed.), *Responding to Latham: the views of the construction team*, Ascot: CIOB, 1995, pp. 37–43.

B.B. Jackson, *Winning and Keeping Industrial Customers*, Lexington: Lexington Books, 1985.

I.L. Janis, *Groupthink: psychological studies of policy decisions and fiascoes*, Boston: Houghton Mifflin, 1982.

P.A. Jarzabkowski, J.K. Lê and M.S. Feldman, 'Toward a theory of coordinating: creating coordinating mechanisms in practice', *Organization Science*, 23 (4), 2012, 907–927.

M.C. Jensen and W.H. Meckling, 'Theory of the firm: managerial behavior, agency cost and ownership structure', *Journal of Financial Economics*, 3, 1976, 305–360.

A.L. Jepsen and P. Eskerod, 'Stakeholder analysis in projects: challenges in using current guidelines in the real world', *International Journal of Project Management*, 27 (4), 2009, 335–343.

J. Johanson and L-G. Mattsson, 'Marketing investments and market investments in industrial marketing', *International Journal of Research in Marketing*, 2 (3), 1985, 185–195.

M.W. Johnson, C.M. Christensen and H. Kagermann, 'Reinventing your business model', *Harvard Business Review*, 86 (12), 2008, 50–59.

S.P. Johnson, L.J. Menor, A.V. Roth and R.B. Chase, 'A critical evaluation of the new service development process', *New Service Development*, J. Fitzsimmons and M. Fitzsimmons (eds.), Thousand Oaks, CA: Sage, 2000, pp. 1–32.

C. Jones and B.B. Lichtenstein, 'Temporary inter-organizational projects: how temporal and social embeddedness enhance coordination and manage uncertainty', *The Oxford Handbook of Inter-Organizational Relations*, S. Cropper, M. Ebers, C. Huxham and P. Smith Ring, (eds.), Oxford: Oxford University Press, 2008, pp. 231–255.

T. Jones, P.A. Dacin and S.F. Taylor, 'Relational damage and relationship repair: a new look at transgressions in service relationships', *Journal of Service Research*, 14 (3), 2011, 318–339.

T.O. Jones and W.E. Sasser, Jr., 'Why satisfied customers defect', *Harvard Business Review*, November–December, 1995, 88–99.

C. Jordi, 'Rethinking the firm's mission and purpose', *European Management Review*, 7, 2010, 195–204.

A. Kadefors, 'Institutions in building projects: implications for flexibility and change', *Scandinavian Journal of Management*, 11 (4), 1995, 395–408.

A. Kadefors, 'Trust in project relationships: inside the black box', *International Journal of Project Management*, 22, 2004, 175–182.

A. Kadefors, 'Fairness in interorganizational project relations: norms and strategies', *Construction Management and Economics*, 23 (8), 2005, 871–878.

D. Kahneman, A. Tversky and P. Slovic, *Judgment under Uncertainty: heuristics and biases*, Cambridge: Cambridge University Press, 1982.

P. Kale, H. Singh and H. Perlmutter, 'Learning and protection of proprietary assets in strategic alliances: building relational capital', *Strategic Management Journal*, 21 (3), 2000, 217–228.

S.H. Kale, 'CRM failure and the seven deadly sins', *Marketing Management*, 13, 2004, 42–46.

R.S. Kaplan and D.P. Norton, 'The balanced scorecard: measures that drive performance', *Harvard Business Review*, 70 (1), 1992, 71–85.

I.O. Karpen, L.L. Bove and B.A. Lukas, 'Linking service-dominant logic and strategic business practice: a conceptual model of a service-dominant orientation', *Journal of Service Research*, 15 (1), 2012, 21–38.

C.J. Kasouf, J. Darroch, C.M. Hultman and M.P. Miles, 'Service dominant logic: implications at the marketing/entrepreneurial interface', *Journal of Research in Marketing and Entrepreneurship*, 11 (1), 2008, 5–21.

H.T. Keh and Y. Xie, 'Corporate reputation and customer behavioral intentions: the roles of trust, identification and commitment', *Industrial Marketing Management*, 38, 2009, 732–742.

I. Keki and H.J. Smyth, 'Investigation of market management in construction: differences between construction contractors and design consultancies in civil engineering business development', *ATINER 8th Annual International Conference on Marketing*, 5th–8th July, Athens, 2010a.

I. Keki and H.J. Smyth, 'Market management in construction: business development differences between construction contractors and cost/project management consultants in the civil engineering market', *24th IPMA World Congress*, 1st–3rd November, Istanbul, 2010b.

J. Kelly and S. Male, *Value Management in Design and Construction*, London: E & FN Spon, 1993.

N. Kelly, A.J. Edkins, H.J. Smyth and E. Konstantinou, 'Reinventing the role of the project manager in mobilising knowledge in construction', *International Journal of Managing Projects in Business*, 6 (4), 2013, 654–673.

P. Kenna, 'Globalization and housing rights', *Indiana Journal of Global Legal Studies*, 15 (2), 2008, 397–469.

C. Kennedy and M. O'Connor, *Managing Major Bid Projects: critical success factors*, Bedford: Policy, 1997.

C.K. Kim, D. Han and S.B. Park, 'The effect of brand personality and brand identification on brand loyalty: applying the theory of social identification', *Japanese Psychological Research*, 43, 2001, 195–206.

C.W. Kim and R. Mauborgne, 'Blue ocean strategy', *Harvard Business Review*, 82 (10), 2004, 76–84.

S.F. King and T.F. Burgess, 'Understanding success and failure in customer relationship management', *Industrial Marketing Management*, 37, 2008, 421–431.

J. Kingman-Brundage, 'Service mapping: gaining a concrete perspective on service system design', *Proceedings of the Third Quality in Services Symposium*, University of Karlstad, 1992.

T.C. Kinnear, 'A perspective on how firms relate to their markets', *Journal of Marketing*, 63, 1999, 112–114.

S. Kirkegaard, *Either/Or: a fragment of life*, 1992 abridged edition, Harmondsworth: Penguin Classic, 1843.

J. Kirsilä, M. Hellström and K. Wikström, 'Integration as a project management concept: a study of the commissioning process in industrial deliveries', *International Journal of Project Management*, 25, 2007, 714–721.

R. Koch, *The 80/20 Principle: the secret of achieving more with less*, New York: Free Press, 1998.

A.K. Kohli and B.J. Jaworski, 'Market orientation: the construct, research propositions, and managerial implications', *Journal of Marketing*, 54, 1990, 1–18.

K. Koskinen and P. Pihlanto, *Knowledge Management in Project-Based Companies: an organic perspective*, Basingstoke: Palgrave Macmillan, 2008.

P. Kotler, *Marketing Management*, New Jersey: Pearson Education, 2003.

P. Kotler and R.A. Connor, 'Marketing professional services', *Journal of Marketing*, 41, 1977, 71–76.

P. Kotler, G. Armstrong, J. Saunders and V. Wong, *Principles of Marketing*, Hemel Hempstead: Prentice Hall, 1996.

D. Krackhardt and J.R. Hanson, 'Informal networks', *Harvard Business Review*, 71, 1993, 104–111.

S. Kraus, R. Harms and M. Fink, 'Entrepreneurial marketing: moving beyond marketing in new ventures', *International Journal of Entrepreneurship and Innovation Management*, 11 (1), 2010, 19–34.

D.R. Krause, R.B. Handfield and B.B. Tyler, 'The relationships between supplier development, commitment, social capital accumulation and performance improvement', *Journal of Operations Management*, 25, 2007, 528–545.

C. Kreiner, 'Comments on challenging the rational project environment: the legacy and impact of Christensen and Kreiner's *Projektledning i en ofulständig värld*', *International Journal of Managing Projects in Business*, 5 (4), 2012, 714–717.

T. Kuhn, *The Structure of Scientific Revolutions*, Chicago, IL: University of Chicago Press, 1996.

S. Kujala, K. Artto, P. Aaltonen and V. Turkulainen, 'Business models in project-based firms: towards a typology of solution-specific business models', *International Journal of Project Management*, 28, 2010, 96–106.

S. Kujala, J. Kujala, V. Turkulainen, K. Artto, P. Aaltonen and K. Wikström, 'Factors influencing the choice of solution-specific business models', *International Journal of Project Management*, 29, 2011, 960–970.

S.A. Kurien, *Business Development Strategies used by General Contracting Construction Companies in Texas for Market Diversification*, Master's Dissertation, College Station: Texas A&M University, 2004.

I. Lakatos, 'Falsification and the methodology of scientific research programmes', *Criticism and the Growth of Knowledge*, I. Lakatos and A. Musgrave (eds.), London: Cambridge University Press, 1970, pp. 91–196.

J. Lampel, 'The core competencies of effective project execution: the challenge of diversity', *International Journal of Project Management*, 19 (8), 2001, 471–483.

D.A. Langford and V.R. Rowland, *Managing Overseas Construction Contracting*, London: Thomas Telford, 1995.

M. Lanning, *Delivering Profitable Value: a revolutionary framework to accelerate growth, generate wealth and rediscover the heart of business*, New York: Perseus, 1998.

R. Lavidge and G. Steiner, 'A model for the measurement of advertising effectiveness', *Journal of Marketing*, 25, 1961, 59–62.

P.R. Lawrence and J.W. Lorsch, 'Differentiation and integration in complex organizations', *Administrative Science Quarterly*, 12, 1967, 1–47.

Leading Edge, *Capturing Clients in the 90s: a benchmark study of client preferences and procurement routes*, Welwyn: Leading Edge, 1994.

L. Lecoeuvre and K. Patel, 'Project marketing implementation and its link with project management and project portfolio management', *Communications of the International Business Information Management Association*, 10, 2009, 50–63.

L. Lecoeuvre-Soudain and P. Deshayes, 'From marketing to project management', *Project Management Journal*, 37, 2006, 103–112.

M.R. Leenders, 'Supplier development', *Journal of Purchasing*, 24, 1966, 47–62.

T. Lehtimäki, H. Simula and J. Salo, 'Applying knowledge management to project marketing in a demanding technology transfer project: convincing the industrial customer over the knowledge gap', *Industrial Marketing Management*, 38 (2), 2009, 228–236.

J-P. Lemaire, 'International projects' changing patters: sales engineers' changing roles', *International Business Review*, 5 (6), 1996, 603–629.

J. Lenskold, 'Marketing ROI, the path to campaign, customer, and corporate profitability', *American Marketing Association*, New York: McGraw-Hill, 2003.

D. Leonard-Barton, 'Core capabilities and core rigidities: a paradox in managing new product development', *Strategic Management Journal*, 3 (SI), 1992, 111–125.

R. Leone and N. Bendapudi, 'How to lose your star performer without losing your customers, too', *Harvard Business Review*, 79, 2001, 104–110.

T. Levitt, 'Marketing myopia', *Harvard Business Review*, 38, July–August, 1960, 24–47.

T. Levitt, *The Marketing Imagination*, New York: Free Press, 1983.

S.A. Leybourne, 'Improvisation within management: oxymoron, paradox, or legitimate way of achieving?' *International Journal of Management Concepts and Philosophy*, 2 (3), 2007, 224–239.

T. Li and R. Calantone, 'The impact of market knowledge competence on new product advantage: conceptualization and empirical examination', *Journal of Marketing*, 62, 1998, 13–29.

S. Liang, *The Bidding Strategies of Chinese Contractors: a marketing perspective*, MSc Dissertation, London: UCL, 2012.

J. Lidstone, 'The marketing of professional services', *Services Industry Journal*, 4 (3), 1984, 463–464.

M.B. Lieberman and D.B. Montgomery, 'First-mover (dis)advantages: retrospective and link with the resource-based view', *Strategic Management Journal*, 19, 1998, 1111–1125.

J. Liinamaa, *Integration in Project Business: mechanisms for integrating customers and the project network during the life-cycle of industrial projects*, Doctorate Dissertation, Turku, Finland: Åbo Akademi University, 2012.

J. Liinamaa and M. Gustafsson, 'Integrating the customer as part of systems integration', *International Journal of Managing Projects in Business*, 3 (2), 2009, 197–215.

M. Linder, *Projecting Capitalism: a history of the internationalization of the construction industry*, Westport: Greenwood Press, 1994.

M. Lindgren and J. Packendorff, 'Deconstructing projects: towards critical perspectives on project theory and projecticised society', *Making Projects Critical: a crisis of instrumental rationality*, April 10th–11th, Bristol: University of the West of England, 2003a.

M. Lindgren and J. Packendorff, 'A project-based view of entrepreneurship: towards action-orientation, seriality and collectivity', *New Movements in Entrepreneurship*, C. Steyaert and D. Hjorth (eds.), Cheltenham: Edward Elgar, 2003b, pp. 86–102.

J.H. Liu, M.S. Wilson, J. McClure and T.R. Higgins, 'Social identity and the perception of history: cultural representations of Aotearoa/New Zealand', *European Journal of Social Psychology*, 29, 1999, 1021–1047.

C. Loch and S. Kavadias, 'Implementing strategy through projects', *The Oxford Handbook of Project Management*, P.W.G. Morris, J.K. Pinto and J. Söderlund (eds.), Oxford: Oxford University Press, 2011, pp. 224–251.

C. Loch, M.T. Pich and A. de Meyer, *Managing the Unknown: a new approach to managing project under high uncertainty*, Hoboken, NJ: Wiley, 2006.

M. Lövblad and A. Bantekas, 'What do you expect? The effect of psychological contracts on affective commitment in industrial marketing relationships', *Journal of Relationship Marketing*, 9, 2010, 161–178.

C.H. Lovelock, 'Classifying services to gain strategic marketing insights', *Journal of Marketing*, 47 (3), 1983, 9–20.

C.H. Lovelock and E. Gummesson, 'Whither services marketing? In search of a new paradigm and fresh perspectives', *Journal of Service Research*, 7 (1), 2004, 20–41.

D. Lowe and R. Leiringer, 'Commercial management – defining a discipline?' *Commercial Management of Projects: defining the discipline*, D. Lowe, and R. Leiringer (eds.), Oxford: Blackwell, 2006, pp. 1–17.

S. Lowe, N. Ellis, S. Purchase, M. Rod and K-S. Hwang, 'Mapping alternatives: a commentary on Cova, B. et al. (2010). "Navigating between dyads and networks" ', *Industrial Marketing Management*, 41, 2012, 357–364.

R.E. Lucas, Jr., 'Some international evidence of output-inflation tradeoffs', *American Economic Review*, 63, 1973, 326–334.

R.A. Lundin and A. Söderholm, 'A theory of the temporary organization', *Scandinavian Journal of Management*, 11 (4), 1995, 437–455.

R.F. Lusch and S.L. Vargo, *The Service Dominant Logic of Marketing: dialog, debate and directions*, Amonk, NY: M.I. Sharpe, 2006.

M. Lycett, A. Rassau and J. Danson, 'Programme management: a critical review', *International Journal of Project Management*, 22, 2004, 289–299.

B. Lyons and J. Mehta, 'Contracts, opportunism and trust: self-interest and social orientation', *Cambridge Journal of Economics*, 21, 1997, 239–257.

S. Macmillan, 'Added value of good design', *Building Research & Information*, 34 (3), 2006, 257–271.

T.J. Madden, F. Fehle and S. Fournier, 'Brands matter: an empirical demonstration of the creation of shareholder value through branding', *Journal of the Academy of Marketing Science*, 34 (2), 2006, 224–235.

P. Madhavji, *An Examination of Client–Contractor Relationships in the Delivery of Projects*, MSc Dissertation, London: The Bartlett School of Construction and Project Management, UCL, 2012.

J. Maheshwaran, *Client Relationship Management: a comparative study between design and non-design service firms*, MSc Dissertation, London: The Bartlett School of Construction and Project Management, UCL, 2012.

D. Maister, 'Marketing to existing clients', *Journal of Management Consultancy*, 5, 1989, 25–32.

S. Mäkinen and M. Seppänen, 'Assessing business model concepts with taxonomical research criteria', *Management Research News*, 30 (10), 2007, 735–748.

W.F. Maloney, 'Construction product/service and customer satisfaction', *Journal of Construction Engineering and Management*, November/December (1), 2002, 522–529.

P. Manchanda, D.R. Wittink, A. Ching, P. Cleanthous, M. Ding, X.J.Dong, P.S.H. Leeflang, S. Misra, N. Mizik, S. Narayanan, T. Steerburgh, J.E. Wieringa, M. Wosinska and Y. Xie, 'Understanding firm, physician and consumer choice behavior in the pharmaceutical industry', *Marketing Letters*, 16 (3/4), 2005, 293–308.

T. Mandják and Z. Veres, 'The D-U-C model and the stages of the project marketing process', *Proceedings of the 14th IMP Annual Conference*, 3, K. Halinen and N. Nummela (eds.), Turku, Finland: Turku School of Economics and Business Administration, 1998, pp. 471–490.

S. Manning, 'The strategic formation of project networks: a relational practice perspective', *Human Relations*, 63 (4), 2010, 551–573.

J.G. March, 'Exploration and exploitation in organizational learning', *Organization Science*, 2 (1), 1991, 71–87.

J.G. March, 'The future, disposable organizations and the rigidities of imagination', *Organization*, 2 (3–4), 1995, 427–440.

C. Markides, 'Six principles of breakthrough strategy', *Business Strategy Review*, 10 (2), 1999, 1–10.

M. Martinsuo and T. Ahola, 'Supplier integration in complex delivery projects: comparison between different buyer–supplier relationships', *International Journal of Project Management*, 28, 2010, 107–116.

P. Matthyssens and W. Faes, 'OEM buying process for new components: purchasing and marketing implications', *Industrial Marketing Management*, 14, 1985, 144–157.

P. Matthyssens and K. Vandenbempt, 'Creating competitive advantage in industrial service', *Journal of Business and Industrial Marketing*, 13 (4/5), 1998, 339–355.

L-G. Mattson, 'Systems selling as a strategy on industrial markets', *Industrial Marketing Management*, 3, 1973, 107–120.

E.J. McCarthy, *Basic Marketing: a managerial approach*, Homewood, IL: Richard D. Irwin Inc., 1964.

M. McDonald, P. Frow and A. Payne, *Marketing Plans for Services*, Chichester: Wiley, 2011.

M. McDonald, T. Millman and B. Rogers, 'Key account management: theory, practice and challenges', *Journal of Marketing Management*, 13, 1997, 737–757.

G.J. McGovern, D. Court, R., J.A. Quelch and B. Crawford, 'Bringing customers into the boardroom', *Harvard Business Review*, 82, 2004, 70–80.

R. McIvor, 'A practical framework for understanding the out-sourcing process', *Supply Chain Management International Journal*, 5 (1), 2000, 22–36.

J. McKean, *Customers are People: the human touch*, Chichester: John Wiley and Sons, 2002.

R.S. McKeeman, *Early Warning Sign of IT Project Failure*, IS SIG, Newtown, PA: PMI, 2002.

G.H. Mead, *Mind, Self and Society*, Chicago: University of Chicago Press, 1934.

M. Mende and R.N. Bolton, 'Why attachment security matters: how customers' attachment styles influence their relationships with service firms and service employees', *Journal of Service Research*, 14 (3), 2011, 285–301.

A. Menon and R.P. Vardarajan, 'A model of marketing knowledge use within firms', *Journal of Marketing*, 56 (4), 1992, 53–71.

A. Menon, S. Bharadwaj, P. Adidam and S. Edison, 'Antecedents and consequences of marketing strategy making: a model and a test', *Journal of Marketing*, 63, 1999, 18–40.

E. Merrow, *Industrial Megaprojects: concepts, strategies and practices for success*, Hoboken, NJ: Wiley, 2011.

M.A. Merz, Y. He and S.L. Vargo, 'The evolving brand logic: a service-dominant logic perspective', *Journal of the Academy of Marketing Science*, 37 (3), 2009, 328–344.

S. Michalski and B. Helmig, 'What do we know about the identity salience model of relationship marketing success? A review of the literature', *Journal of Relationship Marketing*, 7 (1), 2008, 45–63.

C. Midler and P. Silberzahn, 'Managing robust development process for high-tech startups through multi-project learning: the case of two European start-ups', *International Journal of Project Management*, 26 (5), 2008, 479–486.

R.E. Miles and C. Snow, 'Organizations: new concepts for new forms', *California Management Review*, 28 (3), 1986, 62–73.

P. Milgrom and J. Roberts, *Economics, Organization and Management*, New Jersey: Prentice-Hall, 1992.

D. Milin and S. Morača, 'Project organisation culture and its influence on project success,' *Proceedings of the IRNOP 2013: Innovative Approaches in Project Management Research*, 17th–19th June, Oslo: BI Norwegian Business School, 2013.

R. Miller and D.R. Lessard, *The Strategic Management of Large Engineering Projects: shaping institutions, risks, and governance*, Cambridge, MA: MIT Press, 2000.

R. Miller and X. Olleros, 'Project shaping as competitive advantage', *The Strategic Management of Large Engineering Projects: shaping institutions, risks, and governance*, R. Miller and D.R. Lessard (eds.), Cambridge, MA: MIT Press, 2000, pp. 93–112.

S. Min, J.T. Mentzer and R.T. Ladd, 'A market orientation in supply chain management', *Journal of the Academy of Marketing Science*, 35 (4), 2007, 507–522.

H. Mintzberg, *Rise and Fall of Strategic Planning*, New York: Free Press, 1994.

H. Mintzberg, 'The structuring of organizations', H. Mintzberg, J.B. Lampel, J.B. Quinn and S. Ghoshal (eds.), *The Strategy Process*, New Jersey: Prentice Hall, 2003, pp. 209–226.

H. Mintzberg and J.A. Waters, 'Of strategies, deliberate and emergent', *Strategic Management Journal*, 6, 1985, 257–272.

D. Miocevic and B. Crnjak-Karanovic, 'The mediating role of key supplier relationship management practices on supply chain orientation: the organizational buying effectiveness link', *Industrial Marketing Management*, 41 (1), 2012, 115–124.

K. Möller, 'Role of competences in creating customer value: a value-creation logic approach', *Industrial Marketing Management*, 35, 2006, 913–924.

A.B. Moore, *Marketing Management in Construction: a guide for contractors*, Oxford: Butterworth-Heinemann, 1984.

G. Moore, *Crossing the Chasm: marketing and selling products to mainstream customers*, New York: HarperCollins, 1991.

G. Morgan, *Images of Organization*, Thousand Oaks, CA: Sage, 1986.

N.A. Morgan and L.L. Rego, 'The value of different customer and loyalty metrics in predicting business performance', *Marketing Science*, 25 (5), 2006, 426–439.

R.E. Morgan and J.L. Burnicle, 'Marketing communication practices in housebuilding firms', *Building Research & Information*, 19 (6), 1991, 371–376.

R.M. Morgan and S.D. Hunt, 'The commitment-trust theory of relationship marketing', *Journal of Marketing*, July, 58, 1994, 20–38.

R.E. Morgan and N.A. Morgan, 'Marketing consulting engineering services', *Civil Engineering Surveyor*, June, 1990.

R.E. Morgan and N.A. Morgan, 'An appraisal of the marketing development in engineering consultancy firms', *Construction Management and Economics*, 9 (1), 1991, 335–368.

M.H. Morris and D.L. Sexton, 'The concept of entrepreneurial activity: implications for firm performance', *Journal of Business Research*, 36 (1), 1996, 5–13.

M.H. Morris, M. Schinehutte and R.W. LaForge, 'Entrepreneurial marketing: a construction for integrating emerging entrepreneurship and marketing perspectives', *Journal of Marketing Theory and Practice*, 10 (4), 2002, 1–18.

M.H. Morris, M. Schinehutte and J. Allen, 'The entrepreneur's business model: toward a unified perspective', *Journal of Business Research*, 58, 2005, 726–735.

P.W.G. Morris, *The Management of Projects*, London: Thomas Telford, 1994.

P.W.G. Morris, *The Reconstruction of Project Management*, Chichester: Wiley-Blackwell, 2013.

P.W.G. Morris and J. Geraldi, 'Managing the institutional context for projects', *Project Management Journal*, 42 (6), 2011, 20–32.

P.W.G. Morris and G.H. Hough, *The Anatomy of Major Projects*, Chichester: John Wiley and Sons, 1987.

P.W.G. Morris and J.K. Pinto, 'Introduction', *The Wiley Guide to Managing Projects*, P.W.G. Morris and J.K. Pinto (eds.), Hoboken, NJ: John Wiley and Sons, 2004, pp. xiii–xxiv.

P.W.G. Morris, J.K. Pinto and J. Söderlund, 'Towards the third wave of project management', *The Oxford Handbook of Project Management*, P.W.G. Morris, J.K. Pinto and J. Söderlund (eds.), Oxford: Oxford University Press, 2011, pp. 1–11.

P.W.G. Morris, M.B. Patel and S.H. Wearne, 'Research into revising the APM project management body of knowledge', *International Journal of Project Management*, 18 (3), 2000, 155–164.

R. Müller, *Project Governance*, Aldershot: Gower, 2009.

J.F. Muth, 'Rational expectations and the theory of price movements', *Econometrica*, 29, 1961, 315–335.

J. Nahapiet and S. Ghoshal, 'Social capital, intellectual capital, and the organizational advantage', *Academy of Management Review*, 23 (2), 1998, 242–266.

M. Naim and J. Barlow, 'An innovative supply chain strategy for customized housing', *Construction Management and Economics*, 21, 2003, 593–602.

F. Namo and R.F. Fellows, 'The role of advertising in marketing civil/structural engineering consultancy firms', *Construction Management and Economics*, 11 (6), 1993, 431–441.

X. Nan and R. Faber, 'Advertising theory: reconceptualizing the building blocks', *Marketing Theory*, 4, 2004, 7–10.

J.A. Narver and S.F. Slater, 'The effect of market orientation on business profitability', *Journal of Marketing*, 54, 1990, 20–35.

J.A. Narver, S.F. Slater and D.L. MacLachlan, 'Responsive and proactive market and new product success', *Journal of Production Innovation Management*, 25 (5), 2004, 334–347.

B.J. Naylor, M. Naim and D. Berry, 'Leagility: integrating the lean and agile manufacturing paradigms in the total supply chain', *International Journal of Production Economics*, 62, 1999, 107–118.

H.S. Neap and S. Aysal, 'Owner's factor in value-based project management in construction', *Journal of Business Ethics*, 50, 2004, 97–103.

R.R. Nelson and S.G. Winter, *An Evolutionary Theory of Change*, Boston: Harvard Business Press, 1982.

D. Nicolini, 'In search of project chemistry', *Construction Management and Economics*, 20, 2002, 167–177.

R. Normann, *Refraining Business: when the map changes the landscape*, Chichester: Wiley, 2001.

A. O'Donnell, D. Carson and A. Gilmore, 'Competition and co-operation between small firms and their competitors', *Journal of Research in Marketing and Entrepreneurship*, 4 (1), 2002, 7–15.

R. Oliva and R. Kallenberg, 'Managing the transition from products to services', *International Journal of Service Industry Management*, 14 (2), 2003, 160–172.

R.L. Oliver, *Satisfaction: a behavioural perspective on the consumer*, New York: McGraw-Hill, 1997.

E.M. Olsen, S.F. Slater and G.T.M. Hult, 'The performance implications of fit among business strategy, marketing organization structure, and strategic behavior', *Journal of Marketing*, 69, 2005, 49–65.

R. Orr and W. Scott, 'Institutional exceptions on global projects: a process model', *Journal of International Business Studies*, 39 (4), 2008, 562–588.

A. Ostrom, M. Bitner, S. Brown, K. Burkhard, M. Gaul, V. Smith-Daniels, H. Demirkan and E. Rabinovich, 'Moving forward and making a difference: research priorities for the science of service', *Journal of Service Research*, 13 (1), 2010, 4–36.

W.G. Ouchi, 'The relationship between organization structure and organizational control', *Administrative Science Quarterly*, 22, 1977, 95–113.

W.G. Ouchi, 'Markets, bureaucracies and clans', *Administrative Science Quarterly*, 25 (10), 1980, 129–141.

J. Packendorff, 'Inquiring into the temporary organization: new directions for project management research', *Scandinavian Journal of Management*, 11 (4), 1995, 319–333.

A.L. Page and M. Siemplenski, 'Product systems marketing', *Industrial Marketing Management*, 12, 1983, 89–99.

K. Palda, *The Measurement of Cumulative Advertising Effects*, New Jersey: Prentice-Hall, 1964.

D. Palmer, R. Friedland and J.V. Singh, 'The ties that bind: organizational and class bases of stability in a corporate interlock network', *American Sociological Review*, 51, 1986, 781–796.

A. Parasuraman, V.A. Zeithaml and L.L. Berry, 'A conceptual model of service quality and its implications for future research', *Journal of Marketing*, 49 (4), 1985, 41–50.

S.K. Parker and M. Skitmore, 'Project management turnover: causes and effects on project performance', *International Journal of Project Management*, 23, 2005, 205–214.

A. Parmigiani and J. Howard-Grenville, 'Routines revisited: exploring the capabilities and practice perspectives', *Academy of Management Annals*, 5 (1), 2011, 413–453.

D. Partington, S. Pellegrinelli and M. Young, 'Attributes and levels of programme management competence: an interpretive study', *International Journal of Project Management*, 23, 2005, 87–95.

S. Pascale and S. Sanders, 'Supplier selection and partnering alignment: a prerequisite for project management success for the year 2000', *Proceedings of the 28th Annual Project Management Institute 1997 Seminars and Symposium*, Drexel Hill, PA: PMI, 1998, pp. 19–26.

K. Patel, L. Lecoeuvre and J.R. Turner, 'Integrating project marketing with project management', *Paper presented at* EURAM 2012, 6th–8th June, Rotterdam, 2012.

A. Payne and P. Frow, 'Customer relationship management: from strategy to implementation', *Journal of Marketing Management*, 22, 2006, 135–168.

A. Payne, D. Ballantyne and M. Christopher, 'A stakeholder model to relationship marketing strategy: the development and use of the "six markets" model', *European Journal of Marketing*, 39 (7/8), 2005, 855–871.

A. Payne, K. Storbacka and P. Frow, 'Managing the co-creation of value', *Journal of Service Research*, 36 (1), 2008, 83–96.

A. Payne, K. Storbacka, P. Frow and S. Knox, 'Co-creating brands: diagnosing and designing the relationship experience', *Journal of Business Research*, 62 (3), 2009, 379–389.

P. Pearce, *Construction Marketing: a professional approach*, Reston, VA: American Society of Civil Engineers, 1992.

S. Pellegrinelli, 'Program management: organizing project based change', *International Journal of Project Management*, 15 (3), 1997, 141–149.

J. Pels and M. Saren, 'The 4*Ps* of relational marketing, perspectives, perceptions, paradoxes and paradigms: learnings from organizational theory and the strategy literature', *Journal of Relationship Marketing*, 4 (3/4), 2005, 59–84.

E.T. Penrose, *The Theory of the Growth of the Firm*, New York: Wiley, 1959.

E.T. Penrose, 'The growth of the firm: a case study: The Hercules Powder Company', *Business History Review*, XXXIV (1), 1960, 1–23.

R.B. Perry, 'Economic value and moral value', *Quarterly Journal of Economics*, 30 (3), 1916, 443–485.

M.A. Peteraf, 'The cornerstones of competitive advantage: a resource-based view', *Strategic Management Journal*, 14 (3), 1993, 179–191.

C.E. Pettijohn, L.S. Pettijohn and A.J. Taylor, 'The influence of salesperson skill, motivation, and training on the practice of customer-oriented selling', *Psychology and Marketing*, 19 (9), 2002, 743–757.

R. Pettinger, *Construction Marketing: strategies for success*, London: Macmillan, 1998.

L.S. Pheng, 'World market in in construction: a regional analysis', *Construction Management and Economics*, 9 (1), 1991, 63–71.

M.T. Pich, C.H. Loch and A. De Meyer, 'On uncertainty, ambiguity, and complexity in project management', *Management Science*, 48 (8), 2002, 1009–1023.

J.B. Pine and J.H. Gilmore, *The Experience Economy*, Boston: Harvard Business School Press, 1999.

J.K. Pinto and J.G. Covin, 'Project marketing: detailing the project manager's hidden responsibility', *Project Management Journal*, 22 (3), 1992, 29–34.

J.K. Pinto and P.K. Rouhiainen, *Building Customer-based Project Organizations*, New York: John Wiley, 2001.

J.K. Pinto and D.P. Slevin, 'Critical success factors across the project life cycle', *Project Management Journal*, 19 (3), 1988, 67–75.

T. Pitsis, S. Clegg, M. Marosszeky and T. Rura-Polley, 'Constructing the Olympic dream: a future perfect strategy of project management', *Organization Science*, 14 (5), 2003, 574–590.

PMI, *A Guide to the Project Management Body of Knowledge (PMBOK® Guide)*, 5th edition, Newton Square, PA: Project Management Institute, 2013.

K. Polanyi, *The Great Transformation*, New York: Beacon Press, 1944.

L. Poppo, K. Zhou and S. Ryu, 'Alternative origins to interorganizational trust and interdependence perspective on the shadow of the past and the shadow of the future', *Organization Science*, 19 (1), 2008, 562–588.

C. Porath, D. MacInnis and V. Folkes, 'It's unfair: why customers who merely observe an uncivil employee abandon the company', *Journal of Service Research*, 14 (3), 2011, 302–317.

J. Porter, 'Forward', *Industrial Megaprojects: concepts, strategies and practices for success*, E. Merrow (ed.), Hoboken, NJ: Wiley, 2011.

M.E. Porter, 'How competitive forces shape strategy', *Harvard Business Review*, 57 (2), 1979, 137–145.

M.E. Porter, *Competitive Strategy*, New York: Free Press, 1980.

M.E. Porter, *Competitive Advantage*, New York: Free Press, 1985.

M. Powel and J. Young, 'The project management support office', *The Wiley Guide to Managing Projects*, P.W.G. Morris and J.K. Pinto (eds.), Hoboken, NJ: John Wiley and Sons, 2004, pp. 937–969.

W.W. Powell, 'Neither market nor hierarchy: network forms of organization', *Research in Organizational Behavior*, 12, 1990, 295–336.

C.K. Prahalad and G. Hamel, 'The core competencies of the organization', *Harvard Business Review*, 63 (3), 1990, 79–91.

C.K. Prahalad and V. Ramaswamy, 'Co-opting customer competence', *Harvard Business Review*, 78 (1), 2000, 79–90.

C.K. Prahalad and V. Ramaswamy, 'Co-creating unique value with customers', *Strategy & Leadership*, 32 (3), 2004a, 4–9.

C.K. Prahalad and V. Ramaswamy, 'Co-creation experiences: the next practice in value creation', *Journal of Interactive Marketing*, 18 (3), 2004b, 5–14.

B. Prasad, 'Decentralized cooperation: a distributed approach to team design in a concurrent engineering organization', *Team Performance Management*, 4 (4), 1998, 138–165.

C. Preece, K. Moodley and P. Smith, *Corporate Communications in Construction*, Oxford: Blackwell Science, 1998.

C. Preece, P. Smith and K. Moodley, *Construction Business Development*, Oxford: Butterworth-Heinemann, 2003.

A. Prencipe, 'Corporate strategy and systems integration capabilities: managing networks in complex systems industries', *The Business of Systems Integration*, A. Prencipe, A. Davies and M. Hobday (eds.), Oxford: Oxford University Press, 2003, pp. 114–132.

S.D. Pryke (ed.), *Construction Supply Chain Management*, Chichester: Wiley-Blackwell, 2009.

S.D. Pryke, *Social Network Analysis in Construction*, Chichester: Wiley-Blackwell, 2012.

S.D. Pryke and H.J. Smyth, 'Scoping a relationship approach to the management of projects', *Management of Complex Projects: a relationship approach*, S.D. Pryke and H.J. Smyth (eds.), Oxford: Blackwell, 2006, pp. 21–46.

A. Purdy, *Living Beyond Limits*, TEDxOrangeCoast, www.youtube.com/watch?v = N2QZM7azGoA, posted 8th June 2011. Accessed 3rd July 2013.

P. Rad and G. Levin, *Project Portfolio Management Tools and Techniques*, New York: International Institute for Learning, 2007.

Z.J. Radnor and R. Boaden, 'Developing an understanding of corporate anorexia', *International Journal of Operations & Production Management*, 24 (4), 2004, 424–440.

R. Ramírez, 'Value co-production: intellectual origins and implications for practice and research', *Strategic Management Journal*, 20 (1), 1999, 49–65.

S. Read and S.D. Sarasvathy, 'Knowing what to do and doing what you know: effectuation as a form of entrepreneurial expertise', *Journal of Private Equity*, 9 (1), 2001, 45–62.

S. Read, N. Dew, S.D. Sarasvathy, M. Song and R. Wiltbank, 'Marketing under uncertainty: the logic of an effectual approach', *Journal of Marketing*, May, 73, 2009, 1–18.

F.F. Reichheld, *The Loyalty Effect*, Boston, MA: Harvard Business School Press, 1996.

F.F. Reichheld, 'Lead for loyalty', *Harvard Business Review*, 79 (7), 2001, 76–84.

F.F. Reichheld and P. Schefter, 'E-loyalty: your secret weapon on the web', *Harvard Business Review*, July–August, 2000, 105–113.

F.F. Reichheld and W.E. Sasser, 'Zero defections: quality comes to services', *Harvard Business Review*, 68, 1990, 105–111.

W. Reinartz, M. Krafft and W.D. Hoyer, 'The customer relationship management process: its measurement and impact upon performance', *Journal of Marketing Research*, 41, 2004, 293–305.

B. Richardson, *Marketing for Architects and Engineers: a new approach*, London: Chapman & Hall, 1996.

A. Roberts, J. Kelsey, H.J. Smyth and A. Wilson, 'Health and safety maturity in project business cultures', *International Journal of Managing Projects in Business*, 5 (4), 2012, 776–803.

P.W. Roberts and G.R. Dowling, 'The value of the firm's corporate reputation: how reputation helps attain and sustain superior profitability', *Corporate Reputation Review*, 1 (1), 2002, 72–76.

A.G.L. Romme, 'Making a difference: organization as design', *Organization Science*, 14 (5), 2003, 558–577.

L.J. Rosenberg and J.A. Czepiel, 'A marketing approach to customer retention', *Journal of Consumer Marketing*, 1, 1984, 45–51.

A. Rothenberg, 'The process of Janusian thinking in creativity', *Archives of General Psychiatry*, 24, 1971, 311–327.

D.M. Rousseau, 'New hires perspectives of their own and their employer's obligations: a study of psychological contracts', *Journal of Organizational Behavior*, 11, 1990, 389–400.

D.M. Rousseau and R. Schalk, *Psychological Contracts in Employment: cross-national perspectives*, Thousand Oaks, CA: Sage, 2000.

R.T. Rust and A.J. Zahorik, 'Customer satisfaction, customer retention, and market share', *Journal of Retailing*, 69 (2), 1993, 193–215.

R.T. Rust, A.J. Zahorik and T.L. Keiningham, 'Return on quality (ROQ): making service quality financially accountable', *Journal of Marketing*, 59 (2), 1995, 58–70.

L.J. Ryals, 'Are your customers worth more than money?' *Journal of Retailing and Consumer Services*, 9, 2002, 241–251.

L.J. Ryals, 'Making customer relationship management work: the measurement and profitable management of customer relationships', *Journal of Marketing*, 69 (4), 2005, 252–261.

S.D. Sarasvathy, 'Causation and effectuation: toward a theoretical shift from economic inevitability to entrepreneurial contingency', *Academy of Management Review*, 26, 2001, 243–263.

S.D. Sarasvathy, 'Locus of variation in models of new market creation', Paper presented at the *2010 Opening Up Innovation: Strategy, Organization and Technology, Druid Summer Conference*, 15th–18th June, London: Imperial College, 2010.

S.D. Sarasvathy and N. Dew, 'New market creation through transformation', *Journal of Evolutionary Economics*, 15, 2005, 533–565.

S.D. Sarasvathy, N. Dew, S. Read, and R. Wiltbank, 'Designing organizations that design environments: lessons from entrepreneurial activity', *Organizational Studies*, 29 (3), 2008, 331–350.

J-P. Sartre, *Being and Nothingness: a phenomenological essay on ontology*, New York: Philosophical Library, 1943.

C. Sauer, *Why Information Systems Fail: a case study approach*, Henley-on-Thames: Alfred Waller, 1993.

C. Sauer and B.H. Reich, 'Rethinking IT project management: evidence of a new mindset and its implications', *International Journal of Project Management*, 27 (2), 2009, 182–193.

M. Sawhney, 'Going beyond the product: defining, designing and delivering customer solutions', *The Service-Dominant Logic of Marketing: dialog, debate and directions*, R.F. Lusch and S.L Vargo (eds.), Armonk: M.E. Sharpe, 2006, pp. 365–380.

R. Saxe and B.A. Weitz, 'The SOCO scale: a measure of the customer orientation of salespeople', *Journal of Marketing Research*, 19 (3), 1982, 343–351.

R.A. Sayer, *Method in Social Science: a realist approach*, London: Routledge, 1992.

T. Schakett, A. Flaschner, T. Gao and A. El-Ansary, 'Effects of social bonding in business-to-business relationships', *Journal of Relationship Marketing*, 10, 2011, 264–280.

J. Schepers, A. de Jong, K. de Ruyter and M. Wetzels, 'Fields of gold: perceived efficacy in virtual teams of field service employees', *Journal of Service Research*, 13 (3), 2011, 372–389.

M. Schindehutte and M.H. Morris, 'Entrepreneurial marketing strategy: lesson from the Red Queen', *International Journal of Entrepreneurship and Innovation Management*, 11 (1), 2010, 75–94.

M. Schindehutte, M.H. Morris and A. Kocak, 'Understanding market-driving behavior: the role of entrepreneurship', *Journal of Small Business Management*, 46 (1), 2008, 4–26.

D.A. Schön, *The Reflective Practitioner: how professionals think in action*, New York: Basic Books, 1983.

J.A. Schumpeter, *Capitalism, Socialism and Democracy*, (1994 edn.), London: Routledge, 1934.

A. Sen, *On Ethics and Economics*, Oxford: Blackwell, 1987.

J.N. Seth, R.S. Sisodia and A. Sharma, 'The antecedents and consequences of customer-centric marketing', *Journal of the Academy of Marketing Science*, 28 (1), 2000, 55–66.

C. Shearer, 'The marketing of consulting engineering services', *Structural Engineer*, 68 (9), 1990, 177–180.

A.J. Shenhar, D. Dvir, O. Levy and A.C. Maltz, 'Project success: a multidimensional strategic concept', *Long Range Planning*, 34 (6), 2001, 699–725.

G.L. Shostack, 'Service positioning through structural change', *Journal of Marketing*, 51, 1987, 33–43.

H.A. Simon, 'Theories of decision-making in economics and behavioral science', *American Economic Review*, 49 (3), 1959, 253–283.

H.A. Simon, *The Sciences of the Artificial*, Cambridge, MA: MIT Press, 1969.

H.A. Simon, 'Rational decision making in business organizations', *American Economic Review*, 69 (4), 1979, 493–513.

M.A. Skaates and V. Seppänen, 'Market-oriented resource management in customer relationships', *Qualitative Market Research: An International Journal*, 8, 2005, 77–96.

M.A. Skaates and H. Tikkanen, 'International project marketing as an area of study: a literature review with suggestions for research and practice', *International Journal of Project Management*, 21 (1), 2003a, 503–510.

M.A. Skaates and H. Tikkanen, 'International project marketing: an introduction to the INPM approach', *International Journal of Project Management*, 21, 2003b, 503–510.

M.A. Skaates, H. Tikkanen and K. Alajoutsijärvi, 'Social and cultural capital in project marketing service firms: Danish architectural firms on the German market', *Scandinavian Journal of Management*, 18, 2002a, 589–609.

M.A. Skaates, H. Tikkanen and J. Lindblom, 'Relationships and project marketing success', *Journal of Business & Industrial Marketing*, 17 (5), 2002b, 389–406.

M.A. Skaates, H. Tikkanen and K. Alajoutsijärvi, 'The international marketing of professional service projects: to what extent does territoriality matter?' *Journal of Services Marketing*, 17, 2003, 83–97.

M. Skitmore and H.J. Smyth, 'Pricing construction work: a marketing viewpoint', *Construction Management and Economics*, 25 (6), 2007, 619–630.

S.F. Slater and J.C. Narver, 'Market orientation, customer value, and superior performance', *Business Horizons*, 37, 1994, 305–318.

S.F. Slater and J.C. Narver, 'Market orientation and the learning organization', *Journal of Marketing*, 59 (3), 1995, 63–74.

S.F. Slater and E.M. Olsen, 'Strategy and performance: the influence of salesforce management', *Strategic Management Journal*, 21, 2000, 813–829.

S.F. Slater and E.M. Olsen, 'Marketing's contribution to the implementation of business strategy: an empirical analysis', *Strategic Management Journal*, 22, 2001, 1055–1068.

S.F. Slater, G.T.M. Hult and E.M. Olson, 'Factors influencing the relative importance of marketing strategy creativity and marketing strategy implementation effectiveness', *Industrial Marketing Management*, 39, 2010, 551–559.

D.P. Slevin and J.K. Pinto, 'The project implementation profile: new tool for project managers', *Project Management Journal*, 18 (4), 1986, 57–71.

A. Smith, *The Theory of Moral Sentiments*, (1984 edn.), Indianapolis, IN: Liberty Fund, 1759.

A. Smith, *An Inquiry into the Nature and Causes of the Wealth of Nations*, (2003 edn.), London: Bantam Press, 1776.

W. Smith, 'Product differentiation and market segmentation as alternative marketing strategies', *Journal of Marketing*, 21 July, 1956, 3–8.

H.J. Smyth, 'Competitive stakes and mistakes: the position of British contractors in Europe', *Proceedings of the 3rd National Construction Marketing Conference*, 9th July, The Centre for Construction Marketing and CIMCIG, Oxford: Oxford Brookes University, 1998, pp. 19–21.

H.J. Smyth, *Marketing and Selling Construction Services*, Oxford: Blackwell Science, 2000.

H.J. Smyth, 'Competition', *Commercial Management of Projects: defining the discipline*, D. Lowe and R. Leiringer (eds.), Oxford: Blackwell, 2006, pp. 22–39.

H.J. Smyth, 'Developing trust', *Collaborative Relationships in Construction: developing frameworks and networks*, H. J. Smyth and S. D. Pryke (eds.), Oxford: Wiley-Blackwell, 2008a, pp. 129–160.

H.J. Smyth, 'The credibility gap in stakeholder management: ethics and evidence of relationship management', *Construction Management and Economics*, Special Issue in Stakeholder Management in Construction, 26 (6), 2008b, 633–643.

H.J. Smyth, 'Competitive stakes in the "credit crunch": an analysis of strategic polarisation amongst European contractors', *CIB World Congress 2010, Building a Better World*, 10th–13th May, Salford, 2010a.

H.J. Smyth, 'Construction industry performance improvement programmes: the UK case of demonstration projects in the "continuous improvement" programme', *Construction Management and Economics*, 28 (3), 2010b, 255–270.

H.J. Smyth, 'Marketing, programme and project management: relationship building and maintenance over project lifecycles', *Proceedings of the CIB World Building Congress 2013: Construction and Society*, 5th–9th May, Brisbane, 2013a.

H.J. Smyth, 'Deviation, emergent requirements and value delivery: a marketing and "business development" perspective', *Proceedings of the IRNOP 2013: Innovative Approaches in Project Management Research*, 17th–19th June, Oslo: BI Norwegian Business School, 2013b.

H.J. Smyth, ' "Green" or maturing? Environmental sustainability in marketing and business development amongst construction majors', *Proceedings of the 7th Nordic Conference on Construction Economics and Organisation 2013*, 12th–14th June, Trondheim: Norwegian University of Science and Technology, 2013c.

H.J. Smyth, *Relationship Management and the Management of Projects*, London: Routledge, 2015.

H.J. Smyth and A.J. Edkins, 'Relationship management in the management of PFI/PPP projects in the UK', *International Journal of Project Management*, 25 (3), 2007, 232–240.

H.J. Smyth and T. Fitch, 'Application of relationship marketing and management: a large contractor case study', *Construction Management and Economics*, 27 (3), 2009, 399–410.

H.J. Smyth and S. Kioussi, 'Architecture firms and the role of brand management', *Architectural Engineering and Design Management*, 7 (3), 2011a, 205–217.

H.J. Smyth and S. Kioussi, 'Client management and identification', *Managing the Professional Practice*, H.J. Smyth (ed.), Oxford: Wiley-Blackwell, 2011b, 143–160.

H.J. Smyth and I.C. Kusuma, 'The interplay of organisational culture with business development for the TMO: service (in)coherence and the implications for marketing', *Proceedings of the CIB World Building Congress 2013: Construction and Society*, 5th–9th May, Brisbane, 2013.

H.J. Smyth and L. Lecoeuvre, 'Differences in decision-making criteria towards the return on marketing investment: a project business perspective', *International Journal of Project Management*, http://dx.doi.org/10.1016/j.ijproman.2014.03.005, 2014.

H.J. Smyth and R. Longbottom, 'External provision of knowledge management services: the case of the concrete and cement industries', *European Management Journal*, 23 (2), 2005, 247–259.

H.J. Smyth and P.W.G. Morris, 'An epistemological evaluation of research into projects and their management: methodological issues', *International Journal of Project Management*, 25 (4), 2007, 423–436.

H.J. Smyth and S.D. Pryke, 'Managing collaborative relationships and the management of projects', *Collaborative Relationships in Construction: developing frameworks and networks*, H. J. Smyth and S. D. Pryke (eds.), Oxford: Wiley-Blackwell, 2008, pp. 1–24.

H.J. Smyth, M. Gustafsson and E. Ganskau, 'The value of trust in project business', *International Journal of Project Management*, 28 (2), 2010, 117–129.

A. Söderholm, 'Project management of unexpected events', *International Journal of Project Management*, 26, 2008, 80–86.

J. Söderlund, 'Theoretical foundations of project management: suggestions for a pluralistic understanding', *The Oxford Handbook of Project Management*, P.W.G. Morris, J.K. Pinto and J. Söderlund (eds.), Oxford: Oxford University Press, 2011, pp. 37–64.

J. Söderlund and N. Andersson, 'A framework for the analysis of project dyads: the case of discontinuity, uncertainty and trust', R.A. Lundin and C. Midler (eds.), *Projects as Arenas of Learning and Renewal*, Boston, MA: Kluwer Academic, 1998, pp. 181–189.

J. Söderlund and F. Tell, 'The P-form organization and the dynamics of project competence: project epochs in Asea/ABB, 1950–2000', *International Journal of Project Management*, 27, 2009, 101–112.

J. Solomon and A. Solomon, *Corporate Governance and Accountability*, Chichester: Wiley, 2004.

H.E. Sørensen, *Business Development: a market-oriented perspective*, Chichester: Wiley, 2012.

S. Srinivasan and D. Hanssens, 'Marketing and firm value: metrics, methods, findings, and future directions', *Journal of Marketing Research*, 46, 2009, 313–319.

R.K. Srivastava, L. Fahey and K. Christensen, 'The resource-based view and marketing: the role of market-based assets in gaining competitive advantage', *Journal of Management*, 27, 2001, 777–802.

R.K. Srivastava, T.A. Shervani and L. Fahey, 'Market-based assets and shareholder value: a framework for analysis', *Journal of Marketing*, 62, 1998, 2–18.

R.K. Srivastava, T.A. Shervani and L. Fahey, 'Marketing, business processes, and shareholder value: an organizationally embedded view of marketing activities and the discipline of marketing', *Journal of Marketing*, 63 (SI), 1999, 168–179.

H.K. Stahl, K. Matzler and H.H. Hinterhuber, 'Linking customer lifetime value with shareholder value', *Industrial Marketing Management*, 32, 2003, 267–279.

W.H. Starbuck, 'Congealing oil: inventing ideologies to justify acting ideologies out', *Journal of Management Studies*, 19, 1982, 3–27.

K. Storbacka and S. Nenonen, 'Customer relationships and the heterogeneity of firm performance', *Journal of Business & Industrial Marketing*, 24 (5/6), 2009, 360–372.

K. Storbacka, T. Strandvik and C. Grönroos, 'Managing customer relationships for profit: the dynamics of relationship quality', *International Journal of Service Industry Management*, 5 (5), 1994, 21–38.

S. Stremersch and G.J. Tellis, 'Strategic bundling of products and prices: a new synthesis for marketing', *Journal of Marketing*, 66 (1), 2002, 55–72.

J.E. Stryker, 'Identity salience and role performance: the relevance of symbolic interaction theory for family research', *Journal of Marriage and Family*, 30, 1968, 558–564.

H. Tajfel, 'Social identity and intergroup behaviour', *Social Science Information*, 13, 1974, 65–93.

D.J. Teece, G. Pisano and A. Shuen, 'Dynamic capabilities and strategic management', *Strategic Management Journal*, 18 (7), 1997, 509–533.

S. Teerikangas, 'Silent forces shaping the performance of cross-border acquisitions', *The Handbook of Mergers and Acquisitions*, D. Faulkner, S. Teerikangas and R.J. Joseph (eds.), Oxford: Oxford University Press, 2012, pp. 517–542.

K. Tejavanija, *Marketing of Architectural Practices: the role of client relationship management in architectural firms in Thailand*, MSc Dissertation, London: UCL, 2010.

H. Terho, 'A measure for companies' customer portfolio management', *Journal of Business-to-Business Marketing*, 16, 2009, 374–411.

G. Themistocleous and S.H. Wearne, 'Project management top coverage in journals', *International Journal of Project Management*, 18, 2000, 7–11.

G.V. Terry, *After Marketing: how to keep customers for life through relationship marketing*, Homewood, IL: Irwin, 1992.

H. Tikkanen, 'Research on international project marketing: a review and implications', *Marketing and International Business: essays in honour of Professor Karin Holstius on her 65th birthday*, H. Tikkanen (ed.), Turku, Finland: Turku School of Economics and Business Administration, 1998, pp. 261–285.

H. Tikkanen, J. Kujala and K. Artto, 'The marketing strategy of the project-based firm: the four portfolios framework', *Industrial Marketing Management*, 36 (2), 2007, 194–205.

Z.M. Torbica and R.C. Stroh, 'Customer satisfaction in home building', *Journal of Construction Engineering and Management*, 127 (1), 2001, 82–86.

K.R. Tuli and S.G. Bharadwaj, 'Customer satisfaction and stock returns risk', *Journal of Marketing*, 73, 2009, 184–197.

K.R. Tuli, A.K. Kohli and S.G. Bharadwaj, 'Rethinking customer solutions: from product bundles to relational processes', *Journal of Marketing*, 71 (3), 2007, 1–17.

V. Turkulainen, J. Kujala, K. Artto and R.E. Levitt, 'Organizing in the context of global project-based firm: the case of sales–operations interface', *Industrial Marketing Management*, 42, 2013, 223–233.

J.R. Turner, *The Commercial Project Manager*, London: McGraw Hill, 1995.

J.R. Turner, *The Handbook of Project-Based Management*, (2nd edn.), London: McGraw-Hill, 1999.

J.R. Turner and A. Keegan, 'The management of operations in project-based organisation', *Journal of Change Management*, 1 (2), 2000, 131–148.

J.R. Turner, J.K. Pinto and C. Bredillet, 'The evolution of project management research: evidence from the journals', *The Oxford Handbook of Project Management*, P.W.G. Morris, J.K. Pinto and J. Söderlund (eds.), Oxford: Oxford University Press, 2011, pp. 65–106.

W. Ulaga, 'Capturing value creation in business relationships: a customer perspective', *Industrial Marketing Management*, 32 (8), 2003, 677–693.

T. Üstüner and D. Godes, 'Better sales networks', *Harvard Business Review*, 84 (7/8), 2006, 102–113.

B. Uzzi, 'Social structure and competition in interfirm networks: the paradox of embeddedness', *Administrative Science Quarterly*, 42 (1), 1997, 35–67.

A.L. Vaagaasar, 'Development of relationships and relationship competencies in complex projects', *International Journal of Managing Projects in Business*, 4 (2), 2011, 294–307.

S. Vandermerwe and J. Rada, 'Servitization of business: adding value by adding services', *European Management Journal*, 6, 1988, 314–324.

S.L. Vargo and R.F. Lusch, 'Evolving to a new dominant logic for marketing', *Journal of Marketing*, 68, 2004, 1–17.

S.L. Vargo and R.F. Lusch, 'Evolving to a new dominant logic for marketing', *The Service-Dominant Logic of Marketing: dialog, debate and directions*, R.F. Lusch and S.L Vargo (eds.), Armonk: M.E. Sharpe, 2006, pp. 3–28.

S.L. Vargo and R.F. Lusch, 'Service-dominant logic: continuing the evolution', *Journal of the Academy of Marketing Science*, 36 (1), 2008a, 1–10.

S.L. Vargo and R.F. Lusch, 'From goods to service(s): divergences and convergences of logics', *Industrial Marketing Management*, 37, 2008b, 254–259.

S.L. Vargo and R.F. Lusch, 'It's all B2B … and beyond: toward a systems perspective of the market', *Industrial Marketing Management*, 40 (2), 2010, 181–187.

D.S. Vaughan, 'The dark side of organizations: mistakes, misconduct, and disaster', *Annual Review of Sociology*, 25, 1999, 271–305.

V.H. Villenaa, E. Revillaa and T.Y. Choib, 'The dark side of buyer–supplier relationships: a social capital perspective', *Journal of Operations Management*, 29, 2011, 561–576.

D.W. Vorhies, 'An investigation of the factors leading to the development of marketing capabilities and organizational effectiveness', *Journal of Strategic Marketing*, 6 (1), 1998, 3–23.

D.W. Vorhies and N. Morgan, 'Benchmarking marketing capabilities for competitive advantage', *Journal of Marketing*, 69, 2005, 80–94.

M. Voss, 'Impact of relationship value on project portfolio success – investigating the moderating effects of portfolio characteristics and external turbulence', *Paper presented at* EURAM 2012, 5th–8th June, Rotterdam, 2012.

S.A. Waddock and J.E. Post, 'Social entrepreneurs and catalytic change', *Public Administration Review*, 51 (5), 1991, 393–401.

D.H.T. Walker, L. Bourne and S. Rowlinson, 'Stakeholders and the supply chain', *Procurement Systems: a cross-industry project management perspective*, D.H.T. Walker and S. Rowlinson (eds.), Abingdon: Taylor and Francis, 2008, pp. 70–100.

O. Walker and R. Ruekert, 'Marketing's role in the implementation of business strategies: a critical review and conceptual framework', *Journal of Marketing*, 51, 1987, 15–33.

J.E. Wallace, 'Organizational and professional commitment in professional and nonprofessional organizations', *Administrative Science Quarterly*, 40 (2), 1995, 228–255.

K.E. Weick, *Sensemaking in Organizations*, Thousand Oaks, CA: Sage, 1995.

K.E. Weick, 'Organizational design and the Gehry experience', *Journal of Management Inquiry*, 12, 2003, 93–97.

D. Weissbrich, K. Miller and H. Krohmer, 'The marketing–finance interface: an integrative conceptual framework and performance implications', *36th EMAC Conference*, Reykjavik, Iceland, 2007.

H. Wells, *An Investigation into the Contribution of Project Management Methodologies to IT/IS Project Management in Practice*, PhD thesis, London: UCL, 2011.

H. Wells and H.J. Smyth, 'A service-dominant logic – what service? An evaluation of project management methodologies and project management attitudes in it/is project business', *Paper presented at* EURAM 2011, 1st–4th June, Tallinn, Estonia, 2011.

B. Wernerfelt, 'A resource-based view of the firm', *Strategic Management Journal*, 5, 1984, 171–180.

S.C. Wheelwright and K.B. Clark, *Revolutionizing Product Development*, Boston, MA: Harvard Business School Press, 1992.

G. White, 'Towards a political analysis of markets', *IDS Bulletin*, 24 (3), 1993, 4–11.

R. Whitley, 'Project-based firms: new organizational form or variations on a theme?' *Industrial and Corporate Change*, 15 (1), 2006, 77–99.

R. Whittington, 'Strategy as practice', *Long Range Planning*, 29 (5), 1996, 731–735.

R.W. Wideman, *Project and Program Risk Management: a guide to managing project risks and opportunities*, Newton Square, PA: Project Management Institute, 1992.

K. Wikström, M. Hellström, K. Artto, J. Kujala and S. Kujala, 'Services in project-based businesses: four types of business logic', *International Journal of Project Management*, 27, 2009, 113–122.

J. Williams and R. Aitkin, 'Service-dominant logic of marketing and marketing ethics', *Journal of Business Ethics*, 102 (3), 2011, 439–454.

O.E. Williamson, *Markets and Hierarchies: analysis and antitrust implications*, New York: Free Press, 1975.

O.E. Williamson, 'Calculativeness, trust, and economic organization', *Journal of Law and Economics*, 36, 1993, 453–486.

G.M. Winch, *Managing the Construction Project: an information processing approach*, Oxford: Blackwell, 1st edition, 2002.

G.M. Winch, *Managing the Construction Project: an information processing approach*, Oxford: Blackwell, 2nd edition, 2010.

G.M. Winch, 'Is project organising temporary?' *Paper presented at* EURAM 2013, 26th–29th June, Istanbul, 2013.

G.M. Winch and R. Leiringer, 'Client capabilities: the developing research agenda', *Keynote presentation by Graham Winch at the 7th Nordic Conference on Construction Economics and Organisation 2013*, 12th–14th June, Trondheim: Norwegian University of Science and Technology, 2013.

G.M. Winch, A. Usmani and A.J. Edkins, 'Towards total project quality: a gap analysis approach', *Construction Management and Economics*, 16 (2), 1998, 193–207.

Y. Wind, 'Issues and advances in segmentation as alternative marketing strategies', *Journal of Marketing Research*, 15, 1978, 317–337.

A. Windeler and S. Sydow, 'Project networks and changing industry practices: collaborative content production in the German television industry', *Organization Studies*, 22 (6), 2001, 1035–1060.

M. Winter, C. Smith, P.W.G. Morris and S. Cicmil, 'Directions for future research in project management: the main findings of a UK government-funded research network', *International Journal of Project Management*, 24, 2006, 638–649.

R. Wise and P. Baumgartner, 'Go downstream: the new profit imperative in manufacturing', *Harvard Business Review*, September–October, 1999, 133–141.

A. Wölfl, *The Service Economy in OECD Countries*, Paris: OECD Directorate for Science, Technology and Industry, 2005.

J.P. Womack and D.T. Jones, 'Beyond Toyota: how to root out waste and pursue perfection', *Harvard Business Review*, 74 (5), 1996, 140–144.

R.B. Woodruff, 'Customer value: the next source for competitive advantage', *Journal of the Academy of Marketing Science*, 25 (2), 1997, 139–153.

J.P. Workman, Jr., C. Homburg and K. Gruner, 'Marketing organization: an integrative framework of dimensions and determinants', *Journal of Marketing*, 62 (7), 1998, 21–41.

J.C. Yeung, A. Chan and W. Chan, 'Establishing quantitative indicators for measuring the partnering performance of construction projects in Hong Kong', *Construction Management and Economics*, 26, 2008, 277–301.

Y. Yi, 'A critical view of consumer satisfaction', *Review of Marketing*, V. Zeithaml (ed.), Chicago, IL: American Marketing Association, 1990, pp. 68–123.

S.B. Yisa, I. Ndekugri and B. Ambrose, 'A review of changes in the UK construction industry: their implications for the marketing of construction services', *European Journal of Marketing*, 30 (3), 1996, 47–64.

C. Young-Ybarra and M. Wiersma, 'Strategic flexibility in information technology alliances: the influence of transaction cost economics and social exchange theory', *Organization Science*, 10, 1999, 439–459.

S.A. Zahra and D.M. Garvis, 'International corporate entrepreneurship and firm performance: the moderating effect of international environmental hostility', *Journal of Business Venturing*, 15 (5), 2000, 469–492.

S.A. Zahra, D.F. Jennings and D.F. Kuratko, 'The antecedents and consequences of firm-level entrepreneurship: the state of the field', *Entrepreneurship Theory and Practice*, 24 (2), 1999, 45–66.

V.A. Zeithaml and M.J. Bitner, *Services Marketing*, New York: McGraw-Hill, 1996.

C. Zott and R. Amit, *Business Model Design and the Performance of Entrepreneurial Firms*, Working Paper, Fontainebleau: 2003/94/ENT/SM/ACGRD4, INSEAD, 2003.

C. Zott and R. Amit, 'The fit between product market strategy and business model: implications for firm performance', *Strategic Management Journal*, 29 (1), 2008, 1–26.

# INDEX